Brojonath Shaha, Radhika Nath Shaha

The Stylography of the English Language

Brojonath Shaha, Radhika Nath Shaha

The Stylography of the English Language

ISBN/EAN: 9783337086930

Printed in Europe, USA, Canada, Australia, Japan

Cover: Foto ©Paul-Georg Meister /pixelio.de

More available books at **www.hansebooks.com**

THE STYLOGRAPHY

OF

THE ENGLISH LANGUAGE

BY

Dr. BROJONATH SHAHA, L. M. S.,

Medical Officer, Civil Engineering College, Sibpur;
Late Civil Medical Officer, Rangamati;
Sometime Govt. Examiner in
Lushai, &c., &c.

AUTHOR OF "THE GRAMMAR OF THE LUSHAI LANGUAGE,"
"DEHATMIO TATTVA," A DISCOURSE ON MATERIO-SPIRITUALISM BASED ON SCIENCE AND RELIGION, AND "A DISCOURSE ON CAPILLARY BRUIT." &c.

Edited by his son

RADHIKA NATH SHAHA.

Calcutta:

PATRICK PRESS CO.

28, Convent Road.

1897.

[*The right of Translation and Reproduction is reserved.*]

CALCUTTA:
PRINTED BY S. P. GHOSH, AT THE PATRICK PRESS,
28 CONVENT ROAD.

To

J. H. GILLILAND, M. A.,

*Professor of Natural Science, Presidency College, Calcutta;
Registrar and Fellow of the Calcutta University;
&c., &c., &c.*

THIS

BOOK IS DEDICATED,

AS A

Little token of respect, and in recognition of great sympathy for the Author's work.

"Science is the detection of identity."

"Whenever we form a class we reduce multiplicity into unity, and detect as Plato said, the one in the many."—*Jevons*.

"Scientific observation is such as is at once full, precise, and free from unconscious inference."

"Classification facilitates the operations of the mind in clearly conceiving and retaining in the memory the characters of the objects in question, as also to disclose their correlations."—*Huxley*.

PREFACE.

THIS book is intended as a text-book for the Entrance class of our schools, but this system of Analysis and Parsing may be very advantageously and profitably taken up from the 4th class.

As the Author of this work was unable from pressure of other engagements to revise his manuscript and to correct the proof sheets, that task fell upon me.

In the performance of my task, I have always tried to make the book as useful practically as possible, avoiding too great diffuseness on the one hand, and obscurity from over-condensation on the other.

When the Author was Secretary to the Government Boarding School at Rangamati, and in that capacity took an active interest in its progress, a discussion arose between him and the Head Master, the latter having expressed the opinion that Parsing and Analysis could not be done by students without a previous knowledge of the *meaning* of the words of a sentence. The present work is the outcome of an attempt to overcome such a difficulty.

As yet the system of Analysis has been imperfect, cumbrous and not thoroughly scientific. But the present work is a thorough *dissection* of the English language.

The Author has practically found that the arrangement is simple and thoroughly intelligible to juvenile readers by teaching two of his young nephews. If he has deviated from the beaten track it is not at the sacrifice of simplicity. The illustrations and classifications are clear, accurate and perspicuous. The Appendix will be especially useful to Indian students.

A rational course in Analysis and Parsing, whether for younger or older pupils, is something more than a mere assemblage of rules and statements of facts.

Stylography, however, begins from the beginning, helping the pupil *to see* and then think, *to observe* and then reason. In this way the youthful learner is made *observant* and not a mere stock of knowledge. The object is thus to develop powers of observation to enable students to appreciate the *structural beauty* of the English language, and not to force the student by cramming to learn statements and formulas by heart without teaching him to comprehend them.

The stylographic system of Analysis and Parsing, I may add, is not an innovation but an *evolution*.

Some typographical and other obvious inaccuracies, have found their way into the book owing to its scientific and mathematical nature.

It is hoped that all these defects will be removed in the next edition if the system is taken to be intelligible and profitable by the public.

The critic, it is hoped, will be good enough to overlook the shortcomings of the work in consideration of the originality aimed at.

Any suggestions or corrections by way of improvement of the work will be cordially received by the Author.

MEDICAL COLLEGE ;
The 8th December, } RADHIKA NATH SHAHA.
1897.

TABLE OF CONTENTS.

LECTURE I.
The Noun. (N)

	PAGE
1. Noun and verb—the principal parts of speech ...	1
2. Proxies of N, Substitutes of N, Derivatves of V, Analogues of N, Joiners and sub-joiners of N or V, Connective and Absolute parts of speech... ...	ib.
3. Noun Table ; with symbolic and digital representation	2
4. Illustrations of the Noun Table	4
5. Compound Nouns, how formed	5
6. Illustrations of special Ante-joiners to N	6
7. „ of Noun possesive	ib.
8. The noun formula, naked, clothed, & with NP ...	ib.
9. Illustrations of N Formula, naked, clothed, with NP...	7
10. Conversion of joiners to N	8
11. Enumeration of Ante- and Post-joiner words ...	ib.

LECTURE II.
The Verb. (V)

1. The Verb Table, the Verb Formula	11
2. Illustrations of the Verb Table	12
3. „ of the Verb Formula	13
4. The Verb Formula with Auxiliaries	ib.
5. Illustrations of A V Formula...	ib.
6. IV Table, IV Table with A, IV Formula with A ...	15
7. Illustrations to IV Table	16
8. „ to IV Formula	17
9. The PV Table and Formula	18
10. Illustrations of PV Formula	19
11. Enumeration of Aux. Vs, Regular, Irregular and Defective Vs, and Bi-parts of speech group of words ...	20

LECTURE III.

The Simple Sentence. (P)

		PAGE
1.	Minimum Mono-simple sentence—its Formula	22
2.	Illustrations of Ditto to formula	23
3.	Formula of N Medium Mono-simple sentence.	26
4.	Illustrations of Ditto to Formula	27
5.	,, of Gerundial IV ...	29
6.	,, to IV Medium Mono-simple Formula	ib.
7.	,, to PV Medium Mono-simple Formula	30
8.	Maximum Mono-simple sentence Formula	31
9.	*Definition* of Mono-simple sentence	ib.
10.	Illustrations of Maximum Mono-simple Formula	32
11.	,, of Compound Personal Pronoun apposition	34
12.	IV Analogues of N as 1st term	ib.
13.	PV ,, of N as 1st term	35
14.	Alternate IV and PV as First term	36
15-16.	IV Post-joiner of N ; PV Post-joiner of N	37
17.	Alternate IV and PV post-joiners to N	39

ON ABSOLUTE STRUCTURE.

18.	*Definition* of Absolute structure	ib.
19.	Illustrations of N | PV Absolute	40
20.	,, of N | IV Absolute	41
21.	,, of PV Absolute ...	ib.
22.	,, of IV Absolute ...	42
23.	,, of Adjective Absolute	ib.
24.	Governments of Ns and Vs, with illustrations	43

LECTURE IV.

The Conjunction. (C)

1.	The Apposition Ns in Mono simple sentence	45
2.	Development of Punctuation, the comma	ib.
3.	,, of Conjunction	47

TABLE OF CONTENTS.   xi
                                                    PAGE
4. Classification of Conj. into Mono and Bi-groupal;
    Strong and weak compound; and co-ordinate; Proto-
    type conjunctions 'and,' 'or'; Compound symmetrical
    and Asymmetrical Conj.   48
5. Compound and co-ordinate increase of terms, joiners
    or subjoiners by comma and Conjunction   ...   49
6. *Definition* of simple conjunction; comma, a punctua-
    tive connective ...   .   *ib.*
7. Illustrations of *Symmetrical Mono-groupal* conjunction
    between 1st terms   50
8. Illustrations of conj. bet. 2nd terms   51
9.   ,,   of conj. bet. 3rd terms   53
10.   ,,   of conj. bet. 5th terms   ...   ... *ib.*
11.   ,,   of conj. in joiners to Ns and Vs   ... *ib.*
12.   ,,   of conj. in subjoiners to Ns and Vs   ... 56
13.   ,,   of conj. both in terms and joiners   ... 57
14.   ,,   of conj. both in joiners and subjoiners ... 58
15.   ,,   of *Symmetrical Bigroupal* conj. in terms... 59
16.   ,,   of sym. Bi-groupal conj. in joiners   ... 61
17.   ,,   of sym. Bi-groupal conj. in sub-joiners ... 64
18.   ,,   of Apposition connectives, *as* and *such* ... 65
19.   ,,   of *Sym. Mono-* and *Bi-groupal* conj. ... *ib.*
20.   ,,   of *Asymmetrical Mono-groupal* conjunction
                 between V and its post-joiner   ... *ib.*
21. Illustrations of Mono-groupal C bet. N & its post-joiner 66
22.   ,,   of asymmetrical conj. bet. V and IV   ... 67
23.   ,,   of asymmetrical conj. bet. Auxiliary and V *ib.*
24.   ,,   of *Asymmetrical Bi-groupal* conj. bet. A & V 68
25.   ,,   of *Symmetrical* and *Asymmetrical* conj. ... 70
26. Equivalents of capacity in same and different terms 73
27. Difference between Equivalents and Appositions   ... 75
28. A sentence of 11 terms   76

            LECTURE V.
        The Interjection. ⟨ ! ⟩
1. Interjection defined as an Absolute part of speech ... 77
2. The word Interjection structurally a mis-nomer   ... *ib.*

		PAGE
3.	Appearance of Interjections with the mono-simples	*ib.*
4.	The Vocatives, (*Absolute part of speech*)	78
5.	Union of Interjections to Narratives	*ib.*
6.	*Imperative Expression*, defined	80
7.	Union of interjections to Imperatives	*ib.*
8.	*Interrogative Expression*, defined	81
9.	Union of Interjections to Interrogatives	*ib.*
10.	Interrogative Relative in the Interrogatives	82
11.	Definition of *Exclamatory Expression*	83
12.	Union of Interjections to Exclamatory Exp.-	*ib.*

LECTURE VI.
Transposition.

			PAGE
1.	*Emphasis*, one factor of transposition		85
2.	Transposition of Vs in the Narrative		*ib.*
3.	,,	of Ante-joiners of N	86
4.	,,	of Pronominal Adjective	*ib.*
5.	,,	of Ante-joiners of Vs	87
6.	,,	of Ante-joiners of Vs with collateral transposition	*ib.*
7.	Transposition of P. A. Post-joiners to Vs.		88
8.	Prevention of *over-crowding*, second factor		*ib.*
9.	Transposition of Preposition Phrase of Vs		*ib.*
10.	*Perspicuity*, and *preservation of balance* the 3rd and 4th factors		89
11.	Transposition of PV post-joiner of N		90
12.	,,	of 3rd term	91
13.	,,	of 3rd term between V and its post-joiner	*ib.*
14.	,,	of IV terms to 1st seat	92
15.	Gradual Absolute formation from real transposition		94
16.	Illustrations of PV terms to 1st seat		*ib.*

On Absolute Unions.

17.	Independent IV Absolute	95
18.	Adjective absolute...	96

TABLE OF CONTENTS.   xiii

PAGE

19. Transposition of the 4th Term with following Terms   ib.
20. The *Absolute formation*   97
21. Transpositional interchange bet. 1st and 3rd terms   ...   ib.
22. Independent Prep. phrase Absolute & its union with Ps   ib.

On Conversion.

23. Of Active expression of 3 terms into Passive   ...   99
24. Passive-active conversion   100
25. Conversion of Active Exp. of 4 or 5 terms into Passive   101
26. ,, of Active Exp. of 7 terms, how far feasible   102
27. Interchange between 1st and 5th terms in Active-passive conversion   ...   .   ib.
28. Preps. other than 'by' in Passive Exp.   103
29. Conversion of Progessive active into the Passive   ...   104

LECTURE VII.

The Parenthetic Absolutes. "( )"

1. Illustrations of Narrative-Parenthetics   105

The Reported Speech.

2. Distinction between Narrative-Parenthetic and Direct-Narrative   107
3. Illustrations of *positions* of Narrative and Direct in Direct-Narrative ...   .   ib.

LECTURE VIII.

The Subordinate Structure. ( )'

1. Distinction between Incomplete and Complete Complexes   110
2. Relative and Conjunction Subordinates,—R', C', their Character   ...   .   ib.
3. The initial position of Relatives in R'   111
4. Illustrations of *Relative Subordinates*—R'...   ...   112
5. ,, of *Conjunction Subordinates*—C'   ...   113

TABLE OF CONTENTS.

PAGE

The Mono-simple Complexes.

6. Illustrations of PR⁰ Complex by Fractional R⁰—initial, medial, and terminal 116
7. Illustrationss of PC⁰ Complex by fractional C⁰ ... 118
8. C⁰ subordinate as apposition N... 119
9. R⁰—Subordinate to N ; C⁰—Subordinate to V ... 120
10. Illustrations of PR⁰, by integral R⁰ Subordinate ... *ib.*
11. ,, of PC⁰ by integral C⁰ Subordinate ... 121
12. ,, of Relative and Conjunction of R⁰ and C⁰ understood 122
13. Complex of P by Di-Subordination (C⁰ P C⁰) ... 123
14. ,, of P by Bi-Subordination (P R⁰ R²⁰) ... 124
15. ,, of P by Di-bi, Bi-di, and Bi-bi Subordinates 126
16. ,, of P by Poly-Subordinates 127
17. Combinative, locked, riveted Methods of Combination 128
18. Complex of P by c′C‴⁰ *Subordinate Co-ordinate* ... *ib.*
19. ,, of P by elliptical c′C‴⁰ Subordinate ... 130
20. ,, of P by c′R‴⁰ Co-ord. Relative Subordinate 133
21. ,, of P by Co-ordinate, sub-subordinated ... 134
22. ,, of P by *Substitutive* Subordinate Complex ... 137
23. ,, of P by *Substitutive* Co-ordinate ,, ... 138
24. ,, of P by ,, Di-Complex Subordinate ... 139
25. ,, of P by ,, Bi-Complex Subordinate ... *ib.*
26. ,, of P by 2nd Subordinate, Substitutive ... 140
27. ,, of P by *Integral & Fractional* Subordinates... *ib.*
28. ,, of P by mono- and Co-ordinate Subordinate... 141
29. ,, of P by mono- and Co-ordinate Subordinate Sub-subordinated... 142
30. Illustrations of increased connectives in c′C‴⁰ ... *ib.*
31. Complex of P by an *Absolute* and *Subordinate* ... 144
32. ,, of P by Mono-Bi-groupal Connectives ... *ib.*
33. ,, of P by Riveted Relative Subordinate ... 145
34. ,, of P by Expression Subordinate ... 146
35. Illustrations of C⁰ Subordinate as N Analogue ... 147

TABLE OF CONTENTS. xv

PAGE

36. Interrogative relative Subordinate R⁸ as N Analogue... 148
37. ,, relative R⁸ Complex *by Connective* ... *ib.*
38. Apposition Ns to interrogative R⁸ Relative Subordinate *ib.*
39. *Conversion* of C⁸ into Co-ordinate c'C''⁸ Subordinate ... 149

LECTURE IX.

The Absolute Structure. "⟨—⟩"

SUBORDINATES.

1. R⁸ and C⁸ subordinate to the Absolute 150

ABSOLUTE COMPLEXES.

2. Complex of the Absolute N or PV by R⁸ or C⁸ (united to a P) ... ... *ib.*
3. Complex of the Absolute independent of P ... 152
4. Ellipsis in co-ordinate Subordinates and Absolutes compared (three kinds of Ellipsis) 155
5. Complex of the P by *Parenthetic Subordinate* ... 156
6. ,, of the P by elliptical C⁸ Subordinate ... 157

Conversion of Reported Speech.

7. Rules for the conversion of *Assertive* Direct-Narrative into continued Narrative 158
8. Rules for conversion of *Interrogative* Direct-Narrative 159
9. ,, for conversion of *Imperative* Direct-Narrative... 160
10. ,, for conversion of *Exclamatory* Direct-Narrative *ib.*
11. Conversion of *Assertive* Direct-narrative ... ... *ib.*
12. ,, of *Imperative* Direct-narrative ... 163
13. ,, of *Interrogative* Direct-narrative ... 164
14. ,, of *Exclamatory* Direct-narrative ... 167
15. *Active-passive* conversion of R⁸ Subordinate ... 168
16. ,, conversion of C⁸ Subordinate ... 170
17. Proximate position of antecedents to R⁸ ... 174
18. *Recapitulation* with regard to As, Vs, IVs, PVs ... *ib.*
19. Voice and Tenses of Verbs, six types of Vs ... 178
20. Voice and Tenses of IVs and PVs 183

TABLE OF CONTENTS.

PAGE

LECTURE X.
The Di-simple Sentence. (C'P C"P)

1. Di-simple principal, its character 184
2. Illustrations of Di-simple sentence ... ... ib.
3. „ of Di-simple with 2nd co-ordinate conj. understood 186

The Di-simple Complexes.

4. Complex of the Di-simple by fractional Subordinate ... 187
5. The *substitutive combination* 188
6. Complex of the P by substitutive subordinate Di-simple 188
7. „ of the P by direct Di-simple subordinate ... 189
8. Di-simple principals as N Analogue ... ... ib.
9. Complex of P by Mono and substitutive Di-simple ... 190
10. Reference on 4 *kinds of substitutive Subordinates* ... ib.
11. Complex of Di-simple by integral C' Subordinate ... 191
12. Transposition of 1st term of 2nd Co-ordinate ... ib.
13. „ of 1st term of 2nd subordinate Co-ordinate 192

LECTURE XI.
The Compound Sentence.
SYMMETRICAL COMPOUNDS.

1. *Of Mono-simple Ps* by punctuation 194
2. Of Ps by conjunction (P+P.) 195
3. Of Ps by punctuation and conjunction 196
4-5. Of Ps by increased conj. (copulative and adversative) 198
6. Of Ps by Expression Ps ... ... ib.
7-8. Of *Subordinates*—C', R', ... 200
9. Of increased C' or R' Subordinates 201
10. Of co-ordinate Subordinates 202
11. Of Expression „ 203
12. *Of Ps* and *Subordinates* 204
13. Of P and R' complex ... ... ib.
14. Of P and C' complex 205

		PAGE
15.	Of P and co-ordinate Subordinates ...	... 206
16.	Of P and R⋅ and C⋅ both	... ib.
17.	Of P and R⋅ and co-ordinate C″⋅ Subordinate	... ib.
18.	*Of Di-simple Ps* (C′P C″P + C′P C″P.) ...	... 207
19.	Of either co-ordinates of Di-simple ...	... ib.
20.	Simulation of Di-simples to Compound ...	... 208
21.	*Of Compound Ps*	... 209

ASYMMETRICAL COMPOUNDS.

22-23.	Of Ps and R⋅, C⋅, Subordinates ...	... 210
24.	Of Ps and P complex	... 211
25.	Of P complexes and P	... 213
26.	Of PR⋅ and P C⋅ complex	... 214
27.	Of Mono-complex and compounded Mono-complex	... ib.
28.	Of Mono-co-ordinate complex... ...	... 215
29.	Of C⋅ P R⋅ and C⋅ c′C″²⋅ P	... 216
30.	Of Mono-complex and poly-subordinates ...	... ib.
31.	Of Ps and C′P C″P Di-simple... ...	... 217
32.	Of C′P C″P and P c′C″⋅	... 218
33.	Of Di-simples with compounded 1st co-ordinate	... 219

LECTURE XII.
Relation beyond the Period.

1.	Personal pron., and Pron. Adj. relation ...	... 220
2.	Demonstrative Adjective and Adverb relation	... 221
3.	Preposition phrase and Mixed relation ...	... 223
4.	*Complex* of P by Subordinate beyond Period	... 225
5.	*Co-ordinate* of the 2nd co-ordinate in Di-simple	... 228
6.	*Compound* beyond the Period	... ib.
7-8.	„ Of P c′C″⋅ complex and P ...	... 229
9.	„ Of Complex and Complex ...	... ib.
10.	„ Of P and C′P C″P Di-simple ...	... 230
11.	Compound by other Conjunctions beyond the Period ...	ib.

LECTURE XIII.

The Paragraph. (¶)

1. Structures with or without relation *within* Period ... 234
2. Structures ,, relation *beyond* Period ... ib.
3. Structures ,, relation between *Paragraph* ib.
4. Consecutive *Independents* in a Para ... ... ib.

Parts of Speech and Phrase relation.

5. Personal pronoun *relation* between Paras 236
6. Pronominal Adjective *relation* between Paras ... 237
7. Adverb relation between Paras 238
8. Preposition phrase relation between Paras ... 239
9. ,, Of "Place," of "Time" 240
10. ,, Of "Number," and "Place" 241

Structural relation.

11. *Para-complexes* 243
12. *Para-compounds* 246

LECTURE XIV.

Recapitulation.

1. RECAPITULATION.—The Mono-simple sentence, its extent;

(a) Of terms in Subordinates and Co-ordinates; the behavior of Proxy parts of speech; Antecedents of Relative, Compound relative and Pronouns ... 250

(b) The use of *joiners*, as N substitute; IV and PV terms as joiners, Past participle as joiner and term *(Joiner & Term parts of speech)* ... ... ib.

(c) Antecedents of reference of 'the," Pron. Adj. and certain other adjectives and adverbs 251

(d) The three varieties of Government in Parsing ... ib.

(e) The behavior of *Absolute parts of speech* ... ib.

(f) The behavior of *Parenthetic parts of speech* ... ib.

(g) Analogues of N, and its relation to Direct-Narrative 252

TABLE OF CONTENTS. xix

	PAGE
(h) Transposition of terms and joiners ...	... 252
(i) Inversion of 1st two terms ...	... ib.
(j) Transformation of the 1st and 3rd terms	... ib.
(k) The behavior of Direct-Narrative ...	... ib.
(l) Transformation of the "Direct" in Direct-narrative (of 4 expressions)	... ib.
(m) Behavior of *Connective parts of speech* & their classification	... 253

2. Analogy between Conj. and Prep. as connectives   254
3.   „   of dual connection of Prep., Conj., & Adv. ... 256

LECTURE XV.
Transformation.

1. Transformation of N analogues in P   257
2.   „   of several Ps into a P and *Vice-versa* 258
3.   „   of Complex into a Complex and a P ... 259
4.   „   of Simple into Complex by change of joiners and terms   ...   . ib.
   (a) P changed into PR⁵ and *Vice-versa*   ...   ... ib.
   (b) P changed into PC⁵ and *Vice-versa*   261
   (c) P changed into Pc′C‴⁵ and *Vice-versa* 264
   (d) Mutual change of a P into mono-complexes   ... 265
5. Transformation of Absolute united to P into a P, or Complex, or Compound   ...   . ib.
6. Transformation of Complex into Co-ordinate and Compound and *Vice-versa*   268
7. Mutual transformation of all structures 269
8. Transformation of more into less complicated structures *ib.*

LECTURE XVI.
Style of Subjects.

1. Philologico-structural feature of an Author   ... 272
2. The various subjects necessitate various Styles   ... ib.
3. *Table of subjects* with their distinguishing structures... 273

			PAGE
4.	*The subject* of Mathematics	... ...	... 274
5.	,, of Science—Botany	...	... 275
6.	,, of Zoology	... ...	... 276
7.	,, of Experimental Physics and Chemistry		... 277
8.	,, of Law—Indian Penal Code	...	... 278
9.	,, of Medicine—Pharmacopœa	...	... *ib.*
10.	,, of Poetry—Rhyme and Blank-Verse		... 280

Examination Questions on Stylography ... 282

APPENDIX.

RECOGNITION OF WORDS AND THEIR CLASSIFICATION i—xxxviii
CLASSIFICATION OF PARTS OF SPEECH ... xxxix
NOMENCLATURE OF STRUCTURES AND FORMULÆ *ib.*

THE

STYLOGRAPHY

OF THE

ENGLISH LANGUAGE:

INTRODUCTION.

THE basis of this work is *observation*—pure philological observation drawn from examples in writing of possibly diversified character; and its humble pretension is chiefly to arrive at some *short, intelligible,* and at the same time throughly *illustrative system of teaching,* by which students, even those who have not made much advance might become capable of comprehending simultaneously the *Parsing* and *Analysis* of the English language, by certain *mathematical reasonings.* The demonstrations of the government in Parsing and Structure in Analysis are the two principal objects kept in view; these demonstrations are made to depend upon observation, and scarcely any deeper intellectual consideration has been its scope. Observation being prior to reasoning, it has been thought proper to burden the student with its weight antecedent to that of exercising the intellectual powers. The deeper intellectual consideration of any writing, or in other words its *rhetoric,* is *an after-work* that would be easier with the knowledge derived from this condensed but observational sort of study, which this book seeks to lay before beginners.

Language when brought into writing is nothing more than a mathematical demonstration of thought, the alphabet being the basic symbols, an arrangement of grouped symbols its words, a systematic arrangement of these its phrases, while a combination of words, or words and phrases, constitutes the sentence-chain of symbolic thought. Its punctuations on the other hand may be considered as brackets of mathematics. *Language, therefore, is mathematics in its elementary stage*, but unlike the higher sciences, not yet abbreviated into still smaller compass or "*formulæ*" for comprehension. If, therefore, I have borrowed symbols from chemical formulæ, powers and brackets from algebra or conics, perpendicular lines from music-charts, and dots, digits and the plus signs from arithmetic,—leaving the punctuations intact and applied them according to circumstances to formulate writing, it is only because I wish to introduce mathematical reasonings in literature, or, in other words, to substitute *condensation* for expansion.

Attempts have been made at the outset to symbolize the materials of structure, for which *two kinds of stones or bricks* have been introduced : these are the *Noun-stone* with symbol N and the *Verb-stone* with symbol V. As the structure of a sentence is continued by elongation, juxtaposition of these stones one after the other, is all that we have to make, the bonds of union being sidewise, and there being no binding material whatever between them.

The V brick with its auxilliary A is found likewise to exist in two other subsequent varieties of bricks—the Infinitive Verb IV and Participle Verb PV. There are, therefore, *four* essential *symbol-bricks* that have been used—the one of N and the three of Vs excepting their auxiliary. *Ante-* and *post-joiners*, called modifiers or qualifiers to the chief N and V bricks, have likewise been brought in, and the V brick with its preceding auxiliaries may have also an intermediate set of *inter-joiners* between them and between the two or three auxiliaries. These joiners are applicable to all Ns and the three varieties of Vs wherever they may be seen. Ante- and post-joining Adverbs may be considered as *sub-joiners* to Adjective-joiners of Ns, while Prepositional Phrases may sometimes be sub-joiners to other prepositional phrases or to adjective post-joiners of Ns too.

Adverb post-joiners of V may sometimes be sub-joiners to other adverbs or adjective post-joiners of Vs, while Prepositional Phrases may sometimes be sub-joiners to other prepositional phrases, or to adjective or adverb post-joiners of Vs too. *Digital representation* of the Joiners and Sub-joiners and the *Symbolic representation* of the bricks have been framed for the four essential *Formulæ of Ns*, and *three Vs*.

One grand, almost general rule however pervades the whole as regards the arrangement of materials used in structure, and this is *the alternate juxtaposition of the N and V bricks* to the extent of the 9th *Term*, *i.e.*, four-and-a-half pairs of them—unless increased by the same alternate arrangements by the addition of IV or IV | N and PV or PV | N, *i.e.*, 10th or 10th and 11th terms. This construction (Structure 1) is the simplest one, and is called the simple or **Mono-simple sentence** in its narrative or assertive character, the word "mono" being used with reference to the first pair of N | V in contrast with two such first pairs in Di-simple or Co-ordinate sentence. From the minimum, medium and maximum number of such groupal arrangements, these sentences have been named **Minimum, Medium** and **Maximum** simple sentences with their respective rational formulæ as P_2, P_4, P_9. One variety of Medium and two varieties of Maximum sentences may, however, be incomplete when their Vs are wanting in their N governments.

Increase in the number of terms or bricks of each set or kind, or increase in the number of joiners (qualifiers or modifiers) or sub-joiners (qualifiers or modifiers of joiners) of each variety or their respective analogues even, necessitates the use of cement or mortar, *i.e.*, Conjunctions, in these simple sentences. As exceptions of the modifier class, Pronominal Adjective, Adjective, Adverb and Prepositional Phrases are repeated where no conjunctions become visible, while their absence between the two N bricks of a term so increased, with or without an Article to the second N whether preceded or not by a comma, indicates that they are apposition Ns. In these Ns, therefore, the *first development of a punctuative comma* appears in their midst. *Appositions* by the connectives 'as', by past participles 'called' or 'named' and both by past participle and connective 'known as' are also shown. Apposition Ns are *equivalents of capacity* in one and the *same* term, while *equivalent Ns* are but apposition Ns in *different* terms with intermediate V term of 'Be' or 'the Passive form' as the case may be. *Conjunctions* of Mono-simple sentences are met with in two distinct groups—the *mono-groupal* and the *bi-groupal*—the former is seen as single, dual, triple or phrasial ; the latter as dual-separate or co-ordinate. The first co-ordinate, however, when the post-joiner of V is increased or compounded by two or three words, is repeated in as many places as the number of those words are when compound conjunction 'and' of the mono-groupal variety combine with the last of the 1st co-ordinates forming here the conjoined *bi-mono-groupal* variety ; and hence Conjunction connectives may become *tri-* or *quadri- groupal* when viewed along with the second Co-ordinate. Conjunctions of simple sentences have likewise been called 'minor or simple conjunctions' (*Conjunction, Class 1*), firstly—the mono-groupal variety which place themselves *between* similar terms, joiner or sub-joiner Parts of Speech and Phrases, or between such parts of speech and their analogous phrases, and secondly—the bigroupal variety, which form similar or dissimilar Unions. *Similar Minor Co-ordinate Conjunctions* form similar unions in the dual increase of a term, joiner or sub-joiner one before each such increase, while *Dissimilar Co-ordinate Minor Conjunctions*, one before Adverb and another before Adjective, are seen with post-joiners of Vs, the latter being subordinate to the former. Similar positions of first co-ordinate Conjunction before an adverb, or an adjective, or both adverb and adjective after Vs and the second co-ordinate before the subordinate and governed IVs, are seen ; thus showing, that besides Parsing government a *term may be subordinate to its predecessor.* When *Term Subordinations* of this kind exist, extension of the Principal Sentence P beyond the 9th term is visible. Then again, when the increase in terms or their joiners is beyond two or more than two in number, both punctuative and (compound) conjunctional intervention becomes necessary,—the punctuative comma between all but the last of their pairs and the Conjunctions between the last pairs of such consecutive increase.

Now as to the *recognition of words* for their Parts of Speech it is to be remarked that except the Ns, the Vs and their adjective-joiners (for adverbs derived from adjectives are easy of recognition by the suffix 'ly') the number of words in the remaining Parts of Speech are but a handful (151+119 =270) in the language, while they themselves are most numerous and constitute its main bulk. It is a fortunate circumstance, however, that though adjectives may appear plentiful and difficult to be grasped by beginners, their suffixial and prefixial recognition with such list given, is enough for learners to know them on the whole, while strange to remark there are only 285 unrecognizable words of this kind (of which a list is also given for complete reference) and thus the great bug-bear of *recognizing Adjectives* has been made to disappear. The same method of suffixial and prefixial *recognition of Ns and Vs* given in lists being adopted, there remain but 1,181 pure Ns and 562 pure Vs whose lists are also given. The *Bi-tri-quadri-quinque Parts of Speech group of words* are, 1,930 in all as given in the appendix. In the whole range of words, therefore, the English language presents but 4,228 unrecognizable words which beginners may commit to memory when learning their spelling and fortunately too these are mostly or all mono-syllabic.

Loose, emphatic, or *absolute*, ungoverning or ungoverned *bricks* of different nature, allied or not to those already described, are sometimes seen beginning the simple structure (Interjection, Vocative Pronoun, Vocative Noun) but they are self-sufficient and do not hold any bond of union in Parsing to the main structure, and either remain loose there or under certain circumstances go at its termination in different expressions. These Parts of Speech have been called Absolute ones, for they neither join any term nor have any Parsing relation with the main sentence. Nevertheless they begin to show forth traces of union to P by way of development from loose absolute bricks to those of the *Absolute Incomplete Structures* that go to unite with them.

'And', the proto-type of Conjunction, is seen between the Vocative Nouns which also take their *ante-* and *post-*joiners and these latter also in their turn may take 'and' too, according to necessity.

Loose incomplete structure with N but without V and followed by PV and its suite are seen and they are the *absolute* N | PV *incomplete structures* that take their place either before or after a simple sentence. Analogous to the N | PV *Absolute*, N | IV *Absolute* exists. They form independent unions but no subordinate combinations to the Ps.

The alternate arrangement of the bricks is departed from, however, in the first pair of N and V, by *inversion* into V and N, by the system of arrangement called '*Transposition*'—seen even *in the Narrative Expression* under certain conditions, (as first position of certain Adverbs, and Pronominal Adjectives) but as a rule this *inversion* is *methodic* in the Imperative, Interrogative, and sometimes in the *Exclamatory Expressions* in their simple form. When in the Interrogative and Imperative, V has an auxiliary seated before it, N takes its seat between them.

Transposition of the bricks or joiners in a simple sentence with or without inversion is only possible either by reason of emphasis, preservation of balance, when there is an absolute or incomplete structure, or for prevention of elongated repetition of post-joining phrases of V by overcrowding. Adjective modifiers of first N alone change its seat by emphasis from ante to post-position. This variety of transposition is *Transposition posterior* and must be recognized from the general method which is *anterior*. Other transpositions amongst ante-joiners of the N are also visible. Transposition of V itself separating from its auxiliary to the first seat in the sentence, inseparable adverbs or prepositions of V, its separate adverbs, adjective or post-joining prepositional phrases may also obtain their first seats in the sentence by virtue of emphasis or prevention of overcrowding, or when the N at the end of a preposition phrase-joiner to V, requires enlargement by Relative or Conjunction Subordination. A second N may have by emphasis this first seat likewise. It may have its seat between V and post-joiners, especially when the second N is a Personal Pronoun or when it has its ante-joiner only. PV or IV may get transposed with its suite of government to the first seat in the sentence as independent stone by emphasis or always retaining its first seat by sequence or precedence of action of V to that of PV or IV in which cases they are Absolute. When PV is seen to follow any N it becomes its post-joiner. IV likewise becomes post-joiner to any N.

Unlike the algebraic x, *N is a fixed but varied quantity*.

Substitute or proxy bricks for the Noun-brick or their analogues together with their symbols have also been mentioned :—

(Pers. Pron.)^N, (Adject.)^N, (Pron. Adj.)^N, (IV)^N, (PV)^N, (R')^N, (C')^N, (C'·C'·)^N, (quotation)^N.

The N may be substituted by PP (personal pronoun) or when it becomes absent it is represented by such of its ante-joiners as the adjective or PA (pronominal adjective) ; IV and PV with their suites may also take the functions of N. The three subordinate sentence-substitutes or *sentence-analogues* of N have, moreover, been considered, and later on *quotation analogues* are shown as N substitutes.

In structural consideration a Mono-simple sentence has been seen to be made up of N and V in a group of two terms or such repetition to 4½ groups or nine terms; but when Parsing is to be considered, we must look upon them in groups of firstly of two, subsequently of three for three times and lastly of two again as depicted in this formula and diagram :—

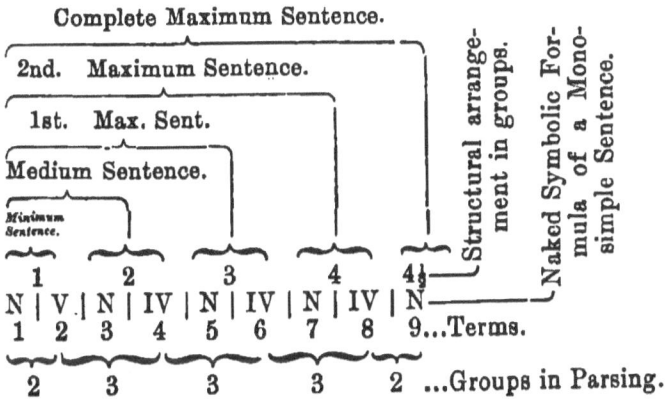

PVs may take the places of IVs in the above term. Also second or subsequent N bricks may be wanting when they form a group of two instead of three in the aforesaid Parsing group.

The first term governs the second term as shown in the diagram, the second governs the third and fourth, the fourth governs the fifth and sixth, the sixth governs the seventh and eighth, and lastly the eighth governs the ninth term only.

Ante-, inter-, and post-joiners should be parsed as *joiners* to Ns and Vs the independent bricks, and the sub-joiners as joined to the *joiners*. In the prepositional phrase-joiner or sub-joiner the Preposition governs the ending N, personal pronoun PP, pronominal adjective PA, or the adjective.

Having thus considered the structure of a Mono-simple sentence and its government in parsing, we have taken up the consideration of other structures. A Mono-simple sentence has been observed not to begin with a Relative or with a Conjunction but that a N stone is its basis in its untransposed form. Structures of the same Mono-simple type are seen, however, to begin with a Relative-stone or Relative-joiner or with a Conjunction mortar; but they never remain alone and are always placed after or before the Mono-simple sentences already described. Hence they are Mono-simple Subordinates and have been styled the **Relative Subordinate** R' (Structure 2) and the **Conjunction Subordinate** C' (Structure 3) both being subordinate to the principal or chief Mono-simple structure. Both these Subordinates may be subordinate to the whole of the Principal or subordinate to certain terms or joiners (Parts of Speech) in the Principal. Hence they are **Integral** or **Fractional** Subordinates with two distinct sets of mono-groupal Conjunction (Conjunction Class 2, *Integral Subordinate*), (Conjunction Class 3, *Fractional Subordinate*), one respectively for each. Relative Fractional Subordinates unconnected by any conjunction to the Principal are subordinates to N, PP, or PA and Adjective taking the functions of N. They are subordinates to such chief Ns or such minor Ns in post-joining prepositional phrases of Ns and Vs. At the blending of the Antecedent and the Relative in the Compound Relative Pronouns 'what', 'whoever' &c., a distinct and riveted variety of combination of the principal to the subordinate structure is shown; and

all these by single C' or R' are **complexes by Mono-Subordinate** with rational formula as for instance :—
(a) $P_2C'_3$; $P_2 2C'_4$; (b) $P_4R'_3$; $P_3 1R'_3$. Conjunction Subordinates are subordinates to Vs and to such post-joiners of Vs, as Adjective or Adverb or to both by mono-groupal conjunctions. Subordinates to Adjective positive and Adjective superlative which are the post-joiners to verb 'Be' are also shown. The Adjectives here being analogous to Past Participle verbs, form the 'passive' by their sense. All the above are the mono-groupal subordinate structure series—Fractional and Integral. Subordination to joiners in the Principal also occurs by bi-groupal or co-ordinate conjunction (*Conjunction Class 4, Co-ordinate*) ; and the Subordinate sentence (Co-ordinate Conjunction Subordinate) elliptical or non-elliptical, becomes subordinate to adjective positive compared in its own positive state (comparison of equality) or to positive adjective or adverb un-compared or to un-compared adverb and adjective combined, (the Subordinate being non-elliptical here) all of which are nevertheless post-joiners to Vs in the Principal. Here the first co-ordinate conjunctions take their seat before these post-joiners of Vs and the second co-ordinate conjunction begins the Mono-simple Subordinate with rational formula as for instance :—$P_2c'\frac{2}{3}C''_3$. The first co-ordinate conjunction, however, when the post-joiner of V is increased or compounded by two or three words, is repeated in as many places, as the number of these words are, and hence conjunction connectives may become *tri-* or *quadri-groupal* when viewed along with the second co-ordinate which begins the subordinate sentence. Besides the pure conjunction co-ordinate, the adverb and conjunction or *vice versâ* co-ordinates, comparative adjective and conjunction co-ordinates exist. The com-

parative prefixes and suffixes of diminution or excess, or the irregular and regular comparative adjectives themselves co-ordinate with the pure conjunctions of the elliptical or non-elliptical Subordinate Sentences. Certain Pronominal Adjective, co-ordinate with certain Relative Subordinates too with rational formula as for instance—$P_2 c'\frac{2}{2} R''^s{}_5$. All these are the (Structure 4) *Fractional* **Co-ordinate Subordinate Structures**.

In combination again of the Principal P and the Subordinate S, the fractional Relative and Conjunction *Subordinates*, besides being *Initials* or *Terminals*, are *Intermediates* ⓢ to the Principals. Conjunction Subordinate sentences simple when intermediately placed in the Principal are in fact *apposition-sentences* to the chief (1st) Ns of the Principal. When Mono-simple Subordinates are terminals or when such terminals can be made into initials to the P, we have called these combinations respectively as *Simple Combinative* (P)(S) or *Permutative* (P)(S), (S)(P). The co-ordinately subordinate combination has been called "*Locked*" ⓟⓢ in contrast to the Simple Combinative or Permutative which are outside the pale of the P. Instances have been shown that simple Co-ordinate Subordinate sentence might be dissolved into the simple Combinative variety of integral Subordination by the first Co-ordinate Conjunction going to approximate the second Conjunction Co-ordinate and thus become an Integral Conjunction Subordinate. Again Co-ordinate Subordinate structures may simulate Mono-co-ordinate Principal structures by taking this first Co-ordinate Conjunction in its transposition by emphasis to the first seat in the P. *Combination by Rivetment* ⓟⓢ, occurs in the P and Compound Relative Subordinate when the antecedents in the compound relative go to terminate or begin the P and the relative to begin the Relative Subordinate structure.

The basis C and R of the two kinds of Subordinates has been shown to remain 'understood' thus showing analogy of their structural combination. Punctuative isolation is absent in both from the Ps when they are understood ; but when expressed, it is in R' that a comma may sometimes precede it.

By the different kinds of combination (the Terminal or Simple Combinative, the Initial or Terminal Permutative, the Intermediate, the Locked, and the Riveted) of the Subordinates to the P, the structures so combined are called **Complex of the Mono-simples.** When both initial and the terminal Conjunction Subordinations exist to the V of the P principal sentence with rational formula as for instance : $2C'_3 P_2 2C'_4$ or when a medial R' to N first term and a terminal C' to the V term of the P with rational formula as for instance :— $P_2 1R'_3 2C'_4$ or when a medial R' to first N and another R' to post-joiner N of Vs or to subsequent N terms with rational formula as for instance :—$P_2 1R'_3 \frac{2}{3} R'_4$ or $P_3 1R'_3 3R'_4$ exist too—**Complexity by Di-subordination** happens. In this former instance both the Subordinates are subordinates to the one V thus differentiating the Conjunction Subordinate from the Relative Subordinate which cannot similarly be dual subordinate to the one N. Subordination of C' and R' singly, on either or both sides of P are the Mono or Di-Subordinate series. The compounds of Mono or Di-subordinates happen by repetion of the subordinates by Compound Conjunctions dealt with later on (R'+R' or C'+C'). Sub-subordination by a second repeated subordination to the first is also shown, the structure being then called **Complex by Bi-subordination** with rational formula—$P_2 2C'_3 \, 2C^{2'}_3$. The word di- is used when there are two subordinates, one on each side, or on medial and terminal side of the P ; bi- is used when both subordinates are on any side but the second subordinate is sub-subordinate to the first. Both the Relative and Conjunction Subordinates follow the same rule of this Sub-subordination with rational formula for example :—$P_3 R'_3 3 R^{2'}_4$; $P_2 2C'_2 2C^{2'}_3$. They are the Bi-subordinate series. But when the same repetition of Sub-subordination occurs beyond the second or third up to the fifth such repetition, the Relative and Conjunction Subordination must alternate to bring them about to these terminations. They are *the Poly-subordinate series*. All these are **Complexes by tri-** and **Quadri-Sub-subordinations** with a rational formula as for instance :—$P_2\ 2C'_3 2C^{2'}_4 4R^{3'}_2 2C^{4'}_3 3R^{5'}_3$. **Di-Bi-** or **Bi-Di-Subordination** to the P happen also, the first one having a single Subordination before and a sub-subordinated Subordinate after the P, while in the second the Subordinate and sub-subordinate Subordinate are *vice versâ* in their position to the P. Another class of complexity arises by substitution of a mono, di or co-ordinate Complex Structure in place of a Mono-simple Subordinate. Hence they are **Complex of Complexes** by mono, di- or co-ordinate Complex Subordinations with rational formulæ for example :—

(1) $P_2 2C(P_2 2C'_3)'$.

(2) $P_2 2C(2C'_3 P_2 2C'_3)'_3$.

(3) $P_2 2C(C' P_3 C'' P_2)'$.

We come now to the next Structure in which two P structures of the Mono-simple type each headed by corresponding or Co-ordinate Conjunction (*Conjunction* Class 5, the chief *Co-ordinates*) are seen (Structure 5). They have been called **Di-simple** or **Mono-co-ordinate Principals** in contrast to the Mono-simple P variety and these Di-simple principals are *co-ordinate compounds* of Grammarians with rational formula as :—$C'P_2 C''P_3$. By increase of the second co-ordinate conjunction at times by a third or more of the same, Di-simple P may be termed *Tri-*or *Poly-co-ordinates*. Certain complexities of each of these Ps, by subordination analogous to the Mono-simple Ps, have also been shown to happen equally or unequally with rational formulæ as for instance :—

(1) $C'P_3\frac{2}{3}C'_2,\ C''P_2\frac{1}{3}R'_3$.
(2) $C'P_2,\ C''P_2 2C'_3$.

Sub-subordinations and Compounds of subordination in these Ps, do also occur and these are not rare with rational formulæ as for instance :—

(1) $C'P_2, C''P_2\frac{2}{3}R'_3 3R^{2\prime}_2 2C'_2 2C^{2\prime}_2 2C^{3\prime}_2$.
(2) $C'P_2 \overline{2C'_2 + C'_5}, C''P_5 4C'_3$.

Substitution of a Mono-co-ordinate like the Complex Subordinate in place of a Mono-simple Subordinate already described is likewise seen with rational formulæ as for instance :—$P_2 2C(C'P_2 C''P_2)'$.

Mono-co-ordinates by 'wheather-or' are always subordinate to Ps, and at time the analogue of N with rational formulæ as for instance :—

(1) $P_2 2C(C'P_2\ C''P_2)'$
(2) $(C'P_3\ C''P_3)^N$ in a P_4.

Mixed complexity both by Mono-simple and Mono-co-ordinate substitutive subordination are visible which might be reckoned as belonging to the Di-subordinate variety with rational formulæ as for example :—$2C'_4 P_2 2C(C'P_2 C''P_2)'$.

The next structure (Structure 6) is the **Mono-compound** sentence $P_3 + P_4$ in which two or more Mono-simple Ps alone or with their respective Mono-subordinates as in $\overbrace{P_2 2C'_3} + \overbrace{P_2 1R'_3}$ or Substitutive subordinates as in

$$\overbrace{P_2 2C(P_3 1R'_3)'} + \overbrace{P_2 2C(P_2 2C'_3)'},$$

two or more Mono-co-ordinates first or second as in

(1) $\overbrace{C'P + C'P_4 C''P_3}$ (2) $\overbrace{C'P_3 C''P_3 + C''P_4}$,

both the complexes of Mono-co-ordinates as in

$$\overbrace{C'P_2 2C'_3 + C'P_3 1R'_3} + \overbrace{C''P_2 2C'_3 + C''P_3 1R'_3},$$

and other Complexes might be brought *in union* (but *not combined* as the above described Complexes or Co-ordinates) each to each or with each other by certain conjunctions called Compound or uniting conjunctions (the *Compound conjunction*, Class 6). The compound unions besides being conjunctional may be punctuative by—, ; : or both punctuative and conjunctional. The differentiation of the powerful or strong compound conjunctions from others of its class is that they are omissible by punctuative substitutes, while no others admit of this omission and substitution. The less powerful or strong compound conjunctions among them unite only two structures, while the more powerful or strong ones unite two or more.

In considering the combination and union of structures we have till now observed only the 'Period', the note of Interrogation and Admiration that *terminate* each variety. But

pronominal parts of speech relation as those of PP and PA besides being within the period, might also go *beyond* it, while independent or distinct sentences or sentence, each ended by a *period*, may so combine or unite according as the Conjunctions are Integral Subordinate or Compound, to form Complexes or Compounds. The consideration of period has led again to call sentences as **Mono, Di-** and **Poly singles** in the same Paragraph. Analogous relations, unions, and combinations do likewise occur in consecutive Paragraphs.

Parenthetic words, phrases, and sentence structures go between the details of the P, and like loose stones or incomplete absolute structures, bear no relation or rarely apposition relation in Parsing with the P. Parenthetics are Narratives thrown between Narratives (*Narrative-Parenthetic*) and analogous to them are the *Direct-Narratives*, the Narrative in which exactly plays the Parenthetic roll—being itself mostly a (Minimum) Mono-simple P_2 thrown at the end. A modification of it, the *Narrative-Direct*, occurs in which the Direct speech is thrown at the end of the structure, so that the whole Direct might be considered as a third Term in continuation of the Narrative. The exact counterpart of a Narrative-Parenthetic in Direct-Narrative with medial Narrative is very frequent. Transformation of *Active Expressions* into *Passive* in Ps and Subordinates and *vice versá* and the Direct-Narrative or Narrative-Direct into Narrative have been shown.

Classification of Conjunctions and Structures have thus been shown to go hand in hand, and this *dual method of recognition*, I believe, would not be a small gain to beginners in learning the roll which conjunctions play in the various structures. Apposition of Terms and Joiners to form *the Mono-simples*; of

Di-simple sentences each headed by a Co-ordinate Conjunction to form *the Mono-co-ordinate*; the substitution of Relative in place of Noun and initial or co-ordinate position of Conjunctions in Mono-simples again to form *the different Subordinates* to both Mono-simple and Mono-co-ordinate Principals; the combination of a Mono-simple and a Mono-co-ordinate Subordinate to a Mono-simple Principal to form a *Mixed Complex*; and the *Compounds* formed by uniting conjunctions in Mono-simples, in Mono-subordinates, and in Mono-co-ordinates have all been thus shown to be in gradual series of development—the knowledge or comprehension of the one bringing on knowledge or comprehension of the other. How far or to what extent Conjunctions, Prepositions, and Adverbs are connectives have also been shown by way of analogy. And lastly **Transformation** of various **structures** one from the other or between each other so far as is structurally feasible or in other words Casting and Recasting of Structures have been shown.

Having thus related in philological bearing the various structures that constitute writing, it becomes necessary now to dwell cursorily on the *symbols, digits, brackets,* and *powers* used in this work for favouring **the art of stylography**. In the Detail or Graphic Formulæ the symbols are but initial letter or letters of the Parts of Speech. The *brackets large,* and *small* at the same time *single, double,* and *triple* have been used as distinctive indicators of each variety of sentences, the different Principals and Subordinates; and the *powers* to indicate their principal and subordinate character in each combination or union. The *small plus* or c expresses 'minor or simple conjunction' which is mono-groupal, and c′ c″ bi-groupal (co-ordinate), within simple sentences.

Large C' C" before each P indicate the Co-ordinate Principals. The *large plus* alone remains isolated as distinguisher of really compound or united sentences, Principals, Subordinates, or Co-ordinates &c. *Dashes* ' and " are put above each of the Co-ordinate Conjunction. *Perpendicular lines* have been used as separators of individual stones or terms, being large in simple, and small in subordinate and in sub-subordinate structures. *Small figures* between perpendicular lines and one on each side of symbols denote Parts of Speech and Phrases and *italics* or *thick symbols* have been put or made to point out the relation firstly—of Antecedent and Relative; secondly—of Parts of Speech or Phrases or a part of speech and its analogous phrases on each side of a minor Conjunction; thirdly—in apposition Ns. A large *Asterisk* in the middle of a sentence between perpendicular lines shows the position of chief brick removed by transposition to initial or other places in the sentence which again begins at the transposed place with its indicative asterisk. In case of transposition of joiners *a small one* is thus utilized. To prevent elongation of a Graphic Formula, the repetition of analogous and apposition parts of speech, phrases, terms, and sentence structures has been written digitally, or symbolically one beneath the other *in different lines* being followed by continuation of its suite if any. *Figure before* R' or C' in the Rational formula indicates the respective Term in the P to which R' or C' is subordinate. The *numerator of fraction* in like place indicates the same but its *denominator* or *sub-denominator* indicates joiner or sub-joiner to which R' or C' is subordinate. In the Rational or Abstract Formula *figure beneath* and a little in front of the Structure symbol, represents the number of Terms in the Structure.

Thus is shown the *stylographic demonstration* or general application of digits, symbols, symbolic powers, and brackets to writing; with the Detail or **Graphic Formulæ** of Parsing and Analysis combined through these agencies and eventually the different character of the writings of different authors by the **Rational Formulæ** alone. It may be pertinently remarked that Sentences are but *Sums for work*, Detail or Graphic Formulæ are the *Processes of work* and the Abstract or Rational Formulæ are but *Answers* worked out. Criticism on Detail or Graphic formulæ and the Abstract or Rational formulæ concludes the peculiar or general *character of the writings of individual authors* as regards structure and thus these conclusions are arrived at, I might be permitted to say, by mathematical reasonings based upon examples and pure observation.

The chief *utility of this work* besides its conspicuousness on points of Philology, is as help to memory, recitation, and composition by showing forth gradual landmarks in each. This would, I may venture to say, be a great gain to students; while the teachers will derive the same amount of relief in their works during the hours of literature as they do now when engaged in teaching mathematics. How far I have succeeded in giving mathematical reasoning to philological demonstration of any writing, remains for the student to grasp or the teacher to impress upon the student, but all I desire is that they should not desert this method of *scientific demonstration* till they find it practically useless or beyond juvinile comprehension or till the teacher cannot invent modification and addition more intelligible.

RANGAMATI;
The 25th Dec. 1894.   } THE AUTHOR.

LECTURE I.

STUDENTS AND GENTLEMEN,

It is known to all that the principal Parts of Speech in a language are the **Noun** and the **Verb**, all others being their *Proxies, Substitutes, Derivatives* or *Varieties, Analogues, Joiners, Sub-Joiners* and *Connectives*, while an independent series exists also which may be called the Emphatic or *Absolute series*. With a view to arrive at a complete method of the process intended to demonstrate gradually on the arrangement of all these with reference to Parsing and Analysis in the English language, by means of symbols, signs, and formulæ, you have first of all to work up a **Noun Table** and then base upon it the **Noun Formula**. You will find with very little trouble of observation that a Noun may be alone, or that it has got certain other Parts of Speech qualifiers or modifiers as *Ante-joiners*, and the same with phrase complements as *Post-joiners* in series. Taking, therefore, those that place themselves before, as well as those that come after in groups, the expanded table of a noun may be struck as follows :—

Proxies of N:
   Personal and Relative Pronouns.
Substitutes of N:
   Pronominal Adjectives and Adjectives, when the Ns are absent; Adverbs.
Derivatives or *Varieties of V:*
   Infinitives and Participles.
Analogues of N:
   The IVs and PVs.
Joiners of N:
   Article Adjectives, Pronominal Adjectives, Possessives and Prepositional Phrases.
Joiners of V:
   Adverbs, Adjectives, and Prepositional Phrases.
Sub-joiners (joiner's joiner):
   Adverbs to Adjectives; Prepositional Phrases to Adjective, Adverb, and other Prepositional Phrases.
Connectives: Conjunctions.
Absolute Series: Interjections.

The Noun Table with Symbolic and Digital Representation.

Ante-Joiners or Sub-joiners.   NOUN   Post-Joiners or Sub-joiners.

(Parts of Speech Series.)   *(Parts of Speech and Phrase Series.)*

Special first Joiner	Sub-joiner	Second Joiner		First Sub-joiner	Second Joiner	Third special Joiner or Sub-joiner.
	ADVERB	ADJECTIVE		ADVERB	ADJECTIVE	PREPOSITION PHRASE

ADJECTIVES:—

- Article Adjective ….1¹   (comparable or non-comparable)   1
- Pronominal Adjective ….1²   (comparable or non-comparable)   2

POSSESSIVES:—

1. Personal Pronoun Possessive ….1³
2. Pronominal Adjective Possessive ….1⁴
3. Noun Possessive ….NP
4. Relative Pronoun Possessive ….RP

     N   (comparable or non-comparable)   1   (comparable or non-comparable)   2   ………   3

N.B.—The Alphabetical Abbreviations NP, RP, in this table denote symbolic Representation and those represented by numerical figures are their Digital Representation.

The Post Joiners 3 (=prep. phrase) on repetition may sometimes take 1 (=Adverb) and 2 (=Adjective) between them thus: |…N ₁ ₂ ₃ |; or in other words the total Post Joiners would be then in groups of three thus:—

$$\{\ldots N\ _1\ _2\ _3\ \}\quad\{\ _1\ _2\ _3\ \}$$

STYLOGRAPHY OF ENGLISH LANGUAGE.

REMARKS :—It is seen that the different series placed before the Noun are series of distinct Parts of Speech while those that follow it are combined series of parts of speech and phrases. Pronominal Adjectives, Adjectives, Adverbs and the Preposition Phrases may be repeated to certain consecutive numbers though the preposition phrases in some instances might admit an adverb, an adjective or both between them. It may be remarked also that an Adverb alone cannot exist as *ante-joiner* to a Noun but that an adjective must always follow it to which it is directly joined. Hence this series may be called the *sub-joiner* series. Adjective rarely takes its place alone (unless for emphasis) after a noun or with its predecessor adverb. When an adjective is placed after a noun it has sometimes to be followed by a preposition phrase. In parsing, therefore, the Adverb *before*, and the Preposition Phrase *after* an Adjective, should be joined to it but both collectively should be joined to the Noun. Repetitions of preposition phrases occur as Sub-Joiners to their predecessor and when an adverb, adjective, or both intervene between them these become *Sub-Joiners* to the final N of the preceding prepositional phrase. Sub-Joiners, therefore, should be *hyphened* together to show their qualifying or modifying character to the joiners in general writing.

A noun alone or with its ante-joiners if preceded by a preposition becomes the *Preposition Phrase* and when so formed has always to *come after a noun.* A preposition phrase, therefore, cannot precede a noun. When so found it must be understood that it is placed there by transposition as will be seen afterwards, in consideration of emphasis on them.

As an exception to the general rule a Preposition Phrase, the substitute of an Adjective, may take the *ante-place* of an adjective. Ante- and post joining adverbs may be considered as sub-joiners to adjective-joiners of Ns, while preposition phrases may sometimes be sub-joiners to other preposition phrases or to adjective or adverb post-joiners of Ns. Adverb post-joiners of V may sometimes be sub-joiners to other adverbs and adjectives, while preposition phrases may sometimes be sub-joiners to other preposition phrase or adjective or adverb post-joiners of Vs as will be shown later on.

Let me now illustrate the Noun Table to examples.

STYLOGRAPHY OF ENGLISH LANGUAGE.

Application of illustrations to the Noun Table.

	Ante-joiners.			NOUN.	Post-joiners.		
1st Special.	Sub-joiner. Adv.	2nd Adj.			1st Adv.	2nd Adj.	3rd Prep. Ph.
1. A	...	good	...	*man.*			
2. A	very	poor	...	*peasant.*			
3. An	intellectually	weak	...	*son.*			
4. A	...	simplest	...	*son*	...	weak	in intellect.
5. The	...	honest	...	*form*	...	imaginable.	
6. Our	...	own	...	*brother*			of the church.
7. One's	...	first	...	*way.*			
8. The	...		...	*stage*	...		of the journey to Petersburgh.
9. A	...		...	*change*	...		of religion on the part of a mahometan.
10. A	...	little	...	*daughter*	only		four years
11. A	...	great	...	*peril*	purely	old.	for the sake of loyalty.
12. The	...		...	*reception*	duo		of all kindness to a friend.
13. Their	...		...	*arrival*	not	furthest	at a place from the prison.
14. All such	...		...	*methods.*			
15. Kali's	...		...	*mother.*			
16. The	...		...	*mother*	...	remote.	
17. A	...		...	*thought*	very		of Kali.
18. An	...	out-of-the-way	...	*place.*			

In example 3 you find the adverb ante-joiner 'intellectually' is changed in example 4 into the preposition phrase 'in intellect', thus showing that when an adverb ante-joiner is changed into a preposition phrase it can no longer retain its place as such but must go to be a post-joiner. In examples 8 and 9 you see that the preposition phrases have increased in number and in 10 'four years' shall have to be reckoned as a preposition phrase with its preposition 'by' understood though transposed before the adjective 'old'. Examples 12, 13 show the position of the adjective 'due', adverb-adjective 'not furthest' between two preposition phrases. In example 14 pronominal adjectives have been repeated. Example 15 gives a noun possessive as ante-joiner which as it changes into the preposition phrase in 16 has to come with the post-joiner series. Thus is proved the analogy between adverb, noun possessive, and the preposition phrase. Post-joining preposition phrases go also to take ante-position to a noun to form *compound nouns* which have been illustrated as follow :—

1. The   beams   of the sun.
     1^1 N   3
     The   *sun-beams.*

2. The   watch   for the night.
     1^1 N   3
     The   *night-watch.*

Now as the first series of ante-joiners which are special to Ns are of five varieties certain remarks seem necessary about them. The general rule is that when one of these varieties is present another will not be so. Definite Pronominal Adjectives 'All,' 'Whole,' 'Both,' 'Former,' 'Latter' and 'Such' come together with Article Adjectives sometimes in their serial number and sometimes transposed on account of emphasis. The first three of these Definites goes also to be together with the next variety 'the pronominal possessive.'

Application of such illustrations to the Noun Table.

Ante-joiners.		Noun.	Post-joiners.		
1st	subjoiner. 2nd		1st	2nd	3rd
1. ALL THE	...	*men* ...	...		of Ranga-
					mati. (J.)
2. THE WHOLE	...	*affair* ...	...		of this
					kind. (J.)
3. BOTH THE	... loving	*brothers.*			
4. SUCH AN	...	*act* ...	injurious-to inter-		
			est. (S.J.)		
5. SUCH A	... brilliant	*career.*			
1. ALL OUR	...	*misery.*			
2. MY WHOLE	...	*life.*			
3. BOTH THEIR	...	*comrades.*			

Noun possessive in its capacity of a noun may have all the three series of ante-joiners. But the Possessed Noun then will be in want of its first ante-joiner series, the other two series becoming the Inter-joiners.

Application of NP Table to illustration.

Ante-joiners.			Inter-joiners.		Post-joiners.		
1st	Subjoiner 2	NP	Subjoiner	2 N	1	2	3
The	... poor	*villager's*	...	humble cottage	... in the		
					field.		

Such being our table of a noun to which illustrations have been applied, our next endeavour would be to deduce from it the **Noun Formula** as we may choose to call it. Let the chief Parts of Speech be represented by symbols for their initial capital letters and the phrases and joiners by their digital abbreviations. The formula will therefore run thus :—

Naked : | N |

$$\text{Clothed : (1)} \quad \left| \begin{array}{c} 1^1 \\ 1^2 \\ 1^3 \\ 1^4 \end{array} \right\} 1\,2\, N \,1\,2\,3 \, |$$

$$\text{When a NP is present : (2)} \quad \left| \begin{array}{c} 1^1 \\ 1^2 \\ 1^3 \\ 1^4 \end{array} \right\} 1\,2\, NP \,1\,2\, N \,1\,2\,3 \, |$$

J.=Joiner.
S.J.=Sub-joiner.

Joiners between NP and N may be termed *Inter-joiners* (both Joiners and Sub-joiners) to distinguish them from the ante-joiners of NP and post-joiners of N though the whole is really ante-joiners to N ; the NP may also be digitally represented by 1^5.

For the purpose of separating the Noun from the other independent parts of speech we have isolated the formulæ by *perpendicular lines.*

Application of the Noun Formula to illustrations.

Illustrations.	Graphic Formulæ.
1. These Quarries of ivory	$\mid 1^2$ N 3 $\mid$
2. A bed of hard stalagmite- of very ancient formation	$\mid 1^1$ N 3 3 $\mid$
3. The twenty years of James' captivity	$\mid 1^1$ 2 N 3 $\mid$
4. Our author's opinion of British artists	$\mid 1^3$ NP N 3 $\mid$
5. The charming philosopher with his head erect	$\mid 1^1{}_2$ N 3 $\mid$
6. Superior officers uncertain- of the tenure of their appointment	$\mid$ 2 N 2 3 3 $\mid$
7. The enormous extent of granite rocks- in Scandinavia	$\mid 1^1{}_2$ N 3 3 $\mid$
8. The belief of Scientific men in the present day	$\mid 1^1$ N 3 3 $\mid$
9. All these molecules of oxygen	$\mid 1^21^2$ N 3 $\mid$
10. The metal* sodium in the common salt- upon the earth	$\mid 1^1{}_2$ N 3 3 $\mid$
11. This pursuit of the actions- of men to their very sources	$\mid 1^2$ N 3 3 3 $\mid$
12. All these simple elementary processes	$\mid 1^21^2{}_2$ 2 N $\mid$
13. No amount of experience- of the sway- of motives	$\mid$ 2 N 3 3 3 $\mid$
14. The labours of students- of the early history- of institutions	$\mid 1^1$ N 3 3 3 $\mid$

* Here two nouns coming together in apposition the first behaves like an adjective.

The next thing for consideration is—the Mutual Conversion of Joiners and Sub-joiners, from Ante- to Post and *vice versâ*, and their Ante- and Post Transposition.

1. Ante-joiner $1+2=2+3$ Post-joiner.
2. ,, $=3$,,
2. ,, $2 = 2+3$,,
3. ,, $2 = 3$,,
4. 2 (of compd. N)= 3 to the 2nd N.
5. NP $= 3$,,

N.B. Adverb, adjective, and NP are convertible to Preposition Phrases.

Illustrations of the above.

1. An intellectually-weak man = A man weak-in-intellect.
 1^1 1   2   N $=1^1$ N   2 3

(3 sub-joiner to 2).
= A man of weak intellect.
 1^1 N   3

2. A delightful entertainment = An entertainment full-of de-
 1^1 2   N 1^1 N   2 3

light (3 sub-joiner to 2).

3. An intelligent person = A person of intelligence.
 1^1 2   N 1^1 N   3

4. The sun-beams = The beams of the sun.
 1^1 N 1^1 N   3

5. A man's life = The life of a man.
 1^1 1^5 N 1^1 N   3

It will not be out of place here to enumerate the words of each series of the noun table so far as they can be known or recognized.

The first or special ante-joiner series have but 42 words and one variety of words in all. Thus—

1. Article Adjective   AA has 3 words ⎫ Non-recogniz-
2. Pronominal Adjective   PA   25 do. ⎬ able.
3. Personal Pronoun Possessive PPP 14 do. ⎭ *(See Appendix)*

4. Noun possessive   NP ⎫ 1 Variety of words
5. Pronominal Adjective   ⎬ (Recognizable by suffix's &c.).
    Possessive   PAP ⎭

LECTURE I. 9

The Sub-joiner series (Adverbs) have but 15 words and one variety of words as follow :—

15 words non-recognizable. *(See Appendix).*

One variety of words recognizable by suffix 'ly'.

The second ante-joiner series (Adjectives) very plentiful in number have the following methods of recognition :—

A.—Adjectives (recognizable).

1. Suffixial   80 varieties.
2. Prefixo-suffixial   54 words.
3. Prefixial with Roots   31 varieties.
4. Prefixial with words (non-recognizable
   first group)   9 words.

B.—Adjectives (non-recognizable).

1. Pure, Regular 285 words ; Irregular 54 words.
2. Irregular Past Participial Adjectives 27 words.
3. Irregular Past Participle with adverb Prefix 9 varieties.

The Noun itself also very numerous may be recognized by the following methods.

A.—Recognizable Nouns.

1. Suffixial 158 varieties (Derivatives and Observational).
   Word Suffixial 9 varieties.

2. Prefixo-suffixial
3. Prefix with Roots } 140 varieties.
4. Prefix with Words

B.—Non-recognizable Nouns.

1. Pure   1,181 words.
2. Participle, Present   1 variety.
3. Do.,   Past   1 variety.

The Post-joiner first and second Series are recognized as the Ante-sub-joiner and 2nd series.

The third series of Post-joiners are recognised by their initial prepositions which are 55 non-recognizable words and one recognizable variety.

References for all recognitions should be made at the **Appendix**. Besides the above reference another important point for **recognition of words** are their position with reference to the different series, the recognition of either the one that precedes or the one that follows being sufficient for the purpose. Lastly the Dictionary or the teacher may be consulted as the case may be.

The *proxy part of speech of N* is the Personal Pronoun which is always naked. As first term or chief N its number is only 8. For the *Substitutes* or Representatives of N we have the parts of speech Pronominal Adjective and Adjectives, the former always anteriorly naked but the latter ante-joined by 'the' while both may have their Post-joiners like those of Noun. The proxy of N belongs to the class of independent parts of speech while the substitutes are but from the class of Ante-joiners of N both belonging to the Adjective class un-inflexible or inflexible. *Analogues of N* in IVs and PVs and in different kinds of sentence structures and *Quotations* will be dealt with in their proper places. IV and PV alone or with their suites of government will also be dealt with after their descriptions in the simple sentence.

———o———

LECTURE II.

STUDENTS AND GENTLEMEN,

IT has already been shown to you in the preceding table and formula that the Sub-joiners and second Joiners of Ante- and the first and second of Post-joiners of Nouns are alike. Analogy and observation will lead you now to construct the **Verb Table** and the **Verb Formula**, the verb being the next independent and important part of speech we have to deal with. You have thus the following as the verb table :—

Ante-joiners. (Parts of Speech and Phrase Series.)			Post-joiners. (Parts of Speech and Phrase Series.)		
Special first Joiner.			1st J. or Sub-joiner.	2nd J.	3rd J. or Sub-joiner.
Adv.	Prep. Phrase.	**Verb**	Adv.	Adj.	Prep. Phrase.

Remarks :—The only Part of Speech that precedes a Verb is the Adverb. It may be single or dual; it alone is the *special ante-joiner* to the verb. Sometimes a prepositional phrase may become its substitute. The joiners that follow a verb and are almost exclusive for it, are the combination of the adverb with the prepositional phrase. The other combinations (1 2 3) are alike to Ns and Vs. We may have all, any, or some of them absent from the Verb as we have remarked before regarding the joiners of the Noun. The repetitions of prepositional phrases are alike common to Ns and Vs.

In Parsing those joiners should be joined to the Vs, and the Sub-joiners to the Joiners. Joiners of other varieties of Vs and Ns should be so parsed anywhere.

From the table we come now to the V formula; it is as we have done with that for the N. Thus :—

- Naked : (1) | V | ; Clothed : (2) | $_1$ $_3$ V $_1$ $_2$ $_3$ |.

Application of illustrations to the Verb Table.

	Ante-joiners.		Verb.	Post-joiners.		
	Adverb. (1)	Prepositional phrase. (3)		Adverb. (1)	Adjective. (2)	Prepositional Phrase. (3)
1.	—	...	resides	altogether	...	within our dwellings.
2.	—	...	was	never	...	of a strong body.
3.	—	...	set	off	...	on horse-back.
3.	—chiefly	...	ascribe	...	...	to the growth of vegetables.
4.	—never	...	return	again	...	to their former nature.
5.	—	...	was	not	handsome.	
6.	—	...	converse-with	...	...	after the third bottle.
7.	—	...	is	so exceedingly	little.	
8.	—	...	is	...	...	in comparison of the whole.
9.	—	at no time	appears	...	imperceptible	to the eye.
10.	—	...	cleaves	...	...	in some degree to creatures of the highest capacities.
11.	—	...	are	...	natural	to the mind of man.
12.	—	...	is	not	less-present	with us.
13.	—	...	grows	...	big	with the inspiring demon.
14.	—very often	...	comes	...	...	to my room.
16.	—	...	roars	...	...	with terror upon his captive.

In certain of the above examples you will find adverbs and preposition phrases have been repeated.

Application of illustrations to Verb Formula.

Illustrations. Graphic Formulæ.

1. —*stood* on the floor- of the great saloon ... | V 3 3 |
2. —now *bloom* on the spot ... ... | 1 V 3 |
3. —*was* very numerous ... ... | V 1 2 |
4. —*thronged* to the capital ... ... | V 3 |
5. —*presided* in person over the assembly- of his own kindred ... ... | V 3 3 3 |
6. —*supped* with him last night ... ... | V 3 3 |
7. —perhaps only *feels* by fits ... ... | 1 1 V 3 |
8. —*is* clever within the limits- of our own acquaintance ... ... | V 2 3 3 |
9. —*are* guilty of a very uncharitable censure- upon the rest- of the world ... ... | V 2 3 3 3 |
10. —*is* so true in the present instance ... | V 1 2 3 |
11. —*ran* into the hall for a hoe- with a long handle ... ... | V 3 3 3 |

As the Noun Formula had to suffer modification by a second formula for NP, the V Formula has to do the same on account of the Verb auxiliaries As. This modification brings on another set of joiners, the *Inter-joiners*. They may place themselves between the A and V or between any two of the three As that are their maximum grouping. Taking into consideration also the rare substitution of prepositional phrase as ante-joiner the expanded **V formula with Auxiliaries** would run thus :—

| 1 3 A 1 3 A 1 3 A 1 3 V 1 2 3 |

Application of illustrations to AV Formula.

Illustrations. Graphic Formulæ.

1. —*had* now *arrived*... ... ... | A 1 V |
2. —*could* ever *have expected* ... ... | A 1 A V |
3. —*was reported* to him ... ... | A V 3 |
4. —*would dine* with him the next day ... | A V 3 3 |
5. —*could* not possibly *have apprehended* ... | A 1 1 A V |
6. —*were* not *wanted* at the guns ... | A 1 V 3 |

7. —*had better gone down* ... ... | A 1 V 1 |
8. —*was wrapped-* up in its one strong purpose | A V 3 |
9. —*was* very much *overcome* by her kindness | A 1 1 V 3 |
10. —*should be at once revised* ... ... | A A 1 V |
11. —*had* so often *dreamt* ... ... | A 1 1 V |
12. —*was* so much *exhausted* by the strength of her feelings ... ... | A 1 1 V 3 3 |
13. —*had been* so kind to her ... ... | A V 1 2 3 |
14. —*had been issued* for her father's pardon... | A A V 3 |
15. —*might* not *be attempted* ... ... | A 1 A V |
16. —*had been* very little *regarded* ... | A A 1 1 V |
17. —*would* probably *have* easily *been saved* ... | A 1 A 1 A V |
18. —*shall* quickly *fall* into their hands ... | A 1 V 3 |
19. —*must be* entirely free from minor errors | A V 1 2 3 |
20. —*can be* successfully *extricated* from the region of hypothesis ... ... | A A 1 V 3 3 |
21. —*may be* contemporary in the same country | A V 2 3 |
22. —*do* not *lie* very deep in the Hindu mind... | A 1 V 1 2 3 |
23. —*is* seldom very much *mistaken* ... | A 1 1 1 V |
24. —*were* in some way *related* to the present inhabitants of Thibet ... ... | A 3 V 3 3 |
25. —*was* no- doubt *adopted* in its fullest development directly from the Persian ritual ... | A 1 V 3 1 3 |

You see, therefore, in the AV Formula in which the antijoiners of the simple V formula changed into inter-joiners, the introduction of Prepositional Phrases besides the Adverbs.

We come now to the two other independent Parts of Speech which are but varieties or derivatives of V. They are the **Infinitive verb IV** and the **Participle verb PV**. One peculiarity is that they have blended with them *Intimate Prepositions* that go before each. This intimacy is so much in the case of IV that to think of its *preposition* apart would be sin and in case of the PV to think of any intimacy at all not to exist on the bare face of analogy would be sin too. In IVs after certain Vs and in certain PVs these prepositions do not exist at all. We shall have, therefore, to respect these intimate prepositions before framing the formulæ.

IV Table and Formula.

A.—Table :—

$$\underbrace{\text{Adverb} \quad \text{Adjective Preposition Phrase.}}_{\text{Ante-Joiners.}} \quad \text{IV} \quad \underbrace{\text{Adverb} \quad \text{Adjective} \quad \text{Preposition Phrase.}}_{\text{Post-Joiners.}}$$

B.—Graphic Formula :— | 1 2 3 IV 1 2 3 |

IV Table with Auxiliaries.

$$\underbrace{\text{Adv. Adj. Prep. Phrase.}}_{\text{Ante-joiners.}} \underbrace{\text{Aux. Adv. Prep. Phrase.}}_{\text{Inter-joiners.}} \text{Aux. Prep. Ph. Adv.} \quad \text{IV} \underbrace{\text{Adv. Adj. Prep. Phrase.}}_{\text{Post-joiners.}}$$

IV Formula with Auxiliaries.

| 1 2 3 A 1 2 A 1 2 IV 1 2 3 |

N.B.—Here the ante- and post-joiners coincide.

Application of illustrations to IV Table.

	Anto-joiners.			Verb.	Post-joiners.		
	Adv.	Adj.	Prep. Ph.		Adverb.	Adjective.	Prep. Ph.
1.	...	...	...	to come	quickly.	visible.	...in the shade.
2.	...	...	...	to become	...	...	...from the labour- of the farm.
3.	...	...	...	to sit	...	...	...with one hand.
4.	...	...	...	to hold up	...	...	
5.	...	...	...	to hold up	...	...	
6.	...	...	...	to look	exceedingly	knowing.	...in the fields.
7.	...	...	...	to grow	...	quicker	...betwixt my duty- to yonder unhappy man.
8.	—How	...	...	to act	...	...	...across the bridge.
9.	—...	...	...	to dash	briskly	...	...to the opposite side-of the road
10.	—Only	...	...	to plunge	...	...	into a thicket- of brambles.
11.	—...	Ready	...	to spring	...	...	...upon the traveller.
12.	—...	Sure	...	to succeed	...	...	...in his efforts.
13.	—Not	...	...	to sit	idly	...	
14.	—...	...	In-order-	to sleep.			...at home.
15.	—...	...	With-a-view-to	amuse.			

Rarely *Intra-joiners* become visible between the intimate Preposition and the IV as :—

1. — *to* constantly *run* before the door ... ... | I ı V s |

Application of illustrations to IV Formula.

Illustrations.	Graphic Formulæ.
1. —*to be executed*	| A IV |
2. —*to be prolonged* under tortures ...	| A IV 3 |
3. —*to be haunted* by the ghost- of the unfortunate pedagogue	| A IV 3 3 |
4. —not *to be discovered*	| 1 A IV |
5. —still *to be heard* in that church ...	| 1 A IV 3 |
6. —*to have prevailed* from very early times ...	| A IV 3 |
7. —chiefly *to be attributed*	| 1 A IV |
8. —virtually *to have connected*	| 1 A IV |
9. —*to have led* eventually to very surprising results	| A IV 1 3 |
10. —*to be* ever in affinity- with scientific truth	| IV 1 3 3 |
11. —in-order-*to have foreseen*	| 3 A IV |
12. —*to have been predicted*	| A A IV |
13. —*to be done* for the sake- of the agent's everlasting happiness hereafter ...	| A IV 3 3 1 |
15. —*to have studied* accordingly	| A IV 1 |
16. —liable *to be robbed* of the fruits- of his labour	| 3 A IV 3 3 |
17. —*to have been* very greatly *misunderstood*	| A A 1 1 IV |
18. —with-a-view *to have said* enough on the subject	| 3 A IV 1 3 |

In chief Vs the *three consecutive Auxiliaries* are *visible* while *in IVs two* are seen. This points out that auxiliaries other than 'Have' and 'Be' are distinct in their capacities. They may be considered as chief Vs forming compounds with other chiefs or auxiliaries and chiefs.

In V Formula with auxiliaries a past participle of chief V is seen after 'Be' to form the Passive so is seen a present participle to form the Progressive. An adjective after 'Be' is analogous to these participles and hence the IVs have been seen ante-joined in excess by adjectives when we consider the 'Be' to have ended by itself and the adjective to have begun the IVs. The extra appearance of the adjectives is thus explained in the IV Formula.

Before we proceed to frame the **Table** and **Formula** of the **Participles** certain remarks seem desirable. Like the present and perfect Infinitives the Participles take or do not take under circumstances intimate prepositions but unlike the IVs they have an additional tense, the Past. This Past Participle goes to be joined to auxiliaries of 'Have' to form different tenses and to those of 'Be' to form the Passive and thus become the chief V whose illustration has already been shown in the V Formula. But when the past participle becomes apparently independent or separate part of speech after Neuter Verbs, it always drops, *i.e.*, not requires its intimate preposition and becomes analogous to adjective (Joiner).

PV Table and Formula.

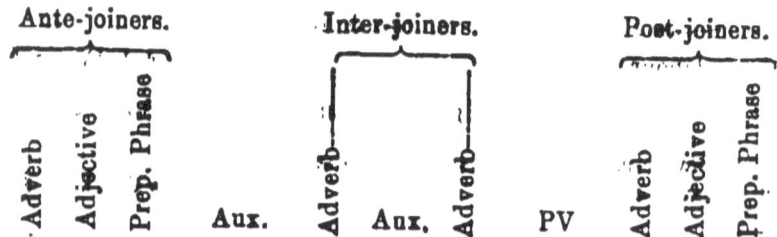

(rarely 1ˢ becomes ante-joiner to PV in its N capacity).

Formula :—| ₁ ₂ ₃ A ₁ A ₁ PV ₁ ₂ ₃ |

N.B.—Here the ante- and post- joiners coincide.

Application of illustrations to PV Formula.

Illustrations.	Graphic Formulæ.
1. —*in being* bituminous	| PV 2 |
2. —*vibrating* at the same rate ...	| PV 3 |
3. —*pushed* onwards from behind ...	| PV 1 3 |
4. —*in going* northwards to Canada ...	| PV 1 3 |
5. —*by going* still further to the north ...	| P 1 1 3 |
6. —*stretching-across* from Prince Patrick Island by Bathurst Island to North Devon	| PV 3 3 3 |
7. —*scarcely capable of moving* ...	| 1 2 PV |
8. —*only doubtfully recognized* in Spitzbergen alone	| 1 1 PV 3 1 |.
9. —*capabale of living* in a considerable amount- of cold	| 2 PV 3 3 |
10. —*continued* into the cretaceous rocks ...	| PV 3 |
11. —*instead of remaining* at home ...	| PV 3 |
12. —most-convenient *for finding-out* from them	| 2 PV 3 |
13. —*without being struck* with the similarity- of the two sets- of artificers ...	| A PV 3 3 3 |
14. —not *having been stopped* by the side	| 1 A APV 3 |
15. —*in not having* come to conclusion	| A 1 PV 3 |
16. —*in passing* from the liquid to the solid state (co-ordinate prep. phrases)	| PV 3 3 |
17. —*separating-up* into smaller parts	| PV 3 |
18. —*even while* for the last time *alluding* to it	| 1 1 3 PV 3 |

It may be remarked here that Adjectives do not go to form as *ante-joiners* to Vs but they may in certain cases be considered as such to IVs, when the V is 'Be' and followed by an apparently adjective post-joiner. In cases of PVs both the ante- and post-joiners can coincide as in IVs. This is *bilateral symmetry*. Partial, but not whole, bilateral symmetry in ante- and post-joiners of Ns is visible too.

The recognition of verbs of the auxiliary series is done as follows :— (*See Appendix.*)

A.—Non-recognizable irregular Auxiliaries As.

1. Those Principal As that take Past Participles :—14 words (Have 6 and Be 8).

2. Those Principal that take un-modified V :—5 words (Do 5).

3. Those As that take un-modified V :—17 words (will, can, must, shall, may).

4. Combination of the above 17 with Have and Be :— Group Duals.

5. Combination of the 17 with conjoined Have and Be :— group Triples.

The total of Auxiliaries :—70 words; Single, Dual, Triples.

B.—Defective Verbs.

1. Both Auxiliary and Defective :—1 word.
2. Only Defective :—6 verbs.

C.—Irregular Verbs.

These are 176 words.

N.B.—All words mentioned above are non-recognizable and 252 in number.

D.—Regular Verbs.

These are recognized by the following methods :—

(*See Appendix.*)

(a).—Verbs, recognizable.
(Derivatives and Observational.)

1. Suffixial ... 13 varieties.
2. Prefixo-suffixial ... 3 varieties.
3. Prefix with roots ... 13 varieties.
4. Prefix with words ... 63 varieties.

(b).—Verbs, Non-recognizable.
Pure Verbs ... 478 words.

Bi-parts-of-speech group of words.

(a).—Verb and Adjective.

1. With common suffix 'ate' ... 19 words (verb and adjective and *vice versâ*).
2. Non-recognizable ... 10 words (verb and adjective).
3. Ditto. ... 59 words (adjective and verb).

(b).—Noun and Adjective.

1. With common suffixes ... 62 varieties of different words.
2. With common suffixes ... 28 varieties of the same words.

(c).—Noun or Verb.
975 words (non-recognizable).

(d).—Verb or Noun.
716 words (non-recognizable).

LECTURE III.

STUDENTS AND GENTLEMEN,

In the two preceding lectures I have shown you naked and clothed formulæ of N, naked and clothed formulæ of V, and those of IV and PV. I have shown you the Post-joiners of all these to be one and the same and that the Ante-joiners varied substantially in N and V though very little in the different varieties of V, IV, and PV. I have shown you that the ante-joiners are all dependent *Parts of Speech* but solitarily a *Prepositional Phrase* in the case of the Vs, IVs, and PVs ; for, the prepositional phrase and the adverb are to be borne in mind to be analogous joiners. In the present lecture I go now to relate to you of the combinations of these four Formulæ and thus get up structures known as *sentences*. The combinations by apposition of the naked or unexpanded and of the clothed or expanded formulæ respectively of N and V constitute the **Minimum Mono-simple sentence**, the word 'minimum' being used in reference to no more than these two terms of N and V ; the word 'mono' being used in reference to Di- and Poly in which this first group of N | V | multiplies to two or more than two, and the word 'simple' being used in reference to combination of parts of speech and not of structures : the first in contrast to medium and maximum, the second in contrast to Di-simples, or Poly-simples which are the Co-ordinate structures, and the last in contrast to Complexes and Compounds (structures)—all of which will be considered in their gradual series of development. The **Formulæ** of Minimum Mono-simple sentence, therefore, run to :—

1. Naked or unexpanded :— | N | V |
2. Clothed or expanded :—

$$\left| \begin{matrix} 1^1 \\ 1^2 \\ 1^3 \\ 1^4 \end{matrix} \right\} {}_1 {}_2 N {}_1 {}_2 {}_3 \left| {}_1 {}_2 V {}_1 {}_2 {}_3 \right|$$

LECTURE III.

3. Clothed or expanded with NP to N :—

$$\left.\begin{array}{l}1^1\\1^2\\1^3\\1^4\end{array}\right\} 1\ 2\ \text{NP}\ 1\ 2\ \text{N}\ 1\ 2\ 3\ |\ 1\ 3\ \text{V}\ 1\ 2\ 3\ |$$

4. Clothed or expanded with Auxiliaries to V :—

$$\left.\begin{array}{l}1^1\\1^2\\1^3\\1^4\end{array}\right\} 1\ 2\ \text{N}\ 1\ 2\ 3\ |\ 1\ 3\ \text{A}\ 1\ 3\ \text{A}\ 1\ 3\ \text{A}\ 1\ 3\ \text{V}\ 1\ 2\ 3\ |$$

5. The fully expanded, Logical :—

$$\left.\begin{array}{l}1^1\\1^2\\1^3\\1^4\end{array}\right\} 1\ 2\ \text{NP}\ 1\ 2\ \text{N}\ 1\ 2\ 3\ |\ 1\ 3\ \text{A}\ 1\ 3\ \text{A}\ 1\ 3\ \text{A}\ 1\ 3\ \text{V}\ 1\ 2\ 3\ |$$

From the naked to the fully expanded formula there exist all sorts of gradation and the fully expanded one is only a matter of inferential myth.

In the Abstract or Rational Formulæ below, P is for Mono-simple Principal and Integer 2 represents the number of Terms in it.

Application of Minimum Mono-simple sentence illustrations to Formula.

With Graphic and Rational Formulæ respectively.

1. John | sleeps. $|\ \underset{1}{\text{N}}\ |\ \underset{2}{\text{V}}\ | = \text{P}_2$

2. *He* | runs (here N is represented by Proxy).
   $_1_2$

   $|\ \underset{1}{\text{N}}\ |\ \underset{2}{\text{V}}\ | = \text{P}_2$

3. *Good* | might proceed from evil (N represented by
   $_1_2$

   Adjective). $|\ \underset{1}{\text{N}}\ |\ \underset{2}{\text{AV}}\ _3\ | = \text{P}_2$

4. *This* | is desirable (N by Pronominal Adjective).
   $\quad_1\quad\quad_2$

$$|\ \underset{1}{N}\ |\ \underset{2}{V}\ 2\ |=P_2$$

5. The flames | are within a quarter- of a mile of us.
   $\quad\quad\quad_1\quad\quad_2$

$$|\ 1^1\ \underset{1}{N}\ |\ \underset{2}{V}\ 3\ 3\ 3\ |=P_2$$

6. The interior of the vessel | is hollowed.
   $\quad\quad\quad\quad_1\quad\quad\quad\quad\quad_2$

$$|\ 1^1\ \underset{1}{N}\ 3\ |\ A\ \underset{2}{V}\ |=P_2$$

7. The experience of the trapper | was in the right.
   $\quad\quad\quad_1$

$$|\ 1^1\ \underset{1}{N}\ 3\ |\ \underset{2}{V}\ 3\ |=P_2$$

8. The subtle element | seized with avidity upon its new fuel.
   $\quad\quad\quad_1\quad\quad\quad_2$

$$|\ 1^1\ 2\ \underset{1}{N}\ |\ \underset{2}{V}\ 3\ 3\ |=P_2$$

9. The old man | was rather perplexed.
   $\quad\quad_1\quad\quad\quad\quad_2$

$$|\ 1^1\ 2\ \underset{1}{N}\ |\ A\ 1\ \underset{2}{V}\ |=P_2$$

10. The light combustible | kindled at the flash.
    $\quad\quad\quad_1\quad\quad\quad\quad_2$

$$|\ 1^1\ 2\ \underset{1}{N}\ |\ \underset{2}{V}\ 3\ |=P_2$$

11. The eyes of many of the lower animals | are doubtless very
    $\quad\quad_1\quad\quad\quad\quad\quad\quad\quad\quad\quad_2$
    beautiful. $\quad|\ 1^1\ \underset{1}{N}\ 3\ 3\ |\ \underset{2}{V}\ 1\ 1\ 2\ |=P_2$

12. It | may be compared to the cup of an acorn.
    $\ _1\quad\quad\quad_2$

$$|\ \underset{1}{N}\ |\ A\ \underset{2}{A\ V}\ 3\ 3\ |=P_2$$

LECTURE III.   25

13. The eyelids | may perhaps be better compared to a pair- of outside shutters- for this window.
$\quad$ | 1^1 $\underset{1}{N}$ | A 1 A 1 $\underset{2}{V}$ 3 3 3 | $=P_2$

14. We | are most-familiar with this portion of the eye.
$\quad$ | $\underset{1}{N}$ | $\underset{2}{V}$ 2 2 3 3 | $=P_2$

15. Its empire over time | is scarcely less bounded.
$\quad$ | 1^3 $\underset{1}{N}$ 3 | A 1 1 $\underset{2}{V}$ | $=P_2$

16. A furnace fire | would not last long.
$\quad$ | 1^1 2 $\underset{1}{N}$ | A 1 $\underset{2}{V}$ 1 | $=P_2$

17. Some of these elements | are more- abundant in vegetables.
$\quad$ | $\underset{1}{N}$ 3 | $\underset{2}{V}$ 2 3 | $=P_2$

18. The woman's boat | is usually about twenty feet long.
$\quad$ | 1^1 NP $\underset{1}{N}$ | $\underset{2}{V}$ 1 3 2 | $=P_2$

19. Animals of this class | swarm in countless millions in all the Northern Seas. | $\underset{1}{N}$ 3 | $\underset{2}{V}$ 3 3 | $=P_2$

20. Many a brave life | has thus been given away.
$\quad$ | 2 1^1 2 $\underset{1}{N}$ | A 1 A $\underset{2}{V}$ 1 | $=P_2$

21. The ship | was fast breaking-up (Progressive).
$\quad$ | 1^1 $\underset{1}{N}$ | A 1 $\underset{2}{V}$ | $=P_2$

22. *They* | were | *all* | hanging-on by ropes to the ship (First N is dual here). | $\underset{1}{N}$ | A | $\underset{1}{N}$ | $\underset{2}{V}$ 3 3 | $=P_2$

It will be oberved that the thought in the Minimum Mono-simple sentence is narrowed only to two terms consisting of the Government of N only to V but its expansion necessitates increase in the number of these terms. An increase by a third and a fourth term of the Independent Parts of Speech, being the dual complete Government of V, thus becomes visible in sentences which might properly be called the **Medium Mono-simple sentences**. You see the third term to be an N, the fourth to be an IV or PV. Thus comes the grand observation that if the combination of the N and V Formulæ is to be extended it must be done by the recurring process of the same two N | V Formulæ one after the other, the only difference being that the Vs are IVs or PVs. You will find the third term to be a single N, a dual N, or a dual of N and its Proxy Parts of of Speech. The expanded, Logical or Beau-ideal **Formulæ** of the N Medium Mono-simple sentence are, therefore, as follow :—

With single second N irrespective of NP and Auxiliary in the Formulæ :—

1. $\left| \begin{matrix} 1^1 \\ 1^2 \\ 1^3 \\ 1^4 \end{matrix} \right\} \begin{matrix} 1\ 2\ N\ 1\ 2\ 3 \\ 1 \end{matrix} \left| \begin{matrix} 1\ 3\ V\ 1\ 2\ 3 \\ 2 \end{matrix} \right| \left| \begin{matrix} 1^1 \\ 1^2 \\ 1^3 \\ 1^4 \end{matrix} \right\} \begin{matrix} 1\ 2\ N\ 1\ 2\ 3 \\ 3 \end{matrix} \right|$

With dual second N :—

2. $\left| \begin{matrix} 1^1 \\ 1^2 \\ 1^3 \\ 1^4 \end{matrix} \right\} \begin{matrix} 1\ 2\ N\ 1\ 2\ 3 \\ 1 \end{matrix} \left| \begin{matrix} 1\ 3\ V\ 1\ 2\ 3 \\ 2 \end{matrix} \right| \left| \begin{matrix} 1^1 \\ 1^2 \\ 1^3 \\ 1^4 \end{matrix} \right\} \begin{matrix} 1\ 2\ N\ 1\ 2\ 3 \\ 3 \end{matrix} \right|$

$\left| \begin{matrix} 1^1 \\ 1^2 \\ 1^6 \\ 1^4 \end{matrix} \right\} \begin{matrix} 1\ 2\ N\ 1\ 2\ 3 \\ 3 \end{matrix} \right|$

With dual second N and its Proxy, Personal Pronoun :—

3. $\left| \begin{matrix} 1^1 \\ 1^2 \\ 1^3 \\ 1^4 \end{matrix} \right\} \begin{matrix} 1\ 2\ N\ 1\ 2\ 3 \\ 1 \end{matrix} \left| \begin{matrix} 1\ 3\ V\ 1\ 2\ 3 \\ 2 \end{matrix} \right| \left| \begin{matrix} 1^1 \\ 1^2 \\ 1^3 \\ 1^4 \end{matrix} \right\} \begin{matrix} 1\ 2\ N\ 1\ 2\ 3 \\ 3 \\ N \\ 3 \end{matrix} \right|$

LECTURE III.

Application of the N Medium Mono-simple Sentence Illustrations to Formula.

With Graphic and Rational Formulæ respectively.

1. The chiefs of both | were | men already of honurable fame·
   $\quad$ 1 $\qquad\quad$ 2 $\qquad$ 3

   $$\mid 1^1 \underset{1}{N} 3 \mid \underset{2}{V} \mid \underset{3}{N} 1\ 3 \mid = P_3$$

2. The portion of the heights nearest the town on the west | is
   $\qquad\qquad$ 1

   called | the Plains of Abraham.
   $\quad$ 2 $\qquad\;$ 3

   $$\mid 1^1 \underset{1}{N} 3\ 3\ 3 \mid A \underset{2}{V} \mid 1^1 \underset{3}{N} 3 \mid = P_3$$

3. The rowers | scarcely *stirred* | the water | *with* their oars.
   $\qquad$ 1 $\qquad\qquad$ 2 $\qquad\qquad$ 3

   $$\mid 1^1 \underset{1}{N} \mid 1. \underset{2}{V} * \mid 1^1 \underset{3}{N} \mid * 3 \mid = P_3$$

4. This beautiful animal | resembles in shape | the common
   $\qquad\qquad$ 1 $\qquad\qquad\quad$ 2

   fox of England. | $\quad 1^2\ 2\ \underset{1}{N} \mid \underset{2}{V} 3 \mid 1^1\ 2\ \underset{3}{N} 3 \mid = P_3$
   $\quad\quad$ 3

5. They | *gave* | him a faithful servant | *for* a conductor
   $\;\;$ 1 $\quad\;\;$ 2 $\quad\;$ 3 $\qquad\qquad\qquad\quad\;$ 3

   (Pronoun-Noun, dual third Term).

   $$\mid \underset{1}{N} \mid \underset{2}{V} * \mid PP\ 1^1\ 2\ \underset{3}{N} \mid * 3 \mid = P_3$$

6. It | *keeps* | the earth itself | *moist* (Noun and Compound
   $\;$ 1 $\;\;\;$ 2 $\qquad\quad$ 3 $\qquad\;\;$ 3

   PP, Apposition third Term).

   $$\mid \underset{1}{N} \mid \underset{2}{V} * \mid 1^1\ \underset{3}{N}\ \underset{3}{PP} \mid * 2 \mid = P_3$$

7. I gave yesterday | Ram two rupees (Noun-Noun, dual
   $\;$ 1 $\;\;$ 2 $\qquad\qquad\quad$ 3 $\qquad\;$ 3

   third Term). $\mid \underset{1}{N} \mid \underset{2}{V} 1 \mid \underset{3}{N} 2 \underset{3}{N} \mid = P_3$

8. The tire-women were *preparing* | her *for* the night's rest.
   $\qquad\quad$ 1 $\qquad\qquad$ 2 $\qquad\qquad$ 3

   $$\mid 1^1 \underset{1}{N} \mid A \underset{2}{V} * \mid \underset{3}{N} \mid * 3 \mid$$

---

* Indicates *transposition* of a Term or Joiner.

You have seen in the Minimum variety of examples a 'Be' verb as independent and the same as Auxiliary forming the Passive and the Progressive. You have seen besides in those examples other Verbs, called Neuter, and in all of them there was no necessity of the second N, for the thought was limited. But here you see the same 'Be' verb, the same Passive as well as Progressive, and another variety of V called the Active which requires the second N for completion by an increased term of the thought.

The second N recurs because its necessity arises from the Voice of the V and its character regarding Case is explained thus. When the second N is absent the V is *Neuter;* when this is present and retains its Nominative designation the V is the verb 'Be' (in which case the third Term becomes equivalent to the first); when it takes its Nominative or Objective designation the verb is *Passive* or *Progressive* and is recognized by the presence of the Auxiliary of 'Be'. When however 'Be' in any shape is absent and still the V has this N after it, it is an *Active* V. We thus come to the conclusion that while the first N is only Nominative, the second is either a Nominative or Objective. It is a general rule to be remembered now that every Proxy, Representative or Analogue of N may take the capacity of this second N as it did in the case of the first.

So far as the formula has till now been shown to extend to three terms in consideration of the present stretch of thought the government in parsing of these terms may be regulated thus : The first term or first N has but one government only, *i.e.*, upon the second term V but V except the Neuter has its government on the third term or second N. Unlike the single government of the first N upon V and the first V upon second N, there exists but a second set of V's government upon V, *i.e.*, its government on the fourth or the IV or PV term. You must remember, therefore, that N *has but one set of government* but V *has got two.* The government upon IV or PV is of all Vs, the Active, Passive, Progressive, and Neuter. These are *action government of Vs* while the N government are *object government of Vs*. The third or odd Terms when equivalent to first or other odd terms after 'Be', are governing and not governed terms.

When the third Term of a Mono-simple is absent the fourth term IV may be determined as a **Gerundial,** or even in the presence of a third term, if the IV could be considered as a post-joiner to the third term, it is still a *Gerund.* For example—

1. He | came | to dance.
   1   2   4

   $$|\ \underset{1}{N}\ |\ \underset{2}{V}\ |\ \underset{4}{IV} = P_4$$

2. They | obtained | a net | to fish-with.
   1   2   3   4

   $$|\ \underset{1}{N}\ |\ \underset{2}{V}\ |\ 1^1\ \underset{3}{N}\ |\ \underset{4}{IV}\ | = P_4$$

Application of illustrations to IV Medium Mono-simple Formula.

With Graphic and Rational Formulæ respectively.

1. The lieutenant | told | his men | to halt.
         1   2   3   4

   $$\rfloor\ 1^1\ \underset{1}{N}\ |\ \underset{2}{V}\ |\ 1^3\ \underset{3}{N}\ |\ \underset{4}{IV}\ | = P_4$$

2. The natives | seldom learn | to shoot (minus 3rd term).
          1   2   4

   $$|\ 1\ \underset{1}{N}\ |\ 1\ \underset{2}{V}\ |\ \underset{4}{IV}\ | = P_{4-3rd}$$

3. Three Spanish line-of-battle ships in the upper part- of
                            1

   Gibralter | were observed | also to be in motion.
               2   4

   $$|\ 2\ 2\ 2\ \underset{1}{N}\ 3 \cdot 3\ |\ \underset{2}{AV}\ |\ 1\ \underset{4}{IV}\ 3\ | = P_{4-3rd}$$

4

4. They | made | him | start back.
      1   2   3   4

$$\left|\underset{1}{N}\left|\underset{2}{V}\right|\underset{3}{N}\right|\underset{4}{IV}\,1\right|=P_4$$

5. Justice | required | this assent | to be given.
      1   2   3   4

$$\left|\underset{1}{N}\left|\underset{2}{V}\right|1^2\underset{3}{N}\right|A\,\underset{4}{IV}\right|=P_4$$

6. This | was sure | to have led to the accident.
      1   2   4

$$\left|\underset{1}{N}\left|\underset{2}{V}\,2\right|A\,\underset{4}{IV}\,3\right|=P_{4-3rd}$$

7. His whole action | seemed | to have been upon the impulse-
               1   2   4

of those- around him.

$$\left|1^3\,1^3\underset{-1}{N}\left|\underset{2}{V}\right|A\,\underset{4}{IV}\,3\,3\,3\right|=P_{4-3rd}$$

Application of illustrations to PV Medium Mono-Simple Formula.

With Graphic and Rational Formulæ respectively.

1. The naturalist | stood | looking at the awful spectacles with
            1   2   4

composure.

$$\left|1^1\underset{1}{N}\left|\underset{2}{V}\right|\underset{:4}{PV}\,3\,3\right|=P_{4-3rd}$$

2. He | may continue | his progress through the night | un-
      1   2   3

interruptedly | certain of reposing.
                                    4

$$\left|\underset{1}{N}\left|\underset{2}{AV}*\right|1^3\underset{3}{N}\,3\right|*1\left|2\,\underset{4}{PV}\right|=P_4$$

3. He | saw | his own proud flag | still floating everywhere.
      1   2   3   4

$$\left|\underset{1}{N}\left|\underset{2}{V}\right|1^3\,2\,2\underset{3}{N}\right|1\,\underset{4}{PV}\,1\right|=P_4$$

4. He $\underset{1}{|}$ gently chided $\underset{2}{|}$ her $\underset{3}{|}$ *for* not *having informed* of her
   $\underset{4}{}$
wishes in time.

$$\Big|\underset{1}{N}\Big|\, \underset{2}{1\, V} \,\Big|\, \underset{3}{N} \,\Big|\, 1\, A\, \underset{4}{PV}\, 3\, 3\,\Big| = P_4$$

5. One $\underset{1}{|}$ affirmed $\underset{2}{|}$ his having lived *half a century* back.
   $\underset{4}{}$

$$\Big|\underset{:1}{N}\Big|\, \underset{2}{V} \,\Big|\, 1^3\, A\cdot \underset{4}{PV}\, 3\, 1\,\Big| = P_{4\text{-}3rd}$$

6. The animal $\underset{1}{|}$ seemed $\underset{2}{|}$ to be reviving slowly.
   $\underset{4}{}$

$$\Big|\, 1^1\, \underset{1}{N}\,\Big|\, \underset{2}{V}\,\Big|\, A\, \underset{4}{PV}\, 1\,\Big| = P_{4\text{-}3rd}$$

In the Minimum Mono-simple you saw the last term to be a V, so in the Medium you have seen the IVs or PVs as terminals too. In the Medium, additional governed terms—the 3rd and the 4th have been seen added to the Minimum for its complete formation and it is by the same addition or repetition of N and IV or PV terms that you hope to arrive at the **Maximum Mono-simple sentence.** Only you are to repeat the N and IV or PV terms to the final IVs or PVs. The continuation or alternate and continued repetitions are, however, allowed to certain number of these pairs, say 2 more to the Medium and an additional half pair by N for its last term. The naked, Logical Formula of a Maximum Mono-simple sentence, therefore, by terms may be depicted thus :—

$$\Big|\underset{1}{N}\Big|\underset{2}{V}\Big|\underset{3}{N}\Big|\underset{4}{IV}\Big|\underset{5}{N}\Big|\underset{6}{IV}\Big|\underset{7}{N}\Big|\underset{8}{IV}\Big|\underset{9}{N}\Big|$$

From the Formula we might generalize a definition of the Mono-simple sentence thus :—

A *Mono-simple sentence* is one that starts with an initial N which governs the next V and this final V of its *minimum* variety in its gradual expansion of government, increases the structure by governing and adding to it the subsequent pair of

N and IV or PV, complete or by halves (*medium*) and this IV or PV alternately, or alternately and continually, governs and thus adds to it in its turn subsequent half or complete pairs of N and IV or PV up to the extent of two such groupal additions and a half (*maximum*). The IVs may continue thrice while PVs only twice in the above arrangement.

You may thus view the structure as made up of N|V groups and consider *all Ns as odd terms* and *all Vs as even terms*, not that 2nd or subsequent Ns may not be absent and thus show an apparent advance to the next reduced number of IV or PV terms, for, their consideration as *even terms* remains the same. Extension by N means extension by *half a group* and extension upto the IV or PV just after it, a *full group* of extension. We thus have structures that are formed by one group of N|V in the Minimum, $1\frac{1}{2}$ to 2 in the Medium $2\frac{1}{2}$ to 3 in the 1st portion of the Maximum, $3\frac{1}{2}$ to 4 in the 2nd portion of it, while $4\frac{1}{2}$ completes the structure by *half a group* of expansion in the 3rd Maximum portion. Further extension, I have seldom been fortunate enough to hit at without the intervention of connectives but when it does it is to be by the same recurring process of groupal addition.

Application of illustrations to the Maximum 1st, 2nd and 3rd Mono-simple sentence Formula.

With Graphic and Rational Formulæ respectively.

I.—MAXIMUM FIRST (*up to 6th Term*).

1. They | requested | my brother | to tell | them the story of
    1   2   3   4   5   6

   the ghost.

   $$\left| \underset{1}{N} \left| \underset{2}{V} \right| 1^3 \underset{3}{N} \left| \underset{4}{IV} \right| \underset{5}{N} \, 1^1 \underset{6}{N} \, 3 \right| = P_6$$

2. The trapper | was | the first | to shake-off | its influence.
       1   2   3   4   5

   $$\left| 1^1 \underset{1}{N} \left| \underset{2}{V} \right| 1^1 \underset{3}{N} \left| \underset{4}{IV} \right| 1^3 \underset{5}{N} \right| = P_5$$

LECTURE III.   33

3. You | may hear | the fire | begin | to roar already.
   $\underset{1}{\text{}}$ $\underset{2}{\text{}}$ $\underset{3}{\text{}}$ $\underset{4}{\text{}}$ $\underset{6}{\text{}}$

$$\left|\underset{1}{N}\right|\underset{2}{AV}\left|\underset{3}{1^1 N}\right|\underset{4}{IV}\left|\underset{6}{IV\,1}\right| = P_{6-5th}$$

II.—MAXIMUM SECOND   (*up to 8th Term*).

1. His companions | try | to dissuade | him | from attempting |
   $\underset{1}{\text{}}$ $\underset{2}{\text{}}$ $\underset{4}{\text{}}$ $\underset{5}{\text{}}$ $\underset{6}{\text{}}$

   this dangerous feat.
                   $\underset{7}{\text{}}$

$$\left|\underset{1}{1^3 N}\right|\underset{2}{V}\left|\underset{4}{IV}\right|\underset{5}{N}\left|\underset{6}{PV}\right|\underset{7}{1^2\,_2 N}\right| = P_7$$

2. The captain of the *Terrible* | suddenly shortened | sail | in-
   $\underset{1}{\text{}}$ $\underset{2}{\text{}}$ $\underset{3}{\text{}}$

   order-to allow | his consort | to join | him.
   $\underset{4}{\text{}}$ $\underset{5}{\text{}}$ $\underset{6}{\text{}}$ $\underset{7}{\text{}}$

$$\left|\underset{1}{1^1 N\,3}\right|\underset{2}{1\,V}\left|\underset{3}{N}\right|\underset{4}{IV}\left|\underset{5}{1^3 N}\right|\underset{6}{IV}\left|\underset{7}{N}\right| = P_7$$

3. Candles | are lighted | to give | us light | to see | to
   $\underset{1}{\text{}}$ $\underset{2}{\text{}}$ $\underset{4}{\text{}}$ $\underset{5\;5}{\text{}}$ $\underset{6}{\text{}}$

   work at night.
         $\underset{8}{\text{}}$

$$\left|\underset{1}{N}\right|\underset{2}{AV}\left|\underset{4}{IV}\right|\underset{5\;5}{N\;N}\left|\underset{6}{IV}\right|\underset{8}{IV\,3}\right| = P_8$$

4. Governments | employ | the military | to assist | in keepin
   $\underset{1}{\text{}}$ $\underset{2}{\text{}}$ $\underset{3}{\text{}}$ $\underset{4}{\text{}}$ $\underset{6}{\text{}}$

   the laws | from being broken.
   $\underset{7}{\text{}}$ $\underset{8}{\text{}}$

$$\left|\underset{1}{N}\right|\underset{2}{V}\left|\underset{3}{1^1 N}\right|\underset{4}{IV}\left|\underset{6}{PV}\right|\underset{7}{1^1 N}\left|\underset{8}{PV}\right| = P_8$$

III.—MAXIMUM THIRD   (*up to 9th Term*).

1. Thouzel | called out | to entreat for some drink | to enable |
   $\underset{1}{\text{}}$ $\underset{2}{\text{}}$ $\underset{4}{\text{}}$ $\underset{6}{\text{}}$

   him | to endure | the stifling.
   $\underset{7}{\text{}}$ $\underset{8}{\text{}}$ $\underset{9}{\text{}}$

$$\left|\underset{1}{N}\right|\underset{2}{V\,1}\left|\underset{4}{IV\,3}\right|\underset{6}{IV}\left|\underset{7}{N}\right|\underset{8}{IV}\left|\underset{9}{1^1 N}\right| = P_9$$

2. She | cheerfully went about her work all-day | endeavouring
   1   2   4

to prevent | her father | from perceiving | their injuries.
   6   7   8   9

$$|\underset{1}{N}|\underset{2}{{}_1V}{}_{33}|\underset{4}{PV}|\underset{6}{IV}|\underset{7}{{}_1{}^3N}|\underset{8}{PV}|\underset{9}{{}_1{}^3N} = P_9$$

I have shown you second or subsequent Ns to be duals distinct, but emphatic parts of speech as the *Compound Personal Pronouns* render all Ns *dual* by emphasis. These Compound PPs may be considered as *in apposition to* Ns.

Illustrations with Graphic and Rational Formulæ respectively.

1. Ram *himself* | had | to do | this work.
   1   1   2   4   5

$$|\underset{1}{N}\ \underset{1}{N}|\underset{2}{V}|\underset{4}{IV}|\underset{5}{{}_1{}^2N}| = P_5$$

2. It | keeps | the earth *itself* | from becoming | a waste.
   1   2   3   3   4   5

$$|\underset{1}{N}|\underset{2}{V}|\underset{3}{{}_1{}^1N}\ \underset{3}{N}|\underset{4}{PV}|\underset{5}{{}_1{}^1N}| = P_5$$

You have been told already of the Proxy and Representative parts of speech of N, I go now to show to you the Analogues of N in certain terms and their continuation. Such Analogues are the 4th terms alone or with their suites as phrases or continued terms as seen in the Maximum Formula.

IV Analogues of N as first Term.

Illustrations with Graphic and Rational Formulæ respectively.

1. To *forgive* | is divine.
      1   2

$$|\underset{1}{IV}|\underset{2}{V}{}_2| = P_2$$

LECTURE III.   35

2. (*To believe* in objective truth)$^N_1$ | is | to throw | ourselves'
               $_2$ $_4$ $_5$
   forward upon the partially mastered subjective.

$$|\ IV_{3}\ |\ V\ |\ IV*\ |\ N\ |*1\,3\ |=P_{5}$$
$$\ _1\ \ \ \ \ _2\ \ \ \ \ _4\ \ \ \ \ _5$$

3. (*To know* | the god of nature | in part)$^N_1$ | is | a poor thing |
      $_4$ $_5$ $_2$ $_3$
   in-comparison- of knowing | the laws of nature in full.
           $_4$ $_5$

$$|\ \overbrace{IV*\ |\ 1^1N_3\ |*3}\ |\ V\ |\ 1^1{,}2\ N\ |\ PV\ |\ 1^1\ N\,3\,3\ |=P_5$$
$$\ \ \ \ \ \ _1\ \ \ \ \ \ \ \ \ \ \ \ \ \ \ \ \ \ \ _2\ \ \ \ \ \ \ \ _3\ \ \ \ \ \ _4\ \ \ \ \ \ _5$$

4. (*To retreat* from the world to a monastery | there to await |
      $_4$ $_6$
   the awful event)$^N_1$ | seemed | the only course.
     $_7$ $_2$ $_3$

$$|\ \overbrace{IV_{33}\ |\ 1\ IV\ |\ 1^1\,2\,N}\ |\ V\ |\ 1^1\,2\,N\ |=P_3$$
$$\ \ \ \ \ \ \ \ \ \ _1\ _2\ \ \ \ \ \ \ \ _3$$

5. (*To have said* | a word for the heretic)$^N_1$ | would have
      $_4$ $_5$
   been | to incur | imminent risk of the fate of the heretic.
   $_2$ $_4$ $_5$

$$|\ \overbrace{A\ IV\ |\ 1^1N_3}\ |\ AA\ V\ |\ IV\ |\ 2\ N\,3\,3\ |=P_5$$
$$\ \ \ \ \ \ \ \ \ \ _1\ _2\ \ \ \ \ _4\ \ \ \ \ \ _5$$

6. (*To watch* | an Amœba | literally flowing from one shape to
      $_4$ $_5$ $_6$
   another)$^N_1$ | is | to behold | one of the most perplexing
        $_2$ $_4$ $_5$
   sights.

$$|\ \overbrace{IV\ |\ 1^1\,N\ |\ 1\,PV\,3\,3}\ |\ V\ |\ IV\ |\ N\,3\ |=P_5$$
$$\ \ \ \ \ \ \ \ \ \ _1\ _2\ \ \ \ \ _4\ \ \ \ \ _5$$

PV Analogues of N as first Term.

Illustrations with Graphic and Rational Formulæ respectively.

1. *Riding* | is | a pleasant exercise.
    $_1$ $_2$ $_3$

$$|\ PV\ |\ V\ |\ 1^1\,2\,N\ |\ =P_3$$
$$\ \ \ _1\ \ \ \ \ _2\ \ \ \ \ \ \ _3$$

2. (His *betraying* | the secrets of Government | to the enemy)^N
    has rendered | him | highly treasonable to the eye of the people.

$$| 1^3 \, PV_1 * | 1^1 \, N \, 3 | * 3 | A\underset{2}{V} * | \underset{3}{N} | * 1 \, 2 \, 3 \, 3 | = P_3.$$

3. (The *refining* of the fine arts)$^N_1$ | was vehemently undertaken by the mass about this time.

$$| 1^1 \, PV_1 \, 3 | A \, 1 \, \underset{2}{V} \, 3 \, 3 | = P_2$$

You see in these examples, PV the naked analogue of N, you see also the first series of special ante-joiners of N placed before it to exhibit its N character and you see again its PV character by its suite N as sub-term.

In conclusion I have to point out to you that the same IV and PV terms respectively alone, or their suite as in the Maximum may be post-joiners to N or its Representatives. In the following Graphic Formulæ small iv and pv and n is used as symbolic representations of sub-terms.

Alternate IV and PV as first N.

Illustrations with Graphic and Rational Formulæ respectively.

1. To leave the cottage for even a minute *without one of us staying* with her | was impossible.

$$| IV | 1^1 \, n_1 | 3 \, 3 \, 3 \, pv \, 3 | \underset{2}{V} \, 2 | = P_2$$

In this example the intimate preposition of a PV joiner has admitted also its formation into a preposition phrase, thus giving its dual functions together.

IV Post-joiners of N.

Illustration with Graphic and Rational Formulæ respectively.

1. The thought *to proceed* to England by the next mail | had |
   $\quad\quad\quad\quad\quad\quad\quad$ 1 $\quad\quad\quad\quad\quad\quad\quad\quad\quad\quad\quad$ 2

   thus to be abandoned by him.

   $$| \; 1^1 \; \underset{1}{N} \; iv \; 3 \; 3 \; | \; \underset{2}{V} \; | \; 1 \; \underset{4}{A} \; IV \; 3 \; | = P_4$$

2. The idea *to analize* the structure of the English language
   $\quad\quad\quad\quad$ 1

   by means of scientific Formulæ | originated with the
   $\quad\quad\quad\quad\quad\quad\quad\quad\quad\quad\quad\quad\quad\quad$ 2

   author.

   $$| \; 1^1 \; \underset{1}{N} \; iv \; | \; 1^1 \; n \; 3 \; 3 \; 3 \; | \; \underset{2}{V} \; 3 \; | = P_2$$

3. A man *to reach* Chittagong from Rangamati by peda-
   $\quad\quad\quad$ 1
   strainism | will take but | 24 hours in all.
   $\quad\quad\quad\quad\quad\;$ 2 $\quad\quad\quad\quad\quad$ 3

   $$| \; 1^1 \; \underset{1}{N} \; iv \; | \; n \; 3 \; 3 \; | \; \underset{2}{AV} \; 1 \; | \; 2 \; \underset{3}{N} \; 3 \; | = P_3$$

4. This | is | the easiest method *to learn*.
   $\;\;$ 1 $\quad$ 2 $\quad\quad\quad\quad\quad\quad\quad\quad$ 3

   $$| \; \underset{1}{N} \; | \; \underset{2}{V} \; | \; 1^1 \; 2 \; \underset{3}{N} \; iv \; | = P_3$$

5. You | ought | to inculcate to the boys | sound principles *to*
   $\;\;$ 1 $\quad\;\;$ 2 $\quad\quad\quad\;$ 4 $\quad\quad\quad\quad\quad\quad\quad\quad\quad\quad$ 5
   base their future career *upon*.

   $$| \; \underset{1}{N} \; | \; \underset{2}{V} \; | \; \underset{4}{IV} \; 3 \; | \; 2 \; \underset{5}{N} \; iv \; 1^3 \; 2 \; n \; | = P_5$$

In the first two examples you might consider the IVs not only as N analogues but take them as dual 1st Ns though they are apparently as post-joiners.

PV Post-joiners of N.

Illustrations with Graphic and Rational Formulæ respectively.

1. This very pride, *in* not *wishing* to accept unfair emolu-
   $\quad\quad\quad\quad\quad\quad\quad$ 1
   ment | did | the cause all the good in the world. (PV as
   $\quad\;\;$ 2 $\quad\;\;$ 3 $\quad\quad\quad$ 3
   N analogue by apposition to N).

   $$| \; 1^2 \; 2 \; \underset{1}{N} \; | \; pv \; | \; iv \; | \; 2 \; n \; | \; \underset{2}{V} \; | \; 1^1 \; \underset{3}{N} \; 1^2 \; 1^1 \; N \; 3 \; | = P_3$$

2. The traveller *hemmed-in*$_1$ between their steep precipices | sees only$_2$ | the dark grandeur of the chasm.$_3$

$$\mid 1^1 \underset{1}{N} \text{ pv } 3 \mid \underset{2}{V} 1 \mid 1^1 2 \underset{3}{N} 3 \mid = P_3$$

3. Every island$_1$ | is$_2$ | a Paradise *accommodated* to its respective inhabitants.

$$\mid 1^2 \underset{1}{N} \mid \underset{2}{V} \mid 1^1 \underset{3}{N} \text{ pv } 3 \mid = P_3$$

4. That melancholy intermittant now capable *of being expelled*$_1$ by excitement | was not allowed$_2$ | to be interposed-with.$_4$

$$\mid 1^2 \underset{1}{N} 2 1 2 \text{ pv } 3 \mid \underset{2}{A} 1 V \mid \underset{4}{IV} \mid = P_4$$

5. The valleys of Nepaul besides *being* very narrow$_1$ | belong$_2$ rather to the region of the lower hills.

$$\mid 1^1 \underset{1}{N} 3 1 \text{ p v } 1 2 \mid \underset{2}{V} 1 3 3 \mid = P_2$$

6. No mortal foot | has yet ascended to the highest springs *situated* in the most elevated recesses of the mountain.

$$\mid 1 2 \underset{1}{N} \mid \underset{2}{A} 1 V 3 \text{ n pv } 3 3 \mid = P_2$$

7. Our only chance then *remaining* of *accomplishing* our ends,$_1$ | was$_2$ | to be united again.$_4$

$$\mid 1^3 2 \underset{1}{N} \mid 1 \text{ pv } \mid \text{pv} \mid 1^3 \text{ n} \mid \underset{2}{V} \mid \underset{4}{IV} 1 \mid = P_4$$

8. | Niger *having* now suddenly *paused*$_1$ | had again cast$_2$ | his net.$_3$

$$\mid \underset{1}{N} 1 1 \text{ pv} \mid \underset{2}{A} 1 V \mid 1^3 \underset{3}{N} \mid = P_3$$

LECTURE III.

Alternate IV and PV Post-joiner of N.

Illustrations with Graphic and Rational Formulæ respectively.

1. | A Bishop *issuing* forth *to convert* the heathen | evolves | a
    1   2

Church | from himself by his apostolic power.
3

$$\left| 1^1 \underset{1}{N} \mid pv\ 1 \mid iv \mid 1^1\ n \right| \underset{2}{V} * \left| 1^1 \underset{3}{N} \right| * 3\ 3\ \left| = P_3 \right.$$

Thus you see now that both the IVs and PVs have their Present and Perfect Tenses. The IV has got no Past Tense of its own, while the PV has got its. You have seen also the chief roll played by the Past Participle in the 2nd term of the formula, being preceded by auxiliaries of 'Have' to form the different Perfect and the Pluperfect tenses and by the auxiliaries of 'Be' to form the Passive. As an independent PV in the fourth term, whose peculiarity of never being followed by a fifth term and always getting an advance to apparently the third term, proves that it belongs to the Adjective class and is really not a term but a post-joiner to second term V. In fact there is no independent past participle as a term unless as Absolute, to be dealt with afterwards. The next great roll played by it is as post-joiner to N only presently shown to you.

Examples, therefore, of all the three tenses of Participles have been shown as post-joiners of N though its perfect tense as such bears semblance to Absolutes.

When the first term N is followed by a fourth term PV alone, clothed or with its suite, provided there be no second term in the Formula, an incomplete structure is formed which is known by the name of N incomplete *Absolute structure*.

This absolute structure is never alone but precedes or follows a Mono-simple sentence. For it, this '{ }' bracket is used and the larger digits within it in the Rational formula indicate the number of Terms.

Application of illustrations to N Absolute formula.

Illustration with Graphic and Rational Formulæ respectively.

1. The sun$_1$ | appearing$_4$ on the horizon,

$$\zeta \mid 1^1 \underset{1}{N} \mid \underset{4}{PV} \, 3 \mid \zeta = \zeta \; N \; PV \, \zeta \; \text{or} \, \zeta \, 1 \, 4 \, \zeta$$

2. His dreams$_1$ of royalty | being$_4$ at an end,

$$\zeta \mid 1^3 \underset{1}{N} \, 3 \mid \underset{4}{PV} \, 3 \mid \zeta = \zeta \; N \; PV \, \zeta \; \text{or} \, \zeta \, 1 \, 4 \, \zeta$$

Illustrations of Union of the 1st N Absolute structure and the Mono-simple sentence with their Formulæ.

A.—Initial 1st N Absolute to Mono-simple.

Illustration with Graphic and Rational Formula respectively.

1. ζNight$_1$ | approaching$_4\zeta$ { my guide$_1$ | conducted$_2$ | me$_3$ | to a hut for shelter }.*

$$\zeta \mid \underset{1}{N} \mid \underset{4}{PV} \mid \zeta \{ \mid 1^3 \underset{i1}{N} \mid \underset{2}{V} * \mid \underset{3}{N} \mid * 3\,3 \mid \} = \zeta \, 1\,4 \, \zeta \, P$$

B.—Terminal 1st N Absolute to Mono-simple.

1. {We$_1$ | walked-out$_2$ of the house } ζ all the entreaties$_1$ of the owner | being$_4$ of no avail | to detain | us | for the night there.ζ

$$\{ \mid \underset{1}{N} \mid \underset{2}{V} \, 3 \mid \} \zeta \mid 1^2 \, 1^1 \underset{1}{N} \, 3 \mid \underset{4}{pv} \, 3 \mid \underset{6}{iv} * \mid \underset{7}{n} \mid * 3\,1 \mid \zeta = P_2 \zeta \, 1\,4\,6\,7 \, \zeta$$

C.—Both initial and terminal N Absolute to Mono-simple.

1. ζThe day$_1$ | having dawned$_4\zeta$ { only two of the company$_1$ | left$_2$ | the Restaurant$_3$ } ζ the rest$_1$ | being$_4$ still in bed under the influence of mighty sleep.ζ

$$\zeta \, 1^1 \underset{1}{N} \mid \underset{4}{pv} \, \zeta \{ \mid 2 \underset{1}{N} \, 3 \mid \underset{2}{V} \mid \underset{3}{1^1 N} \mid \} \zeta \mid 1^1 \underset{1}{N} \mid \underset{4}{pv} \, 1\,3\,3\,3 \mid \zeta$$
$$= \zeta \, 1\,4 \, \zeta \, P_3 \zeta \, 1\,4 \, \zeta$$

---

* Large braces enclose mono-simple Principals.

LECTURE III.

PV being analogous to IV, N | PV Absolute must have its analogy in N | IV Absolute. For Example :—

1. $\Big($ This method of practical teaching | in-order-to be con-
   $\underset{1}{\text{demned}}$ by our staff of teachers $\Big)$ {their sole endeavour |
   $\underset{2}{\text{ought}}$ | $\underset{4}{\text{to be}}$ | $\underset{6}{\text{to give}}$ | $\underset{7}{\text{it}}$ a thoroughly proper $\underset{7}{\text{exercise}}$
   upon the $\underset{}{\text{pupils}}$ | $\underset{8}{\text{before pronouncing}}$ | such a judgment | $\underset{9}{\text{at}}$
   all upon it.}

$$\Big(\underset{1}{|\,1^2\,\underset{1}{N}\,3\,|\,\underset{4}{IV}\,3\,3\,|}\Big)\{1^3\,2\,\underset{1}{N}\,|\,\underset{2}{V}\,|\,\underset{4}{IV}\,|\,\underset{6}{IV}\,|\,\underset{7}{N_1^1}\,1\,2\,\underset{7}{N}\,3\,|$$
$$\underset{8}{PV}*|\,1^2\,1^1\,\underset{9}{N}\,|*3\,3\,|\,\}=\Big(1\,4\,\Big)P_9$$

PV has been shown to be a governed Term to V, IV, or PV; or PV has also been shown to be a post-joiner to N; it has just lately been shown as a suite N Absolute. I go now to show you that it is an un-governed term or absolute incomplete structure by its initiative. To recognize it as such you will find it almost generally drop its intimate preposition: and its action to be distinct and antecedent or subsequent to that of the Principal V, whose action is but a sequence or precedence. Its position with regard to P is analogous to that of the Absolutes.

1. $\Big(\underset{1}{\text{Saying}}\,|\,\underset{4}{\text{nothing}}\,|\,\underset{5}{\text{in the mean time to any one}}\Big),\,\{\underset{1}{\text{he}}$
   | $\underset{2}{\text{went in the evening to the garden-house.}}$}

$$\Big(\,|\,\underset{4}{PV}*|\underset{5}{N}|*3\,3\,|\,\Big)\{\,|\,N\,|\,V\,3\,3\,|\,\}=\Big(4\,5\Big)P_2$$

2. $\Big(\text{Before comunicating}\,|\,\underset{4}{\text{the happy}}\,\underset{5}{\text{news}}\,|\,\text{to his wife}\Big)\,\{\underset{1}{\text{he}}$
   | $\underset{2}{\text{went out personally}}$ | to $\underset{4}{\text{enquire into its truth.}}$}

$$\Big(\underset{4}{PV}*|\,1^1\,2\,\underset{5}{N}\,|*3\Big)\,\{\underset{1}{N}\,|\,\underset{2}{V}\,1\,1\,|\,\underset{4}{IV}\,3\}=\Big(4\,5\Big)P_4$$

PV absolute by analogy brings us to IV absolute. Thus :—

1. ζ To mark also | his gratitude $\rangle$ { he | recommended | the
     $\quad\;\;\,4\qquad\qquad\;\;\,5\qquad\qquad\;\;1\qquad\quad\;\;2$
honest Jew | to various European Sovereigns.}
$\quad\;\;3$

$$\zeta IV_4 \,{}_1|\,{}_1{}^3 N_5 \rangle \;\{\,|\,N_1\,|\,V_2\,|\,{}_1{}^1\,{}_2\,N_3\,|\,{}_3\,|\,\} = \zeta 4\;5\rangle P_3$$

Absolute with Adjective initiative is also seen though it may be considered as a PV absolute with an understood PV before the Adjective. Thus :—

1. ζ (Being) Indignant at Uberto, $\rangle$ { he | passed | the
     $\qquad\qquad\qquad\qquad\qquad\qquad\qquad\;\;1\qquad\;\;\,2$
sentence | in very insolent terms.}
$\quad\;\;3$

$$\zeta(PV)\,{}_2\,{}_3 \rangle \{\,|\,N_1\,|\,V_2*\,|\,{}_1{}^1\,N_3\,|\,*{}_3\,|\,\} = \zeta(PV)_2\,{}_3\rangle P_3$$

2. ζ Weak, unwell, $\rangle$ { Vincent was sold cheap to a fisherman.}

$$\zeta(PV)_2\,{}_2\rangle \{\,N_1\,|\,AV_2\,{}_2\,{}_3\,|\,\} = \zeta{}_2\,{}_2\rangle P_2$$

The first developmental combination that P Mono-simple goes to make, is thus shown by its union with the absolute, un-governed and incomplete structures and phrases. Absolute parts of speech unions to P by the Interjections, Vocative Nouns, and Prepositional Phrases will be shown after finishing the consideration of the different expressions, the Narrative, the Imperative, the Interrogative, and the Exclamatory ones. It must be borne in mind as a philological fact that Absolute Parts of Speech, Phrases, and Structures are Independent Incomplete *Unions* to the P while Complete (R' and C') Structures are *Combinations*, subordinate to it.

The combination of the P by way of increased development deals with complete but so-called Subordinate Structures and rarely with such elliptical ones, which will be considered later on. Subordinate unions occur within all the Absolutes except *Interjection Absolutes*, thus showing that interjections are only isolated vociferations, while the other Absolutes approach gradually more to complete Mono-simple Phrases.

You have been told before, that in Parsing 1st N governs the 1st V (*1st government, of single upon single term*) and this and other Vs (IVs & PVs) govern their subsequent Ns and IVs (*2nd government, of single upon double terms*). You will see here exceptionally that a 2nd and a 3rd term conjointly govern the 4th (*3rd government, double upon single term*). In these instances, however, the 4th may also be considered as Post-joiner to the 3rd term.

2nd and 3rd Terms governing 4th Term :—

1. Dr. Kane | had sent out | parties | to make | stores of
   $\quad$ 1 $\qquad$ 2 $\qquad$ 3 $\qquad$ 4 $\qquad$ 5

   provisions at various intervals.

   $$|\underset{1}{N}|\underset{2}{AV}\,_1|\underset{3}{N}|\underset{4}{IV}|\underset{5}{N}\,_3\,_3\,|=P_5$$

2. She | wanted | a volume | to illustrate | her thought.
   $\;$ 1 . $\quad$ 2 $\qquad$ 3 $\qquad\quad$ 4 $\qquad\quad$ 5

   $$|\underset{1}{N}|\underset{2}{V}|\,_1{}^1\underset{3}{N}|\underset{4}{IV}|\,_1{}^3\underset{5}{N}=P_5$$

3. They | took | three-fourth of an hour | in going | the distance.
   $\quad$ 1 $\quad$ 2 $\qquad\qquad$ 3 $\qquad\qquad$ 4 $\qquad\quad$ 5

   $$|\underset{1}{N}|\underset{2}{V}|\underset{3}{N}\,_3|\underset{4}{PV}|\,_1{}^2\underset{5}{N}=P_5$$

Lastly comes the 2nd term with its Post-joiner 3 that governs the 4th Term :—

1. A sledge | was despatched with eight men | to arrange | one
   $\qquad$ 1 $\qquad\qquad$ 2 $\qquad\qquad\qquad$ 4 $\qquad\quad$ 5

   of these depôts for future use.

   $$|\,_1{}^1\underset{1}{N}|\underset{2}{AV}\,_3|\underset{4}{IV}|\underset{5}{N}\,_3\,_3\,|=P_5$$

2. Many a life | *has been lost in the attempt* | to discover | the North-west passage.
        1   2   4   5

$$\mid 2\,1^1\,\underset{1}{N} \mid \underset{2}{AA}\ V\ 3 \mid \underset{4}{IV} \mid 1^1\ 2\,\underset{5}{N} \mid = P_5$$

The 4th term here may also be considered as Sub-Post-joiner to the N of Post-joiner 3 of 2nd term (3rd *government, of single with its post-joiner upon single*).

LECTURE IV.

STUDENTS AND GENTLEMEN,

. IN the N Formula you have seen *double* or *triple increase* in words of the *pronominal adjective* and *adjective classes*; you have seen even, more *repetitions of preposition phrases* in the same. You have seen also *dual Ns*, or dauls of N proxy and N, in the third or subsequent odd Term of the Mono-simple Formula. You have been shown again duals of any N, the second being the emphatic Compound Personal Pronoun series. In all these, however, you do not see the interference or developement of any mark of Punctuation or connective classes of words—the Conjunctions. I go now presently to show to you another class of N dauls in which *comma* may take its first appearance. These are *duals by apposition* of like Cases of N— the Nominative or Objective. Mark that this second N is either preceded by a comma and followed by a preposition phrase, or the comma dropping is preceded by the Article adjective 'The'. The comma may again be followed by any of the A A and the second N sometimes by preposition phrases, or that the second N is represented by one of the pronominal adjectives and followed by a preposition phrase; mark also that these two Ns may suffer *inversion* in position and these points will settle with you about their recognition.

Application of Apposition Ns in Mono-simples.

Illustrations with Graphic and Rational Formulæ respectively.

1. Charles I, *king* of England | was beheaded by the order
   $\quad\;\;$1 $\qquad\qquad\qquad\qquad\qquad$ 2
   of the first-formed Parliament.

$$\mid \underset{1}{N}\, 2,\, \underset{1}{N}\, 3 \mid \underset{2}{AV}\, 3\, 3 \mid = P_2$$

2. Cicero the *orater* | lived in the first century B.C.
   $\quad$ 1 $\qquad\qquad$ 2

$$| \underset{1}{N} 1^1 \underset{1}{N} | \underset{2}{V} 3\,3 | = P_2$$

3. Babu Hurry Podo Ghose, a *member* of the Meeting
   $\qquad\quad$ 1
   | seconded | the proposition.
   $\quad$ 2 $\qquad\quad$ 3

$$| 2\underset{1}{N}, 1^1 \underset{1}{N} 3 | \underset{2}{V} | 1^1 \underset{3}{N} | = P_3$$

4. Dr. King, the great *Botanist* | is | Professor of Botany
   $\qquad$ 2 $\qquad\qquad$ 1 $\quad$ 2 $\qquad\quad$ 3,
   in the Medical College, Calcutta.

$$| 2\underset{1}{N}, 1^1\,2\underset{1}{N} | \underset{2}{V} | \underset{3}{N}\,3\,3\,3 | = P_3$$

5. Mr. Roy, an *individual* of great renown in the city
   $\quad$ 1 $\qquad\qquad$ 1
   | spoke in favor of widow-marriage.
   $\quad$ 2

$$| \underset{1}{N}, 1^1 \underset{1}{N}\,3\,3 | \underset{2}{V}\,3\,3 | = P_2$$

6. The District Engineer, *Babu Sasibhusan Dutta* | left |
   $\qquad\qquad\qquad\quad$ 1 $\qquad\qquad\qquad$ 1 $\quad$ 2
   this station | on inspection duty.
   $\qquad$ 3

$$| 1^1\,2\underset{1}{N}, 2\underset{1}{N} | \underset{2}{V} * | 1^2 \underset{3}{N} | * 3 | = P_3$$

7. Thomas Clarkson, *one of the students* | took | pains | to
   $\qquad\qquad\quad$ 1 $\qquad\quad$ 1 $\qquad\qquad$ 2 $\quad$ 3
   acquire | information on the subject.
   $\;\;$ 4 $\qquad$ 5

$$| \underset{1}{N}, \underset{1}{N}\,3 | \underset{2}{V} | \underset{3}{N} | \underset{4}{IV} | \underset{5}{N}\,3 | = P_5$$

8. He | asked for some trifling thing—a pair of gloves.

$$| \underset{1}{N} | \underset{:2}{V}\,3n - 1^1 n 3 = P_2$$

9. The youth | is named | Crawford—a relation to Sir George
   $\quad$ 1 $\qquad\;$ 2 $\qquad\;$ 3 $\qquad\qquad\quad$ 3
   Mornay.

$$| 1^1 \underset{1}{N} | \underset{2}{AV} | \underset{3}{N} - 1^1 \underset{3}{N}\,3 | = P_3$$

10. Lady Cornelia | is | a nice girl, the eldest daughter
    $\underset{1}{}$ $\underset{2}{}$ $\underset{3}{}$ $\underset{3}{}$
of Thomas William Steven Conway, Marquis of
Sittingbourne.

$$\mid \underset{1}{N} \mid \underset{2}{V} \mid 1^1{}_2 \underset{3}{N},\ 1^1\ 2\ \underset{3}{N}\ 3\ n,\ n\ 3 \mid = P_3$$

11. Crawford | beheld | the partner of his villany—Reving-
    $\underset{1}{}$ $\underset{2}{}$ $\underset{3}{}$ $\underset{3}{}$
stone. $\mid \underset{1}{N} \mid \underset{2}{V} \mid 1^1 \underset{3}{N}\ 3 - \underset{3}{N} \mid = P_3$

It may be remarked here that Apposition Ns of 3rd or subsequent odd terms generally take 'dash' in place of comma before them.

You see also that *Apposition Ns* are but *Equivalents of capacity* to Proper nouns in one and the same term. Consequently, their government in parsing is the same.

In *V* terms again you saw similar repetitions of adverbs and preposition phrases between which no punctuative comma nor conjunction became visible.

All these repetitions it must be borne in mind were but repetition of implied connection between themselves and did not necessitate the advent of punctuations and conjunctions. It is, therefore, that when unconnected words are increased in any N and V terms or in their joiners and sub-joiners they require the intervention of conjunctions and sometimes punctuations or both.

We thus arrive at the development of conjunction in Mono-simple sentences. Before we proceed to apply them to illustrations and then formulate the latter we must remark that **conjunctions** are—

1st, **groupal—Mono-**, and **Bi-**, the former single, dual, triple, and phrasial, the latter in the Bi-groups consisting of pure and pure, adverb and pure, pronominal adjective and pure, comparative adjective or adverb and pure, adverb and adverb, compound adjective or adverb and the same—both preceded by Article adjective 'The'.

2ndly, that they are links between all, except the Article adjective and Interjection (the latter to be dealt with afterwards).

3rdly, that they vary in their capacity as regards union, certain compounds being present between all varieties of increased terms, joiners and subjoiners; some being, such as the Examplary variety, only fit to unite with Ns and others being special to Vs.

4thly, that there are very few **strong compounds** only, which form the connecting link not only between the maximum number of varieties but between the maximum number of words in each variety, being mono-groupals. Others being supposed to be uniter of a pair only in each variety—**weak compounds** and **co-ordinates**, being both *Mono-* or *Bi-groupals*.

Conjunctions with maximum capacity of placing themselves between varieties as well as between maximum number in each variety may be called the **proto-types** of conjunctions. 'And' as well as 'or' belong to this class.

5thly. Besides the above **Uniters of Symmetry** in a pair or more, another class is visible which is **Asymmetrical**, *i.e.*, which place themselves between different terms or different varieties in a term or between a preceding joiner and a subsequent term. Hence proceeds the following classification :—

A. Connectives between symmetry.
- I. In Compound increase of terms, joiners or subjoiners (*Cumulative, Alternative, Adversative &c*).
- II. In Co-ordinate increase of terms, joiners and subjoiners.
- III. In conjoined Compound and Co-ordinate increase of terms, joiners or subjoiners.

B. Connectives between asymmetry.
- In Semblance Subordinate increase between different terms—between A and V or between preceding V joiner and a subsequent IV term &c.

In compound increases, the terms, joiners or subjoiners are increased to two or more than two of each; in cases of four or more even numbers they may be joined in pairs. In the former instances of more than two increases of each, a comma intervenes between each pair and the connective between the last; while in the latter instances of four or more even pairs, connectives may place themselves between each pair followed by *comma* in cases of joiners and subjoiners, except that of the last which may sometimes be punctuated by a period, colon, or semicolon at the end. Co-ordinate increases are only in a pair unless in the consecutives of compound pairs in the Co-ordinate when conjoined increases as described may be visible.

What is good with connectives in terms, joiners and sub joiners in the Mono-simple sentence, will also be seen to hold good with structures. The uniters of the symmetrical, will be seen to develope into Compounds and Co-ordinates and those of the asymmetricals into Subordinate or Co-ordinate Subordinate structures. Analogy leads us therefore to conceive that subordination exists between terms or between joiners and terms in the Mono-simple.

The Proto-types alone admit ellipsis, their omission being represented by *comma* which is hence a *punctuative connective*.

When these Proto-types or Compounds, as they are called, have to deal with increased number of terms or their joiners in a series of more than 2, comma takes its seat between all pairs except the last between which the conjunction takes its seat.

Let the Conjunction in Mono-simples be called *simple conjunction* as they are between Parts of Speech or between Phrases and between parts of speech and their analogous phrases and let *small plus* represent them in the Formula. Reference for these conjunctions might be made at the Appendix.

A.—Connectives of Symmetrical parts.
I.—BY MONO-GROUPALS.
(a).—IN TERMS.

(i.)—*between 1st terms.*

Illustrations with Graphic and Rational Formulæ respectively.

1. (To tie | tin canisters | to the tails of dogs,) *or* (to cause
   $_4 _5 _4$
   | dogs | to worry | cats) *or* (to throw | stones | at birds,)
   $_5 _6 _7 + _5$
   are | all of them cruel kinds of fun made for the purpose
   $_2 _3 _3 _4$
   of amusing ourselves.
   $_6 _7$

$$(IV_4 \mid 2 N_5 \mid 3\ 3)^N_1,$$
$$+ (IV_4 \mid N_5 \mid IV_6 \mid N_7)_1,$$
$$+ (IV_4 \mid N_5 \mid 3)^N_1 \mid V_2 \mid N\ 3\ 2\ N\ 3\ n - pv\ pv\ n \mid = P_3$$

2. Lord Fanmore *and* he | instantly recognised | each-other.
   $_1 + _1 _2$

$$N_1 + N_1 \mid 1\ V_2 \mid N_3 \mid = P_3$$

3. James *and* Sophia | accordingly proceeded *some way* into the
   $_1 + _2$
   country.

$$N_1 + N_1 \mid 1\ V_2\ 3\ 3 \mid = P_2$$

4. The shreiks of the old woman, the crackling of kindled
   $_1 _1$
   timbers, *and* the voice of the raging element, | were alone
   $_1$
   now for a short space heard.
   $_2$

$$\mid 1^1\ N_1\ 3,\ 1^1\ N_1\ 3,+1^1\ N_1\ 3 \quad A\ 1\ 1\ 3\ V_2 \mid = P_2$$

LECTURE IV.

5. All this *and* a good deal more | was speedily meditated.
   $\quad$ 1 $\qquad\qquad$ 1 $\qquad\qquad\qquad$ 2 :

$$\mid 1^2 \underset{1}{N} + 1^1 \, 2 \underset{1}{N} \, 2 \mid A \, 1 \underset{2}{V} \mid = P_2$$

6. (| To enable | Miss Maxwell's fanaticism concerning the
   $\qquad\quad$ 4 $\qquad\quad$ 5 $\qquad\qquad\qquad$ 6
   abjuration by a community of women to work-up $\mid)^N_1$ *and* |
   $\quad$ 7 $\qquad\qquad\qquad\qquad\qquad\qquad$ 8 $\qquad\quad$ +
   (its contemplated connection with a very questionable
   $\qquad\qquad\qquad\qquad\qquad$ 1
   mode | of raising | the necessary pecuniary supplies for
   $\qquad\quad$ 4 $\qquad\qquad\qquad\qquad\qquad\qquad$ 5
   the support of the novel institution to be carried-out $\mid)^N_1$
   required | John Dimmock | to be thoroughly instructed in
   $\qquad\quad$ 2
   the ramifications of the whole mystery).

$$(\mid \underset{4}{IV} \, 1^5 \, n \, 3 \, 3 \, 3 \, 4 \mid)^N_1$$
$$+(\mid 1^3 \, 2 \underset{1}{N} \, 3 \, iv \, 1^1 \, 2 \, 2 \, n \, 3 \, 3 \, 4 \mid)^N_1$$
$$\mid \underset{2}{V} \mid \underset{3}{N} \mid I \, 1 \underset{4}{V} \, 3 \, 3 \mid = P_4$$

Here the 1st term IV and its suite and 1st term N have been compounded.

(ii.)—*between 2nd terms.*

1. The revenue arising from his school | was small *and* would
   $\qquad\qquad$ 1 $\qquad\qquad\qquad\qquad$ 2 $\qquad$ +
   have been scarcely sufficient | to furnish | him | with
   $\qquad$ 2 $\qquad\qquad\qquad\qquad\qquad$ 4 $\qquad\quad$ 5
   daily bread.

$$\mid 1^1 \underset{1}{N} \, 4, 3 \mid \underset{2}{V} \, 2 + AA\underset{2}{V} \, 1 \, 2 \mid \underset{4}{IV} * \mid \underset{5}{N} \mid * 3 = P_5$$

2. The merchant | was astounded | and | for a space was
   $\qquad$ 1 $\qquad\qquad$ 2 $\qquad\quad$ +
   struck-dumb.
   $\quad$ 2

$$\mid 1^1 \underset{1}{N} \mid A\underset{2}{V} \mid + \, 3 \, A \underset{2}{V} \mid = P_2$$

3. Men | started at the intelligence *and* turned pale.
$\underset{1}{\text{Men}}$ $\underset{2}{\text{started}}$ $\underset{+}{\text{and}}$ $\underset{2}{\text{turned}}$

$$\left|\underset{1}{N}\right|\underset{2}{V}3\left|+\left|\underset{2}{V}2\right|=P_2\right.$$

4. Nathaniel | acknowledged | the complement, | felt satisfied in his own mind | how to act | *and* resumed | some old topic of conversation. (Both comma and conjunction between 2nd terms.)

$$\underset{1}{N}\ \Big|\ \underset{2}{V}\ \Big|\ 1^1\ \underset{3}{N}\ \Big|$$

$$,\ \underset{2}{V}\ 4\ 3\ \Big|\ 1\ \underset{4}{1V}\ \Big|$$

$$+\ \underset{2}{V}\ \Big|\ 1^2\ 2\ \underset{2}{N}\ 3\ \Big|=P_3$$

5. The banished merchant | started at the intelligence, | *but* | checked | himself, *and* | hastily walked away. | ('But' and 'and' between Vs.)

$$\Big|\ 1^1\ 2\ \underset{1}{N}\ \Big|\ \underset{2}{V}\ 3\ \Big|$$

$$,+\ \Big|\ \underset{2}{V}\ \Big|\ \underset{3}{N}\ \Big|$$

$$,+\ \Big|\ 1\ \underset{2}{V}\ 1\ \Big|=P_2.$$

6. Rip | shrugged | his shoulders, | shook | his head, | cast-up his eyes | *but* | said | nothing.

$$\underset{1}{N}\ \Big|\ \underset{2}{V}\ \Big|\ 1^3\ \underset{3}{N}\ \Big|$$

$$,\ \underset{2}{V}\ \Big|\ 1^3\ \underset{3}{N}\ \Big|$$

$$,\ \underset{2}{V}\ \Big|\ 1^3\ \underset{3}{N}\ \Big|$$

$$+\ \underset{2}{V}\ \Big|\ \underset{3}{N}\ \Big|=P_3$$

LECTURE IV.   53

7. Many harmless little animals, *as* flies, snails, worms, *and*
$\quad\quad\quad\quad\quad\quad\quad\quad\quad\;\; {}_1\;\;\; + \;\; {}_1 \quad {}_1 \quad\quad {}_1 \quad +$
frogs | are tortured *and* killed by some people.
${}_1 \quad\quad\quad\quad\;\; {}_2 \quad + \quad {}_2$

$$\Big|\; {}_2\, {}_2\, {}_2\, \underset{1}{N} + \underset{1}{N},\; \underset{1}{N},\; \underset{1}{N} + \underset{1}{N} \;\Big|\; A \underset{2}{V} + \underset{2}{V}\, s \;\Big| = P_2$$

(iii.)—*between 3rd terms.*

1. He | associated with himself, | one Robertson *and* two other
$\;\; {}_1 \quad\quad\quad {}_2 \quad\quad\quad\quad\quad\quad\quad\quad\quad {}_3$
idle young men.
$\quad\quad\quad\quad {}_3$

$$\Big|\; \underset{1}{N} \;\Big|\; \underset{2}{V}\, s \;\Big|\; {}_2 \underset{3}{N} + {}_c\, {}_1{}^2\, {}_2\, {}_2 \underset{3}{N} \;\Big| = P_3$$

2. I | kept | lights | at the mast-head | *and* a constant watch
$\;\; {}_1 \quad {}_2 \quad\quad {}_3 \quad\quad\quad\quad\quad\quad\quad\quad + \quad\quad\quad\quad\quad {}_3$
forward | to look-out for fishing smacks.
$\quad\quad\quad {}_4$

$$\Big|\; \underset{1}{N} \;\Big|\; \underset{2}{V} * \;\Big|\; \underset{3}{N} \;\Big|\; * s \;\Big|$$
$$+ {}_1{}^1\, {}_2\, \underset{3}{N}\, {}_2 \;\Big|\; IV\, s \;\Big| = P_4$$
$\quad\quad\quad\quad\quad\quad\quad\quad {}_4$

3. I | admire | the pigs *and* poultry.
$\;\; {}_1 \quad\; {}_2 \quad\quad\; {}_3 \quad + \quad {}_3$

$$\Big|\; \underset{1}{N} \;\Big|\; \underset{2}{V} \;\Big|\; {}_1{}^1 \underset{3}{N} \;\Big| + \Big|\; \underset{3}{N} \;\Big| = P_3$$

(iv.)—*between 5th terms.*

1. Anthony Foster | entered | the apartment, | bearing in his
$\quad\quad {}_1 \quad\quad\quad\quad {}_2 \quad\quad\quad\; {}_3 \quad\quad\quad\quad\quad\; {}_4$
hand | a glass cup *and* a small flask.
$\quad\quad\quad\quad {}_5 \quad\quad + \quad\quad\;\; {}_5$

$$\Big|\; \underset{1}{N} \;\Big|\; \underset{2}{V} \;\Big|\; {}_1{}^1 \underset{3}{N} \;\Big|\; PV\, s \;\Big|\; {}_1{}^1\, {}_2 \underset{5}{N} + {}_1{}^1\, {}_2 \underset{5}{N} \;\Big| = P_5$$
$\quad\quad\quad\quad\quad\quad\quad\quad\quad\quad {}_4$

(*b*).—IN JOINERS BY MONO-GROUPALS.

1. They | dispersed through the city   burning, plundering
$\;\; {}_1 \quad\quad {}_2$
and destroying. (Between post-joiner pv of V.)
$+$

$$\underset{1}{N} \;\Big|\; \underset{2}{V}\, s,\, 4,\, 4, + 4 \;\Big| = P_2$$

2. David outlawed *yet* loyal at the heart, | sent | his aged
   $\underset{1}{\text{David}}$ $\underset{+}{yet}$ $\underset{2}{\text{sent}}$

   parents | to the land of Moab. ('Yet' between 4 and 2
   $\underset{3}{\text{parents}}$

   post-joiners of first term.)

   $$|\underset{1}{N}\; 4 + 2\; 3\; |\underset{2}{V}\; *\; |\; 1^3\; 2\; \underset{3}{N}\; |\; *\; 3\; 3 = P_3$$

3. He | was of a mild *and* equable temper | *and* was seldom *or*
   $\underset{1}{\text{He}}$ $\underset{2}{\text{was}}$ $\underset{+}{and}$ $\underset{+}{or}$

   never seen in a passion. (First 'and' between 2 post-
   $\underset{2}{\text{seen}}$

   joiners of V ; 2nd 'and' between Vs while 'or' between adverbs of V.)

   $$|\underset{1}{N}\;|\;\underset{2}{V}\; 3\; (1^1\; 2 + 2)\; n\;|$$

   $$+\;|\;\underset{2}{A}\; 1 + 1\; \underset{2}{V}\; 3\;| = P_2$$

4. An object of our admiration *and* affection, of our pride *and*
   $\underset{1}{\text{object}}$

   of our hopes, | was suddenly taken from us.
   $\underset{2}{}$

   $$|\; 1^1\; \underset{1}{N}\; 3\; (1^3 n + n)$$

   $$, 3$$

   $$+\;3\;|\;A\; 1\; \underset{2}{V}\; 3\;| = P_2$$

5. Almost all the public affairs of the province | were *more or*
   $\underset{1}{}$ $\underset{+}{}$

   less directed by Benjamin Franklin. (Between Adverb as
   $\underset{2}{\text{directed}}$

   Inter-joiners in the midst of A and V.)

   $$|\; 1\; 1^2\; 1^1\; 2\; \underset{1}{N}\; 3\;|\; A\; 1 + 1\; \underset{2}{V}\; 3\;| = P_2$$

6. Time | grew worse *and* worse with Van Winkle.
   $\underset{1}{\text{Time}}$ $\underset{2}{\text{grew}}$

   $$|\;\underset{1}{N}\;|\;\underset{2}{V}\; 2 + 2\; 3\;| = P_2$$

The bracket after 3 includes details of the preposition phrase.

7. The city of Tunis [was at that time *in friendship* with the
$_1$ $_2$
Venetians *though hostile* to most of the other Italian
+
states. (Analogy between Prepositional phrase and Adjective joiners of V is shown.)

$$\big| 1^1 \underset{1}{N} 3 \big| \underset{2}{V} 3\ 3\ 3$$
$$+ 2\ 3\ 3 \big| = P_2$$

8. He | governed | men by their reason *and* their affection.
$_1$ $_2$ $_3$

$$\big| \underset{1}{N} \big| \underset{2}{V} \big| \underset{3}{N} 3 + 3 \big| = P_3$$

9. The opinions of this junto | were completely controlled by
$_1$ $_2$
Nicholas Vedder, a patriarch of the village *and* landlord
of the inn. (Appositions in Post-joiners of second term
by comma and conjunction.)

$$\big| 1^1 \underset{1}{N} 3 \big| A\ 1\ \underset{2}{V}\ 3n$$
$$, 1^1\ n\ 3$$
$$+ n\ 3 \big| = P_2$$

10. His head | was | small *and* flat at top, with huge ears, large
$_1$ $_2$
green glassy eyes, *and* a long snipe nose.

$$\big| 1^3 \underset{1}{N} \big| \underset{2}{V} 2$$
$$+ 2\ 3$$
$$, 3\ (2\ n)$$
$$, 3(2\ 2\ 2\ n) \cdot$$
$$, + 3\ (1^1\ 2\ 2\ n) \big| = P_2$$

11. We | may be sick *or* hurt ('or' between adjective and parti-
$_1$ $_2$
ciple adjective, but 'hurt' may be considered here as a chief
V thus showing that Adjectives and Vs are analogous after
'Be'). $\underset{1}{N} \big| A\ \underset{2}{V}\ 2 + 2 \big| = P_2$

12. This friend | was | a pleasant, sociable man, of unobtrusive
    manners, *but* possessed of no great qualification for business. (Connective comma between Adjective antejoiners of third term and Conjunction 'but' between 3 and post-joiner 4 of the same, adversative analogous union of 3 and PV.)

$$\big| \; 1^2 \underset{1}{N} \; \big| \; \underset{2}{V} \; \big| \; 1^1 \; 2, \; 2 \underset{3}{N}, \; 3 + 4 \; 5\,3 \; \big| = P_3$$

13. It | is too *old*, or too much fatigued, or too sparingly *fed*, | to go any faster. (This is alternative Compound repeated twice in joiner; the Post-joiners 'old' 'fatigued' and 'fed' of V show analogy between adjective and participle.)

$$\big| \; \underset{1}{N} \; \big| \; \underset{2}{V} \; 1 \; 2$$
$$, +1\;1\;4$$
$$, +1\;1\;4 \; \big| \; \underset{4}{IV} \; 1 \; 1 \; \big| = P_4$$

14. The mineral substances of the earth | are composed of three general groups, *namely*, the eruptive, the crystalline, and the sedimentary rocks.

$$\big| \; 1^1 \; 2 \underset{1}{N} \; 3 \; \big| \; A\underset{2}{V} \; 3, + 3 \; (1^1 \; 2, \; 1^1 \; 2, + 1^1 \; 2) \; n \; \big| = P_2$$

(c).—In Sub-joiners by Mono-groupals.

1. A respect | is due *from* the superior *to* the inferior, *as-well-as from* the inferior *to* the superior. ('As-well-as' between two *co-ordinate preposition phrases* sub-joiners to 'due'.)

$$\big| \; 1^1 \underset{1}{N} \; \big| \; \underset{2}{V} \; 2 \; 3' \; 3''$$
$$+ 3' \; 3'' \; \big| = P_2$$

2. The common people | regarded | it | with a mixture-of
     1   2   3
respect *and* superstition, *partly* out-of sympathy for the
                              +
fate of its ill-starred name-sake *and partly* from the tales
                                    +
of strange sights *and* doleful lamentions-told concerning it.
                    +
('And' between sub-joiner of second term, 'partly', 'and partly' between subsequent sub-joiners of the same).

$$| \; 1^1 \; 2 \underset{1}{N} \; | \; \underset{2}{V} \; | \; \underset{3}{N} \; 3 \; 3 \; (n{+}n)$$
$$+ 3 \; 3 \; 3$$
$$+ 3 \; 3 \; (2 \; n{+}2 \; n) \; \text{pv} \; 3 \; | = P_3$$

(d).—IN TERMS AND JOINERS BY MONO-GROUPALS.

1. Servants, under such circumstances | usually become much
     1   2
attached to their masters *and* mistresses, *and* at length
                            +
perform | thier duties | *partly* from a feeling-of love *as-well-*
   2   3   +   +
as for the sake of wages. (Compound 'and' between two Vs and conjunction 'partly' and 'as-well-as' before the Post-joiners of V.)

$$| \; \underset{1}{N} \; 3 \; | \; 1 \; \underset{2}{V} \; 1 \; \text{pv} \; 3(1^3 n{+}n)$$
$$+| \; 3 \; \underset{2}{V} \; | \; 1^3 \; \underset{3}{N} + 3 \; 3 + 3 \; 3 \; | = P_3$$

2. He | assisted at their sports, | made | their playthings,
    1   2   2   3
 | taught | them | to fly | kites | *and* told | them long stories
     2   3   4   5   +   2   3   3
of ghosts, witches *and* Indians. (Between four second terms, also between post-joiner of 3rd terms.)

$$| \; \underset{1}{N} \; | \; \underset{2}{V} \; 3$$
$$, \underset{2}{V} \; | \; 1^3 \underset{3}{N}$$
$$, \underset{2}{V} \; | \; \underset{3}{N} \; | \; \underset{4}{IV} \; | \; \underset{5}{N}$$
$$+\underset{2}{V} \; | \; \underset{3}{N} \; 2 \; \underset{3}{N} \; 3 \; (n, \; n{+}n) \; | = P_5$$

58   STYLOGRAPHY OF ENGLISH LANGUAGE.

3. His only alternative to escape from the labour of the farm
$\underset{1}{\text{alternative}}$
$\underset{+}{and}$ the clamour of his $\underset{3}{\text{wife}}$ | $\underset{2}{\text{was}}$ | to $\underset{4}{\text{take}}$ | $\underset{5}{\text{gun}}$ in hand
$\underset{+}{and}$ $\underset{4}{\text{stroll}}$ away into the woods. (Between preposition phrase sub-joiners to sub-joinner iv of first and fourth IV terms.)

$$| 1^3 \underset{1}{\text{ } 2\text{ }} N \text{ iv } 3 \text{ } 3(1^1 n + 1^1 n) 3 | \underset{2}{V} | \underset{4}{IV} | \underset{5}{N} 3$$
$$+\underset{4}{IV} 1\,3 \ |= P_5$$

4. $\underset{1}{We}$ | $\underset{2}{\text{keep}}$ | an $\underset{3}{\text{animal}}$ $\underset{+}{as}$ a $\underset{3}{\text{horse}}$ $\underset{+}{or}$ a $\underset{3}{\text{dog}}$ for our convenience or pleasure. (This is Examplary and alternative compound.)

$$\underset{1}{N} | \underset{2}{V} | 1^1 \underset{3}{N} |$$
$$+ 1^1 \underset{3}{N} | \ .$$
$$+ 1^1 \underset{3}{N} 3(1^1 n+n) \ |= P_3$$

(e.)—IN JOINERS AND SUB-JOINERS BY MONO-GROUPALS.

1. The $\underset{1}{\text{county}}$ of five, bounded by two firths on the South and North and by the sea on the East and having a number of small seaports, | was long $\underset{2}{\text{famed}}$ | for maintaining $\underset{4}{\text{successfully}}$ | a contraband $\underset{5}{\text{trade}}$.

$$| 1^1 N 3, 4\,3\,3\,(1^1 n \underset{\cdot\cdot}{+} n)$$
$$+ 3\,3$$
$$+ pv \ 1^1 n\,3 \ | \ A\,1\,\underset{2}{V} \ | \ P\underset{4}{V} \,1 \ | \ 1^1\,2\,\underset{5}{N} \ |= P_5$$

2. Among other places $\underset{2}{\text{was}}$ | the $\underset{1}{\text{city}}$ of Tunis, at that time in friendship with the Venetians, $\underset{+}{though}$ hostile to most of the other Italian states and particularly to Genoa.

LECTURE IV.   59

('Though' between 3 'in friendship', and 2 'hostile', analogous union.)

$$\Big| 3 \underset{2}{V} * \Big| 1^1 \underset{1}{N} 3 \Big| * 3\ 3\ 3$$
$$, +2\ 3\ 3$$
$$+1\ 3\ \Big| = P_2$$

3. We $\underset{1}{|}$ shall $\underset{2}{\text{see}}$ $|$ her $\underset{3}{\text{resolution}}$ equalled, $\overset{+}{though}$ hardly surpassed, by Christian Antigones of equal love *and* surer-faith. ('Though' between 4 post-joiners of 3rd term and 'and' between sub-joiners of the same.)

$$\Big| \underset{1}{N} \Big| \underset{2}{AV} \Big| 1^3 \underset{3}{N} \, 4, +1\ 4,\ 3\ 3(2n+2n) \Big| = P_3$$

Connectives of Symmetrical parts.

II.—BY BI-GROUPALS (CO-ORDINATE).

(a).—IN TERMS.

1. A Golden Deed $\underset{1}{|}$ must be $\underset{2}{|}$ something $\underset{3}{more}$ $\underset{c'}{than}$ mere $_{c''}$ display of fearlessness. ('More' is 1st co-ordinate connective to 'something' and 'than' 2nd co-ordinate connective to 'display' between 3rd terms.)

$$\Big| 1^1\ 2 \underset{1}{N} \Big| \underset{2}{AV} \Big| \underset{3}{N}\ c'\ c''\ 2 \underset{3}{N}\ 3 \Big| = P_3.$$

2. Judas $\underset{+}{and}$ his $\underset{1}{800}$ $|$ were $\underset{c'}{not}$ driven from the field, but $\underset{c''}{lay}\ 2$ dead upon it.

$$\Big| \underset{1}{N+1^3} \underset{1}{N} \Big| A\ c' \underset{2}{V}\ 3$$
$$c''\underset{2}{V}\ 2\ 3\ \Big| = P_2$$

3. Disciplined men $\underset{1}{|}$ should $\underset{c'}{either}$ conquer $\underset{c''}{or}$ submit to their betters. $\Big| 2 \underset{1}{N} \Big| A\ c' \underset{2}{V}$
$$c''V\ 3\ \Big| = P_2$$

---

c'—c'' represent co-ordinate conjunctions.

60 STYLOGRAPHY OF ENGLISH LANGUAGE.

4. With him | $\underset{1}{I}$ | shall $\underset{c'}{never}$ $\underset{2}{want}$ | forces, $\underset{c''}{nor}$ $\underset{2}{have}$ | too many $\underset{3}{enemies}$ | to $\underset{4}{deal}$ ('never' between A V—'nor' before (A) V). | * 3 | $\underset{1}{N}$ | Ac'$\underset{2}{V}$ | $\underset{3}{N}$ |

$$c'' \underset{2}{V} \mid 1\ 2\ \underset{3}{N} \mid \underset{4}{IV} *= P_4$$

5. $\underset{1}{You}$ | $\underset{2}{spoke}$ | $\underset{c'}{as\ confidently}$ of $\underset{4}{seeing}$ | fîve $\underset{5}{hundred}$ | $\underset{c''}{as}$ | of $\underset{4}{seeing}$ | this smaller $\underset{5}{number}$. ('As-as' before PVs.)

$$\mid \underset{1}{N} \mid \underset{2}{V} \mid c' \ 1 \underset{4}{IV} \mid 2 \underset{5}{N} \mid$$

$$c'' \underset{4}{IV} \mid 1^2\ 2\ \underset{5}{N} \mid = P_5$$

6. A savage $\underset{1}{country}$ | rarely $\underset{2}{supports}$ | $\underset{3}{more}$ (persons) $than$ one $\underset{3}{person}$ | * for every square mile. (Co-ordinate in 3rd terms.)

$$\mid 1^1\ 2\ \underset{1}{N} \mid 2\ \underset{2}{V} * \mid c'\ (\underset{3}{N})\ c''\ 1^2\ \underset{3}{N} \mid * 3 \mid = P_3$$

7. The fleets of the $\underset{1}{enemy}$ | were $\underset{c'}{not\ merely}$ defeated $\underset{c''}{but}$ $\underset{2}{destroyed}$.

$$\mid 1^1\ \underset{1}{N}\ 3 \mid Ac'\underset{2}{V}c''\ \underset{2}{V} \mid = P_2$$

8. $\underset{c'}{Better}$ $\underset{2}{is}$ | $\underset{1}{it}$ | to $\underset{4}{be}$ | a dupe through $\underset{5}{life}$, $\underset{c''}{than}$ to be suspicious of our fellow beings. ('Better' before IV 'than' before IV 4th terms).

$$\mid * c' \mid \underset{2}{V} \mid \underset{1}{N} \mid * \underset{4}{IV} \mid 1^1\ \underset{5}{N}\ 3$$

$$c'' \underset{4}{IV}\ 2\ 3 \mid = P_8$$

LECTURE IV.   61

9. They | are disposed | *rather* to refuse | *than* to obey.
   $\underset{1}{\text{They}}$ $\underset{2}{\text{are disposed}}$ $\underset{c'}{rather}$ $\underset{4}{\text{to refuse}}$ $\underset{c''}{than}$ $\underset{4}{\text{to obey}}$

   ('Rather' before 'to refuse'; 'than' before 'to obey'; 4th terms.)

   $$\mid \underset{1}{N} \mid \underset{2}{AV} \mid c' \underset{4}{IV} \mid c'' \underset{4}{IV} \mid = P_4 \ .$$

10. It | stirred *not* | *but* seemed gathered-up in the gloom like some gigantic monster ready to spring upon the traveller. (Co-ordinate conjunctions between 2nd terms.)

    $\underset{1}{\text{It}}$ $\underset{2}{\text{stirred}}$ $\underset{c'}{not}$ $\underset{c''}{but}$ $\underset{2}{\text{seemed}}$

    $$\mid \underset{1}{N} \mid \underset{2}{V} c' \mid c'' \underset{2}{V} \ 4\ 3\ 3\ 2\ 4\ 3 \mid = P_4$$

11. The signs of agony expressed by their movements, | the cruel boy | *neither* understood *nor* would attend-to.
    $\underset{3}{\text{...movements}}$ $\underset{1}{\text{cruel boy}}$ $\underset{c'}{neither}$ $\underset{2}{\text{understood}}$ $\underset{c''}{nor}$ $\underset{2}{\text{would attend-to}}$

    ('Neither—nor' before Vs.)

    $$\mid *1^1 \underset{3}{N} 3\ 4\ 3 \mid 1^1\ 2 \underset{1}{N} \mid c' \underset{2}{V} c'' \underset{2}{AV} * \mid = P_3$$

(b).—IN JOINERS.

1. She | supported * | her griefs | * with *as much* firmness *as* possible.
   $\underset{1}{\text{She}}$ $\underset{2}{\text{supported}}$ * $\underset{3}{\text{her griefs}}$ * with $\underset{c'}{as\ much}$ firmness $\underset{c'}{as}$

   $$\mid \underset{1}{N} \mid \underset{2}{V} * \mid 1^3 \underset{3}{N} \mid * 3\ (c'\ n\ c''\ 2) \mid = P_3$$

2. These | would lead to many a diffuse colloquy *sometimes* informing, *at other occasion* amusing.
   $\underset{1}{\text{These}}$ $\underset{2}{\text{would lead...colloquy}}$ $\underset{c'}{sometimes}$ $\underset{2}{informing}$ $\underset{c''}{at\ other\ occasion}$ $\underset{2}{amusing}$

   $$\mid \underset{1}{N} \mid A \underset{2}{V}\ 3\ c'\ 2\ c''\ 2 \mid = P_2$$

3. Cases of self-devotion brought-together | stand-out remarkably *either* from their hopelessness, their courage *or*
   $\underset{1}{\text{Cases...brought-together}}$ $\underset{2}{\text{stand-out}}$ $\underset{c'}{either}$ $\underset{c''}{or}$

IV or PV post-joiners of Ns and Vs are also represented by integer 4.

6

their patience varying with the character of their age.
('Either—or' before 3s.)

$$\left| \underset{1}{N} \; 3 \; 4 \; \right| \underset{2}{V} \; 1 \; c' \; 3$$

$$c'' \; 3 \; (n \; 4 \; 3 \; 3) \left| = P_2 \right.$$

4. *Not merely* at Rome, *but* in every province of the Empire |
   $\quad\; c' \qquad\qquad\; c''$
   the custom | was utterly abolished. ('Not-merely—but'
   $\;\;\; 1 \qquad\qquad\qquad 2$
   before 3s of V.)

$$\left| * c' \; 3 \; c'' \; 3 \; 3 \; \right| \; 1^1 \underset{1}{N} \; \left| \; A \; 1 \underset{2}{V} \; * \; \right| = P_2$$

5. The school-house | stood in a *rather* lonely *but* pleasant
   $\qquad\quad 1 \qquad\qquad 2 \qquad\quad\; c' \qquad\qquad c''$
   situation. |

$$\left| \; 1^1 \underset{1}{N} \; \right| \underset{2}{V} \; 3 \; (1^1 \; c' \; 2 \; c'' \; 2) n \; \left| = P_2 \right.$$

6. * This time | it | is * *not* under the bright sky, *but* under
   $\qquad\qquad\quad 1 \;\;\; 2 \quad\; c' \qquad\qquad\qquad\qquad\; c''$
   the grey fogs of the Baltic sea. ('Not—but' before 3s |of V.)

$$\left| * 3 \; \right| \underset{1}{N} \; \left| \underset{2}{V} * c' \; 3 \right.$$

$$c'' \; 3 \; 3 \left| = P_2 \right.$$

7. We | will not hearken to the king's words, | to go from
   $\;\; 1 \qquad\qquad\quad 2 \qquad\qquad\qquad\qquad\qquad 4$
   our religion, *either* on the right hand *or* the left. ('Either—
   $\qquad\qquad\quad c' \qquad\qquad\qquad\quad c''$
   or' before 3s.)

$$\left| \underset{1}{N} \; \right| A \; 1 \underset{2}{V} \; 3 \; \left| \underset{4}{I} V_3 \; c' \; 3 \; c'' \; 3 \; \right| = P_4$$

8. *Hotter than* ever was | the fight over his corpse.
   $\; c' \qquad c'' \qquad\quad 2 \qquad\qquad 1$

$$\left| \; c' \; c'' \; 1 \underset{2}{V} \; \right| \; 1^1 \underset{1}{N} \; 3 \; \left| = P_2 \right.$$

LECTURE IV.

9. It | was | a war *not-only* on the men *but* on their gods.
      1   2   3   c'   c''

   ('Not-only—but' between 3s of 3rd term.)

   $$\mid \underset{1}{N} \mid \underset{2}{V} \mid 1^1 \underset{3}{N} \; c' \; 3 \; c'' \; 3 \mid = P_3.$$

10. We | speak *not* here of his victories *but* of his return
                  c'   c''

    march from the banks of the Indus, in B. C. 326. ('Not—but' before 3s of V.)

    $$\mid \underset{1}{N} \mid \underset{2}{V} \; c' \; 1 \; 3$$
    $$c'' \; 3 \; 3 \; 3 \; 3 \mid = P_2.$$

11. It | is incumbent upon us all *both as* individuals *and as*
     1 2   c'   c''

    nations, | to take | an interest in each-other. ('Both as— and as' before Ns.)
                    4   5

    $$\mid \underset{1}{N} \mid \underset{2}{V} \; 2 \; 3 \; n$$
    $$c' \; n$$
    $$c'' \; n \mid \underset{4}{IV} \mid 1^1 \underset{5}{N} \; 3 \mid = P_5$$

12. An honest bankrupt | is entitled •to pity, *rather than* liable
                        1   2   c'   c''

    to blame. ('Entitled' is past participle after 'is', forming the passive; 'rather than' is placed between this and 'liable.' This shows analogy between PV and Adjective.)

    $$\mid 1^1 \; 2 \underset{1}{N} \mid A \underset{2}{V} \; 3 \; c' \; c'' \; 2 \; 3 \mid = P_2$$

13. *Neither* for fear *nor* favour | should | we | allow | our-
             c'   c''   1   2   1

    selves | to be prevented | from executing | these public
                     4   6

    duties |∗faithfully. ('Neither' before 3 'nor' before 3.)
       7

    $$\mid \ast \; c' \; 3 \; c'' \; 3 \mid \underset{2}{A} \mid \underset{1}{N} \mid \underset{2}{V} \mid \underset{3}{N} \mid \underset{4}{IV} \mid \underset{6}{PV} \ast \mid 1^2 \; 2 \underset{7}{N} \mid \ast 1 \mid = P_7$$

14. In *less* (nights) *than* (in) a fortnight | La Tude | found |
                                                          1   2
himself surrounded by 10 large rats. (Co-ordinate conjunc-
       3
tions in joiners 3 exist with N and Preposition ellipsis.)

$$| *3\ c'\ c''\ 3\ |\ \underset{1}{N}\ |\ \underset{2}{V}\ *\ |\ \underset{3}{N}\ 4\ 3\ | = P_3$$

(c).—IN SUBJOINERS.

1. My uncle Toby | was | a man patient of injuries *not*
            1   2   3   c'
from want of courage *nor* from any obstuseness of his
                      c''
intellectual parts.

$$|\ 1^3\ \underset{1}{N}\ |\ \underset{2}{V}\ |\ 1^1\ \underset{3}{N}\ 2\ 3\ c'\ 3\ 3$$
$$c'\ 3\ 3\ | = P_3$$

You have already seen increased number of similar joiners without even the intervention of punctuation; you have seen also the apposition terms of N without punctuation but with the intervention of 'The'; you have been shown just now the increase of similar terms and similar or analogous joiners or subjoiners by intervention of punctuation and conjunction. I have come to show to you presently the apposition Ns with the intervention of certain conjunction connectives in the same terms. The past participle connectives in the same terms have been treated later on.

A.—'As' as apposition connective.

1. He | had only | to shelter | the Major *as* a guest | for
   1   2   4   5   +   6
3 days. (This is apposition of fifth term by connective 'as'.)

$$|\ \underset{1}{N}\ |\ \underset{2}{V}\ 1\ |\ 1\underset{4}{V}\ *\ |\ 1^3\ \underset{5}{N}\ +\ 1^1\ \underset{6}{N}\ |\ *3\ | = P_5$$

2. He | soon after adopted | Leonard *as* his son.
   1   2   3   +   3

$$|\ \underset{1}{N}\ |\ 1\ 1\ \underset{2}{V}\ |\ \underset{3}{N}\ +\ 1^3\ \underset{3}{N}\ | = P_3$$

3. He | affected | to represent | it *as* a lucky hit. (This is
   $\underset{1}{\text{He}}$ $\underset{2}{\text{affected}}$ $\underset{4}{\text{to represent}}$ $\underset{5}{\text{it}}$
   fifth term apposition by connetive 'as' again.)

$$\Big| \underset{1}{N} \Big| \underset{2}{V} \Big| \underset{4}{IV} \Big| \underset{5}{N} + 1^1 \ 2 \underset{5}{N} \Big| = P_5$$

4. Mr. Clarkson *as* secretary | interposed. (This is first term
   $\underset{1}{\text{Mr. Clarkson}} \underset{+}{\ } \underset{1}{\text{secretary}}$ $\underset{2}{\text{interposed}}$
   apposition of capacity.)

$$\Big| \underset{1}{N} + \underset{1}{N} \Big| \underset{2}{V} \Big| = P_2$$

B.—'Such—as' as apposition connective.

1. The force | would have been most-desperate for the attack
   $\underset{1}{\text{The force}}$ $\underset{2}{\text{would have been}}$
   of *such* a city *as* Tarifa. (Here the sub-post-joiner of a
   post-joiner 3 of V has got co-ordinate apposition Ns by
   connectives 'such—as'.)

$$\Big| 1^1 \underset{1}{N} \Big| AA \underset{2}{V} \ 2 \ 3 \ 3 \ (c' \ 1^1 \ n \ c'' \ n) \Big| = P_2$$

Connectives of Symmetrical parts.

III.—BY CONJOINED MONO- AND BI-GROUPALS.

1. My uncle To by | was | a man patient of injuries *not* from
   $\underset{1}{\text{To by}}$ $\underset{2}{\text{was}}$ $\underset{3}{\text{a man}}$ $\underset{c'}{not}$
   want of courage *nor* from any insensibility *or* obtuseness
   $\underset{c''}{nor}$ $\underset{+}{or}$
   of his intellectual parts (*Co-ordinate negative* and *Alternative Conjunction*. 'Not' before sub-joiner 3; 'nor' before sub-joiner 3 also.)

$$\Big| 1^3 \underset{1}{N} \Big| \underset{2}{V} \Big| 1^1 \underset{3}{N} \ 2 \ 3c' \ 3 \ 3 \ c'' \ 3 \ (1^2 \ n + n) \ 3 \Big| = P_3$$

2. From these *and* the like operations | arises | the wealth *both*
   $\underset{+}{and}$ $\underset{2}{\text{arises}}$ $\underset{1}{\text{the wealth}} \ \underset{c'}{both}$
   of individuals *and* of nations. (Co-ordinates 'both—and'
   $\underset{c''}{and}$
   before each prepositional phrase. 'And' gives detail of 'both'. 'These' and 'the like' are analogous union.)

$$\Big| * 3 \ (1^2 + 1^1 \ 2) \ n \Big| \underset{2}{V} * \Big| 1^1 \underset{1}{N} \ c' \ 3 \ c'' \ 3 \Big| = P_2$$

4. We | should encourage | a mild and patient disposition, |
   $\underset{1}{\text{We}}$ $\underset{2}{\text{should encourage}}$ $\underset{+}{\text{and}}$ $\underset{3}{\text{patient disposition}}$,
   rather than a fretful, irritable, and revengeful one.
   $\underset{c'}{\text{rather}}$ $\underset{c''}{\text{than}}$ ... $\underset{+}{\text{and}}$ $\underset{3}{\text{revengeful one}}$.

('Rather—than' (comparative co-ordinate) between compound adjectives to Nouns.)

$$\mid \underset{1}{N} \mid \underset{2}{AV_\cdot} \mid 1^1 \, 2, +2 \underset{3}{N} \, c' \mid$$
$$c'' \, 1^1 \, 2_r 2, +2 \underset{3}{N} \mid = P_3$$

B.—Connectives of Asymmetrical parts.

Between (different) terms and terms, Joiners and terms, and Sub-joiners and terms.

I.—BY MONO-GROUPAL.

(a).—BETWEEN V AND ITS POST-JOINERS.

1. They | are still reaping as *if* by a most agile sickle | an enormous harvest. (Semblance connective 'as if' between V and its post-joiner.)
   $\underset{1}{\text{They}}$ $\underset{2}{\text{are still reaping}}$ $\underset{+}{\text{as if}}$ ... $\underset{3}{\text{harvest}}$

$$\mid \underset{1}{N} \mid A \, 1 \, \underset{2}{V} + 3 \mid 1^1 \, 2 \, \underset{3}{N} \mid = P_3$$

2. He | would be present | to give * | his aid and advice, *if* necessary. ('If' before 2 post-joiner of V.)
   $\underset{1}{\text{He}}$ $\underset{2}{\text{would be present}}$ $\underset{4}{\text{to give}}$ * $\underset{5}{\text{his aid}}$ $\underset{+}{\text{and}}$ $\underset{5}{\text{advice}}$, $\underset{+}{\textit{if}}$

$$\mid \underset{1}{N} \mid A \, \underset{2}{V} \, 2 \mid \underset{4}{IV} * \mid 1^3 \, \underset{5}{N} + \underset{5}{N} \mid * + 2 = P_5$$

3. Donald | advanced | a step | * as *if* for the purpose- of instantly seizing | the person. ('As if' semblance connective between V and PV; preposition 'of' of the PV is strengthened by 3 'for the purpose' and adverb 'instantly' placed between the intimate preposition and PV.)

$$\mid \underset{1}{N} \mid \underset{2}{V} * \mid 1^1 \underset{3}{N} \mid * + \underset{4}{PV} \mid 1^1 \underset{5}{N} \mid = P_5$$

LECTURE IV.   67

(b).—BETWEEN N AND ITS POST-JOINER.

1. We | have | no intention | of exhibiting | Sophia Maxwell
   1   2   3   4   5
as spotlessly perfect.
  +

$$\left|\underset{1}{N}\;\middle|\;\underset{2}{V}\;\middle|\;2\underset{3}{N}\;\middle|\;\underset{4}{PV}\;\middle|\;\underset{5}{N+1\,2}\;\right|=P_5$$

2. Uberto *though* originally poor, | had risen by his talents
   1   +   2
   and industry | to be | one of the most considerable
   +   4
   merchants.

$$\left|\;\underset{1}{N+1\,2}\;\middle|\;\underset{2}{AV}\;3\;(1^1\,n+n)\;\middle|\;\underset{.4}{IV}\;\middle|\;\underset{5}{N\;3}\;\right|=P_5$$

3. This *though* lamentably deficient, *and* false in some points |
   1   +   +
   was | a real religion. ('Though' between first term and
   2   3
   its joiner, 'and' between 2s.)

$$\left|\;\underset{1}{N+1\,2+2\,3}\;\middle|\;\underset{2}{V}\;\middle|\;1^1\;2\underset{3}{N}\;\right|=P_3$$

(c).—BETWEEN V AND IV TERMS.

1. He | turned from the crucifix | *as* unworthy to look upon it
   1   2   +   4

$$\left|\;\underset{1}{N}\;\middle|\;\underset{2}{V\;3}\;\middle|\;+2\;\underset{4}{IV\;3}\;\right|=P_4$$

(d).—BETWEEN AUXILIARIES AND Vs.

1. The audience | was *as if* moved by this persuasive oration
   1   2
(between A and V). $\left|\;1^1\;\underset{1}{N}\;\middle|\;A+\underset{2}{V}\;3\;\right|=P_2$

Connectives between different Terms show subordination
as well. For examples:—

1. The philosopher Empedocles | had leapt into the burning
                  1   2
   crater of Mount Etna | *thereby* to obtain | an imperishable
                               +   4

name. (The fourth Term here is subordinately governed by the second whole, by Connective 'thereby'.)

$$|\ 1^1\ _2\underset{1}{N}\ |\ A\ \underset{2}{V}\ *\ 3\ |+IV\underset{4}{\ }|\ 1^1\ _2\underset{5}{N}\ |=P_5$$

2. He | took * | his nail | * between his teeth | so as to enclose | the egg and hold * | it * firmly. (The second and third whole terms conjointly governing the fourth by Connective dual 'so as'.)
   $\underset{1}{\text{He}}$ $\underset{2}{\text{took}}$ $\underset{3}{\text{his nail}}$ $\underset{+}{}$ $\underset{4}{\text{enclose}}$ $\underset{5}{\text{egg}}\ \underset{+}{and}\ \underset{4}{hold}\ \underset{5}{it}$

$$|\ \underset{1}{N}\ |\ \underset{2}{V}\ *\ |\ 1^3\underset{3}{N}\ |\ *\ 3\ |+\underset{4}{IV}\ |\ 1^1\underset{5}{N}$$
$$+\underset{4}{IV}\ *\ |\ \underset{5}{N}\ |\ *\ 1\ |=P_5$$

II.—BY BI-GROUPALS.

(a).—BETWEEN POST-JOINERS OF V AND ITS SUBSEQUENT
IV TERMS.

1. Few | are so fortunate | as to be able | to do | this. ('So—as' before 2 of V and IV respectively.)
   $\underset{1}{\text{Few}}$ $\underset{2}{\text{are}}\ _{c'}so$ $_{c''}as$ $\underset{4}{\text{to be able}}$ $\underset{6}{\text{to do}}$ $\underset{7}{\text{this}}$

$$|\ \underset{1}{N}\ |\ \underset{2}{V}\ c'\ 2\ |\ c''\ \underset{4}{IV}\ 2\ |\ \underset{6}{IV}\ |\ \underset{7}{N}\ |=P_7$$

2. It | was too good | to be lost. (Here co-ordination takes place between 'too' the post-joiner of V and 'to' the intimate preposition of the IV.)
   $\underset{1}{\text{It}}$ $\underset{2}{\text{was}}\ _{c'}too$ good $_{c''}to$ $\underset{4}{\text{be lost}}$

$$|\ \underset{1}{N}\ |\ \underset{2}{V}\ c'\ 2\ |\ c''\ \underset{4}{IV}\ |=P_4$$

3. It | is a-little too strong | to pretend so much.
   $\underset{1}{\text{It}}$ $\underset{2}{\text{is a-little}}\ _{c'}too$ strong $_{c''}to$ $\underset{4}{\text{pretend so much}}$

$$|\ \underset{1}{N}\ |\ \underset{2}{V}\ 1^1\ 2\ c'\ 2\ |\ c''\ \underset{4}{IV}\ 1\ 1\ |=P_4$$

4. The Roman | was not yet fallen so low as not to remonstrate. ('Not so' before 'low' and 'as not' before IV.)
   $\underset{1}{\text{The Roman}}$ was not $_{c'}$ yet fallen $_2$ $_{c'}$ so low $_{c''}$ as $_{c''}$ not $\underset{4}{\text{to remonstrate}}$

$$|\ 1^1\underset{1}{N}\ |\ A\ c'\ 1\ \underset{2}{V}\ c'\ 2\ |\ c''\ \underset{4}{IV}\ =P_4$$

LECTURE IV.   69

5. It | is generally best | to assist * | a needy person |*⸰in *such*
   $\;\;\;\;$1 $\;\;\;\;$ 2 $\;$ 4 $\;$ 5 $\;\;\;\;\;\;\;\;\;\;\;\;\;\;\;\;$ c'

a way | *as* to enable | him | to help | himself. (The 4th
$\;\;\;\;\;\;\;\;\;$ c'' $\;\;\;\;\;\;\;\;$ 6 $\;\;\;\;\;\;\;\;\;$ 7 $\;\;\;\;\;$ 8 $\;\;\;\;\;\;\;\;$ 9

term in its post-joiner 3 governs co-ordinately the 6th
by Connective 'such......as'.)

$\underset{1}{N} \mid \underset{2}{V} \; 1 \; 2 \mid \underset{4}{IV} * \mid 1^1 \; 2 \underset{5}{N} \mid * 3 \; (c'\;n) \mid c'' \underset{6}{IV} \mid \underset{7}{N} \mid \underset{8}{IV} \mid \underset{9}{N} \mid = P_9$

(b).—BETWEEN V AND IV TERMS.

1. Nothing | pleased | him | *more* | *than* to be holding | con-
   $\;\;\;\;\;\;\;$1 $\;\;\;\;\;\;\;\;\;\;\;$ 2 $\;\;\;\;\;\;\;$ 3 $\;\;\;\;\;$ c' $\;\;\;\;\;$ c'' $\;$ 4 $\;\;\;\;\;\;\;$ 5

verse with her. ('More' as Post-joiner connective of V
and 'than' as anti-joiner connective of IV.)

$\mid \underset{1}{N} \mid \underset{2}{V} \mid \underset{3}{N} \; c' \mid c'' \; PV \mid \underset{5}{N} \; 3 \mid = P_5.$

2. The chilling news | was indeed *more than* enough to over-
   $\;\;\;\;\;\;\;\;\;\;\;\;\;\;\;\;\;\;\;$1 $\;\;\;\;\;\;\;\;\;\;\;\;\;\;$ 2 $\;\;\;\;\;\;\;\;\;\;$ c' $\;\;\;\;\;$ c''

whelm | her | with sorrow.
$\;\;$4 $\;\;\;\;\;\;$ 5

$\mid 1^1 \; 2 \underset{1}{N} \mid \underset{2}{V} \; 1 \; c' \mid c'' \; 1 \underset{4}{IV} * \mid \underset{5}{N} \mid * 3 \mid = P_5$

(c).—BETWEEN A AND Vs.

1. Mr. Benson | could not be *otherwise than* pleased with so
   $\;\;\;\;\;\;\;\;\;\;$1 $\;\;\;\;\;\;\;\;\;\;\;\;$ c' $\;\;\;\;\;\;\;$ c' $\;\;\;\;\;$ c'' $\;\;\;\;\;\;\;\;\;$ 2

faithful an apprentice. (Asymmetrical, negative comparative co-ordinate.)

$\mid \underset{1}{N} \mid A \; c' \; A \; c' \; c'' \; \underset{2}{V} \; 3 \mid = P_2.$

(d).—BETWEEN N AND IV TERMS.

1. There had been | nothing *more* about it | *than* exhibiting
   $\;\;\;\;\;\;\;\;\;\;\;\;\;\;\;\;$2 $\;\;\;\;\;\;\;\;$ 1 $\;\;\;\;$ c' $\;\;\;\;\;\;\;\;\;\;\;\;$ c'' $\;\;\;\;\;\;\;\;\;$ 4

to us | a most-singular young woman in some of the most
$\;$ 5

singular-of situations.

$\mid 1 \; \underset{2}{AV} \mid \underset{1}{N} \; c' \; 3 \mid c'' \; PV \; 3 \mid 1^1 \; 2 \; 2 \underset{5}{N} \; 3 \; 3 \; 3 \mid = P_5$

C.—Connectives both of Asymmetrical and Symmetrical Parts.

I.—BY MONO-GROUPAL.

1. He | considered | himself *as* robbed *and* plundered.
   $\underset{1}{\text{1}} \quad \underset{2}{\text{2}} \qquad \underset{3}{\text{3}} \quad +\qquad +$

   $$\left| \underset{1}{N} \left| \underset{2}{V} \right| \underset{3}{N} + pv + pv \right| = P_4.$$

2. Maclean | was thoroughly tempted | to swim with his last
   $\underset{1}{\text{1}} \qquad \underset{2}{\text{2}} \qquad \underset{4}{\text{4}}$
   companion | *but* conquered | the impulse *as only* leading to
   $\qquad\qquad \underset{2}{\text{2}} \qquad \underset{3}{\text{3}}$
   a needless peril. (Here the third term allows the connective 'as—only' to intervene between it and its pv postjoiner.)

   $$\underset{1}{N} \mid A\,1\,\underset{2}{V} \mid \underset{4}{IV}\,3 \mid$$

   $$+ \underset{2}{V} \mid 1^1\,\underset{3}{N} + 4\,3 \mid = P_4$$

3. It | is proper | to meet * | danger | * with boldness for any
   $\underset{1}{\text{1}} \quad \underset{2}{\text{2}} \qquad \underset{4}{\text{4}} \qquad \underset{5}{\text{5}}$
   good end, *as, for instance*, to save | a fellow-creature from
   $\qquad\qquad\quad +\qquad\qquad \underset{6}{\text{6}} \qquad\qquad \underset{7}{\text{7}}$
   injury or death, to protect | our lives and property from a
   $\qquad\qquad\qquad\quad \underset{6}{\text{6}} \qquad \underset{7}{\text{7}} \qquad\qquad \underset{7}{\text{7}}$
   robber, *and* to defend * | our native country | * from the
   $\qquad\quad +\qquad \underset{6}{\text{6}} \qquad \underset{7}{\text{7}}$
   attacks of enemies. ('As for instance' before 'to save.)

   $$\underset{1}{N} \mid \underset{2}{V}\,2 \mid \underset{4}{IV} * \mid \underset{5}{N} \mid * 3\,3 \mid + \mid \underset{6}{IV} \mid 1^1\,\underset{7}{N}\,3\,(n+n) \mid$$

   $$, \underset{6}{IV} * \mid 1^3 \underset{7}{N} + \underset{7}{N} \mid * 3 \mid$$

   $$+ \underset{6}{IV} * \mid 1^3\,2\,\underset{7}{N} \mid * 3\,3 \mid = P_7$$

4. It | would have been difficult * *when* prompted by Sophia
   $\underset{1}{\text{1}} \qquad\qquad \underset{2}{\text{2}} \qquad\qquad +$
   and led by Dimmock, for the most- skilled and unscru-

pulous prowler upon the town | to have balked | the party.
$\underset{4}{\quad}$ $\underset{5}{\quad}$
(No comma intervenes between 'difficult' and 'when'.)

$$\Big|\underset{1}{N}\Big|\ A\ A\ \underset{2}{V}\ 2 + 4\ 3$$
$$+\ 4\ 3\ ,\ 3\ (1^1\ 2+2)\ 3\ \Big|\ \underset{4}{IV}\ \Big|\ 1^1\ \underset{5}{N}\Big| = P_5$$

5. The King | fixed | his eyes | as if about-to move | but |
$\underset{1}{\quad}$ $\underset{2}{\quad}$ $\underset{3}{\quad}$ $\underset{4}{\quad}$ $\underset{+}{\quad}$
stopped short. | ('As if' between third and fourth, 'but'
$\underset{2}{\quad}$
between second terms.)

$$\Big|\ 1^1\ \underset{1}{N}\ \Big|\ \underset{2}{V}\ \Big|\ 1^2\ \underset{3}{N}\ \Big|\ +\ \underset{4}{IV}\ \Big|$$
$$+\ \underset{2}{V}\ 2\ \Big| = P_4$$

6. The pair of worthies both | paused for sometime keeping
$\underset{1}{\quad}$ $\underset{2}{\quad}$
mute and abstracted | as if beating about for an idea | and
$\underset{4}{\quad}$
endeavouring | to stimulate | their inventive faculties.
$\underset{4}{\quad}$ $\underset{6}{\quad}$ $\underset{7}{\quad}$

$$1^1\ \underset{1}{N}\ 3\ \underset{1}{N}\ \Big|\ \underset{2}{V}\ 3\ \Big|\ \underset{4}{PV}\ 2 + 2\ \Big|\ +\ \underset{4}{PV}\ 1\ 3$$
$$+\ \underset{4}{PV}\ \Big|\ \underset{6}{IV}\ \Big|\ 1^3\ 2\ \underset{7}{N}\ \Big| = P_9$$

II.—BY BI-GROUPAL AND MONO-GROUPAL.

1. (To tell a falsehood respecting a neighbour, either to save
$\underset{4}{\quad}$ $\underset{5}{\quad}$ $\overset{c'}{\quad}$ $\underset{6}{\quad}$
ourselves, or from malice against him,)^N | is | a still more-
$\underset{7}{\quad}$ $\overset{c''}{\quad}$ $\underset{1}{\quad}$ $\underset{2}{\quad}$
wicked and shameful action. ('Either' before IV, 'or'
$\underset{+}{\quad}$ $\underset{3}{\quad}$
before 3.)

$$(\underset{4}{IV}\ |\ 1^1\ \underset{5}{n}\ 3\ |\ \underset{6}{c'}\ iv\ |\ \underset{7}{n}\ |\ c''\ 3\ 3)^N\ \Big|\ \underset{2}{V}\ \Big|\ 1^1\ 1\ 2 + 2\ \underset{3}{N}\ \Big| = P_3$$

2. Railing, satire, and fighting | can do | no good, but | will
$\underset{1}{\quad}$ $\underset{1}{\quad}$ $\underset{+}{\quad}$ $\underset{1}{\quad}$ $\underset{2}{\quad}$ $\overset{c'}{\underset{3}{\quad}}$ $\overset{c''}{\quad}$
certainly make | things worse than before. (Negative ad-
$\underset{2}{\quad}$ $\underset{3}{\quad}$ $\overset{c'}{\quad}$ $\overset{c''}{\quad}$

versative, both second and 3rd terms co-ordinate with next second term; also post-joiner 2 of third, co-ordinate with post-joiner).

$$|\underset{1}{N}, \underset{1}{N} + \underset{1}{N} | A \underset{2}{V} | c' \underset{3}{N} | c'' A_1 \underset{2}{V} | \underset{3}{N} c' c'' _1 | = P_3$$

3. He | conceived * | the most-rancorous dislike | * to him, and
　　1　　　2　　　　　　　　　3　　　　　　　　　　　　　+
longed- for | nothing *so much* | *as* to see | him | lose | the
　2　　　　　3　　c'　　　　　c''　　4　　　5　　　6
acquired credit. ('So much—as' between N and Vs.)
　　7

$$|\underset{1}{N} | \underset{2}{V} * | 1^1 2 \underset{3}{N} | * 3 |$$

$$+ \underset{2}{V} | \underset{3}{N} c' | c'' \underset{4}{IV} | \underset{5}{N} | \underset{6}{IV} | 1^1 2 \underset{7}{N} | = P_7$$

4. They | would *not* sell | their Turkish prisoners, | *but* send |
　　1　　　　c' 2　　　　　　　　3　　　　　　c'' 2
them, | *if possible*, on some part of the African coast ('not
　　　　　　+
—but' symmetrical co-ordinate, 'if possible' asymmetrical connective.)

$$\underset{1}{N} | A c' \underset{2}{V} | 1^3 2 \underset{3}{N} |$$

$$c'' \underset{2}{V} * | \underset{3}{N} | * + 3\ 3 | = P_3$$

5. | In houses *and* ships | rats| sometimes become *so* numerous |
　　　　　　　+　　　　　1　　　　　　　　　2　c'
as to do | much mischief. ('So' before 2 post-joiner of V,
c''　4　　　　5
'as' before IV term.)

$$| * 3 (\text{n+n}) | \underset{1}{N} | 1 \underset{2}{V} c' 2 * | c'' \underset{4}{IV} | 2 \underset{5}{N} | = P_5.$$

6. He | determined | to call again on Crawford *and* question
　　1　　　2　　　　　　4　　　　　　　　　　+　　　4
| him on the subject *but* in *such* a way | *as* to afford | no
　　5　　　　　　　　c'　　　　　　　　c''　　　6

groundfor suspicion relative to his motives | in sounding |
$\underset{7}{}$ $\underset{8}{}$
him.
$\underset{9}{}$

$\underset{1}{N} \mid \underset{2}{V} \mid \underset{4}{IV}$ 1 3 |

$+ \underset{4}{IV} * \mid \underset{5}{N} \mid * 3 + 3C' \mid c'' \underset{6}{IV} \mid 2 \underset{7}{N}$ 3 2 3 $\mid \underset{8}{PV} \mid \underset{9}{N} \mid = P_9.$

Before I conclude my remarks on the Connectives let me speak to you first on the *Equivalence of different Terms* in the government of Parsing—equivalence being an exception to the Parsing government in terms already described. The verb "To be" is as it were *equational* and the N terms preceding and following it are equivalent ones, the former governing the V but the latter *not* governing the third term but is governed by it like the first ; what is good with "Be" is good with the Passive Vs except that they may have sometimes an Objective government.

Besides the Apposition Ns illustrated at the beginning of this lecture, the Past Participle 'called' and 'named' as well as another with connective 'as', *i.e.*, 'known as' show alike that the N terms before and after them as Connectives are equivalent or apposition ones, for past participle alone are analogous to adjectives and can never govern an N ; the government of the first N here determines the government of the second and hence these appositions are *Equivalents of capacity in the same terms.*

ILLUSTRATIONS :—

1. At the time of the French Revolution, | there lived at Frankfort on the Maine, in Germany, | *a Jewish banker*, of limited means *but* good reputation, *named Moses Rothschild.*

| * 3 3 | 1 $\underset{2}{V}$ * 3 3 3 | 1¹ 2 $\underset{1}{N}$ 3 (2n+2n) + $\underset{1}{N}$ | = P

2. Ethelred *called* the unready or uncounselled | quarrelled
   with his clergy.
   $\underset{1}{\text{1}} \quad \underset{}{+} \quad \underset{1}{\text{1}} \quad + \quad \underset{1}{\text{1}} \quad \underset{2}{\text{2}}$

$$| \underset{1}{N} + 1^1 \underset{1}{N} + \underset{1}{N} | \underset{2}{V} 3 | = P_2$$

3. On June 15, 1330, | his first son afterwards so well *known*
   $\underset{1}{} \quad \quad \quad \quad \quad \quad \quad \quad \quad \quad +$
   as the Black Prince | was born.
   $\underset{1}{} \quad \quad \quad \quad \underset{2}{}$

$$| * 3, 3 | 1^3 \; 2 \underset{1}{N} \; 1 \; 1 \; 1 + 1^1 \underset{1}{N} | A\underset{2}{V} | = P_2$$

On the other hand *Equivalents* are but Appositions *in different Terms.* as :—

1. The martin | is | a gentle bird. (The first and third are
   $\underset{1}{} \quad \quad \underset{2}{} \quad \underset{3}{}$
   Equivalent Terms here, both governing the V.)

$$| 1^1 \underset{1}{N} | \underset{2}{V} | 1^1 \; 2 \underset{3}{N} | = P_3$$

2. The book | is entitled | Stylo-graphy. (The first and third
   $\underset{1}{} \quad \quad \underset{2}{} \quad \quad \underset{3}{}$
   Equivalents with Passive V.)

$$| 1^1 \underset{1}{N} | A\underset{2}{V} | \underset{3}{N} | = P_3$$

3. They | were made | members of the meeting. (Here 'mem-
   $\underset{1}{} \quad \quad \underset{2}{} \quad \underset{3}{}$
   bers' is a third term Objective.)

$$| \underset{1}{N} | A\underset{2}{V} | \underset{3}{N} 3 | = P_3$$

4. He | is sure | to be elected | President of the Republic. (Here
   $\underset{1}{} \; \underset{2}{} \quad \quad \underset{4}{} \quad \quad \underset{5}{}$
   the fifth term is equivalent to the first but if you go to
   consider the second to be an Auxiliary and the fourth to be
   principal V, their conjoined formation into the second term
   will make the fifth the same third term as shown before.)

$$| \underset{1}{N} | \underset{2}{V} 2 | I\underset{4}{V} | \underset{5}{N} 3 | = P_5$$

Conjunction connective 'as' stands asymmetrically as initial before the third term equivalent to the first. For examples :—

1. He | was recommended | *as* house-steward.
   $\quad$1$\qquad\qquad$2$\qquad\qquad\qquad$3

$$\underset{1}{N} \mid \underset{2}{AV} \mid + \underset{3}{N} \mid = P_3$$

2. The terrible sights *and* sounds | were | *as* tokens of anger.
   $\qquad\qquad\quad$1$\qquad\qquad\qquad\quad$2$\qquad\qquad$3

$$\mid 1^1 \, 2 \underset{1}{N} + \underset{1}{N} \mid \underset{2}{V} \mid + \underset{3}{N} \, 3 \mid = P_3$$

The equivalent appositions of N and compound PP, of vocative PP and vocative N, have likewise been or will be shown, as-well-as that of Ns by punctuative comma and "the" when placed between the so-called apposition Ns. **Equivalents** are therefore appositions by *interposition of terms* by the same as-well-as connective joiners to terms, while on the other hand **appositions** are equivelents by *non-interposition of terms* but sometimes by interposition of joiners and punctuative comma. Hence both equivalents and appositions cannot but possess the same government in parsing.

From punctuative and article development we come gradually to equivalence, *i.e.*, apposition of terms by connective conjunction '*as*', '*such* as'. Both punctuative connective and symmetrical connective conjunctions mark also the **equivalence of government** in parsing in a marked and distinct degree in the copulative and alternative varieties of them.

Character of other connectives brings us to other relations between terms and terms, and joiners and joiners yet keeping their equivalence in parsing.

We have shown in the above illustrations that some are connectives *par excellence* as regards like terms, joiners, and analogous joiners, others as *intermediates* in such extension of union, while others are but *limited* in such dealings. The class of Mono-groupals have been shown as single, dual, triple, and phrasial, while of this dual variety it will be shown also that some do split themselves into Bi-groupals or Co-ordinates. Bi-groupals in excess to what the Grammarians admit of, have no doubt been shown but these are done with evident reason. You have seen that a certain solitary connective, '*as*' and certain of the Duals '*more than*,' '*such as*' convertible to Bi-groupals, besides placing themselves between like and analogous terms, or between like and analogous joiners, -place themselves asymmetrically between unlike terms—V alone or with its joiners, subjoiners, and their derivatives IV or PV ; or between A and V ; or between N and its post-joiner PV or adjective ; or lastly between PV and IV and its post-joiner PV. The minor connectives of terms and joiners will gradually lead us along with others of the *special* subordinate and co-ordinate classes, to structural Subordinates, Co-ordinates, and Compounds which will be dealt with hereafter.

The subordinate character of IV terms to those of the Vs has been distinct in some of the above illustrations and it is this subordinate character that may sometimes lead us to stretch the **extent of terms beyond 9.** As an illustration of this I give you one of 11 terms in the Mono-simple which by no means alters the grand general principle of the N | V groupal arrangement of terms in the sentence.

1. We | ought | to try | to keep | ourselves | clam *and* watch-
   $_1$ $_2$ $_4$ $_6$ $_7$ $+$

full | *so-as*-to be able | to do | it. (Preposition 'to' streng-
              $_8$ $_{10}$ $_{11}$

thened by 'so-as'.)

| N | V | IV | IV * | N | * 2+2 | IV 2 | IV | N |=P_{11}
  $_1$ $_2$ $_4$ $_6$ $_{-7}$ $_8$ $_{10}$ $_{11}$

LECTURE V.

STUDENTS AND GENTLEMEN,

I have told you enough of the Mono-simples already. There remain now but the loose, emphatic or *absolute parts of speech* to tell you of. Before the narration or description begins in the Mono-simple the ejaculatory utterances of these parts of speech must commence. They are initials or appendages rarely final or medial that hold no Government whatever to the main Mono-simple nor any Government within themselves. They are called **Interjections** though not very properly so, for they begin the speech. Interjections are *pure* and you will find them also as *drived from* other parts of speech as the *Adjectives*, *Adverbs*, and *Verbs*. They may be *phrasial* too. For the recognition of this class of words we have no difficulty at all, for a note of admiration "!" immediately follows each or a *comma* takes the place of the admirative punctuation.

These punctuations will also be taken advantage of during the depiction of the Formula and the absolute bracket '$\{\ \}$' will seggragate them from the Mono-simple.

Application of Interjections to Mono-simples, their illustrations and Formula.

1. *Alas* ! I must finish $*$ | my journey | $*$ *alone*. (Pure)
    $\quad\quad\;\;\, 1 \quad\quad\quad\quad\;\; 2 \quad\quad\quad\;\; 3$

   $\{\,!\,\} \mid \underset{1}{N} \mid \underset{2}{AV} * \mid 1^2\,\underset{3}{N} \mid *1 \mid = \{\,!\,\} = P_3$

2. *Strange* ! it | *aches* $*$ | me | $*$ *to the heart*. (Adjective)
    $\quad\quad\quad\quad\;\, 1 \quad\;\; 2 \quad\;\;\; 3$

   $\{\,2\,!\,\} \underset{1}{N} \mid \underset{2}{V} * \mid \underset{3}{N} \mid * 3 \mid = \{\,2\,!\,\} P_3$

78　　　　STYLOGRAPHY OF ENGLISH LANGUAGE.

3. *See !* my horse $|$ wins $|$ the race. (Verb)
　　　　　　1　　　2　　　3

$$\langle\ V\ !\ \rangle\ 1^3\ \underset{1}{N}\ |\ \underset{2}{V}\ |\ 1^1\ \underset{3}{N}\ | = \langle\ V\ !\ \rangle\ P_3$$

4. "*Yes ! Yes !*" cried James with matchless impatience and alacrity. (Adverb)

$$\langle\ 1\ !\ 1\ !\ \rangle\ \underset{2}{V}\ *\ |\ \underset{1}{N}\ |\ *\ 3\ 3\ | = \langle\ 1\ !\ 1\ !\ \rangle\ P_2$$

5. *By heaven !* William Leo Alfred Stavent ! how $|\ \underset{1}{I}\ |$ love $\underset{2}{\ }$
$|$ that name. (Preposition Phrase)
　3

$$\langle\ 3\ |\ N\ !\ \rangle\ 1\ |\ \underset{1}{N}\ |\ \underset{2}{V}\ |\ 1^2\ \underset{3}{N}\ | = \langle\ 3\ N\ \rangle\ P_3$$

When Ns are allowed to be thought as Interjections they become the *Vocatives*. They may be alone or preceded by Interjections when commencing the Mono-simples. Personal Pronouns also become Vocatives alone or followed by the apposition N Vocatives, the punctuative marks of distinction remaining the same.

Vocative Ns take their Ante and Post joiners also; all these, when they increase in their numbers, take the conjunctions too by the general rule. No government but pronominal relation only of the N Vocative extends to the Mono-simple. Sentence subordinates to Vocatives will be considered afterwards while Interjection Vocatives will be considered just now. Interjections and Vocatives begin to show forth development of absolute structures to be treated later on.

Application of Interjection to Narrative Expressions.

With Graphic and Rational Formulæ respectively.

1. $\langle$ *No, my son,* $\rangle$ a life of independence $|$ is generally $|$ a
　　　　　　　　　　　　　　1　　　　　　　　　2
life of pleasure.
　3

$$\langle\ 1,\ 1^3\ N,\ \rangle\ |\ 1^1\ \underset{1}{N}\ 3\ |\ \underset{2}{V}\ 1\ |\ 1^1\ \underset{3}{N}\ 3\ | = \langle\ 1,\ 1^3\ N,\ \rangle\ P_3$$

LECTURE V.

2. ⟨ *Damsel,* ⟩ it | is not for thee | to question *but* to obey.
   $_1$ $_2$ $_4$ $_+$ $_4$
   (Noun pronominal relation between 'Damsel' and 'thee,' exists here.)

   $$\langle N, \rangle \mid \underset{1}{N} \mid \underset{2}{V} \text{ 1 3} \mid \underset{4}{IV} + \underset{4}{IV} \mid = \langle N, \rangle P_4$$

3. ⟨ *Ay,* ⟩ this | is indeed | testimony.
            $_1$ $_2$ $_3$

   $$\langle !, \rangle \mid \underset{1}{N} \mid \underset{2}{V} \text{ 1} \mid \underset{3}{N} \mid = \langle ! \rangle P_3$$

4. ⟨ *Farewell!* ⟩ I | shall not soon forget | you.
                  $_1$ $_2$ $_3$

   $$\langle ! \rangle \underset{1}{N} \mid A \text{ 1 1} \underset{2}{V} \mid \underset{3}{N} \mid = \langle ! \rangle P_3$$

5. ⟨ *Good yeoman,* ⟩ the Lady Rowena | is desirous | to return
                            $_1$ $_2$ $_4$
   to Rotherwood.

   $$\langle 2 N, \rangle 1^1 \underset{1}{N} \mid \underset{2}{V} 2 \mid \underset{4}{IV} 3 \mid = \langle 2 N, \rangle P_4$$

6. ⟨ *My dear son,* ⟩ It | is | a pleasant task | to give | you
                     $_1$ $_2$ $_3$ $_4$ $_5$
   advice on your enquiring points.
   $_5$

   $$\langle 1^3 2 N, \rangle \mid \underset{1}{N} \mid \underset{2}{V} \mid 1^1 2 \underset{3}{N} \mid \underset{4}{IV} \mid \underset{5}{N} \underset{5}{N} 3 \mid = \langle 1^3 2 N, \rangle P_5$$

7. ⟨ *Ladies and Gentlemen,* ⟩ I | thank * | you | * very much
                                $_1$ $_2$ $_3$
   for offering | the chair to me admidst the crowded assembly.
      $_4$ $_5$

   $$\langle \underset{1}{N} + \underset{1}{N}, \rangle \mid \underset{1}{N} \mid \underset{2}{V} * \mid \underset{3}{N} \mid * \text{ 1 1} \mid \underset{4}{PV} \mid 1^1 \underset{5}{N} 3 3 \mid$$
   $$= \langle N + N, \rangle P_5$$

8. ⟨ *King of outlaws and prince of good fellows!* ⟩ no deed
        $_1$ $_+$ $_1$ $_1$
   done during your absence in these turbulent times | shall
   be commemorated to thy disadvantage.
        $_2$

   $$\langle N \text{ 3} + N \text{ 3} ! \rangle 2 \underset{1}{N} \text{ 4 3 3} \mid AA\underset{2}{V} \text{ 3} \mid = \langle N \text{ 3} + N \text{ 3} \rangle P_2$$

80　　　　STYLOGRAPHY OF ENGLISH LANGUAGE.

9. $\langle\underset{1}{Thou},\,my\,poor\,\underset{1}{knave},\rangle\,\underset{1}{\text{I}}\,|\,\underset{2}{\text{shall go presently}}\,|\,\underset{4}{\text{to reward}}$ | thee. (Vocative PP and N Appositions.)

$$\langle\underset{1}{N},\,1^3\,2\,\underset{1}{N},\rangle\,|\,\underset{1}{N}\,|\,A\underset{2}{V}\,1\,|\,\underset{4}{IV}\,|\,\underset{5}{N}\,|=\langle\underset{1}{PP},\,\underset{1}{N}\rangle\,P_5$$

You have seen then that Interjections and Vocatives take the first seat in speech and this is surmised in consequence of their emphatic nature; You have seen also that naked Vs followed by "!" go to rank amongst the Interjections and thus retain the initial seat but when V begins a Mono-simple followed by N expressed or understood, its expression is changed from the narrative or descriptive to that of the "Imperative." The **inversion** of the first pair of N | V of the Narrative into V | N of the Imperative, differentiates between the two. When A appears with the V, the N in the Imperative intervenes between the A and V. The punctuative termination by a Period is common to both and their precedence by Interjection and Vocative remains common too. In the graphic Formula the ellipsis of first N will be shown by its enclosure within a parenthesis and in the Rational, 'thick symbols' will differentiate it from the Narrative.

Illustrations of Inversion of N | V terms in Imperative Expression and its union to Interjection absolutes.

1. Be wise, and make not | bootless opposition.
   $\underset{2}{}$　　　+　$\underset{2}{}$　　　　$\underset{3}{}$

   $$|\,\underset{2}{V}\,\underset{1}{(N)}\,2\,|\,+\,\underset{2}{V}\,(N)\,1\,|\,2\,\underset{3}{N}\,|=P_2$$

2. Never tell an untruth. (*Imperative* V *rarely takes Adverb Ante-joiner.*)
   $\underset{2}{}$　　$\underset{3}{}$

   $$(\underset{1}{N})\,|\,1\,\underset{2}{V}\,|\,1^1\,\underset{3}{N}\,|=P_3$$

3. Let | your guards | attend | me.
   $\underset{2}{}$　　$\underset{3}{}$　　　$\underset{4}{}$　　　$\underset{5}{}$

   $$|\,\underset{.2}{V}\,|\,\underset{1}{(N)}\,|\,1^3\,\underset{3}{N}\,|\,\underset{4}{IV}\,|\,\underset{5}{N}\,|=P_5$$

LECTURE V.   81

4. Do not *expose* * | thyself | * *to wounds and death.*
       2   3   +

| A 1 (N) V * | N | * 3 + 3 | = P₃
         1   2   3

5. Love | thou | thy neighbours.
    2   1   3

| V | N | 1³ N | = P₃
  2   1   3

6. Look from the window once again, ⟨ *kind maiden.* ⟩
    2

| V | (N) | 3 1 1 | ⟨ 2 N ⟩ | = P₂
  2   1

7. ⟨ *No, my father,* ⟩ let | us | instantly leave | this evil
          1   2   3   4
place.
  5

⟨ 1 , 1³ N , ⟩ | V | (N) | N | 1 IV | 1² 2 N |
                 2   1   3   4   5
= ⟨ 1 , 1³ N , ⟩ P₅

Mono-simples allowing the same inversion in the first pair
of N | V into V | N like that in the Imperative expression, occur
again in the **Interrogative expressions**, when N is, however,
always expressed. This expression has its distinctive final
punctuation, the note of interrogation which will be taken
advantage of in the Rational Formula. Certain Adverb ante-
joiners belong to it while its relation remains the same with
regard to Interjection and Vocative (absolute) as in the two
others,—the Narrative and the Imperative.

**Illustrations of Inversion of N | V terms in Interrogative
Expression and its union to Interjection absolutes.**

Illustrations with Graphic and Rational Formulæ respectively.

1. Have | you | then | a convent | to retire ?
    2   1   2   3   4

| V * | N | * 1 | 1¹ N | IV | = P₄ ?
  2   1   3   4

82   STYLOGRAPHY OF ENGLISH LANGUAGE.

2. Are | you | not then well protected in England ?
            $_1$ $_2$

   $|A|\underset{1}{N}|1\ 1\ 1\ \underset{2}{V}\ 3\ |=P_2?$

3. How call | you | those grunting brutes running about on
         $_2$ $_1$ $_3$
   their 4 legs ?

   $|1\ \underset{2}{V}|\underset{1}{N}|1^2\ 2\ \underset{3}{N}\ pv\ 1\ 3\ |=P_3?$

4. Why do | you | offer me a deference so unusual ?
              $_1$ $_2$ $_3$ $_3$

   $|1\ A|\underset{1}{N}|\underset{2}{V}|\underset{3}{N}\ 1^1\ \underset{3}{N}\ 1\ 2\ |=P_3?$

5. $\langle$ Traveller, $\rangle$ whence comest | thou ?
                                    $_2$ $_1$

   $\langle N, \rangle |\ 1\ \underset{2}{V}|\underset{1}{N}|=\langle N, \rangle P_2?$

6. What | dost thou think of this, $\langle$ friend Gurth, ha ? $\rangle$
      $_3$ $_1$ $_2$ $_1$

   (Here inversion of Terminal Vocative and Interjection
   has taken place.)

   $|\underset{3}{N}|A|\underset{1}{N}|\underset{2}{V}\ 3\ ,|\langle 2\ N, !\ ?\ \rangle=P_3\langle 2\ N!\rangle?$

7. $\langle$ Ha ! proud Templar, $\rangle$ hast | thou | forgotten | your
                                              $_1$ $_2$
   twice-repeated fall before this lance ?
                              $_3$

   $\langle !\ 2\ N, \rangle|\underset{2}{A}|\underset{1}{N}|\underset{2}{V}|1^3\ 2\ \underset{3}{N}\ 3\ |=\langle N\rangle P_3?$

It may be remarked however that interrogative relative
"who" being independent of an antecedent and not subordinate
to the Meno-simple principal, does not admit the inversion of
N | V but retains position as in the narrative. For example :—

1. Who | dares | to arrest | a knight of the Templar of Zion
     $_1$ $_2$ $_4$ $_5$
   within the girth of his own preceptory and in the presence
   of the Grand Master ?

   $|\underset{1}{N}|\underset{2}{V}|\underset{4}{IV}|1^1\ \underset{5}{N}\ 3\ 3\ 3\ 3\ +\ 3\ 3\ |=P_5?$

The fourth **expression** in the Mono-simple is the **Exclamatory** having for its distinctive punctuation, the note of admiration. Both the narrative and the imperative may be recognized as *exclamatory* by their terminal punctuation, the " !". We see then that they may or may not admit inversion in the first pair of N | V. The really exclamatory expression however admits of inversion of N | V. It has got a particular A also as its indicator and it has got also particular adverb as antejoiner to the V. The A is 'may' and the adverb is 'what' or 'how'. An adjective after this adverb is also visible. The *exclamatory parts of speech* behave with it the same way as they did with the other expressions.

Illustrations of Inversion of N | V terms in Exclamatory Expression and its union to Interjection absolutes.

Illustrations with Graphic and Rational Formulæ respectively.

1. Long live | the king ! (Auxiliary 'may' is understood here.)
   $$\mid 1\,\underset{2}{V} \mid 1^1\,\underset{1}{N} \mid = P_2\,!$$

2. May | the king | live forever !
   $$\mid A \mid 1^1\,\underset{1}{N} \mid \underset{2}{V}\,1 \mid = P_2\,!$$

3. ⟨*Farewell,*⟩ may | he | shower-down on you | his choicest blessings !
   $$\langle 1,\rangle \mid A \mid \underset{1}{N} \mid \underset{2}{V}\,3 \mid 1^3\,2\,\underset{3}{N} \mid = \langle 1,\rangle\,P_3\,!$$

4. Heaven, ⟨*my leige,*⟩ hath *taken** | this proud man | *for its victim* ! (This is Narrative admirative with medial vocative.)
   $$\mid \underset{1}{N},\mid \langle 1^3\,N,\rangle \mid \underset{2}{AV}\,* \mid 1^2\,2\,\underset{3}{N} \mid *\,3 \mid = P_2\,!$$

5. ⟨*Child of my sorrow,*⟩ well shouldst | thou$_1$ | be called$_2$ Benoni instead-of Rebecca!

$$\langle \underset{1}{N}3, \rangle \mid 1A \mid \underset{1}{N} \mid A\underset{2}{V} \mid \underset{3}{N}3 \mid = \langle N3, \rangle P_3!$$

6. ⟨ *False Norman,* ⟩ thy money | perish with thee!
$_1$ $_2$

$$\langle 2N, \rangle 1^3 \underset{1}{N} \mid \underset{2}{V}3 \mid = \langle 2N, \rangle P_2!$$

7. ⟨ *Archers,* ⟩ send | me an arrow through yon monk's frock!
$_2$ $_3$ $_3$

$$\langle N, \rangle \underset{2}{V} * \mid (\underset{1}{N}) \mid \underset{3}{N} 1^1 \underset{3}{N} \mid * 3 \mid = \langle N, \rangle P_3!$$

8. ⟨ *Thou, my child,* ⟩ thou | shalt render | the lady this
$_1$ $_1$ $_2$ $_3$
service!
$_3$

$$\langle \underset{1}{N}, 1^3 \underset{1}{N}, \rangle \mid \underset{1}{N} \mid A\underset{2}{V} \mid 1^1 \underset{3}{N} 1^2 \underset{3}{N} \mid = \langle N, 1^3 N, \rangle P_3!$$

9. ⟨ *Sweet Lady of Clery, blessed Mother of Mercy!* ⟩ have |
$_2$
compassion with me a sinner!
$_3$

$$\langle 2N3, 2N3! \rangle \mid \underset{2}{V} * \mid (\underset{1}{N}) \mid \underset{3}{N} \mid 3 (n 1^1 n) \mid$$
$$= \langle 2N3, 2N3 \rangle P_3!$$

It will be shown afterwards that interrogative adverb 'why' and exclamatory adverb and adjective 'how' and 'what' follow the Narrative or Imperative expressions of the Mono-simples as *Expression Subordinates*, keeping however their Narrative style or structure but changing their respective punctuation into periods.

———o———

LECTURE VI.

STUDENTS AND GENTLEMEN,

In the last lecture I have related to you of *inversions* in position *of the* N *and* V *terms* in the Mono-simples in their three different expressions,—the Imperative, the Interrogative and the Exclamatory. I have pointed to you out that these inversions are the rule. But in the Narrative certain considerations make it compulsory to invert these and all the other terms and joiners of the Mono-simple which we better call by the name of **Transposition**, for, inversions shown before are nothing but transpositions; for instance you have seen in them all, the auxiliaries and Vs got transposed to the first seat in the sentences before the Ns; you have seen the emphatic parts of speech by their natural order also take the first seat in the sentence. *Emphasis* therefore is *one of* the *chief factor* of these transpositions. The first N by emphasis may take its seat in the Narrative before its Ante-joiners or between them after the Article adjective series. *Among the ante-joiners of* N themselves the adjectives alone or with their middle or sub-joiner series may get themselves transposed before the Article adjectives; *among the Post-joiners of* N adjectives with their antecedent adverbs get transposed likewise to the first seat. Transpositions of the Auxiliaries and Vs in the three expressions have already been dealt with but *Vs in the narrative* again may by emphasis take the seats before first Ns alone or with their inseparable adverbs transposed or inverted.

Illustrations of Vs in the Narrative transposed to first place with Formula.

1. Learn $|\underset{2}{I}|$ must in-spite-of the difficulties thrown in my way.

$$|\underset{2}{V}|\underset{1}{N}|\underset{2}{A}\ 3\ 4\ 3\ |=P_2$$

Transposition of Ante-joiners of N.

Illustrations with Graphic and Rational Formulæ respectively.

2. *Peter* the Great | was | the first Emperor of Russia.
$\quad\quad$ 1 $\quad\quad\quad\quad$ 2 $\quad\quad\quad\quad\quad\quad\quad\quad$ 3

$$\mid \underset{1}{N} 1^1 \; 2 \mid \underset{2}{V} \mid 1^1 \; 2 \underset{3}{N} \; 3 \mid = P_3$$

3. A rate *so favourable* for the article | was never sanctioned
$\quad\quad\quad\quad\quad\quad\quad 1 \quad\quad\quad\quad\quad\quad\quad\quad\quad\quad 2$
before.

$$\mid 1^1 \underset{1}{N} \; 1 \; 2 \; 3 \mid A \; 1 \underset{2}{V} \; 1 \mid = P_2$$

4. *So-glorious* a victory | has scarcely been won within the
$\quad\quad\quad\quad\quad\quad\quad 1 \quad\quad\quad\quad\quad\quad\quad\quad\quad 2$
past century.

$$\mid 1 \; 2 \; 1^1 \underset{1}{N} \mid A \; 1 \; A \underset{2}{V} \; 3 \mid = P_2$$

5. *Full Many* a flower | is born | to blush unseen.
$\quad\quad\quad\quad\quad\quad\; 1 \quad\quad\quad\; 2 \quad\quad\quad\quad 4$

$$\mid 2 \; 2 \; 1^1 \underset{1}{N} \mid A \underset{2}{V} \mid I \underset{4}{V} \; 4 \mid = P_4$$

Certain *Post Joiners of N* transposable by conversion into Ante-joiners have been shown in Lecture I.

Of the first series of the same Ante-joiners, *the PAs* by emphasis precede the article Adjectives. For examples :—

1. *Such* a conduct in him | is reprehensible to the extreme.
$\quad\quad\quad\quad\quad\quad\quad 1 \quad\quad\quad\quad\quad 2$

$$\mid 1^2 \; 1^1 \underset{1}{N} \; 3 \mid \underset{2}{V} \; 2 \; 3 \mid = P_2$$

2. *All* the crowd of spectators | shouted | their applause
$\quad\quad\quad\quad 1 \quad\quad\quad\quad\quad\quad\quad\quad 2 \quad\quad\quad\quad 3$
upon the victor.

$$\mid 1^2 \; 1^1 \underset{1}{N} \; 3 \mid \underset{2}{V} \mid 1^3 \underset{3}{N} \; 3 \mid = P_3$$

3. *Both* the individuals | trusted to their own abilities.
$\quad\quad\quad\quad\quad\quad 1 \quad\quad\quad\quad\quad\quad 2$

$$\mid 1^2 \; 1^1 \underset{1}{N} \mid \underset{2}{V} \; 3 \mid = P_2$$

LECTURE VI.

Ante-joiners of Vs are not transposable. Adverbs as part of the V may separate from the V's and go to the first seat by the same emphasis while *in separable* **Adverb** out of the *post-joiner of V* take the same first seat for the same reason. For examples :—

1. Out | came∗ | the contemptible mouse | ∗ from its hole.
           2   1

   (Collateral transposition of 1st and 2nd terms also.)

$$\mid 1 \underset{2}{V} * \mid 1^1 \; 2 \underset{1}{N} \mid * 3 \mid = P_2$$

2. ∗ *Onward* | the procession | *marched* ∗ for its destination.
                          1   2

$$\mid * 1 \mid 1^1 \underset{1}{N} \mid \underset{2}{V} * 3 \mid = P_2$$

3. ∗ *Up* | he | *turned* ∗ | the table-cloth *and* found | no letter
          1   2   3   2   3
   there.

$$\mid * 1 \underset{1}{N} \mid \underset{2}{V} * \mid 1^1 \underset{3}{N}$$
$$+ \underset{2}{V} * \mid 2 \underset{3}{N} \mid * 1 \mid = P_3$$

It must be remarked here that the inseparable adverb has brought on transposition in the first pair of N | V between themselves and this holds good with certain *separated adverbs*. This is *double* or collateral *transposition*, Initial and collateral. For examples :—

1. *There* is scarcely | a man | to help | me in my adversity
             2   1   4   5

$$\mid 1 \underset{2}{V} 1 \mid 1^1 \underset{1}{N} \mid \underset{4}{IV} \mid \underset{5}{N} 3 \mid = P_5$$

2. *Here* appears | another argument in support of his views.
          2   1

$$\mid 1 \underset{2}{V} \mid 1^2 \underset{1}{N} \; 3 \; 3 \mid = P_2$$

Certain **Pronominal adjectives,** *the Post-joiners to ·Vs* go to the first seat bringing on transposition similar to the above. For example :—

1. *Such* | should be | the means for the end in view.
           2   1

$$|\ast 1^2\ |\ \underset{2}{AV} \ast |\ 1^1 \underset{11}{N} 3\ 3\ | = P_2$$

Like Adverbs, *post-joining Preposition phrases of* V take the first seat by *Emphasis*. When post-joining preposition phrases of V *overcrowd* so as to create confusion that which refers to time sometimes takes the first seat in the sentence. This is as much for emphasis as for the *second reason* just told.

Transposition of Preposition Phrases of V to First Seat.

Illustrations with Graphic and Rational Formulæ respectively.

1. * *In this un-remitting labour* | he | continued * several days.
                                      1   2

$$|\ast 3\ |\ \underset{1}{N}\ |\ \underset{2}{V} \ast 3\ | = P_2$$

2. * *In one respect at least* | this | is * | a merciful appointment.
                                  1   2   3

$$|\ast 3\ 3\ |\ \underset{1}{N}\ |\ \underset{2}{V} \ast |\ 1^1\ 2\ \underset{3}{N}\ | = P_3$$

3. * *Just before dusk* | they | return * in long strings 'from the
                            1   2
foraging of the day.

$$|\ast 1\ 3\ |\ \underset{1}{N}\ |\ \underset{2}{V} \ast 3\ 3\ 3\ | = P_2$$

4. * *In his whole life* | Nelson | was never known * | to act
                              1   2   4
unkindly towards an officer.

$$|\ast 3\ |\ \underset{1}{N}\ |\ A\ 1\ \underset{2}{V} \ast |\ I\underset{4}{V}\ 1\ 3\ | = P_4$$

5. * *On several occasions* | he | succeeded * | in baffling | the
                                1   2   4
pursuit *and* researches of the king's officer.
    5   5

$$|\ast 3\ |\ \underset{1}{N}\ |\ \underset{2}{V} \ast |\ P\underset{4}{V}\ |\ 1^1\ \underset{5}{N} + \underset{5}{N}\ 3\ | = P_5$$

LECTURE VI.   89

6. ⁕ *For our pleasure and not their own* | they | sweat ⁕ under
                 1   2
a cumberous heap of finery.

$$\mid *3+3 \mid \underset{1}{N} \mid \underset{2}{V} *33 \mid = P_2$$

7. ⁕ *Upon this maxim* | is founded ⁕ | one of the prettiest
               2   1
sayings of Publius Syrus.

$$\mid *3 \mid \underset{2}{AV} * \mid \underset{1}{N\; 3\; 3} \mid = P_2$$

8. ⁕ *At the inner end of this burrow* | does | this bird | deposit ⁕
                   1   2
in a good degree of safety | her rude nest consisting of
                      3
fine grasses and feathers, usually goose feathers very
inartistically laid together.

$$\mid *33 \mid A \mid 1^2 \underset{1}{N} \mid \underset{2}{V} *33 \mid 1^3\; 2\; \underset{3}{N}\; pv\; 3\; (2\; n + n)\; 1\; 2\; n\; 1\; 1\; pv\; 1 \mid = P_3$$

From these examples you will gather that transposition of
preposition phrases like those of adverbs sometimes brings on
collateral transposition of the first pair of N | Vs. You are
to understand also that the *prevention of overcrowding* mentioned
before is also for perspicuity the *third reason* for transposition.
Taking into consideration that V is the pivot upon which the
balance of Mono-simple structure is poised, its arm on the right
of the pivot should be shorter than that on the left but by no
means the left arm should be prolonged beyond a certain limit.

To prevent this unusual prolongation of the left arm you
will find partially here the reason why transposition is needed
though the full stretch of it can only be shown after we have
done with the consideration of the Subordinate structures.
The prevention then of *unusual prolongation of the left arm* is
the *fourth reason* of transposition.

The pv or *adjective phrases posterior to N* suffer transposition
as illustrated below. They may be considered as *absolute phrases*
also.

Transposition of PV Post-joiner of N to First Seat.

Illustrations with Graphic and Rational Formulæ respectively.

1. * Situated on the eastern coast of Sicily | Etna $*_1$ | $_2$ appears at the first glance | to have $_4$ | a very simple structure. $_5$

$$| \text{pv } 3\ 3\ \underset{1}{N} | \underset{2}{V}\ 2 | \underset{4}{IV} | 1^1\ 1\ 2\ \underset{5}{N} | = P_1$$

2. * Excessively variable in its texture | protogine $*_1$ | $_2$ passes from the most perfect granitic aspect to that of a porphyry.

$$| 1\ 2\ 3\ \underset{1}{N} | \underset{2}{V}\ s'\ s''\ 3 | = P_2$$

3. * Consequent on its continual cooling | the star originally $_1$ gaseous $*$ | would attain $_2$ | a liquid state. $_3$

$$| 1\ 3\ 1^1\ \underset{1}{N}\ 1\ 2 | \underset{2}{AV} | 1^1\ 2\ \underset{3}{N} | = P_3$$

4. * Circulating round the sun in obedience to the law of universal gravitation | this incandescent gaseous mass $*_1$ | was necessarily regulated by the laws-governing other $_2$ material substances.

$$| \text{pv } 3\ 3\ 3\ 3 | 1^2\ 2\ 2\ \underset{1}{N} | A\ 1\ \underset{2}{V}\ 3\ n\ \text{pv } 1^2\ 2\ n | = P_2$$

5. * Secure in his own cunning and subtlety | he $*_1$ | $_2$ feared not | the attack of the violated laws of his country. $_3$

$$| 2\ 3\ (1^3\ 2\ n + n) | \underset{1}{N} | \underset{2}{V}\ 1 | 1^1\ \underset{3}{N}\ 3\ 3 | = P_3$$

We come now to the discussion of the **transposition of the third term or second N** in the Mono-simple. This N may take the first seat by emphasis or it may very often intrude itself between the V and its Post-joiners. The latter condition becomes an absolute necessity when this term is a naked Personal Pronoun or when it has but only its Ante-joiners and none of the Post-joiners attached to it.

Illustrations with Graphic and Rational Formulæ respectively.

1. *Thee* $\underset{3}{|\ I\ |}$ love from the core of my heart.
$$\left|\ \underset{3}{N}\ \right|\ \underset{1}{N}\ \left|\ \underset{2}{V}\ 3\ 3\ \right| = P_3$$

2. *This idea* $\underset{3}{|}$ he $\underset{1}{|}$ conceived while meditating upon the aspect $\underset{2}{}$ $\underset{4}{}$ of the country.
$$\left|\ 1^2\ \underset{3}{N}\ \right|\ \underset{1}{N}\ \left|\ \underset{2}{V}\ \right|\ 1\ \underset{4}{PV}\ 3\ 3\ \right| = P_4$$

3. $\underset{1}{I}\ |\ \underset{2}{saw}\ |\ \underset{3}{it}\ |$ with my own eyes.
$$\left|\ \underset{1}{N}\ \right|\ \underset{2}{V}\ *\ \left|\ \underset{3}{N}\ \right|\ *\ 3\ \right| = P_3$$

4. $\underset{1}{Saint\ John}\ |\ \underset{2}{wrote}\ |\ \underset{3}{his\ gospel}\ |$ at the age of ninety.
$$\left|\ \underset{1}{N}\ \right|\ \underset{2}{V}\ *\ \left|\ 1^3\ \underset{3}{N}\ \right|\ *\ 3\ \right| = P_3$$

It suffices here to mention only (for as yet we are not in a position to illustrate) that whichever of the two, the final N of the post-joining preposition phrase of V or the third term N be prolonged by subordination, the one that is not subordinated precedes the other. The transposition of the post-joining preposition phrase of V *then* is a transposition *posteriorly* in contrast to the *anterior* method of third N hitherto shown.

The *fourth term IV* of the Mono-simple gets also transposed to the first seat, but as a post-joiner to the first N it will not be found so transposed. The IV post-joiners to N being its apposition analogue, their transposition is not permissible (unless by Conversion of Structures to be shown afterwards).

Transposition of IV terms to First Seat.

1. *To make-up for this deficiency* | they | are furnished with
   long legs for wading *or* long bills for groping *or* usually
   with both.

$$| \text{IV}_4\ 3 | \underset{1}{\text{N}} | \underset{2}{\text{AV}}\ 3\ 4 |$$
$$+ 3\ 4$$
$$+ 1\ 3\ | = P_4$$

2. *To prevent* | *her* | *falling* | *a victim to so laudable an*
   exercise of her talents | I | interposed in a moment with the
   hoe *and* performed upon him | an act of decapitation.

$$| \underset{4}{\text{IV}} | \underset{5}{\text{N}} | \underset{6}{\text{PV}} | \underset{7}{1^1\ \text{N}\ 3\ 3} | \underset{1}{\text{N}} | \underset{2}{\text{V}\ 3\ 3} | + \underset{2}{\text{V}\ 3} | \underset{3}{1^1\ \text{N}\ 3} | = P_7$$

The *fourth PV term* likewise may take the first seat but its position in the serial term cannot be maintained in some instances on account of the sequence of action of the V to that of the Participle and on account of the Noun-pronominal relation extending to the Mono-simple from the PV. In the latter instances the first position of PV is an apparent transposition or Absolute formation.

Transposition of PV terms to First Seat.

1. *By extending* | *this phenomenon to the whole surface of the*
   globe | the solidification of its entire surface | would be
   produced.

$$| \underset{4}{\text{PV}} | \underset{5}{1^2\ \text{N}\ 3\ 3} | \underset{1}{1^1\ \text{N}\ 3} | \underset{2}{\text{AAV}} | = P_5$$

2. *After lingering there many years* | he | was released under
   an act of insolvency.

$$| \underset{4}{\text{PV}\ 1} | \underset{5}{^2\ \text{N}} | \underset{1}{\text{N}} | \underset{2}{\text{AV}\ 3\ 3} | = P_5$$

3. *In extracting* | *teeth with the forceps,* | three things | should
   ⁴   ⁵   ¹
be kept in view.   (Pure transposition as in Ex. 2.)
   ²

$$\mid \underset{4}{PV} \mid \underset{5}{N} 3 \mid 2 \underset{1}{N} \mid \underset{2}{V} 3 \mid = P_5$$

4. *On standing* | healthy urine | undergoes | change.
   ⁴   ¹   ²   ³

$$\mid \underset{4}{PV} \mid 2 \underset{1}{N} \mid \underset{2}{V} \mid \underset{3}{N} \mid = P_4 \quad \text{(Pure.)}$$

5. *By struggling with misfortunes* | we | are | sure | to receive |
   ⁶   ¹   ²   ³   ⁴
some wounds in the conflict.   (Pure.)
   ⁵

$$\mid \underset{6}{PV} 3 \mid \underset{1}{N} \mid \underset{2}{V} 2 \mid \underset{4}{IV} \mid 1^2 \underset{5}{N} 3 \mid = P_6$$

6. *Before convicting* | *a man of blasphemy* | an intention on
   ⁴   ⁵   ¹
his part to injure | must be proved.
                        ²

(Transposition by interchange of N and PP as in Ex. 1.)

$$\mid \underset{4}{PV} \mid 1^1 \underset{5}{N} 3 \mid 1^1 \underset{1}{N} 3 4 \mid AA\underset{2}{V} \mid = P_5$$

7. *By being* | *the constant companions of her solitary hours* |
   ⁴   ⁵
they | naturally become | the objects of her superstition.
  ¹   ²   ³
                                        (Pure.)

$$\underset{4}{PV} \mid 1^1 2 \underset{5}{N} 3 \mid \underset{1}{N} \mid 1 \underset{2}{V} \mid 1^1 \underset{3.}{N} 3 \mid = P_5$$

8. ⟨*Having waited for nearly an hour* | *without seeing* | *Craw-*
                        ⁴   ⁶   ⁷
ford,⟩ | Henry Hunter | took | his departure.
              ¹   ²   ³

$$\langle \underset{4}{PV} 3 \mid \underset{6}{PV} \mid \underset{7}{N} \rangle \underset{1}{N} \mid \underset{2}{V} \mid 1^3 \underset{3}{N} \mid = \langle 4\ 6\ 7 \rangle P_3$$

8

9. $\langle Taking \mid \underset{5}{care} \mid not\ to\ \underset{6}{frighten} \mid \underset{7}{it}\ by\ any\ violent\ move\text{-}ment\ |\rangle\ \underset{1}{he} \mid \underset{2}{threw} \mid the\ \underset{3}{rat}\ a\ small\ \underset{3}{piece}\ of\ bread\ close\ to\ the\ horizontal\ slit\ in\ the\ wall.$

$$\langle PV \mid \underset{5}{N} \mid 1\ \underset{6}{IV} \mid \underset{7}{N}\ 3\ \rangle\ \underset{1}{N} \mid \underset{2}{V} \mid 1^1\ \underset{3}{N}\ 1^1\ 2\ \underset{3}{N}\ 3\ 2\ 3\ 3 \mid$$

$$\cdot = \langle 4\ 5\ 6\ 7 \rangle P_3$$

The above examples show gradually from *real* transposition to absolute formation. You find in the first seven *transposed examples* that intimate prepositions as a general rule always precede the Participle Terms (though they may be absent from absolute participles). You will find here also that pronominal connection of any antecedent N in suite of the transposed PV extends to that in the Mono-simple, which however on the breaking of the transposition shall have to admit interchanges of antecedent N in the Mono-simple and subsequent PP, that is, personal pronoun in the suite of the PV term. You will find also that the government of the Vs stands good upon the PVs though they are transposed to the first seats.

But in the last two *absolute ones* the intimate prepositions of PV are absent as a general rule (though they may be exceptionally present). The Pronominal relations of antecedents in the PVs do also extend to pronouns in the chief sentences. The government of the V upon the PVs does not exist in them at all but the relations with Ns in terms or post-joiners and PP must be yet conceived. Remark and remember that as these PVs have no government relation in Parsing with Vs but have mere relation of N and PP in the respective structures they are *PV Absolutes*. You remember also that Ns, having PV alone or with its suite and having no V for its government have been already called the first *N Absolutes*. Analogy has thus brought you on again to the PV Absolutes having no government in Parsing. You might consider as well that *Interjections* and *Vocative Nouns*

LECTURE VI.   95

and *Vocative Pronouns* are *absolute parts of speech* having no government of their own in Parsing.

Analogy can lead you again to the finding out of **IV Absolutes** *with no relation to Ps* whose further illustrations I give below.

1. *To be sure*, she | is married, Sir.
       4   1   2   1

$$\langle IV\ 2\rangle \{\underset{1}{N}\ |\ \underset{2}{AV}\}\ \langle N\rangle = \langle 4\rangle\ \{P_2\}\ \langle 1\rangle$$

2. *To be brief*, the hour of midnight | had struck.
                         1   2

$$\langle IV\ 2\rangle \{1^1\ \underset{1}{N}\ 3\ |\ \underset{2}{AV}\} = \langle 4\rangle P_2$$

3. *To tell* | *you the truth*, Rivingstone | should be out of our
        4   .5   5   1   2

   way, | *and* hanged without danger to ourselves.
             +   2

$$\langle \underset{4}{IV}\ |\ \underset{5}{N}\ 1^1\ \underset{5}{N}\rangle \{\underset{1}{N}\ |\ \underset{2}{AV}\ 1\ 3\ |\ +\ |\ \underset{2}{V}\ 3\ 3\} = \langle 4\ 5\rangle P_2$$

4. *To sum-up* | *the foregoing arguments of the freethinkers*, | I
            4   5   1

   | may shortly say of their main object-to establish the
                        2

   supremacy of Reason and the Moral Sense over that of Theological dogmas.

$$\langle \underset{4}{IV}\ |\ 1^1\ 2\ \underset{5}{N}\ 3\rangle \{\underset{1}{N}\ |\ \underset{2}{A}\ 1\ V\ 3\ iv\ 1^1\ n\ 3\ (n+1^1\ 2\ n)\ 3\ 3\} = \langle 4\ 5\rangle P_2$$

Absolute IVs may stand independent of the Mono-simple.
For examples :—

1. *To return to our subject.*
                   4

$$\langle IV\ 3\rangle = \langle 4\rangle$$

2. *But to return to the infatuated, darling daughter of the*
                         4

   opulent and money-making merchant.

$$\langle + \ IV\ 3\ 3\rangle = \langle 4\rangle$$

3. Not to mention | the exchange of a sweet smelling garden for the putrid exhalations of Silver End.

$$\left({}_1 \underset{4}{IV} \mid 1^1 \underset{5}{N}\; 3\; 3\; 3 \right) = \left({}_4\; 5 \right)$$

4. To describe | an equilateral triangle | on a given finite straight line.

$$\left(\underset{4}{IV} * \mid 1^1\; 2\; \underset{5}{N} \mid *\; 3 \right) = \left({}_4\; 5 \right)$$

5. But to continue. $\left(+ \underset{4}{IV} \right) = \left({}_4 \right)$

Adjective absolute with co-ordinate connectives is also seen. For example :—

$$\left(\text{So far, so good.} \right) = \left(c'\; 1\; c''\; 2 \right)$$

The subsequent terms, the fifth, the sixth, the seventh, &c., would follow suite to the fourth IV or PV terms in the transposition when such transposition is feasible. For examples :—

1. To catch | a glimpse of the object of all curiosity | many a clerk | that day managed | to sneak-off half an hour *earlier* than usual from-out-of his dusky office in the Inns of Court.

$$\underset{6}{IV} \mid 1^1 \underset{7}{N}\; 3\; 3 \mid 2\; 1^1\; \underset{1}{N} \mid 3\; \underset{2}{\dot{V}} \mid \underset{4}{IV}\; 3\; c'\; c''\; 2\; 3\; 3\; 3 \mid = P_7$$

2. To keep | him | from laying | violent hands | upon himself | two soldiers | were placed in his apartment.

$$\mid \underset{4}{IV} \mid \underset{5}{N} \mid \underset{6}{PV} * \mid 2\; \underset{7}{N} \mid *\; 3 \mid 2\; \underset{1}{N} \mid \underset{2}{AV}\; 3 \mid = P_7$$

Absolute formation, I may again say, consists, therefore, in the want of the parsing government of a term ; in the extension of its N pronominal relation to the main Mono-simple ; in the antecedent or sequent action of PV and IV to those of the V of the main Mono-simple, when the PV is generally recognized by its dropping the intimate preposition or in any two conditions mentioned above. Conditions other than these or only the pronominal relation existing in terms or in the post-joiners of terms indicate that the structure is a Mono-simple one.

When the third term is naked and the first is prolonged and the V is the verb 'Be', **transpositional interchange** takes place between the two, as :—

1. Many | were | the objections raised against the startling
   $_3$ $_2$ $_1$

   theory of Copernicus.

$$| \underset{3}{N} | \underset{2}{V} | 1^1 \underset{1}{N} \text{ pv } 3 \text{ s}| = P_3$$

Thus in the case of 'Be' the first naked N and the second N with post-joiners are convertible.

Like the PV and IV Absolutes, **Preposition phrase Absolutes** with connectives may begin Paragraphs and stand independent or unite with the Mono-simple. For examples :—

1. So-far-as to the manner of religious beliefs.

2. Now-as to beliefs.
$$\langle c\ 3\ 3\ \rangle$$

3. *As to your son*, I | promise | to do | something | for him
   $_1$ $_2$ $_4$ $_5$
   as speedily as possible.

$$\langle c\ 3\ \rangle$$

$$\langle c\ 3\ \rangle \{\underset{1}{N} | \underset{2}{V} | \underset{4}{IV} | \underset{5}{N} | 3\ c'\ 1\ c'\ 1\ \} = \langle c\ 3 \rangle P_s$$

4. *Fortunately for her situation*, | Arnold and his young com-
   $_1$
   panion | again entered | the room.
   $_1$ $_2$ $_3$

$$\langle 1\ 3\ \rangle \{\underset{1}{N} + 1^3\ 2\ \underset{1}{N} | 1\ \underset{2}{V} | 1^1\ \underset{3}{N}\} = \langle 1\ 3 \rangle P_s$$

5. *Then-as to John Dimmock,* | he | was | to be drugged to stupefaction by the miscreants acting as the servants of Bremer and Barclay.
$\underset{1}{1}

$\langle c\ 3\ \rangle \{ \underset{1}{N} \mid \underset{2}{V} \mid \underset{4}{IV}\ 3\ 3\ pv + 1^1\ n\ 3\ (n + n) \mid \} = \langle c\ 3\ \rangle P_4$

6. *But to her sorrow,* | he | informed | her | in his rejoinder | to sign | certain deeds in his and a lawyer's presence.
$\underset{1}{} \underset{2}{} \underset{3}{} \underset{5}{}$

$\langle 1\ 3\ \rangle \{ \underset{1}{N} \mid \underset{2}{V} * \mid \underset{3}{N} \mid * 3 \mid \underset{4}{IV} \mid 2\ \underset{5}{N}\ 3\ (1^3 + 1^1 1^5 n) \mid \} = \langle 1\ 3\ \rangle P_5$

We have heitherto occupied ourselves with the *Inversions* of first and second terms in the Imperative, Interrogative and Exclamatory expressions and *Transpositions* of each and all the terms and joiners in the Mono-simple of the Narrative,—the former being a rule and the latter, in consequence of various causes already mentioned. We come presently to the consideration of another important philological point which concerns only the first 3 or 5 terms of the Mono-simple structure. This point is the *Transformation* or **Conversion** *first*, of these three terms into others or their Joiners with interchanged transposition, retaining yet the original sense of the structure but changing the Voice Expression of the Vs. A glimpse of such *conversion* and *interchage* has no doubt been shown when we dealt with the Ante- and Post- joiners of Ns, though there we have only represented them as *equational*. This change of the V by conversion along with conversion and interchange of the other two terms concerns the Active and Passive expressions only. The Neuter which is wanting in its third term is not concerned here. *Secondly*, will come the same consideration of structures with 5 terms, the third being wanting. *Thirdly*, we will show how far the 7th term admits such a conversion into the first term with collateral conversions of other terms and their interchanges.

LECTURE VI.

A.—Illustrations of Conversion of the Active expressions of V into Passive *with Conversion and Interchange of the first and third terms in the Mono-simple Structure.*

Active Expression.

1. I | love | John.
   $\underset{1}{\ } \quad \underset{2}{\ } \quad \underset{3}{\ }$

$$\mid \underset{1}{N} \mid \underset{2}{V} \mid \underset{3}{N} \mid = P_3$$

2. Ram | struck | me.
   $\underset{1}{\ } \quad \underset{2}{\ } \quad \underset{3}{\ }$

$$\underset{1}{N} \mid \underset{2}{V} \mid \underset{3}{N} \mid = P_3$$

3. We | might believe | him.
   $\underset{1}{\ } \quad \underset{2}{\ } \quad \underset{3}{\ }$

$$\mid \underset{1}{N} \mid \underset{2}{AV} \mid \underset{3}{N} \mid = P_3$$

Passive Expression.

1. John | is loved *by me.*
   $\underset{1}{\ } \quad \underset{2}{\ }$

$$\underset{1}{N} \mid \underset{2}{AV} \ 3 \mid = P_2$$

2. I | was struck *by Ram.*
   $\underset{1}{\ } \quad \underset{2}{\ }$

$$\underset{1}{N} \mid \underset{2}{AV} \ 3 \mid = P_2$$

3. He | might be believed *by us.*
   $\underset{1}{\ } \quad \underset{2}{\ }$

$$\underset{1}{N} \mid \underset{2}{AAV} \ 3 \mid = P_2$$

Observe here that the preposition 'by' plays an important roll in the formation of the post-joiner of the V by going before the first converted term.

RULE FOR THE ABOVE CONVERSION.—Change the third term into the first, convert the Verb Active into Passive, and lastly change the first term into a prepositional phrase by placing the preposition 'by' before its suited conversion and place them all in their respective places.

B.—Illustrations of Passive-active conversion *in which a first term is made to develope in the Active though its Equivalent third remains elliptical in sense or its third itself remains present in the Passive.*

1. *This* | was kept concealed in a box. (Passive.)
   $\quad\quad 1 \quad\quad\quad\quad\quad 2$

   $$| \underset{1}{N} | \underset{2}{AV} * 3 | = P_2$$

   They | kept | *this* | * concealed in a box. (Active.)
   $\;1\quad\;\;2\quad\;\;3$

   $$| \underset{1}{N} | \underset{2}{V} * | \underset{3}{N} | * * 3 | = P_3$$

2. *They* | were told | to go away. (*Passive.*)
   $\;\;1\quad\quad\quad\;\;2\quad\quad\;\;4$

   $$| \underset{1}{N} | A \underset{2}{V} | \underset{4}{IV} \, 1 | = P_4$$

   Others | told | *them* | to go away. (*Active.*)
   $\;\;1\quad\quad 2\quad\;\;3\quad\quad\;\;4$

   $$| \underset{1}{N} | \underset{2}{V} | \underset{3}{N} | \underset{4}{IV} \, 1 | = P_4$$

3. *We* | have been tempted into the bargain. (*Passive.*)
   $\;1\quad\quad\quad\quad\quad\;\; 2$

   $$| \underset{1}{N} | A \, A \, \underset{2}{V} \, 3 | = P_2$$

   They | have tempted | *us* | into the bargain. (*Active.*)
   $\;1\quad\quad\;\;2\quad\quad\;3$

   $$| \underset{1}{N} | A \underset{2}{V} * | \underset{3}{N} | * 3 | = P_3$$

4.. *He* | was made | a magistrate. (*Passive.*)
   $\;1\quad\quad\;2\quad\quad\quad 3$

   $$| \underset{1}{N} | A \underset{2}{V} | 1^1 \underset{3}{N} | = P_3$$

   They | made | *him* a magistrate. (*Active.*)
   $\;1\quad\;\;2\quad\;\;3\quad\quad 3$

   $$| \underset{1}{N} | \underset{2}{V} | \underset{3}{N} \, 1^1 \underset{3}{N} | = P_3$$

The last example proves that the third term after a Passive Verb is not a convertible objective but an equivalent first term and hence it shifted not from its original place.

RULE FOR THE ABOVE CONVERSION.—Develope a first term which is elliptical in sense, change V Passive into Active, convert the first term into third and place them all in their respective situations. When the third term is present here it is inconvertible and un-transposable.

C.—Illustrations of Active-*Passive or Passive-active Conversion of Mono-simple of first four or five terms, the third being wanting.*

1. He | learnt | to speak * | French | * within 6 months.
   $1 \quad\quad 2 \quad\quad\quad 4 \quad\quad\quad 5$

   (*Active.*)

   $| \underset{1}{N} | \underset{2}{V} | \underset{4}{IV} * | \underset{5}{N} | * 3 | = P_5$

   French | was learnt | to be spoken by him within 6 months.
   $1 \quad\quad\quad 2 \quad\quad\quad 4$

   (*Passive.*)

   $| \underset{1}{N} | A \underset{2}{V} | \underset{4}{IV} \, 3 \, 3 | = P_4$

2. We | intended | to give * | bonbons | * to the children.
   $1 \quad\quad 2 \quad\quad\quad 4 \quad\quad\quad 5$

   (*Active.*)

   $| \underset{1}{N} | \underset{2}{V} | \underset{4}{IV} * | \underset{5}{N} | * 3 | = P_5$

   Bonbons | were intended | to be given by us to the children.
   $1 \quad\quad\quad\quad 2$

   (*Passive.*)

   $| \underset{.1}{N} | A \underset{2}{V} | \underset{4}{IV} \, 3 \, 3 | = P_4$

3. Henry and his Council | sent for him | to examine.
   $\quad\quad\quad 1 \quad\quad\quad\quad 2 \quad\quad\quad 4$

   (*Active.*)

   $| \underset{1}{N} + 1^3 \underset{1}{N} | \underset{2}{V} \, 3 | \underset{4}{IV} | = P_4$

He | was sent-for | to be examined *by Henry and his*
 1   2   4
Council.   (*Passive*.)

$$\mid \underset{1}{N} \mid \underset{2}{AV} \mid \underset{4}{IV} \; 3 \; (n + 1^3 n) = P_4$$

RULE FOR THE ABOVE CONVERSION.—The same as that with three terms except that the IV is also to be rendered Passive or Active as the case may be and the fifth term or the N of post-joiner of fourth term into first term.

D.—Illustration of Active-Passive Conversion with seven terms how far feasible.

1. He | tried | to learn | to speak | French | within six months.
    1   2   4   6   7
                                (*Active*.)

$$\mid \underset{1}{N} \mid \underset{2}{V} \mid \underset{4}{IV} \mid \underset{6}{IV} * \mid \underset{7}{N} \mid * 3 \mid = P_?$$

French | was tried | to be learnt and (to be) spoken by him
   1   2   4   4
within six months.   (*Passive*.)

$$\mid \underset{1}{N} \mid \underset{2}{AV} \mid \underset{4}{IV} \mid + \mid \underset{4}{IV} \; 3 \; 3 \mid = P_4$$

You see then that it is not feasible, as 'and' has to be introduced abolishing the government of IV upon IV.

When the Passive V is followed by Active IV, *the fifth term may be interchanged with the first* and the IV Active changed into Passive. For examples:—

1. Kneller | is said | to have painted | *the figure*.
     1   2   4   5
                                (*Active*.)

$$\underset{1}{N} \mid \underset{2}{AV} \mid \underset{4}{IV} \mid 1^1 \underset{5}{N} \mid = P_5$$

The figure | is said | to have been painted by Kneller.
      1   2   4
                                (*Passive*.)

$$\mid 1^1 \underset{1}{N} \mid \underset{2}{AV} \mid \underset{4}{IV} \; 3 \mid = P_4$$

LECTURE VI.

In Passive expressions prepositions other than 'by' are visible in the post-joining preposition phrases of V. These are 'with,' 'for,' 'of,' 'through,' 'to,' 'on account of,' &c. The following are the examples :—

1. They | were marked out *for* probity. (*Passive.*)
   $_1$ $_2$

$$\underset{1}{N} \mid A \underset{2}{V} 1\ 3 \mid = P_2$$

Probity | marked * | them | * out. (*Active.*)
$_1$ $_2$ $_3$

$$\underset{1}{N} \mid \underset{2}{V} * \mid \underset{3}{N} \mid * 1 \mid = P_3$$

2. The table | was covered *with* fruits and flowers.
   $_1$ $_2$

   (*Passive.*)

$$\mid 1^1 \underset{1}{N} \mid A \underset{2}{V} 3\ (n + n) \mid = P_2$$

Fruits and flowers | covered | the table. (*Active.*)
$_1$ $_1$ $_2$ $_3$

$$\mid \underset{1}{N} + \underset{1}{N} \mid \underset{2}{V} \mid 1^1 \underset{3}{N} \mid = P_3$$

3. Ye | shall be hated *of* all men. (*Passive.*)
            $_2$

$$\mid \underset{1}{N} \mid AA\underset{2}{V} 3 \mid = P_2$$

All men | shall hate | ye. (*Active.*)
$_1$ $_2$ $_3$

$$\mid 1^2 \underset{1}{N} \mid A\underset{2}{V} \mid \underset{3}{N} \mid = P_3$$

4. This favor from the king | could only be obtained *through*
   $_1$ $_2$
   the ministry. (*Passive.*)

$$\mid 1^2 \underset{1}{N} 3 \mid A\ 1\ A\underset{2}{V} 3 \mid = P_2$$

The ministry | could only obtain | this favour from the
$\quad\quad\;\;$1$\quad\quad\quad\quad\quad\quad\quad\;\;2\quad\quad\quad\quad\;$3
king. $\quad\quad\quad\quad\quad\quad\quad\quad$ (*Active.*)

$$|\ 1^1\ \underset{1}{N}\ |\ A\ 1\ \underset{2}{V}\ *\ |\ 1^2\ \underset{3}{N}\ |\ *\ 3\ |=P_3$$

5. He | was saved *on account of* the swiftness of his horse.
$\;\;\;$1$\quad\quad\quad\quad$2

$$|\ \underset{1}{N}\ |\ A\underset{2}{V}\ 3\ 3\ |=P_2 \quad\quad (Passive.)$$

The swiftness of his horse | saved | him. (*Active.*)
$\quad\quad\quad\quad\;\;$1$\quad\quad\quad\quad\quad\quad\;\;2\quad\quad$3

$$|\ \underset{1}{N}\ 3\ |\ \underset{2}{V}\ |\ \underset{3}{N}\ |=P_3$$

E.—Conversion of Progressive-Active into Progressive-Passive and vice versa.

Progressive Active.

1. The groom | was conducting | the horse to the stable.
$\quad\;\;$1$\quad\quad\quad\quad\;\;$2$\quad\quad\quad\quad\;\;$3

$$|\ 1^1\ \underset{1}{N}\ |\ A\underset{2}{V}\ *\ |\ 1^1\ \underset{3}{N}\ |\ *\ 3\ |=P_3$$

2. We | saw | him | profiting in the transaction.
$\quad\;$1$\quad\;\;$2$\quad\;\;$3$\quad\quad$4

$$|\ \underset{1}{N}\ |\ \underset{2}{V}\ |\ \underset{3}{N}\ |\ \underset{4}{PV}\ 3\ |=P_4$$

Progressive Passive.

1. The horse | was being- conducted by the groom to the stable.
$\quad\;\;$1$\quad\quad\quad\;$2

$$|\ 1^1\ \underset{1}{N}\ |\ A\underset{2}{V}\ 3\ 3\ |=P_2$$

2. He | was seen | to be- profiting in the transaction.
$\;\;\;$1$\quad\quad$2$\quad\quad\quad\quad$4

$$|\ \underset{1}{N}\ |\ A\underset{2}{V}\ |\ \underset{4}{PV}\ 3\ |=P_4$$

The above conversions are formed by the same rule.

LECTURE VII.

STUDENTS AND GENTLEMEN,

We have seen what Parts of Speech Absolutes are ; we have seen also Phrase Absolutes and the N Absolutes of grammariáns but these are by no means *Medials* in the Mono-simples. It remains now to tell you of the literal *interjectional absolute* of joiners and terms, or interjectional Mono-simples that are thrown *between* the Chief Mono-simple. These *interjectional medials* are (1) parts of speech and (2) phrases in contrast to the initial Absolutes or terminal Absolutes already described ; while (3) *interjectional Mono-simples* are in every way the same with the Chief Mono-simples except their interjectional or medial position within the latter. We are not in a position to speak to you of the (4) *Subordinate interjectional Mono-simples* as yet but reserve their illustrations for the future. These medial Absolutes, Appositions, Joiners or terms, and the medial Mono-simples are no other than the Parenthetics segregated within the Chief Mono-simples by commas, dashes, brackets single or triple. Of the commas the second is its own while the first belongs but to the Chief Mono-simple. Let us go now to illustrate and formulate them.

Narrative-Parenthetic or Interjectional medial.

Illustrations with Graphic and Rational Formulæ respectively.

1. In the days of Hipparchus $\underset{1}{|}$ the length of the tropical year (*an important astronomical datum*) $\underset{2}{|}$ was supposed $|$ to consist of exactly 365 days and a quarter of a day.
$\underset{4}{}$

(*Term.*)

$| \; 3 \; 3 \; | \; 1^1 \; \underset{1}{N} \; 3 \; n \; (1^1 \; 2 \; 2 \; n) \; | \; \underset{2}{AV} \; | \; \underset{4}{IV} \; 3 \; (1 \; 2 \; n + 1^1 \; n) \; 3 \; | = P_4$

2. In the same year (*1804*) | the same daring endurance and heroism | were evinced by the officers of H. M. S. *Hindostan*.

(N *of a joiner*.)

$$| \text{ 3 n (n) } | \text{ } 1^1 \text{ 2 2 } \underset{1}{\text{N}} + \underset{1}{\text{N}} | \underset{2}{\text{AV}} \text{ 3 3 } | = P_2$$

3. · $\underset{1}{\text{I}}$ | was totally unacquainted *either* with the practice of the law *or* the foundations of it, ζ having never opened | a law book (*except the Bible*) in my life. $\rangle$

(*Joiner*.)

$$| \underset{1}{\text{N}} | \text{ A 1 } \underset{2}{\text{V}} \text{ c' 3 3}$$

$$\text{lc' 3 3 } | \zeta \text{ A 1 } \underset{4}{\text{PV}} 1^1 \text{ 2 } \underset{5}{\text{N}} \text{ (3 n) 3 } \rangle = P_2 \zeta \text{ 4 5 } \rangle$$

4. The death of Captain Cook | took | place at Owyhee (*now more-usually written Hawii*) the principal island of the Sandwich group in a sudden tumult of the natives on the 14th of February 1779.

(*Joiner*.)

$$| 1^1 \underset{1}{\text{N}} \text{ 3 } | \underset{2}{\text{V}} * | \underset{3}{\text{N}} \text{ 3 n(1 1 pv n)}$$

$$1^1 \text{ 2 n 3 } | * 3 3 3 3 3 | = P_3$$

5. His bones, *they say*, were found in Scuros.

$$| 1^3 \underset{1}{\text{N}} | \text{ (N } | \text{ V) } \underset{2}{\text{V}} \text{ 3 } | = P_2 \qquad \text{(Mono-simple.)}$$

6. The Banerjees, ζ *to speak the truth*, $\rangle$ are | very honest folks.

(*Phrase*.)

$$| 1^1 \underset{1}{\text{N}} \text{ (IV } | 1^1 \underset{4}{\text{N}}) \underset{2}{\text{V}} | 1 \text{ 2 } \underset{3}{\text{N}} | = P_3.$$

In order to show some developmental analogy between the Absolutes and Parenthetics, the parenthetic portion on the last sentence when transposed to the first seat will prove it.

LECTURE VII. 107

Analogous to *Narrative-Parenthetics* i.e., parenthetic parts of speech, phrases, and Mono-simples, thrown between the *Mono-simple Narratives*, we have now to deal with the parts of speech, phrases, and Mono-simples of *direct-speech* in their various expressions that combine with the Narrative Mono-simples. The Parenthetics are '*aside narratives*,' within Narrative-Parenthetics while Narratives of the Direct-Narrative speeches are 'aside narratives' too by analogy. Let us, therefore, give to it the combined name of **Direct-Narrative**. As it is the direct speech that concerns here, the *verbs*, it must be remembered, would *in the Narrative* be some words that mean 'to speak' in its various forms or manner. Inverted commas include the direct speech and punctuations characteristic of the various expressions end in them. In the *Narrative-Parenthetic* the parenthetic is placed within the narrative while here it is the narrative that becomes initial, medial, or terminal. Attempts have particularly been made to illustrate *the various positions of the Narratives between the different terms of the Direct*.

Illustrations of the positions of the Narrative and Direct in Direct-Narrative with *Graphic and Rational Formulæ*.

1. "A Hubert! A Hubert!" | shouted | the populace more
                                   2   1   c'
   interested in a known person than in a stranger. (Direct
                                                 c''
   initial phrase ; narrative, *terminal*.)

$$\text{``}| 1^1 N ! 1^1 N ! |\text{''} \{ \underset{2}{V} | \underset{1}{1^1 N} c' 2 3 c'' 3 \} = \text{``}\underset{\cdot}{(} 1^1 N ! 1^1 N ! \underset{\cdot}{)}\text{''} P_2$$

2. "The bravest | were | the Knights of the Temple of St.
           1   2   3
   John," *said* | Sir Brian. (Narrative, *terminal*.)

$$\text{``}| \underset{1}{1^1 N} | \underset{2}{V} | \underset{3}{1^1 N} 3 3 \text{''} (\underset{2}{V} | \underset{1}{N}) = \text{``}P_3\text{''} P_2$$

3. "Fly $\underset{2}{\zeta}$ Rebecca $\underset{1}{\rangle}$ and save | thine own life," $\underset{3}{said}$ | $\underset{2}{Ivanhoe}.$
(Narrative, terminal.)

$$"| \underset{2}{V} | (\underset{1}{N}) | \zeta_{\underset{}{N_{\gamma}}}\rangle$$

$$+\underset{2}{V} | (\underset{1}{N}) | 1^3 \; 2 \; \underset{3}{N}" \; (\underset{2}{V} | \underset{1}{N}) = "\zeta N \rangle P_3" \; P_2$$

4. "The yeomen and commons," $\underset{2}{said}$ | $\underset{1}{De \; Bracy}$, "must not
   $\underset{1}{} \;\;\;\;\; + \;\;\; \underset{1}{}$
be dismissed-discontented for lack-of their share-in the
$\underset{2}{}$
sports." (Narrative, *medial* between 1st and 2nd terms.)

$$"| 1^1 \underset{1}{N} + \underset{1}{N} | (\underset{2}{V} | \underset{1}{N}) | A \; 1 \; A\underset{2}{V} \; 4 \; 3 \; 3 \; 3 \; |" = "P_2" P_2$$

5. "A Smith and a file," $\underset{1}{he}$ | $\underset{2}{cried}$, "to do away | the collar from
   $\underset{1}{} \;\;\; + \;\; \underset{1}{} \;\;\;\; \;\;\;\;\;\;\;\;\;\;\;\; \underset{4}{} \;\;\;\;\; \underset{5}{}$
the neck of a freeman!". (Narrative, *medial* between 1st
and 4th terms; Direct, absolute Incomplete.)

$$"\zeta 1^1 \underset{1}{N} + 1^1 \underset{1}{N} (\underset{1}{N} | \underset{2}{V}) \underset{4}{IV} | 1^1 \underset{5}{N} \; 3 \; 3 \; \rangle" = "\zeta 1 \; 4 \; 5 \rangle" \; P_2$$

6. "I | am |," $\underset{2}{said}$ | $\underset{1}{the\;forester}$, | "a nameless man but a friend
   $\underset{1}{} \;\; \underset{2}{} \; \underset{3}{} \; + \; \underset{3}{}$
of my country and of my country's friend." (Narrative
between 2nd and 3rd terms.)

$$"| \underset{1}{N} | \underset{2}{V} (\underset{2}{V} | 1^1 \underset{1}{N}) \; 1^1 \; 2 \; N + 1^1 \underset{3}{N} \; 3 + 3 \; |" = "P_3" \; P_2$$

7. "It | is | time | * then" |, $\underset{2}{said}$ | $\underset{1}{Fitzurse}$, "to draw* | our party |
   $\underset{1}{} \;\; \underset{2}{} \;\;\; \underset{3}{} \; \underset{4}{} \;\;\;\;\; \underset{5}{}$
*to a head either at York or some other central place."
$c' c''$
(Narrative between 3rd and 4th terms of the direct.)

$$"| \underset{1}{N} | \underset{2}{V} * | \underset{3}{N} | * 1 | (\underset{2}{V} | \underset{1}{N}) \underset{4}{IV} | 1^3 \underset{5}{N} | 3 \; c' \; 3 \; c'' \; 3 \; |" = "P_5" \; P_2$$

LECTURE VII.

8. "A sudden charge of the Royal horse | would," | $\underset{1}{Rupert}$ | $\underset{2}{argued}$, | "$\underset{2}{sweep}$ the $\underset{3}{Roundheads}$ from the field." (Narrative between A and V of 2nd term.)

   "$|\ 1^1\ 2\ \underset{1}{N}\ 3\ |\ A\ (\underset{1}{N}\ |\ \underset{2}{V})\ \underset{2}{V}\ |\ 1^1\ \underset{3}{N}\ 3\ |$" = "$P_3$," P_2

9. "I | should in that case hold | you," replied | the yeoman, "a friend to the weaker party". (Narrative between two 3rd terms.)

   "$|\ \underset{1}{N}\ |\ A\ 3\ \underset{2}{V}\ |\ \underset{3}{N}\ (\ \underset{2}{V}\ |\ 1^1\ \underset{1}{N}\ )\ 1^1\ \underset{3}{N}\ 3\ |$" = "$P_3$" P_2

10. $\langle$"Rebecca,"$\rangle$ said | Ivanhoe, "thou | hast painted | a hero." (Narrative between Vocative N and 1st term.)

    "$|\ \langle\underset{2}{N}\rangle\ (\ \underset{1}{V}\ |\ \underset{1}{N}\ )\ \underset{1}{N}\ |\ A\underset{2}{V}\ |\ 1^1\ \underset{3}{N}\ |$" = "$\langle N\rangle P_3$", P_2

11. $\langle$"Dogs!"$\rangle$ said | De Bracy, | "will | ye | let | two men | win | our only pass for safety?" (Narrative between Vocative N and 2nd term.)

    "$\langle N\rangle(\ \underset{2}{V}\ |\ \underset{1}{N}\ )\ A\ |\ \underset{1}{N}\ |\ \underset{2}{V}\ |\ 2\ \underset{3}{N}\ |\ I\underset{4}{V}\ |\ 1^3\ 2\ \underset{5}{N}\ 3\ |$" = "$\langle N\rangle P_5$," P_2?

12. $\langle$"Thou my poor knave," $\rangle$ said | Cedric, turning-about and embracing | his jester, "how shall | I | reward | thee?" (Narrative between PP and N Vocatives, and 2nd term of direct.)

    "$\langle\ \underset{1}{N},\ 1^3\ 2\ \underset{1}{N},\ \rangle\ (\ \underset{2}{V}\ |\ \underset{1}{N}\ pv+pv\ 1^2\ n\ )\ 1\ A\ |\ \underset{1}{N}\ |\ \underset{2}{V}\ |\ \underset{3}{N}\ ?\ |$"
    = "$\langle N,\ 1^3\ 2\ N\rangle\ P_3$," P_2?

13. $\underset{1}{He}$ | $\underset{2}{exclaimed}$, "$\langle$False Norman,$\rangle$ thy money | perish with thee!" (Narrative, initial.)

    $(\ \underset{1}{N}\ |\ \underset{2}{V}\ )$ "$\langle\ 2\ N\ \rangle\ 1^3\ \underset{3}{N}\ |\ \underset{4}{V}\ 3\ !\ |$" = P_2 "$\langle\ 2\ N\ \rangle P_4$"

LECTURE VIII.

·STUDENTS AND GENTLEMEN,

In the last lecture I have shown you that both the parenthetic and Direct Mono-simples unite with the chief Mono-simples and these unions are indicated by distinct marks of punctuations—the Comma, parentheses, dash or inverted commas. We come now to other groups of Mono-simples that as a general rule do not submit to punctuative interference but unite also with the chief Mono-simples. The Absolutes were before shown to be incomplete Structures that combined with the Principals with punctuative marks of segregation but these would be complete structures in combination with the chief Mono-simples. The union of the Absolutes to Mono-simples may be termed *Incomplete Complexes* while these are *Complete Complexes*, though an elliptical variety of the latter exists also for recognition. These are the two Subordinates to the chief Mono-simples, the first called by the name of **Relative Subordinate** and the second by the name of **Conjunction Subordinate**, the former combining with the Mono-simple neither by punctuation nor conjunction but direct, though the punctuative comma is seen sometimes when the Subordinate is a very enlarged structure, or a Parenthetic structure intervenes between it and the chief Mono-simple (or is itself between 1st and 2nd terms) and the latter by conjunctions alone heading its Mono-simples. Sometimes the conjunction of the Conjunction Subordinate remains *understood* and so does the relative of the Relative Subordinate under circumstances. The analogy of both for combination with the chief Mono-simples is thus proved. Let us now begin with the structures of the Relative Subordinate first, before we go to show its combination with the chief Mono-simple.

That the Relative is always an *initial* term or a subordinate joiner or subjoiner to a term in its Mono-simple can be proved by the following :—

When a Nominative, the arrangement of its terms coincides exactly with those of the Mono-simple Narrative. *When an Objective*, i.e. 3rd term in the Mono-simple, it gets itself transposed to the 1st seat before the first pair of N | V. When in the 5th or other odd terms it behaves the same way though Objective to the IVs or PVs in its Mono-simple. When it also constitutes as a terminal in the preposition phrase-joiner to different varieties of Vs, it conducts itself likwise to retain its first place in its Mono-simple, though the preposition may hold its place after the V or removes itself along with the Relative to the 1st seat. The behaviour of the *Relative Possessive* is the retention likewise of the same first seat though it acts then the part of a joiner, consequently that of a subordinate to a term. As *Possessive* it may join the 1st N. When joined to its 3rd N, it brings that N along with it yet to the same 1st seat in its Mono-simple. The possessive behaviour is alike with the Objective as regards an independent term or a joiner or subjoiner described before.

One thing you must remember therefore that the *Relative* is always in the *first seat* whether a Nominative, Possessive, or Objective ; the *relative possessive* joining either an independent N or the subordinate one in a post-joining preposition phrase to the different Vs, the *relative objective* likewise as independent part of speech or the terminal subordinate in preposition phrases too.

Another confounding point you shall have to remember is that when a *Relative preposition phrase* is a joiner to the first N, this N may be seen as transposed before the phrase as in the ordinary Narrative.

Let us go now to illustrate my assertions above and when formulating them, use R for Relative, the *large parentheses* the *power* 's' to it to indicate its subordinate nature.

I.—Relative Subordinate R'.

Illustrations with Graphic and Rational Formulæ respectively.

1. That | lives in the forest.
   $\quad$ 1 $\qquad$ 2

   $(\underset{1}{R} \mid \underset{2}{V} \text{ 3 })' = R'_2$

2. Who | killed | the snake.
   $\quad$ 1 $\qquad$ 2 $\qquad$ 3

   $(\underset{1}{R} \mid \underset{2}{V} \mid \underset{3}{1^1 N})' = R'_3$

3. Which | you | see here.
   $\quad$ 3 $\qquad$ 1 $\qquad$ 2

   $(\underset{3}{R} \mid \underset{1}{N} \mid \underset{2}{V} \text{ 1 })' = R'_3$

4. Which | you | love | to eat.
   $\quad$ 5 $\qquad$ 1 $\qquad$ 2 $\qquad$ 4

   $(\underset{5}{R} \mid \underset{1}{N} \mid \underset{2}{V} \mid \underset{4}{IV})' = R'_5$

5. Which | we | liked | studying.
   $\quad$ 5 $\qquad$ 1 $\qquad$ 2 $\qquad$ 4

   $(\underset{5}{R} \mid \underset{1}{N} \mid \underset{2}{V} \mid \underset{4}{PV})' = R'_5$

6. That | they | shall be obliged | to abide *with*. (Here R is objective in the post-joiner 3 of the IV.)
   $\quad$ 1 $\qquad$ 2 $\qquad$ 4

   $(*r \mid \underset{1}{N} \mid \underset{2}{AAV} \mid \underset{4}{IV} \text{ 3 } *)' = R'_4$

7. Whose stick | was broken at the centre.
   $\quad\quad$ 1 $\qquad\qquad$ 2

   $(1^5 \underset{1}{N} \mid \underset{2}{AV} \text{ 3 })' = R'_2$

8. * In *whose* house | we | lived. *
   $\qquad\qquad\qquad$ 1 $\qquad$ 2

   $(* 3 (r) \mid \underset{1}{N} \mid \underset{2}{V} *)' = R'_2$

'1⁵' indicates Relative possessive to an independent N.

'r' indicates the Relative in a preposition Phrase.

LECTURE VIII.   113

9. * Towards *which* | you | are | first to go. *
                    1   2   4

$$(* 3 (r) | \underset{1}{N} | \underset{2}{V} | 1 \underset{4}{IV} *)^{\epsilon} = R^{\epsilon}_4$$

10. * From *whence* | these sketches | have flowed. *
                      1   2

$$(* 3 (r) | 1^2 \underset{1}{N} | \underset{2}{AV} *)^{\epsilon} = R^{\epsilon}_2$$

11. * *Where* | they | saw * | that gigantic beast.
                1   2   3

$$(* 3 (r) | \underset{1}{N} | \underset{2}{V} * | 1^1 2 \underset{3}{N})^{\epsilon} = R^{\epsilon}_3$$

12. * Of *which* the cost * | is | Rupees ten.
            1   2   3

$$(* 3 (r) 1^1 \underset{1}{N} * | \underset{2}{V} | \underset{3}{N} 2)^{\epsilon} = R^{\epsilon}_3$$

13. The cost of *which* | is | rupees ten. (Here it behaved like
                  1   2   3
an ordinary Narative. The R term or joiner in the R' is
therefore transposed to first seat as a rule and hence its
name.)

$$(1^1 \underset{1}{N} 3 (r) | \underset{2}{V} | \underset{3}{N} 2) = R^{\epsilon}_3$$

Now comes for consideration the Conjunction Subordinates.
These are also Mono-simples headed by the so-called subordinate conjunctions and their terms remain exactly the same
in their positions as those of the Mono-simple Narratives. Before
illustrating and formulating these let us conceive the insertions
of symbol C in lieu of conjunctions in the Formulae.

II.—Conjunction Subordinate C'.

Illustrations with Graphic and Rational Formulæ respectively.

1. *That* | I | am wrong,
   C   1   2

$$(C | \underset{1}{N} | \underset{2}{V} 2)^{\epsilon} = C^{\epsilon}_2$$

2. *Before* | we | proceed.
   c   1   2

$$(\,C\mid \underset{1}{N}\mid \underset{2}{V}\,)'=C'_2$$

3. *Lest* | you | should feel | pain.
   c   1   2   3

$$(\,C\mid \underset{1}{N}\mid \underset{2}{AV}\mid \underset{3}{N}\,)'=C'_3$$

4. *In-as-much-as* | the people | are poor.
   c   1   2

$$(\,C\mid 1^1\underset{1}{N}\mid \underset{2}{V}\,2)'=C'_2$$

5. *If* | the dead animal | had descended to the bottom of
   c   1   2

   the sea.

$$(\,C\mid 1^1\,2\,\underset{1}{N}\mid \underset{2}{AV}\,3\,3\,)'=C'_2$$

6. *That* in the basin of a modern European sea—the Baltic |
   c

   a curious assemblage of phenomena-bearing on the ques-
                                           1

   tion | is now in operation.
        2

$$(\,C\mid *\,3\,3\,(1^1\,2\,2\,n - 1^1\,n\,)\mid \underset{1}{1^1\,2\,N\,3\,pv\,3}\mid \underset{2}{V\,1\,3\,*}\,)'=C'_2.$$

7. *As-far-as* | angels | can ken.
   c   1   2

$$(\,C\mid \underset{1}{N}\mid \underset{2}{AV})'=C'_2$$

8. *When* | Mammals analogous to those of our epoch | gave * |
   c   1   2

   animation | * to the forests, plains, and shores of the
            3

   ancient world.

$$(\,C\mid \underset{1}{N}\,2\,3\,3\mid \underset{2}{V}\,*\mid \underset{3}{N}\mid *\,3\,n,\,n+n\,3\,)'=C'_3$$

9. *While* | the largest of living Iguanas | scarcely exceeds * |
   $\;\;\;\;$c $\;\;\;\;\;\;\;\;\;\;\;\;\;\;$ 1 $\;$ 2

   a yard | * in length.
   $\;$1

   $(\, C \mid 1^1 \underset{1}{N} \, 3 \mid 1 \underset{2}{V} * \mid 1^1 \underset{3}{N} \mid * 3 \,)^s = C^s_3$

10. *As-if* | the sea | had retired | in-order-to show * | us | * still
    $\;\;\;\;\;\;$c $\;\;\;\;\;\;\;$ 1 $\;\;\;\;\;\;\;\;$ 2 $\;$ 4 $\;\;\;$ 5

    intact | the submarine fauna-of this period.
    $\;\;\;\;\;\;\;\;\;\;\;\;\;$ 5

    $(\, C \mid 1^1 \underset{1}{N} \mid \underset{2}{AV} \mid \underset{4}{IV} * \mid \underset{5}{N} \mid * 1 \, 2 \mid 1^1 \, 2 \underset{5}{N} \, 3 \,)^s = C^s_5$

11. *At-the-moment-that* | the wheel | begins | to move.
    $\;\;\;\;\;\;\;\;\;\;\;\;\;\;\;\;\;\;\;$c $\;\;\;\;\;\;\;\;\;$ 1 $\;\;\;\;\;\;$ 2 $\;\;\;\;\;\;$ 4

    $(\, C \mid 1^1 \underset{1}{N} \mid \underset{2}{V} \mid \underset{4}{IV} \,)^s = C^s_4$

The Relative and Conjunction Mono-subordinates having been thus described, it remains now to point you out that they cannot stand by *alone* but that the chief or Principal Mono-simples have had to be accompained by them or in other words the Mono-simple Principals are said to be subordinated by them. The Mono-simple Principals thus combined with the Mono-simple Subordinates develope a complicated structure known by the name of *Complex*. All Formulae shown before are the detailed or Graphic as well as abstract or Rational of Principal and Subordinate as separate Formulae but in treating the Complexes we shall have recourse to a combined detail or graphic and Abstract or Rational Formulae. The Mono-simple Principal is to be bracketed by a large double bracket '{ }' to indicate its nature and the Subordinates initiated by R or C bracketed by a large single bracket '( )' each powered by 's'; while the summation of the terms in each *placed below and a little in front* of the P and the R or C Subordinates, (as in chemical formula) along with digits or fractions *placed before in a line* with the symbols indicating the antecedent or union of R or C with P, will lead you to the Abstract or Rational Formulae of the complexes. Let us now therefore endeavour to illustrate the Complexes both by the Detailed and Abstract Formulae.

I.—Complex by Fractional Relative Subordination of the Principal.

Illustrations with Graphic and Rational Formulae respectively.

1. { The pleasantest parts of the book | are | those } (in which |
   $\quad\quad\quad\quad\quad\quad\quad\quad\quad 1\quad\quad\quad\quad 2\quad\quad 3\quad\quad\quad\quad\quad R$

   she | treats of her own inner experiences.)
   $\;1\quad\;\; 2$

   $\{ 1^1\; 2\; \underset{1}{N}\; 3\; |\; \underset{2}{V}\; |\; \underset{3}{N}\; \} (* 3\; r\; |\; \underset{1}{N}\; |\; \underset{2}{\overset{\cdot}{V}} * 3\;)^{\iota} = P_3\; 3\; R^{\iota}_2$

2. { Clisson | was burnt to the ground with the very *fire-*
   $\quad\;\; 1\quad\quad\quad\quad 2$
   works } (*which* | had been prepared for the christening of
   $\quad\quad\quad\quad\; 1\quad\quad\quad\quad\; 2$
   its master's eldest child.)

   $\{ \underset{1}{N}\; |\; \underset{2}{AV}\; 3\; 3\; \} (\underset{1}{R}\; |\; \underset{2}{AAV}\; 3\; 3\;)^{\iota} = P_2\; \tfrac{2}{3}\; R^{\iota}_2$

3. { A last resistance | was attempted by the retreating Ven-
   $\quad\quad\quad 1\quad\quad\quad\quad\quad 2$
   deens at *Saveny* } (* *where* | they | fought * nobly but in
   $\quad\quad\quad\quad\quad\quad\quad\quad\quad\quad\; 1\quad\quad 2$
   vain.)

   $\{ |\; 1^1\; 2\; \underset{1}{N}\; |\; \underset{2}{AV}\; 3\; 3\; |\; \} (* 3\; r\; |\; \underset{1}{N}\; |\; \underset{2}{V} * 1+3)^{\iota} = P_2\; \tfrac{2}{3}\; R^{\iota}_2$

4. { He | was now doubly beloved and trusted by the *followers* }
   $\;\;\; 1\quad\quad\quad\quad\quad\quad\quad 2\quad\; +\quad\; 2$
   (*who* | had proved | his worth.)
   $\;\; 1\quad\quad\;\; 2\cdot\quad\quad\; 3$

   $\{ \underset{1}{N}\; |\; A\; 1\; 1\; \underset{2}{V}+\underset{2}{V}\; 3\; \} (\underset{1}{R}\; |\; \underset{2}{AV}\; |\; 1^3\; \underset{3}{N}\;)^{\iota} = P_2\; \tfrac{2}{3}\; R^{\iota}_3$

5. { It | is with the bright *spots* in the dark picture } (*that* |
   $\;\;\; 1\;\; 2\quad\quad\quad\quad\quad\quad\quad\quad\quad\quad\quad\quad\quad\quad\quad\quad\quad\quad\;\; 5$
   we | are | to deal.)
   $\;1\quad\; 2\quad\quad\; 4$

   $\{ \underset{1}{N}\; |\; \underset{2}{V}\; 3\; 3\; \} (\underset{5}{R}\; |\; \underset{1}{N}\; |\; \underset{2}{V}\; |\; \underset{4}{IV}\;)^{\iota} = P_2\; \tfrac{2}{3}\; R^{\iota}_5$

The numerator of the fraction before R^{ι} indicates the term in the P to which it is subordinate; while the denominator points to the *Preposition Phrase* of that term in which the antecedent of R is seen.

LECTURE VIII.   117

6. {The eloquence | was | such } (as charmed | the audience.)'
    $\quad\quad\quad 1 \quad\quad\quad 2 \quad 3 \quad\quad 1 \quad\quad 2 \quad\quad\quad 3$
(Unlocked R' co-ordinate.)

$$\{ 1^1 \underset{1}{N} \mid \underset{2}{V} \mid \underset{3}{N} \} (\underset{1}{R} \mid \underset{2}{V} \mid 1^1 \underset{3}{N})' = P_3\ 3R'_3$$

7. { The chief harbour of Malta | is | a deep bay-turned
    $\quad\quad\quad\quad\quad\quad\quad\quad\quad\quad 1 \quad\quad 2 \quad\quad\quad\quad 3$
towards the North and divided into two lesser bays by a
large tongue of rock } (on-the-point-of which | stood |
                                                       $\quad\quad 2$
a strong castle—called Fort Elmo.)'
    1

$$\{ 1^1\ 2\underset{1}{N}\ 3 \mid \underset{2}{V} \mid 1^1\ 2\underset{3}{N}\ 4\ 3 + 4\ 3\ 3\ 3 \} (*3\ r \mid \underset{2}{V} * \mid 1^1\ 2\underset{1}{N} + \underset{1}{N})$$
$$= P_3\ \tfrac{3}{3}\ R'_2$$

Here the R is a subordinate of 3 joiner of the 3rd term
of the P. And we may consider the preposition of R strengthened by a preposition phrase.

Examples as these show that the **R'** is **terminal** to the P.

We come now to show you examples in which **R'** is **medial**
in the P.

Illustrations with Graphic and Rational Formulæ.

1. { All the richer *inhabitants* | (*who* | had | the means | of
    $\quad\quad\quad\quad\quad\quad\quad 1 \quad\quad\quad 1 \quad\ 2 \quad\quad\quad 3$
quitting | the city) fled with one accord. }
   $\quad 4 \quad\quad\ 5 \quad\quad\ 2$

$$\{ 1^2\ 1^1\ 2\underset{}{N} \mid (\underset{1}{R} \mid \underset{2}{V} \mid 1^1\underset{3}{N} \mid P\underset{4}{V} \mid 1^1 \underset{5}{N})'\ \underset{2}{V}\ 3 \mid \} = P_2\ 1R'_5$$

2. {The *actions* (*which* | follow | the impression made upon
    $\quad\quad 1 \quad\quad 1 \quad\quad 2 \quad\quad\quad\quad\quad 3$
the organ of seeing)' do not end thus.}
                         $\quad\quad\quad 2$

$$\{ 1^1 \underset{}{N} \mid (\underset{1}{R} \mid \underset{2}{V} \mid 1^1 \underset{3}{N}\ 4\ 3\ 3)'\ A\ 1\underset{2}{V}\ 1 \} = P_2\ 1R'_3$$

The **initial** position of **R'** to that of P is a very rare occurrence and this even happens by transposition. For example :—

1. (To whom | much | is given)' { * from him | much | is required.*}
   $\quad$ R $\quad\quad$ 1 $\quad\quad$ 2 $\quad\quad\quad\quad\quad$ 1
   2

$$(\text{s r} \mid \underset{1}{N} \mid \underset{2}{AV})' \{ * \text{s n} \mid \underset{1}{N} \mid \underset{2}{AV} * \} = \tfrac{3}{3} R'_2 P_2$$

2. * Him (that | cometh to me) {I | will in no-wise cast out.*}
   $\quad\;\;$ 3 $\quad$ 1 $\quad\quad$ 2 $\quad\quad\;\;$ 1 $\quad\quad\quad\quad\quad\quad\;$ 2

$$\{ * \underset{3}{N} \mid (\underset{1}{R} \mid \underset{2}{V} \text{s})' \{ \underset{1}{N} \mid A \text{ s } \underset{2}{V\text{-}1} * \} = 3R'_2 P_3$$

Now comes the terminal, medial, initial illustrations of the Fractional Conjunction Subordinates with their Formulae. The rule for Integers in the Formulae remaining the same as detailed above.

II.—Complex by Fractional Conjunction Subordinate.

Illustrations with Formulæ.

1. {I | devoutly prayed to God and the Holy Virgin} (that
   $\;\;$ 1 $\quad\quad\quad\quad$ 2 $\quad\quad\quad\quad\quad\quad\quad\quad\quad\quad\quad\quad\;\;$ +
   $\quad\quad\quad\quad\quad\quad\quad\quad\quad\quad\quad\quad\quad\quad\quad\quad\quad\quad\quad$ c
   | they | would support and help | me.)'
   $\quad$ 1 $\quad\quad\quad$ 2 $\quad\quad\;\;$ + $\quad$ 2 $\quad\quad$ 3

$$\{ \underset{1}{N} \mid 1 \underset{2}{V} \text{s} \mp \text{s} \} (C \mid \underset{1}{N} \mid \underset{2}{AV} + \underset{2}{V} \mid \underset{3}{N})' = P_2 \, 2 \, C'_3$$

2. (While | she | was waiting)' {she | began | to remark on a
   $\;\;\;$ c $\quad\;\;$ 1 $\quad\quad$ 2 $\quad\quad\quad\quad\;$ 1 $\quad\quad$ 2 $\quad\quad\quad$ 4
   strange thing lying by the stove.}

$$(C \mid \underset{1}{N} \mid \underset{2}{AV})' \{ \underset{1}{N} \mid \underset{2}{V} \mid \underset{4}{IV} \text{ s pv s} \} = 4 \, C'_2 \, P_4$$

3. {The Roman Senate (as | he | would not come- in to them)'
   $\quad\quad\quad\quad\quad\;\;\;$ 1 $\quad\;\;$ c $\;\;$ 1 $\quad\quad\quad\quad\quad\;\;$ 2
   came out | to hold | their meeting in their Campagna.}
   $\;\;\;$ 2 $\quad\quad\quad$ 4 $\quad\quad\quad$ 5
   (Medial Subordinate.)

$$\{ \mid 1^1 2 \underset{1}{N} \mid (C \mid \underset{1}{N} \mid A 1 \underset{2}{V} \text{s})' \underset{2}{V} 1 \mid \underset{4}{IV} \mid 1^8 \underset{5}{N} \text{s} \} = P_5 \, 2 \, C'_2$$

4. {Carthage | had, (as | some | say,) been first founded by
      1   c   1   2   2
   the Canaanites.} Here C^s is Parenthetic, not medial.

$$\{ \underset{1}{N} \mid A\ (C \mid \underset{1}{N} \mid \underset{2}{V})^s\ A\ 1\ \underset{2}{V}\ 3\ \} = P_2\ (P_2)$$

5. {The old *saying* (*that* | a dutiful child | has | dutiful
        1   c   1   2
   children)^s N | is well exemplified in the More family.}
        3   1   2
   Here C^s is Apposition N to the 1st term.

$$\mid 1^1\ 2\ \underset{1}{N}\ (C \mid 1^1\ 2\ \underset{1}{N} \mid \underset{2}{V} \mid 2\ \underset{3}{N})^N_1 \mid A\ 1\ \underset{2}{V}\ 3 \mid = P_2$$

6. { Nathaniel *addressed* * | the youth | * with his usual ease }
       1   2   3
   (*as if* | nothing | had happened.)^s
     c   1   2

$$\{\underset{1}{N} \mid \underset{2}{V}\ * \mid 1^1\ \underset{3}{N} \mid *\ 3\}\ (C \mid \underset{1}{N} \mid A\underset{2}{V})^s = P_2\ 2C^s_2$$

7. {Let | us | * then | *suppose*} (*that* | Revingstone and Crawford
      2   3   4   c   1   +   1
   | called on the old man near Bagshot.)
       2

$$\{\underset{2}{V}\ * \mid (\underset{1}{N}) \mid \underset{3}{N} \mid *\ 1 \mid I\underset{4}{V}\}\ (C \mid \underset{1}{N} + \underset{1}{N} \mid \underset{2}{V}\ 3\ 3)^s = P_4\ 4C^s_2$$

The Adjective post-joiner after 'Be' or Passive alone or with its suite conjointly governs the C^s. For examples:—

1. {It | *was found necessary for his cure* } (*that* | he | should
      1   2   c   1
   be carried to the same monastery.)
           2

$$\{ \underset{1}{N} \mid A\underset{2}{V}\ 2\ 3\ \}\ (C \mid \underset{1}{N} \mid AA\underset{2}{V}\ 3\ )^s = P_2\ 2C^s_2$$

2. {He | *is careful*} (*that* | nobody | cheats | him.)
      1   2   1   2   3

$$\{ \underset{1}{N} \mid \underset{2}{V}\ 2\ \}\ (C \mid \underset{1}{N} \mid \underset{2}{V} \mid \underset{3}{N}\ )^s = P_2\ 2C^s_3$$

3. $\{\text{It} \mid \underset{2}{\textit{is becoming and}} \underset{+}{\textit{decorous}}\} \underset{c}{(\textit{that}} \mid \text{due honors} \mid \text{be}$

paid to Wordsworth.)
$_2$

$\{\underset{1}{N} \mid \underset{2}{V}\ _{2+2} \mid \} (C \mid \underset{1}{{}_2 N} \mid (A) A \underset{2}{V}\ _3)' = P_2\ 2C'_2$

Looking deeply into the various illustrations of R' and C', you will find that the R' are subordinates to Ns, their proxies, or their equivalents in the chief terms or such in the terminals of preposition phrases in the P; while the C' are subordinates to Vs in the P whether chief or joiner to any of the chiefs. Such being your observation you see both the Subordinates to be Part-of-Speech or Fractional subordinates to Ps. In contrast to the fractional, I give you now **Integral Subordinate** of the Ps. In the case of the R', you will find Antecedents of the Rs to be *absent* from the Ps, remembering that R has but its Antecedent quite close to it (unless phrases intervened), i.e., *proximate*, in contrast to the Antecedents of personal pronouns which are but *remote*. In the case of C' Integrals the conjunctions are a *distinct* set that head the Subordinates forming the *third class*, the second being already shown. The Integeral Subordinates are in both instances subordinates to the *whole* of the Principal and integers before C or R are not necessary in the Rational Formula. Let me now illustrate to you the R' integrals first.

III.—Complex by Integral Relative Subordinate.

Illustrations with Formulæ.

1. $\{* \text{ During the rains} \mid \text{the water of the river} \mid \underset{2}{\text{gets muddy}} *\}$
$\underset{1}{}$

$(\underset{R\ 1}{\textit{which}} \underset{c}{\text{ when drunk}} \mid \underset{2}{\text{brings-on}} \mid \underset{3}{\text{sure diarrhoea}}.)$

$\{*_3 \mid 1^1 \underset{1}{N}\ _3 \mid \underset{2}{V}\ _2 *\} (\underset{1}{R}\ _1\ pv \mid \underset{2}{V} \mid \underset{3}{_2 N})' = P_2\ R'_3$

2. $\big(\underset{4}{\text{Being}}$ of a sanguine disposition and resolute to perform his $\underset{5}{\text{duty}}\big)$ { $\underset{1}{\text{he}}$ | still $\underset{2}{\text{persisted}}$ | in $\underset{4}{\text{going-out}}$ }; (the consequence of $\underset{R}{which}$ | was | the $\underset{3}{\text{inflammation}}$ of his throat.)

$$\big(\underset{4}{PV}\ 3+2\ \underset{4}{IV}\ |\ 1^3\ \underset{5}{N}\big)\ \{\underset{1'}{N}\ |\ 1\ \underset{2}{V}\ |\ \underset{4}{PV}\ \};$$

$$(*\ 1^1\ \underset{1}{N}\ 3\ r\ |\ \underset{2}{V}\ |\ 1^1\ \underset{3}{N}\ 3)^{\bullet} = \big(4+4\ 5\big)\ P_4\ R^{\bullet}{}_3$$

IV.—Complex by Integral Conjunction Subordinate.

Illustrations with Formulæ.

1. {$\underset{1}{\text{Man}}$ | is $\underset{2}{\text{mortal}}$} (*therefore* | $\underset{1}{\text{we}}$ | must $\underset{1}{\text{all}}$ $\underset{2}{\text{die}}$.)

$$\{\ \underset{1}{N}\ |\ \underset{2}{V}\ 2\ \}\ (C\ |\ \underset{1}{N}\ |\ A\ 1\ \underset{2}{V})^{\bullet} = P_2\ C^{\bullet}{}_2$$

2. {$\underset{1}{I}$ | $\underset{2}{\text{imposed}}$ * | fresh $\underset{3}{\text{taxes}}$ | * upon my $\underset{4}{\text{subjects}}$} (*hence* | they | grew $\underset{2}{\text{clamorous}}$.)

$$\{\ \underset{1}{N}\ |\ \underset{2}{V}\ *\ |\ 2\ \underset{3}{N}\ |\ *\ 3\ \}\ (C\ |\ \underset{1}{N}\ |\ \underset{2}{V}\ 2)^{\bullet} = P_3\ C^{\bullet}{}_2$$

3. {$\underset{1}{I}$ | $\underset{2}{\text{make}}$ | these more-refined $\underset{3}{\text{precepts}}$ | $\underset{4}{\text{follow}}$ in the train of the more obvious and rough ones} (*because* | $\underset{1}{\text{this}}$ | $\underset{2}{\text{appears}}$ | to have been | the traditional $\underset{5}{\text{order}}$ of their establishment.)

$$\{\ \underset{1}{N}\ |\ \underset{2}{V}\ |\ 1^2\ 2\ \underset{3}{N}\ |\ \underset{4}{IV}\ 3\ 3\ \}\ (C\ |\ \underset{1}{N}\ |\ \underset{2}{V}\ |\ \underset{4}{IV}\ |\ 1^1\ 2\ \underset{5}{N}\ 3\ )^{\bullet} = P_4\ C^{\bullet}{}_5$$

4. {No $\underset{1}{\text{one}}$ | would $\underset{2}{\text{undertake}}$ | to $\underset{4}{\text{deal}}$ with his own wife privately,} (*so* | $\underset{1}{\text{it}}$ | $\underset{2}{\text{ended}}$ by a message | being $\underset{4}{\text{sent}}$ to the more distinguished ladies | to $\underset{6}{\text{attend}}$ | the $\underset{7}{\text{Council}}$.)

$$\{\ 2\ \underset{1}{N}\ |\ \underset{2}{AV}\ |\ \underset{4}{IV}\ 3\ 1,\ \}\ (\ C\ |\ \underset{1}{N}\ |\ \underset{2}{V}\ 3\ |\ \underset{4}{PV}\ 3\ |\ \underset{6}{IV}\ |\ 1^1\ \underset{7}{N}\ )^{\bullet}$$
$$= P_4\ C^{\bullet}{}_7$$

5. {Mrs. Pembroke | divided * | her time * between Mrs. and
      1   2   3
Miss Crawford to the utmost of her ability} (notwithstand-
                                                                    c
ing | she | had | private cares of her own and private reasons
       1   2   3
for sorrow | to occupy | her attention and lacerate | her heart.)
                 4   5   4   6

$\{\underset{1}{N} \mid \underset{2}{V}\, _{\text{o}} \mid \, 1^s \underset{3}{N} \mid \, _{\text{o}}\, 3\, 3\, 3\}$

$(C \mid \underset{1}{N} \mid \underset{2}{V} \mid \, 2\, \underset{3}{N}\, 3 + 2\, \underset{3}{N}\, 3 \mid IV \mid \, 1^s \underset{5}{N} \mid + \mid \underset{4}{IV} \lceil 1^s \underset{5}{N} \mid\,) = P_3\, C^{\bullet}{}_5$

The Relative and Conjunction of R• and C• may remain understood under circumstances as :—

Illustrations of Relative and Conjunction of R• and C• Understood.

1. I think I am right.

$\{ \mid \underset{1}{N} \mid \underset{2}{V} \mid \} ((C) \mid \underset{1}{N} \mid \underset{2}{V}\, 2\,)^{\bullet} = P_2\, 2\, C^{\bullet}{}_2$

2. He gave me the book I wanted.

$\{ \mid \underset{1}{N} \mid \underset{2}{V} \mid \underset{3}{N}\, 1^1 \underset{3}{N} \mid \} ((R) \mid \underset{1}{N} \mid \underset{2}{V})^{\bullet} = P_3\, 3\, R^{\bullet}{}_3$

3. (Could | I | but get | her | snared or noosed or muzzled | so
              1   2   3
    as to leave | her within my power in another Gower
    c   4   5
Street) {the thing | would to a dead certainty be achieved.}
                              2

Could I but get = If I could get—*i. e.* 'if' is here understood.

$((C) \mid A \mid \underset{1}{N} \mid 1\, \underset{2}{V} * \mid \underset{3}{N} \mid *\, 4+4+4 \mid c\, \underset{4}{IV} \mid \underset{5}{N} \mid 3\, 3)^{\bullet}$

$\{1^1\, \underset{1}{N} \mid A\, 3\, A\, \underset{2}{V}\} = 2C^{\bullet}{}_5\, P_2$

As yet we have been considering only of *one* Subordinate at a time combining with the P, it has now become necessary to show to you that *two* Subordinates one on each side of the P may occur, the initial being a C• and the terminal an R•, or both the initial and terminal being a C• each but not R•. These double Sub-ordinates may properly be designated as *Di-subordinates* in contrast to the *Bi-subordinates* which we will subsequently have to speak of. As the P is here di-subordinated we might call these Complexes '*Complexes by di-subordination.*'

V.—Complex by Di-subordination.

Illustrations with Graphic and Rational Formulæ.

1. ($As \mid \underset{1}{\text{I}} \mid$ was surveying $\mid$ the moon walking in her bright-
   c $\quad\quad\quad\quad\quad\quad 2 \quad\quad\quad\quad\quad 3$

   ness and taking her progress among the constellations)
   { a $\underset{1}{thought} \mid \underset{2}{rose}$ in me} ($\underset{1}{which} \mid$ very often $\underset{2}{perplexes}$ and

   $\underset{2}{disturbs} \mid \underset{3}{men}$ of serious and contemplative nature.)

$$(C \mid \underset{1}{N} \mid \underset{2}{AV} \mid 1^1 \underset{3}{N} \text{ pv } 3 + \text{pv } 1^3 \text{ n } 3 \mid)^{\bullet} \{ \mid 1^1 \underset{1}{N} \mid \underset{2}{V} 3 \mid \}$$
$$(R \mid 1 1 \underset{2}{V} + \underset{2}{V} \mid \underset{3}{N} 3)^{\bullet} = 2 \, C^{\bullet}_3 P_2 1 \, R^{\bullet}_3$$

2. ($\underset{c}{When} \mid \underset{1}{we} \mid \underset{2}{came} \mid$ to $\underset{4}{cut} * \mid \underset{.5}{it} \mid *$ up) $\{ \underset{1}{we} \mid \underset{2}{found} \} (that \atop c$
   $\mid$ the $\underset{1}{abdomen} \mid$ was $\underset{2}{crowded}$ with young 15 in numbers.)

$$(C \mid \underset{1}{N} \mid \underset{2}{V} \mid \underset{4}{IV} * \mid \underset{5}{N} \mid * 1)^{\bullet} \{ \underset{1}{N} \mid \underset{2}{V} \} (C \mid 1^1 \underset{1}{N} \mid \underset{2}{AV} 3 2 3)^{\bullet}$$
$$= 2 \, C^{\bullet}_5 \, P_2 \, 2 \, C^{\bullet}_2$$

Then on the other hand a Subordinate itself when viewed as a Principal, takes a second Subordinate and the second a third, each to each in series till to even the 5th of such Sub-subordinations. These may receive the generic name of *serial Sub-subordinates*. Let the combination of the Subordinate with the first of the Sub-subordinate receive the name of a *Bi-subordinate*, we might then say of the P to be bi-subordinated and let the Sub-subordinates beyond receive the name of the *Poly-subordinates* and the P to be poly-subordinated. Bi-subordinates are formed by the repetitions of $C^{\bullet}$ or $R^{\bullet}$ or alternations of both ; we go now to illustrate and formulate them. In the Formulae the sub-subordinate will take the integer 2 in its power 's' to show its extent of subordination remote from P.

Analogous to the single Government of N upon V, and dual government of V upon N and IV or PV, you have just seen Subordination single of N by $R^{\bullet}$ and Subordinations dual of V by two $C^{\bullet}$.

VI.—The Complex by Bi-subordination.

(*i.e. Subordinations sub-subordinated.*)

With Graphic and Rational Formulæ.

1. {This | was | a necessary precaution | in- order- to secure |
   $\quad$ 1 $\quad\;$ 2 $\qquad\qquad\qquad$ 3 $\qquad\qquad\qquad\qquad$ 4
   equality betwixt the two *bodies*} (*which* | should be opposed
   $\qquad\qquad\qquad\qquad$ 5 $\qquad\quad\;$ 1 $\qquad\qquad\qquad\;$ 2
   to each-other in the general *encounter*) (*which* | was called |
   $\qquad\qquad\qquad\qquad\qquad\qquad\qquad\qquad$ 1 $\qquad\;$ 2
   a mêlée.)
   $\;$ 3

   $\{\;|\;\underset{1}{N}\;|\;\underset{2}{V}\;|\;1^1\;2\;\underset{3}{N}\;|\;\underset{4}{IV}\;|\;\underset{5}{N}\;3\;|\;\}\;(\underset{1}{R}\;|\;AA\underset{2}{V}\;3\;3)^{\bullet}$

   $\bullet\;(\underset{1}{R}\;|\;A\underset{2}{V}\;|\;1^1\;\underset{3}{N})^{2\bullet} = P_5\;\tfrac{5}{3}\;R^{\bullet}{}_2\;\tfrac{2}{3}\;R^{2\bullet}{}_3$

2. { The most- degraded savage | has *discovered* } (*how* | one |
   $\qquad\qquad\qquad\qquad\;\;$ 1 $\qquad\qquad$ 2 $\qquad\qquad\;\;$ c $\quad\;$ 1
   rubs * | two sticks | * together or *whirls* | the point of one
   $\;\;$ 2 $\qquad\quad$ 3 $\qquad\qquad\quad\;$ + 2 $\qquad\qquad\qquad$ 3
   in a socket in the other) (*till* | the wood | is kindled.)
   $\qquad\qquad\qquad\qquad\qquad\;$ c $\qquad\;\;$ 1 $\qquad\;\;$ 2

   $\{\;|\;1^1\;2\;\underset{1}{N}\;|\;A\underset{2}{V}\;|\;\}\;(\;C\;|\;\underset{1}{N}\;|\;\underset{2}{V}\;*\;|\;2\;\underset{3}{N}\;|\;*\;1\;|+|\;\underset{2}{V}\;|\;1^1\;\underset{3}{N}\;3\;3\;3\;)^{\bullet}$

   $(C\;|\;1^1\;\underset{1}{N}\;|\;A\underset{2}{V})^{2\bullet} = P_2\;2\;C^{\bullet}{}_3\;2\;C^{2\bullet}{}_2$

3. {Adorno | *dropped* | the letter | and | *covered* * | his face
   $\quad\;\;$ 1 $\qquad\quad$ 2 $\qquad\qquad$ 3 $\quad\;$ + $\qquad$ 2 $\qquad\qquad$ 3
   | * with his hand} (*while* | his son | was describing in the
   $\qquad\qquad\qquad\qquad$ c $\qquad\quad$ 1 $\qquad\qquad\;$ 2
   warmest language | the virtues of Uberto | and | the *kind-*
   $\qquad\qquad\qquad\qquad\quad\;\;$ 3 $\qquad\qquad\qquad\quad$ + $\qquad$ 3
   ness) (he | had received from him.)
   $\qquad\;\;$ 1 $\qquad\qquad\qquad$ 2

   $\{\;|\;\underset{1}{N}\;|\;\underset{2}{V}\;|\;1^1\;\underset{3}{N}$

   $+\;|\;\underset{2}{V}\;*\;|\;1^3\;\underset{3}{N}\;|\;*\;\mathrm{s}\;|\;\}$

   $(C\;|\;1^3\;\underset{1}{N}\;|\;A\underset{2}{V}\;3\;|\;1^1\;\underset{3}{N}\;3+1^1\;\underset{3}{N})^{\bullet}\;(\;(R)\;|\;\underset{1}{N}\;|\;A\underset{2}{V}\;3\;)^{2\bullet}$

   $\qquad\qquad\qquad\qquad = P_3\;2\;C^{\bullet}{}_3\;3\;R^{2\bullet}{}_3$

LECTURE VIII.   125

4. {All the hirundines of a village | are-up in arms at the sight
   $_1_2$
   of a *hawk*} (*whom* | they | will persecute)⁎ (*till* | he |
   $_3_1_2_1$
   leaves | that district.)²⁎
   $_2_3$

$$\{ \mid 1^2\,1^1\,\underset{1}{N}\,3 \mid \underset{2}{V}\,3\,3\,3\} (\underset{3}{R} \mid \underset{1}{N} \mid \underset{2}{AV})^{\centerdot} (C \mid \underset{1}{N} \mid \underset{2}{V} \mid \underset{3}{1^2\,N})^{2\centerdot}$$

$$= P_2\, \tfrac{2}{3}\, R^{\centerdot}{}_3\, 2\, C^{2\centerdot}{}_3$$

5. {It | was now} (that | the wine-merchant (*who* | had come
   $_1_2_c_1_1_2$
   | to maintain | a very watchful eye over his daughter's
   $_4_5$
   manner and appearance)²⁎ | thought ⁎ | it | ⁎ necessary |
   $_2_3$
   to call-in | the family physician | in-order-not-merely-to
   $_4_5_{c'}$
   have | his advice as-to the state of her health | but to use
   $_6_7_{c''}_6$
   | his influence over the fair enthusiast| with-the-view-of
   _7
   having | her | to consent to a change of air to a temporary
   $_8_9_{10}$
   removal to some one of Mr. Maxwells' correspondents in
   the island of Madeira)⁎, ⟨ a consumptive tendency ⟨ it
   $_1$
   being believed, ⟩ characterising | her state of health. ⟩
   $_4_5$

$$\{\underset{1}{N} \mid \underset{2}{V}\,1\} (C \mid \underset{1}{1^1\,N} \mid (\underset{1}{R} \mid \underset{2}{AV} \mid \underset{4}{IV} \mid 1^1\,1\,2\,\underset{5}{N}\,3)^{2\centerdot} \mid \underset{2}{V} * \mid \underset{3}{N} \mid * 2$$

$$\mid \underset{4}{IV} \mid 1^1\,2\,\underset{5}{N} \mid c'\underset{6}{IV} \mid 1^3\,\underset{7}{N}\,3\,3$$

$$\mid c''\underset{6}{IV} \mid 1^3\,\underset{7}{N}\,3 \mid \underset{8}{PV} \mid \underset{9}{N} \mid \underset{10}{IV}\,3\,3\,3\,3\,3\,3\,3)^{\centerdot},$$

$$\langle 1^1\,2\,\underset{1}{N} \langle \underset{1}{N} \mid \underset{4}{PV} \rangle \underset{4}{PV} \mid 1^3\,\underset{5}{N}\,3 \rangle$$

$$= P_2\, 2\, C^{\centerdot}{}_{10}\, 1\, R^{2\centerdot}{}_5 \langle 1 \langle 1\,4 \rangle 4\,5 \rangle$$

Bi-subordinates may appear both initially and terminally to P, when they might respectively be called a *Bi-bi-subordinate*; or a *Bi-di-subordinate*, when a Bi-subordinate precedes and a Mono-subordinate follows the P; or a *Di-bi-subordinate*, when these conditions are *vice versâ*.

VII.—Complex by Di-bi, Bi-di, and Bi-bi-subordinations.

(Subordination sub-subordinated.)

1. (*If* | you | follow | the main)· {you | would find} (*that*
         $\quad$ 1 $\quad\quad$ 2 $\quad\quad\quad$ 3 $\quad\quad\quad$ 1 $\quad\quad\quad$ 2

| it | took | a long course up and down beneath the pave-
$\,$1 $\quad\,$2 $\quad\quad\quad\quad$ 3

ment of the streets)· (*until* ∗ at last | it | reached ∗ | the
$\quad\quad\quad\quad\quad\quad\quad\quad\quad\quad\quad\quad\quad$ 1 $\quad\quad$ 2

water-works.)²·   (This is Di-bi-subordination.)
$\quad\quad\quad$ 3

$$(C \mid N \mid V \mid 1^1 \, N)· \{ N \mid AV \} (C \mid N \mid V \mid 1^1 \, 2 \, N \, 1 + 1 \, 3 \, 3)$$
$$\quad\; 1 \quad 2 \quad 3 \quad\quad\quad 1 \quad\quad 2 \quad\;\; 1 \quad 2 \quad\quad 3$$

$$(C \, 1 \mid N \mid V \mid 1^1 \, N) = 2 \, C^·_3 \, P_2 \, 2 \, C^·_3 \, 2 \, C^{2·}_3$$
$$\quad\quad\quad\; 1 \quad 2 \quad\; 3$$

2. (As | he was musing on his present condition and very
   $\quad\quad$ 1 $\quad\quad\quad\quad\quad$ 2
                                                          +
much perplexed in himself on the state)· (he | should
$\quad\quad\quad\quad$ 2 $\quad\quad\quad\quad\quad\quad\quad\quad\quad\quad\quad\quad\quad$ 1

choose)²· {he | saw | two women of a *larger* stature *than*
$\quad\quad\,$ 2 $\quad$ 1 $\quad\,$ 2 $\quad\quad\quad\,$ 3 $\quad\quad\quad\quad$ c′ $\quad\quad\quad\,$ c″

ordinary} (who | approached towards him.)· (Bi-di-subor-
$\quad\quad\quad\quad\,$ 1 $\quad\quad\quad$ 2

dinate.)

$$(\, C \mid N \mid AV \, 3 + 1 \, 1 \, V \, 3 \, 3 \,)·$$
$$\quad\quad\; 1 \quad\; 2 \quad\quad 2$$

$$((R) \mid N \mid AV)^{2·} \{ \mid N \mid V \mid 2 \, N \, 3 \, (1^1 \, c' \, n \, c'' \, 2 \, n) \} (R \mid V \, 3)·$$
$$\;\;\; 3 \quad\; 1 \quad\; 2 \quad\quad\quad\;\; 1 \quad 2 \quad 3 \quad\quad\quad\quad\quad\quad\quad\quad\quad\; 1 \quad 2$$

$$= 2 \, C^·_2 \, \tfrac{2}{3} \, R^{2·}_3 \, P_3 \, 3 \, R^·_2$$

3. (*As* | there is not | the slightest difference in weight
   $\quad\quad\quad\quad\quad$ 2 $\quad\quad\quad\quad\quad\quad\quad\quad$ 1

between a given quantity of water and the ice or the

steam)* (* into which | it | may be converted *)²*{ it | is
         1   1   2   1
clear} (that | the heat (which | is added to or taken from
        2   1   1   2
the water | to give * | rise | * to these several states)²* can
                   4   5
possess | no weight.)*   (Bi-bi-subordinate.)
    2   3

(C | 1 V 1 | 1¹ 2 N 3 3 3 (n+1¹ n+1¹ n))*
       2   1

$$(3\ r\ |\ \underset{1}{N}\ |\ AA\underset{2}{V})^{2*}\ \{\ |\ \underset{1}{N}\ |\ \underset{2}{V}\ 2\ |\ \}$$

(C | 1¹ N (R | AV+V 3 | IV | N | 3 |)²* | AV | 2 N |)*
        1   1   2 2   4   5   2   3

$$= C^{*}{}_{2}\ \tfrac{4}{3}\ R^{2*}{}_{2}\ P_{2}\ 2\ C^{*}{}_{3}\ 1\ R^{2*}{}_{5}$$

Before illustrating the *Poly-subordinate*, I go to remind you that extensions, beyond the IV and PV terms of the Mono-simple are made by repetitions and alternate repetitions of these terms. In like manner poly-subordinations are only feasible by repetitions or alternate repetitions of R* and C* Subordinates.

VIII.—Complex by Poly-subordination.

(*Serial Sub-subordinations.*)

1. {The water | is brought from a large pipe or main in the
        1   2
street by smaller house-pipe } (which | is often made | to
                                    1   2
twist-about in various directions)* (before | it | reaches
          4   2
the cistern at the top of the house)²* (into which it | delivers
         3   2
| the water.)³*
       3

{1¹ N | AV 3 (1¹ 2 n+n) 3 3 } (R | A 1 V | IV 3)*
    1   2   1   2   4

(C | N | V | 1¹ N 3 3)²* (* 3 r | N | V * | 1¹ N)³*
     1   2   3   1   2   3

$$= P^{*}_{2}\ \tfrac{2}{3}\ R^{*}_{4}\ 4\ C^{2*}{}_{3}\ \tfrac{2}{3}\ R^{3*}{}_{3}$$

128   STYLOGRAPHY OF ENGLISH LANGUAGE.

2. {It | does not follow however} (*that* | it | really possesses
   1   2   1   2
none)⁰ (*for,* | there are | many *things*)²⁰ (*which* | seem | to
     3   2   1   1   2
be | the same throughout or homogeneous)³⁰ (*which* | yet
 4   5   1
show | structures)⁴⁰ (*if* | they | are examined with a
  2   3   1   2
magnifying glass.)⁵⁰

{N | A ₁ V ₁ } (C | N | ₁ V | N)¹⁰ (C | ₁ V | ₂ N)²⁰
 1   2   1   2   3   2   1

(R | V | IV | 1¹ N 2 + 2)³⁰ (R | ₁ V | N)⁴⁰ (C | N | AV 3)⁵⁰
 1   2   4   5   3   2   3   1   2

=P₂ 2 C⁰₄C²⁰₂ 1 R³⁰₅ 3 R⁴⁰₃ 2 C⁵⁰₂

In considering the **Methods of Combination** of the Mono-
subordinates as seen before to Mono-principals, R⁰ may be
thought to be '*simple combinative*', and C⁰ to be '*combinative*' and
'*permutative.*' We come now to a third variety of combination,
which we might very properly call *the 'locked.*' Co-ordinating
Conjunctions and co-ordinating Relatives play the roll of lock-
ing here. Fractional subordination to Ns and Vs has been played
by Relatives or mono-groupal Conjunctions, but the co-ordinating
or bi-groupal ones play double roll by throwing towards the
tail or any part of the P, its first conjunction C' as the post-
joiner of V or ante-joiner of N and placing at the *head* of
the Subordinates, its 2nd one C" or R". In these Complexes
c'-c" go to form the 4th Class of conjunctions. Here the
c' is connective to Adjective, Adverb, or both Adverb and
Adjective post-joiners to Vs, IVs, or PVs ; or as inter-joiner
between them and their auxiliaries in case of C"; or as ante-
joiner connective to N in case of R'. It is but these Subordinates which are non-elliptical or elliptical in terms, or joiners,
or both, that I go now to illustrate and formulate.

IX.—Complex by co-ordinate c' C"⁰ subordination.

1. NON-ELLIPTICAL CO-ORDINATE SUBORDINATES.

1. { They | descended to *so* many labours and also minor studies
     1.   2   c'   +

to *such* a variety of ramifications and strange agencies }
   c'   +

LECTURE VIII.

(*that* | to go into every particular | would be | to prolong |
 c'' 1   2:   4

these pages | * out of all due proportion.)*
       5

(Here ante-joiner Adjectives to final Ns of 3s to V get
co-ordinately subordinated.)

$$\{ \underset{1}{N} \mid \underset{2}{V} \; 3(c' \; 2 \; n+12 \; n) \; 3 \; (c' \; 1^1 \; n) \; 3 \; (n+2 \; n) \}$$

$$(C'' \mid \underset{1}{IV} \; 3 \mid \underset{2}{AV} \mid \underset{4}{IV} \mid 1^2 \underset{5}{N} \mid 1 \; 3)^\epsilon = P_2 \; c' \atop c' \} \; C''_5$$

2. { His ideas of moral justice | were *such* } (*that* | he | could
         1   2   c'   c''   1

not for a moment allow | himself | to be in the least pre-
                2   3   4

judiced against the innocent Catharine.)*

$$\{1^2 \underset{1}{N} \; 3 \mid \underset{2}{V} \; c' \} \; (C'' \mid \underset{1}{N} \mid A \; 1 \; 3 \; \underset{2}{V} \mid \underset{3}{N} \mid A \; 3 \; IV \; 3 \;)^\epsilon = P_2 \; c' \; C''_4$$

3. {The back of a chair placed opposite to a bright fire |
              1

gets *so* hot } (*that* | you | can hardly touch | it.)
  2   c'   c''   1   2   3

$$\{1^1 \underset{1}{N} \; 3 \; pv \; 2 \; 3 \mid \underset{2}{V} \; c' \; 2 \} \; (C'' \mid \underset{1}{N} \mid A \; 1 \; \underset{2}{V} \mid \underset{3}{N})^\epsilon = P_2 \; c' \; \tfrac{2}{3} C''_3$$

4. { The earth | has | to travel over *so* wide a circuit or orbit}
          1   2   4   c'   +

(*that* | it | takes | rather more than 365 days | to perform
 c''   1   2   3   4

the journey.)*
      5

$$\{1^1 \underset{1}{N} \mid \underset{2}{V} \mid \underset{4}{IV} \mid 3(c' \; 2 \; 1^1 \; n+n) \} \; (C'' \mid \underset{1}{N} \mid \underset{2}{V} \mid c' \; c'' \; 2 \; \underset{3}{N} \mid \underset{4}{IV} \mid 1^1 \underset{5}{N})^\epsilon$$

$$= P_4 \; c' \; \tfrac{4}{3} \; C''_5$$

130   STYLOGRAPHY OF ENGLISH LANGUAGE.

5. { He | did so carefully go through the proof-sheets } (that
     1   2   c′   c″
   there could not possibly be | any mistakes in them.)
           2   1

   {N | A c′ 1 V 3} (C″ 1 A 1 1 V | 1² N 3)·= P₂ c′ C″·₂
    1   2   2   1

6. { Every material substance | tends *·| to approach | every
                    1   2   4
   other material substance | * just in the same way } (as | a
                  5   c′   c″
   drop of rain | falls towards the earth.)·
        1   2

{| 1² 2 N | V | IV | 1² 1² 2 N | 2 3} (C″ 1¹ N 3 | V 3) = P₅ c′ C′″·₂
       1   2   4   5 c′   1   2

7. {This | was done *oftener* on the whole} (than | we | expected.)·
     1   2   c′   c″   1   2

   {N | A V (c′ 3 } C″ | N | V)·= P₂ c′ 2 C′″·₂
    1   2   1   2

2. ELLIPTICAL CO-ORDINATE SUBORDINATES BY TERMS OR JOINERS.

1. { They | were found *less-cheerful*} (than | we | expected |·
     1   2   c′   c″   1   2
   them | to be)·. (Joiner 'cheerful' elliptical in IV.)
     3   4

   { N | V 2 } (C″ | N | V | N | IV)·= P₂ c′ C′″·₄
     1   2 c′   1   2   3   4

2. {It | is just *as* hard | to reason accurately} (*as* | it | is | to
    1   2   c′   4   c″   1   2
   observe accurately.)·
        4

{| N | V 2 c′ 2 | IV 1 |} (C″ | N | V | IV 1)·= P₄ c′ C′″·₄
   1   2   4   1   2   4

   (This is comparison of equality ; here joiner ellipsis " hard"
is visible.)

LECTURE VIII.

3. { The parson | could not make | * her | dearer or nearer
      1   2   3   c'   +   c'
   to me } (than | she | is.)* ('dear or near to me' joiner
              c"   1   2
   ellipsis.)

$\{1^1 \underset{1}{N} | A \underset{2}{1} \underset{3}{V} | \underset{c'\ c'}{N} | 2+2\ 3 \}(C'' | \underset{1}{N} | \underset{2}{V} (2+2\ 3)))^* = P_3\ c\ '+c'\ C''^*_2$

4. {The elephant | is stronger } (than the camel.)*
        1   2   c'   c"   1

$\{1^1 \underset{1}{N} | \underset{2}{V}\ \underset{c'}{2}\ \} (C'' | 1^1 \underset{1}{N} | (\underset{2}{V}))=P_2\ c'\ C''^*_2$

5. {To speak the truth | is | a better sign of civilisation} (than
         1   2   c'   3   c"
   to wear | English boots and stockings.)* (Terms ellipsis
       4   5   +   5
   "it is" in the Subordinate.)

$\{(\underset{4}{IV} | 1^1 \underset{5}{N})^N | \underset{1}{V} | \underset{2}{1^1}\ \underset{c'}{2}\ \underset{3}{N}\ 3\} (C''\ (\underset{1}{N} | \underset{2}{V} |)\ \underset{4}{IV} | \underset{5}{2}\ \underset{6}{N+N})^*$

$= P_3\ c'\ C''^*_5$

6. {We | are not in a worse position} (than | we | were
     1   2   c'   c"   1   2
   before.)*

$\{\underset{1}{N} | \underset{2}{V}\ 1\ 3\ c'\} (C'' | \underset{1}{N} | \underset{2}{V}, 1)^* = P_2\ c'\ C''^*_2$

7. {He | managed in better style (than could have been
    1   2   c'   c"
   expected)* to ask | pardon | for calling at such an unsea-
         3   4   5   6
   sonable hour. } (C''* medial in position, with Term ellipsis
   of 'it'.)

$\{\underset{1}{N} | \underset{2}{V}\ 3\ c' | (C''\ | (\underset{1}{N}) | \underset{2}{A\ A\ A\ V})^* | \underset{4}{IV} | \underset{5}{N} | \underset{6}{PV}\ 3\ \}$
$= P_6\ c'\ \tfrac{2}{3}\ C''^*_2$

8. {He | drew | his chair | somewhat *closer* to Catherine's}
   1   2   3   c′

   (*than* | was necessary.)*
     c″   2

   { $\underset{1}{N}$ | $\underset{2}{V}$ * | $1^2 \underset{3}{N}$ | 1 c′ 3 } (C* (N) | $\underset{2}{V}$ 2) = P_3 c′ C″*$_2$

9. {She | would certainly *rather* be | his mistress} (*than* | the
    1   c′   2   3   c″

   Captain's bride.)* (both N and V terms elliptical.)
              3

   { $\underset{1}{N}$ | A 1 c′ $\underset{2}{V}$ | $1^1 \underset{3}{N}$ } (C* ($\underset{1}{N}$ | A $\underset{2}{V}$) | $1^1 1^5 \underset{3}{N}$)* = P_3 c′ C″*$_3$

10. {The effort | required | to bring * | it | * into the horizontal
          1

    position | will be the-greater } (the-greater the weight of
              2   c′   c″

    the body in the opposite scale.)

   { | $1^1 \underset{1}{N}$ * | 6 | * 7 | * 3 | A $\underset{2}{V}$ c′ } (C″ | $1^1 \underset{1}{N}$ 3 3 | ($\underset{2}{V}$))= P_2 c′ C‴*$_2$

11. { That | is *as* good | to dispel | all doubts } (*as* a regiment
      1   2   4   6   1
    of king's soldiers | to dispel | mobs.)* (Second term with
                         4   6
    - post-joiner elliptical in the Subordinate.)

   { $\underset{1}{N}$ | $\underset{2}{V}$ c′ 2 | $\underset{4}{IV}$ | $1^2 \underset{5}{N}$ } (C* | $1^1 \underset{1}{N}$ 3 | ($\underset{2}{V}$ 2) | $\underset{4}{IV}$ | $\underset{5}{N}$)* = P_5 c′ C‴*$_5$

Or in Ex. 7 and 8 here "C* *than*" by analogy may be considered as a Relative like "R* *as*" when followed by a V. (vide Ex. 1 and 2 p. p. 133.)

LECTURE VIII.   133

12. {He | sat down despite of the cold | to chase-away | the
     $_1$ $_2$ $_4$
   intervening minute as well} (as | he | could | with his
                          $_5$ $_{c'}$ $_{c''}$ $_1$ $_2$
   reflections till the appearance of his sister.)*   (2nd Term
   elliptical in the Subordinate though 'auxiliary' present.)

($\underset{1}{N}$ | $\underset{2}{V}$ 1 2 3 | $\underset{4}{IV}$ * | 1¹ 2 $\underset{5}{N}$ | * c' 1 } (C* | $\underset{1}{N}$ | A $\underset{2}{(V)}$ 3 3 3)*

$\hspace{6cm} = P_5 \; c' \; C''*_2$

13. { The outer surface of the window-glass | will get cool
                                        $_1$ $_2$
   sooner } (than | the surface within.)*
   $_{c'}$ $_{c''}$ $_1$

{1¹ 2 $\underset{1}{N}$ 3 | A$\underset{2}{V}$ 2 c' } (C'' | 1¹ $\underset{1}{N}$ 3 | (A$\underset{2}{V}$ 2))* = P$_2$ c' C''*$_2$

X.—Complex by co-ordinate c' R** subordination.

1. {It | would no longer support | such vegetation at least}
    $_1$ $_2$ $_{c'}$ $_3$
   (as | previously lived upon it.)*
   $_{R''}$ $_2$

{ | $\underset{1}{N}$ | A 1 1 $\underset{2}{V}$ * | 1² $\underset{c'\;3}{N}$ * 3 | } ($\underset{1}{R}$ | 1 $\underset{2}{V}$ 3)* = P$_3$ c' R''*$_2$

2. { The same kind of movement of the air | takes | place}
         $_{c'}$ $_1$ $_2$ $_3$
   (as | can be watched by the fireside.)*
   $_{R''}$ $_2$

{ 1¹ c' $\underset{1}{N}$ 3 3 | $\underset{2}{V}$ | $\underset{3}{N}$ | } ($\underset{1}{R}$ | A A $\underset{2}{V}$ 3)* = P$_3$ c' R''*$_2$

3. { It | is | the same thing } (that | we | see in our midst.)
    $_1$ $_2$ $_{c'}$ $_3$ $_{R''}$ $_1$ $_2$

{ | $\underset{1}{N}$ | $\underset{2}{V}$ | 1¹ (c' $\underset{3}{N}$ | } $\underset{3}{R}$ | $\underset{1}{N}$ | $\underset{2}{V}$ 3)* = P$_2$ c' R''*$_2$.

4. $\{$ *As-much* water ($\underset{R'}{\underset{1}{as}}$ | will fill | the tube 2 ft. 3¼ inches)
$\underset{C'}{}$
| will weigh | a pound.$\}$
      2   3

$\{\,|\,c'\,\underset{1}{N}\,|\,(\,\underset{1}{R}\,|\,A\,\underset{2}{V}\,|\,1^{1}\,\underset{3}{N}\,s\,)^{\bullet}\,A\,\underset{2}{V}\,|\,1^{1}\,\underset{3}{N}\,|\,\}=P_{3}\,c'\,R''\!\cdot_{2}$

5. $\{$ The ritual of the Incas | involved | a routine of obser-
           1   .2   3
vances *as* complex and elaborate $\}$ ($\underset{R'}{as}$ | ever distinguished
         $\underset{C'}{}$ 2
| that of any nation whether Pagan or Christian.)$^{\bullet}$
   3                              $\underset{C'}{}$ $\underset{C''}{}$

$\{\,|\,1^{1}\,\underset{1}{N}\,s\,|\,\underset{2}{V}\,|\,1^{1}\,\underset{3}{N}\,s\,c'\,2{+}2\,|\,\}\,(\,\underset{1}{R''}\,|\,1\,\underset{.2}{V}\,|\,\underset{3}{N}\,s\,(1^{2}\,n\,c'\,n\,c''\,n))^{\bullet}$

$$=P_{3}\,c'\,R'''\!\cdot_{3}$$

XI.—Complex of P by Co-ordinate subordination sub-subordinated.

1. $\{$ It | was | *such* a spot $\}$ (as that)$^{\bullet}$ (*where* in the poetry of
      1   2 $\underset{C'}{}$ 3 $\underset{C''}{}$· $\underset{R}{}$
Persian Bards | we | read of fond Megnoun-whispering
                 1   2
tales of love to his beautiful Leilah.)$^{2\bullet}$

$\{\underset{1}{N}\,|\,\underset{2}{V}\,|\,\underset{C'}{1^{2}\,1^{1}\,N}\}\,(C''\,|\,\underset{1}{N}\,|\,\underset{2}{(V)})^{\bullet}\,(\,^{*}\,\underset{R}{1\,3}\,s\,|\,\underset{1}{N}\,|\,\underset{2}{V}\,*\,3\,pv\,n\,3\,s\,|\,)^{2\bullet}$

$$=P_{3}\,c'\,3\,C''\!\cdot_{2}\,\tfrac{2}{3}\,R^{2\bullet}\!\cdot_{3}$$

2. $\{$ The sharp flint | is softer $\}$ (than the heart)$^{\bullet}$ (that bosom
                    1   2 $\underset{C'}{}$ $\underset{C''}{}$ 1   1
| contained.)$^{2\bullet}$
  12

$\{\,1^{1}\,2\,\underset{1}{N}\,|\,\underset{2}{V}\,\underset{C'}{2}\,\}\,(C''\,|\,1^{1}\,\underset{.1}{N}\,|\,\underset{2}{(V)})^{\bullet}\,(\,(\underset{3}{R})\,|\,1^{2}\,\underset{1}{N}\,|\,\underset{2}{V})^{2\bullet}$

$$=P_{2}\,c'\,C''\!\cdot_{2}\,1R^{2\bullet}\!\cdot_{3}.$$

(Ex. 1 and 2 are Bi-subordinated co-ordinate Subordinates.)

LECTURE VIII.   135

3. { *Such* were | the reflections } (*which* | kept | him | awake
         2   1   1   2   3
    till an hour in the morning) (*when* slumber | cut short | his
                                           1   2
    meditation.)
         3

    { c' | V | 1¹ N } (R" | V* | N | *2 3 3)·(C | N | V 1·| 1³N)²·
           2   1   2   3   1   2   3
                                                  = c' P₂ R"·₃ $\frac{1}{3}$ C²·₃

4. { They | float } (*because* | each ship | weighs less)· (than | a
         1   2   1   2   c'   c''
    quantity of water of the same bulk | does (weigh).)²·
         1   2

    { N | V }(C | 1² N | V c')· (C" | 1¹ N 3 3 | A (V))²· = P₂ C·₂ c' C"²·₂
      1   2   1   2   1   2

    (This is Complex by Integral C· subordination co-ordinately
    sub-subordinated.)

5. (*As* | he | had completely failed | in meeting with the arch-
      c   1   2   4
    miscreant)· (save-on-one-occasion-*when* | the wretch |
                                        c'   )
    managed | to elude | his grasp)²· { he | penned | such a letter}
        2   4   5   1   2   c'   3
    (*that* | any one-possessing the pride and proper feelings
       c"   1
    of a man | could not help | responding to it in a hostile
                      2   4
    manner indeed in the way)· (*which* | Hunter | desired.)²·
                                    3   1   2

    (C | N | A 1 V | PV 3)·(C | 1¹ N | V | IV | 1³ N)²·
          1   2   4   1   2   4   5
    { N | V | c' 1¹ N | }
      1   2   3

         (C" | 1² N 4 1¹ n +·2 n 3·| A 1 V | PV 3 3 1 3)·
                    1   2   4
         (R | N | V)²· = 2 C·₄ 4 C²·₅ P₃ c' C"·₄ $\frac{4}{3}$R²·₃
           3   1   2

    (This is Bi-di-co-ordinate subordination sub-subordinated.)

.6 {He | found * | his slave's learning and intelligence | * so
    1   2   3   +   3   c′

useful} (that | he | grew very fond of him and tried hard
         c′   1   2   +   2

| to persuade | him | to turn | Mahometan | offering | him |
      4   5   6   7   8   9

not-only liberty but | the inheritance of all his wealth and
  c′   9   c″   9   +

the secrets) (that | he | had discovered.)
                3   1   2

$\{\underset{1}{N} \mid \underset{2}{V} * \mid 1^3\ 1^5\ \underset{3}{N} + \underset{3}{N} \mid * c'\ 3\}$

$(C' \mid \underset{1}{N} \mid \underset{2}{V}\ 1\ 2\ 3 \mid + \mid \underset{2}{V}\ 2 \mid \underset{4}{IV} \mid \underset{5}{N} \mid \underset{6}{IV} \mid \underset{7}{N} \mid \underset{8}{PV} \mid \underset{9}{N}\ c'\ \underset{9}{N}\ c''\ 1^1\ \underset{9}{N}$

$3(\ 1^2\ 1^2\ n + 1^1\ n\ ))\cdot (R \mid \underset{1}{N} \mid AV)^{2\cdot} = P_3\ c'\ 2\ C'^{\cdot}_{\scriptscriptstyle 6}\ \underset{8}{8}\ R^{2\cdot}_{\scriptscriptstyle 3}$

7. (When | they | again sought | the drawing room)· {Emily
              1   2   3   1

had so far composed | herself} (that | her aunt | failed | to
    c′   2   3   c″   2

notice | any little alteration)· (there might have been in
  4   5   2

her looks.)·

$(C \mid \underset{1}{N} \mid 1\ \underset{2}{V} \mid 1^1\ 2\ \underset{3}{N})\cdot \{\underset{1}{N} \mid A\ c'\ 2\ \underset{2}{V} \mid \underset{3}{N}\}$

$(C'' \mid 1^3\ \underset{1}{N} \mid \underset{2}{V} \mid \underset{4}{IV} \mid 1^2\ 2\ \underset{5}{N})\cdot (\ (R) \mid 1\ A\ A\ \underset{2}{V}\ 3)^{2\cdot}$

$= C^{\cdot}_3\ P_3\ c'\ C''_5\ ^{\cdot}\ R^{2\cdot}_2$

8. { That (which | is lighter) · (than | water) ²· | floats
      1   1   2   1   2

upon it.}

$\{\underset{1}{N}\ (\underset{1}{R} \mid \underset{2}{V}\ c')\cdot (C'' \mid \underset{1}{N} \mid (\underset{2}{V}\ 2))\ ^{2\cdot} \mid \underset{2}{V}\ 3\} = P_2\ 1\ R^{\cdot}_2 c'\ C\ ^{2\cdot}_2$

LECTURE VIII.   137

9. { There is | no funeral *so* sad | to follow} (*as* the funeral of
     $_2$ $_1$ $_4$ $_1$
our own *youth*) (*which* | we | have been pampering with
                    $_3$ $_1$ $_2$
fond *desires, ambitions, hopes* and all bright *berries*) (*that* |
                                                            $_1$
hang in poisonous clusters over the path of our life.)
 $_2$

$$\{ _1 \underset{2}{V} \mid _2 \underset{1}{N} c' _2 \mid \underset{4}{IV} \} (C'' \mid _1{}^1 \underset{1}{N} _3 \mid \underset{2}{(V)})^\bullet$$

$$(\underset{3}{R} \mid \underset{1}{N} \mid A A \underset{2}{V} _3 (_2 n, n, n+_1{}^2 {}_2 n))^{2\bullet} (\underset{1}{R} \mid \underset{2}{V} _3 {}_3 {}_3)^{3\bullet}$$

$$= P_4 \, c' \, C''_{\bullet 2} \tfrac{1}{3} \, R^{2\bullet}{}_3 \, \tfrac{2}{3} R^{3\bullet}{}_2$$

All along Subordinates have been shown as Mono-simple structures either in their mono- or poly-subordinations (sub-subordinations), but here we go to see that the assertive "that" is followed by a subordinate Complex structure, consisting of a P and a Subordinate.

This variety may therefore be called Complex by Subordinate Complex structure. Hence this combination is *combination by substitution*, *i.e.*, Complex in lieu of a Mono-simple Subordinate.

XII.—Complex of P by Complex substitutive subordination in the first Subordinate.

1. {It | has been ascertained} (that | (if | water | be confined in
    $_1$ $_2$ $_1$ $_2$
a closed vessel or space) a pressure amounting to 15 pounds
                                $_1$
on the square inch | diminishes | its volume | by only one
                         $_2$ $_3$
20,000th part.)

$$\{ \mid \underset{1}{N} \mid A A \underset{2}{V} \mid \} (C (C \mid \underset{1}{N} \mid \underset{2}{A V} _3)^\bullet \{_1{}^3 \underset{1}{N} \, pv \, _3 \, _3 \mid \underset{.2}{V} \mid _1{}^3 \underset{3}{N} \mid _3\})^\bullet$$

$$= P_2 \, 2 \, C \, (2 \, C'_2 \, P_2)^\bullet$$

138   STYLOGRAPHY OF ENGLISH LANGUAGE.

2. { It | has been seen } (*that* (when a cubic inch of water |
   $_1$ $_2$ $_1$

is dissipated by heat) it | merely changes * | its form | *
      $_2$ $_1$ $_2$ $_3$

from the fluid to the gaseous state.)*

{| N | A A V |}(C (C | 1^1 $_2$ N 3 | A V 3^*_1)*{N | $_1$ V | 1^3 N 3 3})*
   $_1$ $_2$ $_{f1}$ $_2$ $_1$ $_2$ $_3$

$$= P_2\ 2C\ (2C^*_2\ P_3)^*$$

The assertive "that" may also take a subordinately
co-or-dinated Complex substitute to the Mono-simple. For
examples:—

1. { It | is certain} (*that* {solid bodies | may be divided into
   $_1$ $_2$ $_1$ $_2$

particles so minute} (*that* | the best microscopes | show |
          $_{c'}$ $_{c''}$ $_1$ $_2$

no trace of them.))*
         $_3$

{| N | V $_2$ |} (C {$_2$ N | A A V 3 1 2 }(C″ | $1^1 2$ N | V | $_2$ N 3))
   $_1$ $_2$ $_1$ $_2$ $_{c'}$ $_1$ $_2$ $_3$

$$= P_2\ 2\ C\ (P_2\ c\ C^*_2)^*$$

2. { It | may merely mean } (*that* { the particles | are so
   $_1$ $_2$ $_1$ $_2$ $_{c'}$

extremely small } (that | they | cannot be distinguished
            $_{c''}$ $_1$ $_2$

even by the most powerful microscopes.)*)*

{| N | A 1^*_2 V }(C {1^1 N | V c' $_1$ $_2$}(C' | N | A A V 1 3 |)*)*
   $_1$ $_2$ $_1$ $_{12}$ $_1$ $_2$

$$= P_2\ 2\ C\ (P_2\ c'\ C''^*_2)^*$$

XIII.—Complex by substitutive Di-complex subordination.

1. { He | often told | his friends } (that (unless he | had
   $_1$ $_2$ $_3$ $_1$

   found-out | this mode of employing himself) { he | verily
   $_2$ $_3$ $_1$

   believed | } (he | should have lost | his senses.))
   $_2$ $_1$ $_2$ $_3$

$$\{N_1 \mid {}_1 V_2 \mid {}_1{}^3 N_3\} (C(C \mid N_1 \mid V_2 \mid {}_1{}^2 N_3 \text{ 4 5})$$

$$\{N_1 \mid {}_1 V_2\}(N_1 \mid V_2 \mid {}_1{}^3 N_3))^\iota \ = P_3 \, 2 \, C \, (\, C^\iota{}_3, P_2 \, 2 \, C^\iota{}_3)^\iota$$

XIV.—Complex of P by substitutive Bi-complex subordination.

1. { I | belive } (that { | there have been | few men } (who |
   $_1$ $_2$ $_2$ $_1$ $_1$

   have done | great things in the world) (who | have not had
   $_2$ $_3$ $_1$ $_2$

   a large power of imagination.))$^{2\iota}$
   $_3$

(The Sub-subordinate R in R$^{2\iota}$ has here for its Antecedent an R or R$^\iota$ as a whole.)

$$\{N_1 \mid V_2\}(C \{ {}_1 V_2 \mid {}_2 N_1 \}(R_1 \mid V_2 \mid {}_2 N_3)^\iota (R_1 \mid A \, {}_1 V_2 \mid {}_1{}^1 \, {}_2 N \, 3)^{2\iota})$$

$$= P_2 \, 2 \, C \, (P_2 \, R^\iota{}_3 \, 1 \, R^{2\iota}{}_3)^\iota.$$

Having then just shown to you that Mono- or first Subordinate in the complex structure allows substitution by a complex, a Di-complex, or a Bi-complex within its C$^\iota$, I go now to illustrate to you that the Bi- or second Subordinate may similarly be substitutively subordinated. As for example :—

XV.—Second Subordinate substitutively subordinated.

{ He$_1$ | was$_2$ | a European loafer$_3$ } (who$_1$ | explained$_2$)^{c} (that$_\text{c}$ (when$_\text{c}$ | he$_1$ | heard$_2$ | the strange noise coming up the road)^{c}$_3$ (he$_1$ | had run and hidden$_{2+2}$ | himself$_3$ } (because$_\text{c}$ | he$_1$ | thought)^{c} ((C) it$_1$ | was$_2$ | the mutineers.)$^{2\text{c}}$$_3$)$^{2\text{c}}$

{ N$_1$ | V$_2$ | 1^1 2 N$_3$ } (R$_1$ | V$_2$)^{c} (C (C | N$_1$ | V$_2$ | 1^1 2 N 4 3)^{c}

{ N$_1$ | A V$_2$ + V$_2$ | N$_3$ | } (C | N$_1$ | V$_2$)^{c} ((C) | N$_1$ | V$_2$ | 1^1 N)$^{2\text{c}}$)$^{2\text{c}}$

$$= P_3 \; 3 \; R^{\text{c}}_2 \; C \; (\; 2 \; C^{\text{c}}_3 \; P_3 \; C^{\text{c}}_2 \; 2 \; C^{2\text{c}}_3)^{2\text{c}}$$

In Subordination, *fractional subordinations* have been shown *distinct*, but I give you presently an illustration in which both the Integral and Fractional Subordinates will combine with the P.

XVI.—Complex of P by Integral and Fractional Subordinates.

1. (When | conical bullets, with high velocity$_1$ | are used,)^{c}$_2$ {the aperture of entrance$_1$ | is not readily distinguished from that of exit}$_2$, (for, | the apertures$_1$ | differ little in size and have$_2$ | a somewhat triangular shape.)^{c}$_3$

(C | 2 N 2$_1$ | V$_2$) {1^1 N 3$_1$ | A 1 1 V 3 2$_2$ }

(C | 1^1 N$_1$ | V 2 3 + V$_2$ | 1^1 1 2 N$_3$)

$$= 2 \; C^{\text{c}}_2 \; P_3 \; C^{\text{c}}_3$$

LECTURE VIII.   141

XVII.—Complex by an initial Mono- and final Co-ordinate-subordinate to P.

1. (If one of the pupils of the class | is got | to read,) {he |
   $\underset{1}{\text{ }}$ $\underset{2}{\text{ }}$ $\underset{4}{\text{ }}$ $\underset{1}{\text{ }}$
   profits at least (as much} as | his fellows.)
   $\underset{2}{\text{ }}$ $\underset{c'}{\text{ }}$ $\underset{c''}{\text{ }}$ $\underset{1}{\text{ }}$

$$(C \mid \underset{1}{N} \text{ } 3 \text{ } 3 \mid \underset{2}{AV} \mid \underset{4}{IV}) \{\underset{1}{N} \mid \underset{2}{V} \text{ } 1 \text{ } (c' \text{ } 1\} \text{ } C'' \mid 1^3 \underset{1}{N} \mid (\underset{2}{V}))^*$$

$$= 2 \text{ } C^*_4 \text{ } P_2 \text{ } c' \text{ } C''^*_2$$

2. (When | he | shook | him | hastily) * {Fitzgerald | almost
   $\underset{c}{\text{ }}$ $\underset{1}{\text{ }}$ $\underset{2}{\text{ }}$ $\underset{3}{\text{ }}$ $\underset{1}{\text{ }}$
   died of fright and was almost (as helpless from actual
   $\underset{2}{\text{ }}$ $\underset{2}{\text{ }}$ $\underset{c'}{\text{ }}$
   alarm } as | an infant child.)*
   $\underset{c''}{\text{ }}$ $\underset{1}{\text{ }}$

$$(C \mid \underset{1}{N} \mid \underset{2}{V} \mid \underset{3}{N} \mid 1) \cdot \{\underset{1}{N} \mid 1 \underset{2}{V} \text{ } 3 \mid + \mid \underset{2}{V} \text{ } 1 \text{ } (c' \text{ } 2 \text{ } 3\}^*$$

$$C'' \mid 1^1 \text{ } 2 \underset{1}{N} \mid (\underset{2}{V} \text{ } 2))^* = 2 \text{ } C^*_3 \text{ } P_2 \text{ } c' \text{ } C''^*_2$$

3. (When | he | had gained | the gate)* {he | partially roused
   $\underset{1}{\text{ }}$ $\underset{2}{\text{ }}$ $\underset{3}{\text{ }}$ $\underset{1}{\text{ }}$ $\underset{2}{\text{ }}$
   himself | and | gaged wistfully up the road towards London,
   $\underset{3}{\text{ }}$ $\underset{2}{\text{ }}$
   (as well} as the increasing duskiness of the evening | would
   $\underset{c'}{\text{ }}$ $\underset{c''}{\text{ }}$ $\underset{1}{\text{ }}$
   permit.)*
   $\underset{2}{\text{ }}$

$$(C \mid \underset{1}{N} \mid \underset{2}{AV} \mid 1^1 \underset{3}{N}) \{\underset{1}{N} \mid 1 \underset{2}{V} \mid \underset{3}{N} \mid + V \text{ } 1 \text{ } 3 \text{ } 3 \text{ } c' \text{ } 2\}$$

$$(C'' \mid 1^1 \text{ } 2 \underset{1}{N} \text{ } 3 \mid \underset{2}{AV})$$

$$= 2 C^*_3 \text{ } P_3 \text{ } c' \text{ } C''^*_2$$

In Di-bi-subordination the 1st of the Bi-subordinate is simple combinative. I go now to illustrate to you this Sub-subordinate as being "locked." We might name these as Di-subordinates co-ordinately sub-subordinated.

11

XVIII.—Complex by an initial mono- and a final co-ordinate Subordinate to P sub-subordinated.

1. (If | the bag | were taken away) { it | would retain | its
        $\quad$ 1 $\qquad$ 2 $\qquad$ 1 $\qquad\quad$ 2

shape | so long } (as | it | was kept as hot)^a (as | boiling
  3 $\;$ c' $\qquad$ c'' $\;$ 1 $\qquad\quad$ 2 $\;$ c' $\qquad\quad$ c''
water.)^{2a}
   1

(C | 1^1 N | AV 1)^a { N | AV | 1^3 N c' 1 } (C'' | N | AV c' 2)^a
$\qquad\;$ 1 $\quad$ 2 $\qquad\quad$ 1 $\quad$ 2 $\quad$ 3 $\qquad\qquad\quad$ 1 $\quad$ 2

(C'' | 2 N | (V))^{2a} $\quad$ = 2 C$\cdot_2$ P$_3$ c' C$'_2 \cdot^a$ c' C$'^{2a}_2$
$\qquad\quad$ 1 $\;$ 2

In the Co-ordinate c' before joiner or subjoiner of Equal Comparison or otherwise by adjective and adjective with its preceding adverb, when the adjective post-joiner of V increases into two words, the c' conjunction co-ordinate may not repeat itself between them, but it allows a compound conjunction to intervene for the increase as usual. Or when the adjective increases to more than two words, the first co-ordinate is repeated before each increased post-joiner, while the compound conjunction is added but before the last of the first co-ordinate. These lead to *tri-* and *quadri-groupal series of connectives* whose illustrations I give below.

XIX.—Illustrations of groupal increase of connectives in Complexes by co-ordinate subordination.

(a) *By as...as.*

1. {John | is *as* honest and polite} (*as* his neighbour James.)^a
   $\;\;$ 1 $\quad$ 2 c' $\qquad\qquad\qquad\quad$ c'

{N | V c' 2 + 2} (C'' | 1^3 2 N | (V))^a
 1 $\;$ 2 $\qquad\qquad\qquad\;\;$ 1 $\quad$ 2

= P$_2$ c' 2 + 2 $\tfrac{2}{3}$ C''$\cdot_2$

LECTURE VIII.

2. {John$_1$ | is *as* honest and *as* polite}$_2$ (*as* his neighbour James.)

$$\{N_1 \mid V_2 \, c'\,2 + c'\,2\}(C'' \mid 1^3 \, 2 \, N_1 \mid (V)_2)^{\bullet}$$

$$= P_2 \, c'\, 2 + c'\, 2\, \tfrac{2}{3}\, C''\cdot_2$$

3. {John$_1$ | is *as* honest, *as* polite and *as* generous}$_2$ (*as* his neighbour James.)

$$\{N_1 \mid V_2 \, c'\,2,\, c'\,2 + c'\,2\} (C'' \mid 1^3 \, 2 \, N_1 \mid (V)_2)^{\bullet}$$

$$= P_2 \, c'\,2,\, c'\,2 + c'\,2\, \tfrac{2}{3}\, C''\cdot_2$$

(b) *By so...that.*

1. {James$_1$ | is *so* honest and polite}$_{2\ c'\ 2\ +\ 2}$ (*that* | all his neighbours$_1$ | like$_2$ | him.)$_3$

$$\{N_1 \mid V_2 \, c'\,2 + 2\} (C'' \mid 1^2 \, 1^3 \, N_1 \mid V_2 \mid N_3)^{\bullet}$$

$$= P_2 \, c'\,2 + 2\, \tfrac{2}{3}\, C''\cdot_3$$

2. {James$_1$ | is *so* honest and *so* polite}$_2$ (that all his neighbours$_1$ | like$_2$ | him.)$_2$

$$\{N_1 \mid V_2 \, c'\,2, + c'\,2\}(C'' \mid 1^2 \, 1^3 \, N_1 \mid V_2 \mid N_3)^{\bullet}$$

$$= P_2 \, c'\,2 + c'\,2\, \tfrac{2}{3}\, C''\cdot_3{}^{\bullet}$$

3. {James$_1$ | is *so* honest, *so* polite and *so* generous}$_2$ (that all his neighbours$_1$ | like$_2$ | him.)$_3$

$$\{N_1 \mid V_2 \, c'\,2,\, c'\,2, + c'\,2\,\} (C'' \mid 1^2 \, 1^3 \, N_1 \mid V_2 \mid N_3)^{\bullet}$$

$$= P_2 \, c'\,2,\, c'\,2 + c'\,2\, \tfrac{2}{3}\, C''\cdot_3$$

The repetitions of first co-ordinate c' are for emphasis.)

It is the joiners then as the Article adjective, the comparative adjective, the adverb, certain adjectives and the pronominal adjectives that *subordinately co-ordinate* with each other, or with the pure conjunctions (besides the co-ordinations of the pure conjunctions with the pure), or with the relative.

Lastly, I show to you *the union and combination of both the Absolute and Subordinate to* P.

XX.—Complex of P by an Absolute and Subordinate.

1. {A North American Indian, $\binom{\text{upon returning home to his}}{4}$

cabin,$\big\rangle$ discovered} (that | his venison | was stolen.)
$\quad\quad\quad 2 \quad\quad\quad\quad\quad 1 \quad\quad\quad\quad 2$

$\{1^1 \; 2 \; \underset{1}{N} \;|\; \big(P \; \underset{2}{V} \; 8 \; 3\big) \underset{2}{V}\} \; (C \;|\; 1^3 \; \underset{1}{N} \;|\; A \; \underset{2}{V})^{\bullet} = P_3 \; \big(pv\big) \; 2 \; C^{\bullet}_2$

XXI.—Complex of P by conjoined Mono- and Bi-groupal connectives.

1. {All | seemed quite intent on their respective duties}
$\quad\;\; 1 \quad\quad 2$

(*when not-only* | were | they | being-shot-down every
$\quad\;\; c \quad\quad c' \quad\quad\quad\quad\;\; 1 \quad\quad\quad\quad 2$

moment)• (*but when* | each comparatively harmless ball, |
$\quad\quad\quad\quad\;\; c'' \quad\; c \quad\quad\quad\quad\quad\quad\quad\quad\quad\quad\quad 1$

rocked | the gun-boat, | sent | splinters | flying | or | brought
$\;\;\; 2 \quad\quad\quad 3 \quad\quad\quad 2 \quad\quad 3 \quad\quad\; 4 \quad\; + \quad\quad 2$

| the yards | down upon their heads.)•
$\quad\quad 3$

$\{\underset{1}{N} \;|\; \underset{2}{V} \; 1 \; 2 \; 3 \;\}(C\text{-}C' \;|\; A \;|\; \underset{1}{N} \;|\; \underset{2}{V} \; 3)(C^{\bullet}\text{-}C \;|\; 1^2 \; 1 \; 2 \; \underset{1}{N} \;|\; \underset{2}{V} \;|\; 1^1 \; \underset{3}{N} \;|,$

$|\; \underset{2}{V} \;|\; \underset{3}{N} \;|\; \underset{4}{IV} \;|\; + \;|\; \underset{2}{V} \;|\; 1^1 \; \underset{3}{N} \;|\; 1 \; 3) = P_2 \; C\text{-}C^{\bullet}_2 \; C''\text{-}C^{\bullet}_4$

Do not fail to observe that the mono-groupal has here preceded the bi-groupal connective in the 1st Co-ordinate, while this condition is *vice versâ* in the 2nd Co-ordinate.

Complexes other than those described in this lecture, may be visible in various writings, but they would by no means deviate from the general principles thus laid down.

We come now to the 4th variety of combination, *the 'Riveted'*. It occurs in relative subordination of the P consisting of a N term or joiner antecedent in it blending with the initial Relative, the odd term or joiner of the Subordinate. This blending of the *antecedent* and the *relative* into one word has introduced the word "Compound" to the wrong denomination of the Relative alone, when it includes the antecedent also. The word "what" is the *compound relative* of the Neuter gender which alone admits of median rivetment (unless by emphasis), but here are others of the masculine or faminine variety that are inital or medial in rivetment viz.—"whoever," "whosoever," "whomsoever". "Whichever," "whichsoever", "whatsoever" go also to group with "what". Let us illustrate them.

XXII.—Complex by Riveted Relative Subordinates.

(a).—Rivetment of two terms.

1. {He | does (*what*) his *friends* | advise | him | to do.)*
     1   2   3 5   1   2   3   4
   (Neuter).

   $\{ \underset{1}{N} \mid \underset{2}{V} \mid \underset{3}{N} \} (R \mid \underset{1}{1^3 N} \mid \underset{2}{V} \mid \underset{3}{N} \mid \underset{4}{IV} \mid)^*$

   $= P_3 \; 3 \; R^*_5$

2. {(*Whoever* | talks much)* must talk in vain.}
      1   1   2   2

   (Masculine and Faminine.)

   $\{ \underset{1}{N} (\underset{1}{R} \mid \underset{2}{V} \; 1 \mid)^* \mid A \; \underset{2}{V} \; 1 \} = P_2 \; R^*_2$

(b).—Rivetment of a joiner and a term.

1. {*What* little protection (the common people | had received
     1² 3   1   1   2
   from the crown,) | was now at an end by the king's captivity
                      2
   and the general confusion throughout the kingdom.}

1. { *That* little protection (*that* or *which* | the common people &c.) was now &c. } (This *initial* "what" is a compound of the *Pronominal adjective* and *Relative*.)

$$\{1^2 \; 2 \; \underset{1}{N} \; ((R)) \; | \; 1^1 \; 2 \; \underset{1}{N} \; | \; \underset{2}{A} \underset{}{V} \; 3\;)^{\boldsymbol{\cdot}} \; | \; \underset{2}{V} \; 1 \; 3 \; 3 \; 3\}$$
$$= P_2 \; 1 \; R^{\boldsymbol{\cdot}}_3$$

Besides the Narrative C⋅ by "that", Interrogative C⋅ by "why", "when", and that by exclamatory "how" are seen to commence the Subordinates, and the variety commencing with 'what' becomes visible too. All these Subordinates alone become *Analogues of N* and as such their illustrations in both the capacities seem desireable here.

XXIII.—Complex by Expression Subordinate.

1. {You | remember} (*that* | you | did | it.)
   $$\{\; | \; \underset{1}{N} \; | \; \underset{2}{V} \; | \; \} \; (C \; | \; \underset{1}{N} \; | \; \underset{2}{V} \; | \; \underset{3}{N})^{\boldsymbol{\cdot}} = P_2 \; 2 \; C^{\boldsymbol{\cdot}}_3$$

2. {You | remember} (*why* | you | did | it.)
   $$\{\; | \; \underset{1}{N} \; | \; \underset{2}{V} \; | \; \} \; (C \; | \; \underset{1}{N} \; | \; \underset{2}{V} \; | \; \underset{3}{N})^{\boldsymbol{\cdot}} = P_2 \; 2 \; C^{\boldsymbol{\cdot}}_3$$

3. {You | remember} (*how* | you | did | it.)
   $$\{\; | \; \underset{1}{N} \; | \; \underset{2}{V} \; | \; \} \; (C \; | \; \underset{1}{N} \; | \; \underset{2}{V} \; | \; \underset{3}{N})^{\boldsymbol{\cdot}} = P_2 \; 2 \; C^{\boldsymbol{\cdot}}_3$$

4. {You | remember} (*what* an amount of trouble | we | had | to undergo for the occasion.)
   $$\{\; | \; \underset{1}{N} \; | \; \underset{2}{V} \; | \;) \; (\; \underset{R}{2}\; 1^1 \; \underset{5}{N} \; 3 \; | \; \underset{1}{N} \; | \; \underset{2}{V} \; | \; \underset{4}{IV} \; 3)^{\boldsymbol{\cdot}} = P_2 \; 2 \; R^{\boldsymbol{\cdot}}_5$$

5. {He | asked} (*what* ransom | was expected for the youth.)
   $$\{\underset{1}{N} \; | \; \underset{2}{V}\} \; (\; \underset{R}{2}\; \underset{1}{N} \; | \; \underset{2}{V} \; 3)^{\boldsymbol{\cdot}} = P^{\boldsymbol{\cdot}}_2 \; R^{\boldsymbol{\cdot}}_2$$

LECTURE VIII.   147

6. { The banker at the same time | related } (by *what* means
         $\underset{1}{}$ $\underset{2}{}$
he | had saved | it.) .
$\underset{1}{}$ $\underset{2}{}$ $\underset{3}{}$

$$\{1^1 \underset{1}{N} \text{ s } | \underset{2}{V}\} \text{ (s r } | \underset{1}{N} | \underset{2}{V} | \underset{3}{N})^\bullet = P_2 R^\bullet{}_3$$

Illustrations of C' as N Analogue.

1. {(*That* | the molecules of water | do take-up | a particular
            $\underset{1}{}$ $\underset{2}{}$
order | in assuming | the solid condition) $_1^N$ | is shown by
$\underset{3}{}$ $\underset{4}{}$ $\underset{5}{}$ $\underset{2}{}$
the crystalline form of ice.}

$$\{(\ | \ C \ | \ 1^1 \underset{1}{N} \text{ s } | \ A\underset{2}{V} \ | \ 1^1 \text{ 2 } \underset{3}{N} \ | \ P\underset{4}{V} \ | \ 1^1 \text{ 2 } \underset{5}{N} \ |)_1^N \ | \ A\underset{2}{V} \text{ s s } | \ \}$$
$$= P_2$$

2. { (*Why* | his own friends | turned against him at this
              $\underset{1}{}$ $\underset{2}{}$
crisis)$_1^N$ | is yet | a mystery.}
         $\underset{2}{}$ $\underset{3}{}$

$$\{ (C \ | \ 1^3 \text{ 2 } \underset{1}{N} \ | \ \underset{2}{V} \text{ s s } | \ )_1^N \ | \ \underset{2}{V} \text{ 1 } \ | \ 1^1 \underset{3}{N} \ | \ \} = P_3$$

3. {(*How* | he | came-by | so much wealth)$_1^N$ | is not known
               $\underset{1}{}$ $\underset{2}{}$ $\underset{3}{}$ $\underset{2}{}$
to any.}

$$\{(C \ | \ \underset{1}{N} \ | \ \underset{2}{V} \ | \ 1 \text{ 2 } \underset{3}{N})_1^N \ | \ A \text{ 1 } \underset{2}{V} \text{ s } | \ \} = P_2$$

4. { (*How* | it | came | to pass)$^\bullet$ (*that* | your brother | is at
               $\underset{1}{}$ $\underset{2}{}$ $\underset{4}{}$ $\underset{1}{}$ $\underset{2}{}$
Cheltenham)$^{2\bullet}$ $\underset{1}{N}$ | was } (as | follows.)$^\bullet$ (Here N is equal
                            $\underset{2}{}$ $\underset{1}{}$ $\underset{2}{}$
to C'$_4$ C$^2{}'_2$.)

$$\{ | (C \ | \ \underset{1}{N} \ | \ \underset{2}{V} \ | \ \underset{4}{IV})^\bullet (C \ | \ 1^3 \underset{1}{N} \ | \ \underset{2}{V} \text{ s })^{2\bullet} \underset{1}{N} \ | \ \underset{2}{V} \} (\underset{1}{R} \ | \ \underset{2}{V})^\bullet$$
$$= P_2 R^\bullet{}_2$$

The Interrogative relative Mono-simple may be a subordinate as well as an N Analogue. For examples :—

148   STYLOGRAPHY OF ENGLISH LANGUAGE.

1. $\{I_1 \mid \underset{2}{\text{know not}}\}$ (*who* $\mid$ first brought * $\mid$ this news $\mid$ * to us.)*
   $\underset{1}{}$ $\underset{2}{}$ $\underset{3}{}$

   $\{\mid \underset{1}{N} \mid \underset{2}{V}\ _1 \mid\} (\underset{1}{R} \mid\ _1 \underset{2}{V} \mid\ _1{}^2 \underset{3}{N} \mid\ _3 \mid) = P_2\ R^*_3$

2. $\{($ *Who* $\mid$ committed $\mid$ the murder$)^N_1 \mid$ may well be imagined.$\}$
   $\underset{1}{}$ $\underset{2}{}$ $\underset{3}{}$ $\underset{2}{}$

   $\{(\mid \underset{1}{R} \mid \underset{2}{V} \mid\ _1{}^1 \underset{3}{N} \mid)^N_1 \mid A\ _1 \underset{2}{AV} \mid\} = P_2$

Interrogative Subordinates instead of ending in their characteristic '?' are terminated by Periods. Contrary to the general rule again *connectives intervene between* P *and the Interrogative* R*. For example :—

1. $\{$They $\mid$ agreed $\mid$ to try $\mid$ their strength $\mid$ upon a traveller$\}$
   $\underset{1}{}$ $\underset{2}{}$ $\underset{4}{}$ $\underset{5}{}$
   (as to $\mid$ which $\mid$ should be able $\mid$ to get off * $\mid$ his cloak $\mid$
   $\underset{c}{}$ $\underset{1}{}$ $\underset{2}{}$ $\underset{4}{}$ $\underset{5}{}$
   * first.)*

   $\{\underset{1}{N} \mid \underset{2}{V} \mid \underset{4}{IV} * \mid\ _1 \underset{5}{N} \mid * 3\} (C \mid \underset{1}{R} \mid \underset{2}{AV}\ _2 \mid \underset{4}{IV} * \mid\ _1{}^3 \underset{5}{N} \mid * 1)*$

   $= P_5\ R^*_5$

Like N appositions of Ns and PPs, the Interrogative Rs have N appositions too, showing that Rs may be *Antecedents to Ns.*

1. (*Which* $\mid$ was most-marvelous) $\{$it $\mid$ is hard $\mid$ to say$\}$, *the*
   $\underset{1}{}$ $\underset{2}{}$ $\underset{1}{}$ $\underset{2}{}$ $\underset{4}{}$
   force of will (that $\mid$ actuated $\mid$ her)²* or $\mid$ *the force of under-*
   $\underset{1}{}$ $\underset{1}{}$ $\underset{2}{}$ $\underset{3}{}$ +
   standing $\mid$ (that $\mid$ gave $\mid$ value to such presence and
   $\underset{1}{}$ $\underset{2}{}$ $\underset{3}{}$
   commands.)*) (*The Interrogative Rs takes here the first seat by emphasis in the* P.)

   $(\underset{1}{R} \mid \underset{2}{V}\ _2 \mid)^* \{\underset{1}{N} \mid \underset{2}{V}\ _2 \mid \underset{4}{IV}\}$

   $_1{}^1 \underset{1}{N}\ _3 \mid (\underset{1}{R} \mid \underset{2}{V} \mid \underset{3}{N} \mid)^{2*}$

   $+_1{}^1 \underset{1}{N}\ _3 \mid (\underset{1}{R} \mid \underset{2}{V} \mid \underset{3}{N}\ _3\ (_1{}^2\ n+n))^{2*}$

   $= 4\ R^*_2\ P_4\ (\underset{1}{N})\ R^2_3 + (\underset{1}{N})\ R^{2*}_3$

You have seen that the *third* term in the Mono-simple transforms itself to the *first*, with vanishment of the first term which is changed into a post-joining preposition phrase, when the Active form of Voice is changed into the Passive. In the C• or Interrogative R• subordinate structures when the Subordinates are subordinate to Vs which are Active, they are in fact the 3rd terms if the complex is considered as one P structure only; and their conversion into the 1st terms is nothing more than their transformation into the Passive voice.

You go now to see how an integral Subordinate with dual conjunction becomes a co-ordinate Subordinate by certain emphasis, and by extreme emphasis goes to simulate in structure a Di-simple or co-ordinate P, which would be the subject for the next lecture.

Conversion of integral C• into co-ordinate C• subordination.

{1. The gap$_1$ | was$_2$ very wide} (*so that* | no body$_1$ | could jump$_2$ across it.)

$\{1^1 \ N_1 \ | \ V_2 \ 1\ 2\ | \ \} \ (C \ | \ 2\ N_1 \ | \ AV_2 \ s) = P_2 \ C^{\bullet}{}_2$

1. {The gap$_1$ | was$_2$ *so* very wide} (*that* no body$_1$ | could jump$_2$ across it.)

$\{1^1 \ N_1 \ | \ V_2 \ (c'\ 1\ 2\ | \ \} \ C'' \ | \ 2\ N_1 \ | \ AV_2 \ s) = P_2 \ c'\ C''{}_2$

1. {*So* very wide was$_1$ | the gap$_2$} (*that* | no body$_1$ | could jump$_2$ across it.)

$\{c'\ 1\ 2\ V_1 \ | \ 1^1 \ N_2 \ | \ \} \ (C'' \ | \ 2\ N_1 \ | \ AV_2 \ s)^{\bullet} = c'\ P_2 \ C''{}_2$

Here both the structures have initial conjunctions and apparently will lead one to confound them with the Di-simples in which each of the Mono-simples have initial conjunctions. Remark here the different transpositions that have occured and this will lead you to their distinction by observation.

LECTURE IX.

STUDENTS AND GENTLEMEN,

Having now shown to you the Subordinates of the Mono-simple P in their various stretches, it remains for me to point out to you that as the *Absolute incomplete Strcuctures* gradually approach the Principal Mono-simple, they allow to certain extent the same R* and C* subordinations, R* in case of Vocative N or PP Absolute, and C* in cases of PV or IV Absolutes, the continuations in these last by subsequent Terms to that of the fourth having already been shown. PVs or IVs, however, when post-joined by Preposition phrase, *its* final N may take an R* or may do so to any of the subsequent N terms after IV or PV.

I.—Complex of the Absolutes.

I.—BY C* and R* SUBORDINATIONS UNITED TO P.

a. *Of N Absolute.*

1. ζ You, you, the son of a base *mechanic*, (*who* | have dared
   $\quad$ 1 $\quad\;$ 1 $\quad\;\;$ 1 $\qquad\qquad\qquad\qquad$ 1 $\qquad\quad$ 2
   | to trample on the nobles of Genoa) $\}$ { you, * by their
   $\;\;$ 4 $\qquad\qquad\qquad\qquad\qquad\qquad\qquad\;\;$ 1
   clemency, | are only doomed * | to shrink again into the
   $\qquad\qquad\qquad\quad\;\;$ 2 $\qquad\qquad$ 4
   nothing } (* from which | you | sprang ! *)*
   $\qquad\qquad\qquad\qquad\qquad\;\;$ 1 $\quad\;\;$ 2

ζ PP—PP—$_1^1$ N 3 (R | AV | IV 3 3).$\}$
$\;\;$ 1 $\quad\;\;$ 1 $\quad\;\;$ 1 $\;\;\;$ 1 $\qquad$ 2 $\qquad$ 4

{N | *3 | A 1 V * | IV 1 3 } (3r | N | V)* = ζN-N-$_1^1$N 3 R*$_4$ $\}$ P*$_4$ $\frac{4}{3}$ R*$_2$
$\;$ 1 $\qquad\qquad\;\;$ 2 $\qquad$ 4 $\qquad\qquad\;\;$ 1 $\;\;$ 2

b. *Of PV Absolute.*

1. ζ Allowing then (that | such cruelties | were perpetrated
   $\quad\;\;$ 4 $\qquad\qquad\qquad$ c $\qquad\;\;$ 1 $\qquad\qquad\qquad\;\;$ 2
   by Britons upon the poor Africans)* { he | could not help
   $\qquad\qquad\qquad\qquad\qquad\qquad\qquad\qquad\;\;\;$ 1 $\qquad\qquad\;\;$ 2

LECTURE IX.   151

| feeling} (that | it | was | an important duty in some one
         4   1   2   3
| to undertake | the task of awakening public feeling to
         4   5
a just sense of the case.)⁎

$$\left\{ \underset{4}{PV} \ 1 \ (C \ | \ 1^2 \underset{1}{N} \ | \ \underset{2}{AV} \ 3 \ 3)^{\cdot} \right\} \{ \underset{1}{N} \ | \ A \ 1 \ \underset{2}{V} \ | \ \underset{4}{PV} \}$$

$$(C \ | \ \underset{1}{N} \ | \ \underset{2}{V} \ | \ 1^1 \ 2 \ \underset{3}{N} \ 3 \ | \ \underset{4}{IV} \ | \ 1^1 \ \underset{5}{N} \ 4 \ 5\text{-}3\text{-}3 \ | \ )^{\cdot} = \left\{ PV \ C^{\cdot}{}_{2} \right\} P_4 \ 4 \ C^{\cdot}{}_5$$

2. ⟨ Supposing however (that | the supply of good nourish-
         4   1
ment | is adequate) ⟩ {people | are apt | to err in various
         2   1   2   4
ways} (when | they | come | to use | it.)⁎
                1   2   4   5

$$\left\{ PV \ 1 \ (C \ | \ 1^1 \underset{1}{N} \ 3 \ | \ \underset{2}{V} \ 2) \right\} \{ \underset{1}{N} \ | \ \underset{2}{V} \ 2 \ | \ \underset{4}{IV} \ 3 \}$$

$$(C \ | \ \underset{1}{N} \ | \ \underset{2}{V} \ | \ \underset{4}{IV} \ | \ \underset{5}{N}) = \left\{ PV \ 4 \ C^{\cdot}{}_2 \right\} P_4 \ 4 \ C^{\cdot}{}_5$$

3. ⟨ Supporting ⁎ | her | ⁎ to a seat, (which | happened | to
         4   5   1   2
be hard-by)⁎ ⟩, { he | told ⁎ | her | ⁎ in a few syllables |
       4   1   2   3
enough to satisfy | her immediate curiosity.}
         4   5

$$\left\{ \{ \underset{4}{PV} \ast \ | \ \underset{5}{N} \ | \ \ast \ 3 \ \ast \} (\underset{1}{R} \ | \ \underset{2}{V} \ | \ \underset{4}{IV} \ 1)^{\cdot} \right\}$$

$$\{ \underset{1}{N} \ | \ \underset{2}{V} \ast \ | \ \underset{3}{N} \ | \ \ast \ 3 \ | \ 1 \underset{4}{IV} \ | \ 1^3 \ 2 \underset{5}{N} \} = \left\{ 4 \ 5 \ {}_3^4 R^{\cdot}{}_4 \right\} P_5$$

4. ⟨ Without attempting | to describe | the various stages of
                                 4   6   7
the Revolution | and | the different committees (that | under
                                                              1
different titles carried-on | the work of destruction)⁎ ⟩,
                 2   3
{we | will mention | some of the deeds} (that | shine-out)⁎
   1   2   3   1   2

STYLOGRAPHY OF ENGLISH LANGUAGE.

(as | we | look into that abyss of horror, the Paris of
$\underset{1}{}$ $\underset{2}{}$
1792 and the following year.)²•
$\overset{+}{}$

$\zeta \{ PV_4 \mid IV_6 \mid 1^1 \underset{7}{\approx} N \; 3{+}1^1 \underset{7}{\approx} N \} (R_1 \mid 3 \underset{2}{V} \mid N_3 \mid) \succ$

$\{ N_1 \mid AV_2 \mid N_{(3} 3 \} (R_1 \mid V_2)\cdot (C \mid N_1 \mid V_2 \; 3(1^2 \; n) \; 3,$

$1^1 \; n \; 3(n{+}1^1 \underset{\ldots}{\approx} n))^{2\cdot}$

$= \zeta 4 \; 6 \; 7 \; \tfrac{3}{3}R\cdot_3 \succ P_3 \; 3 \; R\cdot_2 \; 2 \; C^{2\cdot}_2$

5. ζ Being on one occasion applied to, | to save * | an
$\underset{4}{}$ $\underset{6}{}$
young officer | * from a court-martial, (which | he | had
$\underset{7}{}$ $\underset{3}{}$ $\underset{1}{}$
provoked by his misconduct)• $\succ$ {his reply | was} (that
$\underset{2}{}$ $\underset{1}{}$ $\underset{2}{}$ c
| he | would do | every thing in his power | to oblige |
$\underset{1}{}$ $\underset{2}{}$ $\underset{3}{}$ $\underset{4}{}$
so gallant and good an officer as Sir John Warren.)
$\underset{5}{}$ $\overset{+}{} \underset{6}{}$

$\zeta \{ A \; 3 \; PV_4 \mid IV_6 * \mid 1^1 \underset{7}{\approx} N \mid * \; 3 \; n \} (R_3 \mid N_1 \mid V_2 \mid 3)\cdot \succ \{ 1^3 N_1 \mid V_2 \}$

$(C \mid N_1 \mid AV_2 \mid 1^2 \; N_3 \; 3 \mid IV_4 \mid 1 \; 2{+}2 \; 1^1 \; N{+}N)\cdot$
$\underset{5}{} \underset{5}{}$

$= \zeta 4 \; 6 \; 7 \; \tfrac{3}{3}R\cdot_3 \succ P_3 \; 2 \; C\cdot_5$

These subordinated Absolutes are sometimes seen to stand alone without the Ps.

II.—By C• and R• SUBORDINATIONS INDEPENDENT OF P.

a. Of N Absolute.

1. {No wonder (that | the people of Paris | have ever since
$\underset{3}{}$ $\underset{1}{}$
looked back to Genevieve as their protectress)• and (that
$\underset{2}{}$ $\overset{+}{}$ $\overset{+}{}$
| * in after ages | she | has grown | to be * | the patron
$\underset{1}{}$ $\underset{2}{}$ $\underset{4}{}$
saint of the city.)•}
$\underset{5}{}$

$\zeta \; 3 \; N_3 \; (C \mid 1^1 \; N_1 \; 3 \mid A \; 1 \; 1 \; V_2 \; 1 \; 3 \; (n{+}1^3 \; n))\cdot$

$+ (C \mid * \; 3 \mid N_1 \mid AV_2 \mid IV_4 \mid 1^1 \underset{5}{\approx} N \; 3)\cdot \succ = \zeta N \; (C\cdot_2 {+} C\cdot_5 \;) \succ$

LECTURE IX.   153

2. ⟨ What an awakening! alone in a frail boat, their compani-
   ₁   ₁
ons gone, water all round, and swarming with the cruel
           ₁   ₄
sharks,—the sun | burning over head, | and themselves
            ₁   ₄   ₄
now 36 hours without food, and parched with the deadly
                             ₄
thirst (which | they | had | the resolution | not to attempt |
       ₅   ₁   ₂   ₃   ₄
to slake with salt water, | well knowing |)* (that | the
   ₆   ₈   c
temporary relief | would be followed by worse suffering,
          ₁   ₂
perhaps by phrenzy.)²*⟩

⟨ ₂ ₁¹ N ! ⟩ ⟨ ₁ ₃, ⟩ ⟨ ₁³ N | PV ⟩ ⟨ N ₃+₄ ₃ ⟩ ⟨₁¹ N | PV ₃ ⟩
    ₁   ₁   ₁   ₄   ₁   ₄

+⟨N ₁ ₃ ₃+PV ₃ ⸸ (R | N | V | ₁¹ N | ₁ IV | IV ₃ | ₁ PV)³
   ₁   ₄   ₅   ₁   ₂   ₃   ₄   ₆   ₈

(C | ₁¹ ₂ N | A A V ₃, ₁ ₃)⟩²*
      ₁   ₂

=⟨ 1 ⟩−⟨ ₁ ₃, ⟩ ⟨ 14, ⟩ ⟨ 1, ⟩−⟨ 14, ⟩+⟨ 1, + 4 ⸸ R*₃ 8 C²*₂⟩

Here the 1st Absolute has in apposition 5 conjoined Absolutes.

b. of IV *Absolute.*

1. ⟨{"To shoot | the *villain*} (*who* | has destroyed | my sister")
        ₄   ₅   ₁   ₂   ₃
returned James, ⟨ rising hastely from his chair ⟩ ⟨{"To
         ₂   ₁   ₄
rid * | the world | * of the *villain*} (*who* | has made | me
    ₄   ₅   ₁   ₂
what)* (| I | am)²*, (who | drew * | me | * *from* the
      ₃₃   ₁   ₂   ₁   ₂   ₃
paths of rectitude *to* the ways of crime)* (who | has
                                              ₁
blasted | my character)*, (who | has heaped | misery on
   ₂   ₃   ₁   ₂   ₃
my mother)*, (who | has beguiled | my sister)*, (who |
                ₁   ₂   ₃   ₁
has done | all, all) ((R) | he | could | to trample * | us | * in
   ₂   ₃   ₃   ₃   ₁   ₂   ₄   ₅

STYLOGRAPHY OF ENGLISH LANGUAGE.

the dust, and reduce * | us | * to the level, aye, below the
$\quad\quad\quad\quad\; \underset{+}{} \;\; \underset{4}{} \;\;\;\;\;\; \underset{5}{}$
level of the vilest of mankind !")·⟩

"⟨ { $\underset{4}{IV}$ | $1^1 \underset{5}{N}$ } ($\underset{1}{R}$ | $\underset{2}{AV}$ | $1^3 \underset{3}{N}$)· ⟩" $\underset{2}{V}$ | $\underset{1}{N}$ ⟨ $\underset{4}{PV}$ 1 3 ⟩

"⟨ { $\underset{4}{IV}$ * | $1^1 \underset{5}{N}$ | * 3 } ($\underset{1}{R}$ | $\underset{2}{AV}$ | $\underset{3}{N}$ | $\underset{3}{N}$)· ($\underset{3}{R}$ | $\underset{1}{N}$ | $\underset{2}{V}$)²·

, (R | V * | N | * 3'-3 3"-3)·

, (R | AV | 1³ N)·

, (R | AV * | N | * 3)·

, (R | AV | 1⁸ N)·

, ($\underset{1}{R}$ | $\underset{2}{AV}$ | $\underset{3}{N}$, $\underset{3}{N}$)

, ($\underset{3}{R}$) | $\underset{1}{N}$ | A ($\underset{2}{V}$) | $\underset{4}{IV}$ * | $\underset{5}{N}$ | * 3

$\quad\quad\quad\quad\quad\quad\quad$ IV * | $\underset{5}{N}$ | * 3 ! 3-3 3)·⟩

=" ⟨ 4 5 5R·₃ ⟩" P₂ ⟨ 4 ⟩ " ⟨ 4 5 R·₃ R²·₃ ⟩"

$\quad\quad\quad\quad$ " R·₃, R·₃, R·₃ R·₃ R·₃, R·₅ "

It must be remembered thus that Absolutes are Indepedent Unions and not Subordinates to Ps as the Subordinates are, which is an important philological point.

2. ⟨How much *better* | to give | any thing⟩ (we | can spare
$\quad\quad\;\; \underset{c'}{}\quad\quad \underset{4}{}\quad\quad \underset{5}{}\quad\quad\; \underset{1}{}\quad\quad\;\; \underset{2}{}$
to the deserving poor)·, *than* | either | to misspend | it | on
$\quad\quad\quad\quad\quad\quad\;\; \underset{c''}{}\;\; \underset{c'}{}\quad\quad\quad \underset{4}{}\quad\; \underset{5}{}$
frivolities, or | waste | the good things⟩ (we | buy with it !)
$\quad\quad\;\; \underset{c''}{}\quad\; \underset{4}{}\quad\quad\quad\;\; \underset{5}{}\quad\quad \underset{1}{}\;\; \underset{2}{}$

⟨ 1 1 2 | $\underset{4}{IV}$ | $1^2 \underset{5}{N}$ ⟩ ((R) | $\underset{1}{N}$ | A $\underset{2}{V}$ 3)·
$\;\; \underset{c'}{}$

⟨ c'' ((c' | $\underset{4}{IV}$ | $\underset{5}{N}$ | * 3 c'' | $\underset{4}{IV}$ | 1^1 2 $\underset{5}{N}$ ⟩

$\quad\quad$ (($\underset{3}{R}$) | $\underset{1}{N}$ | $\underset{2}{V}$ 3)²·=⟨ c' $\underset{4}{IV}$ | $\underset{5}{N}$ ⟩ 5 R·₂

$\quad\quad\quad\quad\quad\quad$, ⟨ c'' c' IV | N

$\quad\quad\quad\quad\quad\quad\quad\quad$ c'' IV | N ⟩ 3 R·₃

LECTURE IX.   155

c. *of Absolute preposition phrase Subordinate.*

I. ⌜After mutual temporary adieus, and after a fond though timid glance from Emily to him (she | loved)• ⌝ { the whole
                                                      $_1$ $_2$
party | retired to their respective chambers. }
$_1$ $_2$

$$\langle 3, +3\ (1^1\ 2 + 2\ n)\ 3\ 3\ ((R)_3\ |\ N_1\ |\ V_2\ )\rangle\ \{1^1\ 2\ N_1\ |\ V_2\ 3\}$$

$$= \langle\ 3\ +3\ 3\ 3\ (R)^\bullet_2\ \rangle P_2$$

COMPARISON OF ELLIPSIS IN CO-ORDINATE SUBORDINATES
AND ABSOLUTES.

Co-ordinate subordinate structures of higher or lower comparison with co-ordinating " Comparative adjectives" as Joiners to V Term of the P and "Than" as initiative Subordinate have been shown. Co-ordinate sub-structures by way of Equality of of Comparison, having Co-ordinating Conjunction "as" before Positive Adjectives in the V Term of the P and initiative "as" to Subordinates, have also been shown. *Ellipsis in these co-ordinate Subordinates* occurs by joiners or by one Term only ; in the case of the presence of the N Term, V alone or with its joiners is elliptical; and in the case of the presence of the V Term, N alone or with its joiners remains elliptical too. An elliptical N term followed by an auxiliary V term in the Co-ordinate Subordinate is also shown before.

Ellipsis of both N and V terms *before the second* N *Absolute* is possible also, for in the above illustrations of the Independent Absolutes it is to be pointed out that ellipsis consists in the absence of two Terms together, the first and the second, which may be filled up by "it is" thus rendering the Absolutes incomplete into Ps complete. There is no reason why they should not be considered as *Double Ellipsis*. Ellipsis in Absolutes goes therefore to be more so over Co-ordinate Subordinate structures, which is another philological point to be remembered. But if *want* and not ellipsis be the sole rule of Absolute formation these examples might be considered as elliptical Ps.

156   STYLOGRAPHY OF ENGLISH LANGUAGE.

Parenthetic parts of speech, phrases and Mono-simples having been shown before; Parenthetic Subordinates come here for illustration.

II.—Complex by Parenthetic subordination of the Principal.

1. $\{$These Sophists, $|$ as they were called, $|$ detested $|$ Socrates.$\}$
   $\phantom{\{}$ 1 2

   $\{1^2 \underset{1}{N}, (C \mid \underset{1}{N} \mid \underset{2}{AV,}) \underset{2}{V} \mid \underset{.3}{N} \} = P_3 (C^._2)$

2. $\langle$ * In the winter of the year 1776, $|$ the Count and Countess Podotsky being on their way *from* Vienna *to* 1 4

   Cracow $\rangle$ $\{$the wolves, (*which* $|$ *are very numerous in the* 1 1 2

   Carpathien Mountains and, (*when the cold* $|$ *is very severe,*)
    + 1 2

   are more bold and savage than usual,)' $|$ came down in
    2 2

   hordes and pursued $|$ the carriage between the towns of
    + 2 3

   Osweik and Zator.$\}$

   r $\langle$ 3 3 (n) $|$ $1^1 \underset{1}{N} + \underset{1}{N} \mid \underset{4}{PV}$ 3 3'-3'' $\rangle$

   $\{1^1 \underset{1}{N} (\underset{1}{R} \mid \underset{2}{V} 1 2\text{-}3 \mid + \mid (C \mid 1^1 \underset{2}{N} \mid \underset{2}{V} 1 2)^. \underset{}{V} c' 2 \dotdiv c'' 2)^. \mid$

   $\underset{2}{V} 1 3 + \underset{2}{V} \mid 1^1 \underset{3}{N} 3 3(n+n)\} = \langle \underset{4}{N} \mid \underset{5}{PV} \rangle P_3 (R^._2 C^._3)$

In the 1st sentence 'as they were called' is parenthetic, isolated by commas. In the 2nd sentence from 'which' to 'usual' isolated by commas with Vs in the present Tense is a parenthetic R', and within this R' another parenthetic C', isolated likewise by commas, is visible too. Parentheses, commas or dashes are *parenthetic indicators*, and the present Narration within the past one is another philological point of distinction.

I have just then shown to you that Absolute N Vocative is subordinated by R⁵ and Absolute IV or PV by C⁵, the former being 1st, and the latter, 4th term of the Absolutes. I have shown to you also that 3rd term N Absolutes with elliptical 1st and 2nd terms stand as independent Mono-simples. I have shown to you too that *Absolutes* as regards ellipsis are *more elliptical than co-ordinate Subordinate* structures by two absent terms to render them complete, though rarely the co-ordinate Subordinates, which are generally elliptical by one term, may be seen to be elliptical by two absent terms also.

I believe that you have, by this time, been able to discern that Mono-simple Ps are subordinated by complete R⁵ and C⁵, and that Absolute combinations to the Ps are but independent unions to the same by incomplete Absolute structures; the former, is a *complete Complexity*; the latter, an union of incomplete structure to the P, and hence an *incomplete Complexity*.

I go presently to point out to you that complete C⁵ Subordinate Structures to Ps may stand as Absolute incomplete by *two* absent or elliptical terms. And this C⁵, I presume, completes the narration, of the *3rd kind of ellipsis*, which I go to impress upon you by way of differentiation.

III.—Complex of the P by Elliptical C⁵ Subordinate.

1. (ζWhen | a little boy at school $\rangle$) { he | surprised * | every
       c   3   1   2
   body | * by the curious little *machines* } (*which* | he
     3   3   1
   | made with his own hands.)⁵
     2

(C | 1¹ 2 N 3)⁵ { N | V * | 1² N | * 3 } (R | N | V 3)⁵
           3   1   2   3   3   1   2

$= C^{\cdot}_3, P_3 \, \S \, R^{\cdot}_3$

12

158   STYLOGRAPHY OF ENGLISH LANGUAGE.

2. ($(\mathrm{If}\mid$ not formally punished by law$\mathop{\rangle})^{\bullet}$ { he | is punished
$\qquad\qquad\qquad\qquad\qquad{}_2\qquad\qquad\quad{}_1\ {}_2$
by his neighbours } (who | avoid | dealing again with one)$^{\bullet}$
$\qquad\qquad\qquad\quad\ {}_1\qquad\ {}_2\qquad\quad\ {}_4$
(who | has once imposed upon them.)$^{2\bullet}$
$\ \ {}_1\qquad\ {}_2$

$(C \mid (\underset{1}{N}) \mid (A)\ {}_1\ {}_1\ \underset{2}{V}\ {}_3)^{\bullet}\ \{\ \underset{1}{N} \mid \underset{2}{AV}\ {}_3\ \}\ (\underset{1}{R} \mid \underset{2}{V} \mid \underset{4}{PV}\ {}_1\ {}_3)^{\bullet}$

$(\underset{1}{R} \mid A\ {}_1\ \underset{2}{V}\ {}_3)^{2\bullet} = 2C^{\bullet}_2\, P_2\ \tfrac{2}{3}\ R^{\bullet}_4\ \tfrac{4}{3}\ R^{2\bullet}_2$

The two terms "he was", "he is" are elliptical after "when" and "if" respectively in the above two examples.

Like the elliptical 3rd and 4th term initial Absolutes which have been considered as Elliptical Ps, these two examples might be considered as *initial* Elliptical Subordinates, in contrast with *final* Elliptical Co-ordinate Subordinates already described.

We come now to the consideration of the *Direct-Narratives* for their **conversion** into the *continued Narratives*, for, such conversions of the 'direct' concern the C$^{\bullet}$ and R$^{\bullet}$ Subordinates in these continuations. So long as the Direct Speech is a part of speech or phrase alone, we might consider each as N Analogue in the narrative and as a third term N to it, and hence inconvertible. When however the Direct portion is a sentence this might as well be considered as the same 3rd term N to the Narrative, for here the sentence has become the Analogue of N too. Before you go to convert the Direct, (if Assertive here,) into Narrative in continuation, you have only to develope the *Narrative* or *objective Conjunction* "that" before the Direct in case the V Tenses are Present and the N or PP persons agreed or disagreed with both the Narrative and the Direct. No further change than this developmental "that" is necessary to convert the whole into a Narrative except by omission of the punctuative 'inverted Commas,' for, we must consider the Direct as Narrative with *understood* conjunction "that" as related before. Provided that V in the Narrative is Present or auxiliaried by an

Auxiliary Present, the arrangement for Conversion remains the same even if the V Tense disagreed in the Direct with that of the former.

But when the *Tenses* of the Vs in both differ we must *equalize* them, or when the *Persons* of the Ns or PPs differ we must *equalize* them too (except the inequality of 2nd Person of the Direct to 1st Person in the Narrative), the *standard for equalization* in both being with the V Past and N or PP *(personal pronoun)*, as the case may be, *of the Narrative.*

When again the Auxiliaries appear before the Vs in the Direct, their Tenses, no matter whether in the Indicative or Potential, shall have the same standard of equalization. The Present auxiliaried V in the Narrative must agree with the Present Auxiliary in the Direct and the Past with its Past, though this brings about wide grammatical changes of Indicatives into Potentials (*i.e.*, Indicative Future to Potential Past) or only the Tense changes of the Present into Past, and Perfect into Pluperfect in these respective moods.

Then comes the consideration of the post-joining preposition phrases, of V the 2nd term in the Narrative, or of the 3rd term itself from which the N, and PP equalizations must extend to those of the 'direct'. The persons of these N or PP must tally with the persons of N or PP of the Direct for the continued conversion, but the Rule of Tense will hold good as before, though the Vs may change themselves into totally different but appropriate words keeping the original sense.

Proximate PAs 'this', 'these' and proximate Adverbs 'here', 'hither', 'hence', 'now', &c., in the 3rd or subsequent terms of the Direct must change into *distant* PAs 'that', 'those' and distant adverbs 'there', 'thither', 'thence', 'then', &c., respectively in the converted Narrative, unless the proximity be so distinct that it cannot bear distant relation.

So far we have considered only of the Narrative of the Direct. Let us now see how the *Interrogative Direct* behaves in the Narrative conversion. All the above rules hold good in this case except that the V-changes in the Narrative into appropriate Vs are constant, and that the conjunction narrative 'that', cannot intervene here but is substituted by 'whether', or 'if', changing the Interrogative into the Narrative as C' Subordinate,— whether the first place is occupied by the Interrogative V or an Adverb. The interrogative initial Relatives become, as they should be, the subordinate R' simple, combinative, or riveted. The inversion of 1st and 2nd into 2nd and 1st term of the Direct comes as a consequence and sometimes its emphatic Auxiliary vanishes too when present.

The third expression, *Imperative of the Direct*, comes next for consideration. In this conversion the old rules of the Narrative remain the same while the imperative V changes into 4th term in continuation of the Narrative.

The 4th expression, *Exclamatory of the Direct* in its Optative variety, converts its 1st term into that of the 3rd of the Narrative and its V term into the 4th term. The V of the Narrative, like that of the V of the Interrogative, changes into an appropriate V. Other varieties of it allow conversion in most independent ways and do not belong to the observational system of teaching.

IV.—Conversion of Assertive-Direct-Narrative into continuous Narrative by C' subordination.

(*a*).—IN WHICH NARRATIVE 1ST TERM IS IN THE 1ST PERSON AND V IN THE PRESENT TENSE.

Illustration of 1st term in the 1st Person and V in the Present tense of Narrative having Direct speech as a Sentence in continuation is considered as a *continued Narrative*. The Narrative here is the Principal and the Direct speech without inverted comma enclosure, the C' Subordinate,—in which the subordinate narrative conjunction 'that' remains understood.

I say $\begin{cases} \text{I am right} \\ \text{you are right} \\ \text{he is right} \end{cases}$ I say $\begin{array}{l} \text{that I am right} \\ \text{that you are right} \\ \text{that he is right} \end{array}$

(b).—IN WHICH NARRATIVE 1ST TERM IS IN THE 2ND PERSON AND V IN THE PRESENT.

you say $\begin{cases} \text{I was wrong} \\ \text{you were wrong} \\ \text{he was wrong} \end{cases}$ $\begin{array}{l} \text{that I was wrong} \\ \text{You say that you were wrong} \\ \text{that he was wrong} \end{array}$

(c).—IN WHICH NARRATIVE 1ST TERM IS IN THE 3RD PERSON AND V IN ANY TENSE.

He says $\begin{cases} \text{'I have been kind'} \\ \text{'you will be kind'} \\ \text{'Hari is cruel'} \end{cases}$ $\begin{array}{l} \text{that he has been kind} \\ \text{He says that I will be kind} \\ \text{that Hari is cruel} \end{array}$

(d).—IN WHICH NARRATIVE 1ST TERM IS IN THE 3RD PERSON AND V IN THE PAST TENSE.

1. { "I$_1$ | am bound$_2$ by my vow | to do so,$_4$" } {replied$_2$ | the knight.$_1$ } $= $ " P$_4$ " P$_2$

1. { The knight$_1$ | replied$_2$ } (that | he$_1$ | was bound by his vow$_2$ | to do so.$_4$) $= $ P$_2$ 2 C'$_4$.

2. { "I$_1$ | should in that case hold$_2$ | you$_3$ |" {replied$_2$ |the yeoman,$_1$} "a friend to the weaker party."$_3$ }

$= $ " P$_3$ " P$_2$

2. { The yeoman$_1$ | replied$_2$ } (that | he$_1$ | should in that case hold$_2$ | me a friend$_3$ to the weaker party.$_3$)

$= $ P$_2$ 2 C'$_3$

3. "{ Treason | hath been with us,} ⟨ Ivanhoe ⟩" { said | the
    1   2   2   2
    king.} (Narrative after Direct narrative and its Absolute;
    1
    remark that N Vocative in Direct converts itself into 3rd
    Term of the Narrative.)

$$= \text{``}P_2 \langle N \rangle\text{''} P_2$$

3. {The king | told | Ivanhoe } (that | treason | had been with
    1   2   3   1   2
    them)².

$$= P_3 \, 2 \, C^{\bullet}{}_2$$

4. "{ He (that | is in lion's clutch,)" { answered | Fitzurse, }
       1   2   2   1
    "knows } (it | were needless.") (Narrative between R⁰ of
     2   1   2
    1st Term and the 2nd of Direct.)

$$= \text{``}P_2 \, 1 \, R^{\bullet}{}_2\text{''} \, P_2 \, \text{``}2 \, C^{\bullet}{}_2\text{''}$$

4. { Fitzurse | replied } (that { he | (that | was in the lion's
    1   2   1   1   2
    clutch)⁸ knew }⁰ (it | were needless.))⁰
             2   1   2

$$= P_2 \, C \, (P_2 \, 1 \, R^{\bullet}{}_2 \, 2 \, C^{\bullet}{}_2)^{\bullet}$$

5. "{I | will do | my best}, (as | Hubert | says)," {answered |
     1   2   3   1   2   2
    Locksley.} (Narrative after Direct-complex.)
    1

$$= \text{``}P_3 \, 2 \, C^{\bullet}{}_2\text{''}, \, P_2$$

5. {Locksley | replied} (that | he | would do | his best (as |
    1   2   1   2   3
    Hubert | said.)²ᵃ)⁰
    1   2

$$= P_2 \, 2 \, C^{\bullet}{}_3 \, 2 \, C^{2a}{}_2$$

6. "{It | is not for myself }" {she |said,} ("that | I | pray | this
    1   2   1   .2   1   2
favor.)
 3

(Narrative between Direct Complex *i.e.* its P and C^s.)

$= $"P$_2$" P$_2$ " 2 C$^s{}_3$"

6. {She | said} (that | it | was not for herself) (that | she
   1   2   1   2   1
prayed | that favor.)*
   2   3

$=$ P$_2$ 2 C$^s{}_2$ 2 C$^{2s}{}_3$

V.—Conversion of Imperative-Direct-Narrative into Continued Narrative.

Narrative 1st term in the 3rd Person and V past, with Imperative Direct, besides its conversion by the above method, may be continued into the Narrative not by Subordination, but by continuation of the *Terms* of the Narrative.

1. "{Forgive | me, ⟨ lady ⟩}" {replied | De Bois-Guillbert.}
         2   3   2   1

$=$"P$_3$ ⟨N !⟩" P$_2$

1. { De Bois-Guillbert | asked | the lady | to forgive | him.}
         1   2   3   4   5

$=$ P$_5$

2. "⟨Elgitha⟩," {said * | he | * to the maid of the Lady
            2   .1
Rowena}, "{let | thy lady | know} (we | shall not this
            2   3   4   1
night expect | her in the hall),* (unless | such | be | her
          2   3   b   1   2
especial pleasure.)" Narrative between ⟨ N !⟩ and P of
               3
Direct.

$=$"⟨N !⟩" P$_2$ "P$_4$ 4 C$^s{}_3$ 2 C$^{2s}{}_3$"

2. {He | told | Elgitha, the maid of the Lady Rowena | to
    1   2   3   3
let | her lady | know} (that | they | should not that night
  4   5   6   1
expect | her in the hall),* (unless | such | would be | her
  2   3   1   2
especial pleasure.)²*
   3

$$= P_6 \; 6 \; C^*_3 \; 2 \; C^{2*}_3$$

VI.—Conversion of Interrogative-Direct-Narrative into Continued Narrative.

1. "{Have | you, | then, | convents}, (to one of which | you
        2   1   3   1
mean | to retire!")* {asked | Rowena}.
  2   4   2   1

$$= \text{``}P_3 \; \tfrac{2}{3} \; R^*_4\text{''} \; P_2$$

1. { Rowena | asked | (the Jewess)} (whether | she | had|
       1   2   3   1   2
then | convents)* (into one of which | she | meant | to
          3   1   2
retire.)²* $= P_3 \; 2 \; C^*_3 \; \tfrac{2}{3} \; R^{2*}_4$
   4

2. "{What | mean" {said | I }| " those great flights of birds
      1   2   2   1   3
(that | are perpetually hovering about the bridge and|
   1   2   +
settling upon it from time to time.")*
   2

$$= \text{``}P_3\text{''} \; P_2 \; \text{``}\tfrac{2}{3} \; R^*_2\text{''}$$

2. { I | asked} (what | those flights of birds | meant)*, (that
     1   2   1   3   2   1
were perpetually hovering about the bridge and settling
              2   +   2
upon it from time to time.)²*

$$= P_2 \; R^*_3 \; \tfrac{2}{3} \; R^{2*}_2$$

3. "{What | is | the reason}" {said |I} ("that | the tide (I | see)
   $_1$ $_2$ $_3$ $_2$ $_1$ $_1$ $_1$ $_2$
   | rises out of a thick mist at the one end and again loses |
   $\quad\;\;_2$ $+$ $_2$
   itself in a thick mist at the other?")[*] (Narrative between
   $_3$
   P and C[•] of Interrogative Direct.)

   $=\text{``}P_3\text{''} \; P_2 \; \text{``}2 \; C\text{•}_3 \; R^{2\text{•}}_3\text{''}$

3. {I | asked} (what | the reason | was)[•] (that the tide (I | saw)
   $_1$ $_2$ $_1$ $_3$ $_2$ $_1$ $_1$ $_2$
   | rose out of a thick mist at the one end and lost itself in a
   $\;\;_2$ $_2$
   thick mist at the other.)[2•]

   $= P_2 \; R\text{•}_3 \; 2 \; C^{2\text{•}}_2 \; 1 \; R^{3\text{•}}_3$

4. "{How shall | I | reward | thee?}" {said | Cedric} ⟨turning
                $_1$ $_2$ $_3$ $_2$ $_1$ $_4$
   about and embracing | his Jester.⟩
        $_4$ $_5$

   $= \text{``}P_3\text{''} \; P_2 \; \langle 4 \dotplus 4 \; 5 \rangle$

4. ⟨Turning about and embracing | his jester,⟩ { Cedric |
        $_4$ $+$ $_4$ $_5$ $_1$
   asked } (how | he | should reward | him.)[•]
    $_2$ $_1$ $_2$ $_3$

   $= \langle 4 + 4 \; 5 \rangle \; P_2 \; 2 \; C\text{•}_3$

5. "{ Who | can | this | be? }" { whispered | the yeoman to
       $_1$ $_3$ $_2$ $_2$ $_1$
   each other }; "{ such archary | was never seen } (since | a
                            $_1$ $_2$
   bow | was first bent in Britain.)" (Narrative between
   $_1$ $_2$
   Direct Interrogative and Direct Narrative.)

   $= \text{``}P_3\text{''} \; P_2 \; \text{``}P_2 \; 2 \; C\text{•}_2\text{''}$

5. {The yeomen | asked * | each other | * whisperingly } (who
          $_1$ $_2$ $_3$ $_1$
   | could | this | be; } { for, such &c. }
     $\;\;_3$ $_2$

   $= P_3 \; 2 \; R\text{•}_3 \; ; \; P_2 \; 2 \; C\text{•}_2$

STYLOGRAPHY OF ENGLISH LANGUAGE.

NARRATIVE WITH INTERROGATIVE AND IMPERATIVE DIRECT CONTINUED TO THE NARRATIVE. FOR EXAMPLES :—

1. "{ How mean | you ⟨ knave ? ⟩ }" { said | the knight} ;
          2   1   .2   1
   "{ restore | me the bugle. }"
        2   3   3

$$= \text{``} P_2 \langle N \rangle \text{''} \; P_2 \; \text{``} P_3 \text{''}$$

1. { The knight | asked | the knave (how | he | meant)• and
          1   2   3   1   2   +
   ordered | to restore | him the bugle. }
      2   4   6   5

$$= P_5 \; C^{\bullet}{}_2$$

2. "{ Why do | you | sob, ⟨ Fanny ⟩" {demanded | the mother}
                1   2   2   1
   "{ tell | me | its reason. }"
      2   3   3

$$= \text{``} P_2 \langle N \rangle \text{''} \; P_2 \; \text{``} P_3 \text{''}$$

2. { The mother | asked | Fanny | to tell | her | the reason }
         .1   2   3   4   5   5
   (why she | did sob.)
        1   2

$$= P_5 \; 5 \; C^{\bullet}{}_2$$

NARRATIVE WITH EXCLAMATORY DIRECT BY PARTS OF SPEECH OR PHRASES AS *Inconvertible*. FOR EXAMPLES :—

1. { A hundred voices | exclaimed, } ⟨ "a champion ! a cham-
                  1   2
   pion !"⟩ $= P_2 \text{``} \langle N ! N ! \rangle \text{''}$

2. ⟨ "St. George !" ⟩ { he | cried } ⟨ "merry St. George for
              3   1   2   3
   England !"⟩, $= \text{``} \langle N ! \rangle \text{''} \; P_2 \; \text{``} \langle N ! \rangle \text{''}$

LECTURE IX. 167

NARRATIVE WITH EXCLAMATORY DIRECT AS ABSOLUTE
CONVERTIBLE. FOR EXAMPLE :—

1. $\{$ "A singular novelty" {muttered | the knight }, | "to
            1   2   1
advance | to storm | such a castle without pennon or
   4   6   7
banner displayed!" $\}$

$= "\{ 1 \}" P_2 "\{ 4\ 6\ 7 \}"$

1. { The knight | muttered } (that | it | was a singular
          1   2   1   2
novelty | to advance | to storm | such a castle without
   3   4   6   7
pennon or banner displayed.)*

$= P_2\ 2\ C^*_7$

VII.—Conversion of Exclamatory-Direct-Narrative into Continued Narrative.

1. { "The castle | burns!" } { said | Rebecca. }
           1   2   2   1

$= "P_2" P_2$

1. { Rebecca | said } (that | the castle | burnt.)*
       1   2   1   2

$= P_2\ 2\ C^*_2$

2. { The conqueror | exclaimed }, ("were | I | not | a victor)*
         1   2   2 1   3
{ I | should have wished | thus to die ! }"
  1   2   4

$= P_2\ "2\ C^*_3\ P_4"$

2. { The conqueror | exclaimed } (that (if | he | were not | a
         1   2   1   2
victor) { he | should have wished | thus to die. })*
  3   1   2   4

$= P_2\ C\ (C^*_3\ P_4)^*$

3. {" Beshrew | thy Spanish steel coat!}" { said | Locksley. }
        2   3   2   1

$= "P_3" P_2$

3. { Locksley | told | De Bracy | to beshrew | his Spanish
      1   2   3   4
   steel coat.} ('Direct' is exclamatory and imperative.)
         5
   $= P_5$

We have considered in a previous Lecture conversion of the Active expressions of the V into passive and *vice versa* in the Mono-simple; our present task is to show the same by the same rule as it is feasible in the R' and C' Subordinates. For examples:—

VIII.—Conversion of R' Subordinates active into passive and *vice versâ*.

1. { The king | took much | the same *view* of the case } (*which*
     1   2   3   3
   | the English captain at Majorca | had taken.)
       1   2

   $\{ 1^1 \underset{1}{N} \mid \underset{2}{V} 1 \mid 1^1 \; 2 \underset{3}{N} \; 3 \} (R \mid 1^1 \; 2 \underset{1}{N} \; 3 \mid \underset{2}{AV})' = P_3 \; 3 \; R'_3$

1. { The king &c. } (which | had been taken by the English
                        1   2
   Captain at Majorca.)
   $= P_3 \; 3 \; R'_2$

2. { The English crew | then began | to grumble at the
                   1   2   4
   danger } (to *which* | they | were exposed by their
                     1   2
   superiors.)' $= P_4 \; \tfrac{4}{3} \; R'_2$

2. { The English &c. } (to which | their superiors exposed |
                                    1   2
   them.)' $= P_4 \; \tfrac{4}{3} \; R'_3$
      3

3. { Favorable winds | brought * | the vessel | * quickly to
                   1   2   3
   England } (*where* | the story of the captured Turks | was
                          1
   already known.)' $= P_3 \; \tfrac{3}{3} \; R'_2$
             2

LECTURE IX.   169

3. { Favorable &c. } (where | every body | knew already | the
                              1   2
story of the captured Turks.)*
       3

$$= P_3 \tfrac{2}{3} R'_3$$

4. { Some persons from a light or wanton disposition | do |
          1   2
things } (*which* | a little thought | would shew | to be very
   3   3   1   2   4
mischievous.)* $= P_3 \ 3 \ R'_4$

4. { Some &c. } (which | on a little thought would be shown |
                   1   2
to be very mischievous.)
     4

$$= P_3 \ 3 \ R'_4$$

5. { There is | yet another species of *falsehood* } (*which* |
            2   1   1
ought | to be at all times avoided as scrupulously)* (as
   2   4   c'   c''
positive lying.)** $= P_2 \tfrac{1}{3} R'_4 \ c' \ C''^*_4$
     1

5. { There &c. } (which | we | ought | at all times to avoid as
                    5   1   2   4   c'
scrupulously) (as &c.)

$$= P_2 \tfrac{1}{3} R'_5 \ c' \ C''^*_4$$

6. { The family | might have starved but for the eldest *son* }
         1   2
(*whom* from a child | the father | had brought-up | to
    3   1   2
help * | him | * in his work.)
   4   5

$$= P_2 \tfrac{2}{3} R'_6$$

6. { The family &c. } (who from a child | had been brought-up
                                    1   2
by the father | to be helped in his work.)*
                      4

$$= P_2 \tfrac{2}{3} R'_4$$

7. { The company | assembled and were introduced into the
   $_1$ $_2$ $+$ $_2$
   great room } (where | the light | had just been fully
                          $_1$
   admitted | by drawing-up | a curtain.)•
   $_2$ $_4$ $_5$

$$= P_2 \tfrac{2}{3} R^\bullet_5$$

7, { The company &c. } (where | a curtain-by being drawn-
                                  $_1$
   up | had just fully admitted | the light.)
                      $_2$ $_3$

$$= P_2 \tfrac{2}{3} R^\bullet_3$$

8. { His enemies | knew well (what} | the ignorant multitude |
     $_1$ $_2$ $_{33}$ $_1$
   would think of him.)•
         $_2$

$$= P_3 \; 3 \; R^\bullet_3$$

8. {His &c. (what} | would be thought of him by the ignorant
              $_1$ $_2$
   multitude.)• $\quad = P_3 \; 3 \; R^\bullet_2$

9. { He | told * | the lady | * voluntarily, } (who | was buy-
     $_1$ $_2$ $_3$ $_1$ $_2$
   ing | silk | of him) (that | the goods | were damaged.)•
          $_3$ $_1$ $_2$
   (Progressive Active.)

$$= P_3 \; 3 \; R^\bullet_3 \; 2 \; C^\bullet_2$$

9. { He &c. } (by whom | silk | was being bought of him)
                        $_{1\cdot}$ $_2$
   (that | the goods | were damaged.) (Progressive Passive.)
           $_1$ $_2$

$$= P_3 \; 3 \; R^\bullet_2 \; 2 \; C^\bullet_2$$

10. { The Dutch | (whom | we | are apt | to despise for want of
         $_1$ $_5$ $_1$ $_2$ $_4$
    genius,) show | an infinitely greater taste of antiquity
              $_2$ $_{c'}$ $_3$
    and politeness in their buildings and works of this nature }
    (than what (we | meet-with in those of our own country.)$^{2\bullet}$)•
     $_{c''}$ $_{3}$ $_3$ $_1$ $_2$

$$= P_3 . c'' \; 1 \; R^\bullet_5 \; C''^\bullet_3 \; 3 \; R^{2\bullet}_3$$

LECTURE IX.   171.

10. {The Dutch, (who | are apt | to be despised by us for want
       1   2   4
&c.,) show &c.} &c. $= P_4 \, c' \, 1 \, R'_4 \, C''_3 \, 3 \, R^{2'}_3$

11. { They | are the *men* } (*whom* | we | have | to punish.)
      1   2   3   5   1   2   4
$= P_3 \, 3 \, R'_5$

11. { They &c. } (who | have | to be punished by us.)
                  1   2   4
$= P_3 \, 3 \, R'_4$

12. {These | relate to certain *facts*} (*which* | we | have | to
      1   2   5   1   2
shift out very carefully.)
     4
$= P_2 \, \tfrac{2}{3} \, R'_5$

12. {These &c.} (which | have | to be shifted out very care-
                  1   2   4
fully by us.)' $= P_2 \, \tfrac{2}{3} \, R'_4$

The examples from 10 to 12 are turned into 'Passive' only by change of the gerundial IV after 'Have', or 'be', the third term being absent. They prove that the IVs are principal Vs after 'be' and 'have', when Gerundial. The IVs behaved here exactly as participles of principal Vs though apparently 'be' and 'have' are principal.

IX.—Active-passive or passive-active conversion in C' Subordinates.

1. { It | *was found necessary for his cure* } (that | he | should
     1   2   1
be carried to the same monastery.)'
 2

$= P_2 \, 2 \, C'_2$

1. { It &c. } (that | they | should carry | him | to the same
                      1   2   3
monastery.)' $= P_2 \, 2 \, C'_3$

2. { Men in general | work } (that | they | may enjoy | the
$\underset{1}{\text{Men}}$ $\underset{2}{\text{work}}$ $\underset{1}{\text{they}}$ $\underset{2}{\text{enjoy}}$
fruits of their labours.)*
$\underset{3}{\text{fruits}}$

$$= P_2 \; 2 \; C'_3$$

2. { Men &c. } (that | the fruits of their labours | may be
$\underset{1}{\text{fruits}}$
enjoyed by them.) $= P_2 \; 2 \; C'_2$
$\underset{2}{\text{enjoyed}}$

3. {He | was so pious} (that | he | undertook | nothing | without
$\underset{1}{\text{He}}$ $\underset{2\;\;c'}{\text{was}}$ $\underset{c''}{\text{that}}$ $\underset{1}{\text{he}}$ $\underset{2}{\text{undertook}}$ $\underset{3}{\text{nothing}}$
asking | counsel of the gods.)*
$\underset{4}{\text{asking}}$ $\underset{5}{\text{counsel}}$

$$= P_2 \; c' \; 2 \; C''_5$$

3. { He &c. } (that | nothing | was undertaken by him with-
$\underset{1}{\text{nothing}}$ $\underset{2}{\text{undertaken}}$
out &c.) $= P_2 \; c' \; C''_5$

4. { Their fruitless attacks | always end in retreats,} (till |
$\underset{1}{\text{attacks}}$ $\underset{2}{\text{end}}$
we | have learnt | to laugh | them | to scorn.)*
$\underset{1}{\text{we}}$ $\underset{2}{\text{learnt}}$ $\underset{4}{\text{laugh}}$ $\underset{5}{\text{them}}$ $\underset{6}{\text{scorn}}$

$$= P_2 \; 2 \; C'_6$$

4. {Their &c.} (till | they | have taught | us | to laugh | them
$\underset{1}{\text{they}}$ $\underset{2}{\text{taught}}$ $\underset{3}{\text{us}}$ $\underset{4}{\text{laugh}}$ $\underset{5}{\text{them}}$
to scorn.)* $= P_2 \; 2 \; C'_6$
$\underset{6}{\text{scorn}}$

This is Conversion of Active into *Passive without 'be'* but with appropriate change of V, by *sense* only, the 1st into 3rd term interchange remaining intact.

5. {Ivan's suspicious mind | took-up | an idea} (that |.Feeleep |
$\underset{1}{\text{mind}}$ $\underset{2}{\text{took-up}}$ $\underset{3}{\text{idea}}$ $\underset{1}{\text{Feeleep}}$
had been excited by the nobles | to request | the abolition
$\underset{2}{\text{excited}}$ $\underset{4}{\text{request}}$ $\underset{5}{\text{abolition}}$
of the Oprichnina.)*

$$= P_3 \; 2C'_5$$

5. { Ivan's &c. } (that | the nobles | had excited | Feeleep to
$\underset{1}{\text{nobles}}$ $\underset{2}{\text{excited}}$ $\underset{3}{\text{Feeleep}}$
request &c.) $= P_3 \; 2 \; C'_5$
$\underset{4}{\text{request}}$

6. {He | resolved} (that no private pique | should hinder | him |
   1   2   1   2   3
   from doing | his duty.)⁵
        4   5

$$= P_2 \ 2 \ C^5_5$$

6. {He &c.} (that | his duty | should be hindered by no private
                    1   2
   pique | from being done.)⁵ (Passively converted.)
              4

$$= P_2 \ 2 \ C^5_4$$

7. { Once again | he | was led before the Emperor | to hear |
        1   2   2   4
   the monstrous sentence }, (that | for sorcery and other
                    5
   heavy charges | she | was | to be imprisoned for life.)⁵
        1   2   3   4

$$= P_5 \ 4 \ C^5_4$$

7. { Once &c. } (that | for sorcery and other heavy charges |
   they | were | to imprison | her for life.) (Gerundial passive
    1   2   4   5
   IV after 'be' changed to active IV.)

$$= P_5 \ 4 \ C^5_5$$

8. (When | she | was watching | the beheading of 63 vassals
          1   2   3
   of another of the murderers)⁵ { she | repeatedly ex-
                                     1
   claimed }, {"Now I | bathe in May dew."}
       2   1   2

$$= 2 \ C^5_3 \ P_2 \ ``P_2\text{''}$$

8. (When | the beheading of 63 vassals of another of the
                 1
   murderers | was being watched by her)⁵ { she | repeatedly
                              2   2
   exclaimed } (that | she | was then bathing in May dew)⁵
        2   1   2

$$= 2 \ C^5_2 \ P_2 \ 2 \ C^5_2$$

This is Progressive Active changed into Progressive Passive of V expression, and Direct Exclamatory changed into continued Assertive.

9. { These | make | us | so much honor and admire | the good
      1   2   3   4   4
women } (that | we | cannot refrain | from telling | the
      5   1   2   4
story.)* $= P_5\ 4\ C^*_5$
      5

9. { These &c. } (that | the story | cannot be refrained | from
                               1   2
being told by us.)* $= P_5\ 4\ C^*_4$
      4

Lastly, I go to show to you by way of illustrations tha whichever of the two, the N of the post-joining Preposition phrase of a V or the 3rd term N with no post-joiner, is enlarged by R* subordination, that which requires enlargement keeps to the last, for the Subordinate in general is but a governed structure to the whole P, or to any of its terms, or to any post-joiner of its terms, and consequently has to take the last seat in the P. The R* Subordinate besides, should always be proximate to its antecedent to prevent ambiguity.

1. { He | returned * | the book | * to his *friend* } (* from *whom*
     1   2   3
   | he | got | it for perusal.)*
     1   2   3

$$= P_3\ \tfrac{2}{3}\ R^*_3$$

1. { He | returned to his friend | the book } (which | he | got
     1   2   3   3   1   2
from him for perusal.)*

$$= P_3\ 3\ R^*_3$$

RECAPITULATION :—Before I close this lecture, let me recapitulate to you certain points in connection with *As*, *Vs*, *IVs*, bnd *PVs* which you have already known or seen. Vs unallied ay As, reveal themselves in the forms, the present and the past

(Indicative) active or neuter, and to this class belong also the three As 'have' active or neuter, 'be' neuter, and active 'do', which behave as principal Vs in their present or past forms. Like the principal Vs, As are present and past too (Indicative or Potential). All As including 'do' are followed by the present tense of principal Vs in their alliances, while As 'have' and 'be' are followed by past participle Vs. Of the last two alliances the former is active or neuter and the latter passive.

Present participle type of principal Vs active or neuter (progressive or incomplete) follows the auxiliary 'be' and not 'have.' Present passive participle of principal Vs (Progressive passive) does the same. 'Have' as A precedes 'have' or 'be' when principal, but 'be' cannot be A to 'have' or to itself except in progressive present participle. Auxiliary by enumeration of one, two, or three, past or present, may precede a principal V in the union. All As present or past when one or single, take such precedence; when two or dual, the initial As may be present or past with the 2nd auxiliary 'have' or 'be' unchanged; and when three or triple, which is the maximum of auxiliary enumeration, the initials may be present or past followed by 'have' the 2nd and 'be' the 3rd as 'been'. Thus it follows that the principal V is immediately preceded in the *Tripple Alliance-first*, by 'been'; *secondly*, by 'have'; and *thirdly*, back-wards by other As than these in their present or past forms. It must be remembered however that the A 'do' does not share in the dual or triple alliance but only in the single of the *Assertive expression.*

In the *Imperative expression* V is only present and its As are simply 'do' or 'be.' 'Have' cannot be an A in this expression. In the *Interrogative* and *Exclamatory expressions* all As play their roll as in the Assertive.

Besides the *present type*, the *past participle type* and the the *present participle type of* Vs after As, another type not yet recognised is the *IV type of* Vs active or neuter or passive as principal which follows 'have' or 'be.' The latter type should be reckoned as principal Vs though the As 'have' and 'be' are only apparently so. The inference of 'have' and 'be' as auxiliaries here, had already been drawn when we dealt with their IV conversions from active to passive by the presence of the 5th term, in which 'have' and 'be' could not play the roll in the conversion but allowed it to the IVs which thus acted as Principal Vs.

Having thus reminded you of the **conjugation** of the Principal Vs present and past, of As present and past with Present type of Vs as Principal, and of Principal Vs formed by the Participle present or past with auxiliary present or past and also IVs present with intimate preposition and present type of Vs, or intimate preposition with As present only in their single, dual, and triple alliances as the case may be, we come now to the *governed* IVs and PVs. The As of IV which have only present and auxiliaried present tenses are 'have' and 'be' and their dual 'have been.' The IVs are active, neuter, and passive and governed alike by active, neuter, and passive progressive Vs or the preceeding IVs or PVs though with the intervention of their governed Ns, which however become absent in the case of neuter Vs, IVs, or PVs. The triple alliance of As is wanting in IVs. Unlike the As in the principal Vs, which precede the Principal, these As take their seat between them and their intimate prepositions, or only precede the IVs when the preposition is absent. The As of governed PVs are exactly analogous to those of the IVs in their tenses and in their active, neuter, or passive, or progressive forms. Their intimate Prepositions, more numerous than those of IVs, may or may not remain expressed also. The only tense wanting analogy is the superfluous Past of the PV. As the IVs and PVs are the 4th governed terms to 2nd and rarely to conjoined 2nd and 3rd, all varieties of present, past, and the present and past auxiliaried V Principals (except the non-observational varieties) may precede them. PVs governed or ungoverned (absolute) have their intimate prepositions (the time prepositions) expressed or understood likewise, but when the Past PVs follow immediately their As, they never retain their intimate prepositions and thus become the Principal. Denuded of its intimate preposition when a PV follows a neuter and passive V it behaves as a Post-joiner to it and not as a governed term. In this denuded condition it is never active but always retains a neuter or passive status or condition of the Principal Vs, IVs or PVs like their modifying or qualifying adverbs or adjectives. Analogous Post-joining condition to N terms are also visible with the PV Past.

In the *ungoverned* or absolute IVs and PVs, the IVs and PVs carry separate and independent actions in themselves unconnected with those of the principal Vs which bear no continued but sequential or precedential actions to the foregoing, for such independent actions in the IVs and PVs, and the sequential or precedential actions in Vs have been shown in the combined, absolute incomplete and the principal structures.

Tense sequences of Vs in the Subordinate (complete) have already been shown in the conversion of the Direct speech in continuation of the P. There, in some instances the V present or auxiliaried present of the P has had all varieties of present, past, or auxiliaried present or past in their subordinate conversions; and in other instances the V past in the P, is equalised by V past or auxiliaried V past of the Direct in their changes to Subordinates. You have simply therefore to remember the non-equalisation or equalization in the sequential tenses of the Subordinate to those of the P when present, and equalization only when the sequential tenses of the Subordinate follow those of V past in the P. Remember also that the converted Subordinates and the assertive Subordinates are one and the same.

It will not be out of place here to conclude this Lecture with the following *conjugation tables* of Vs, IVs, and PVs irrespective of their moods.

A.—Voice and Tenses of Verbs.
(Irrespective of Mood.)

Voice.

(a).—*Active* or *neuter*.

By present type and past participle type of V.

	A.—Present Series	B.—Past Series
	Call or hear	*Called or heard*
Without As =	Have called	Had called
With one As =	Will call	Would call
	Shall call	Should call
	May call	Might call
	Can call	Could call
	Must call	Must call
With two As =	*Will have* heard	Would have heard
	Shall have heard	Should have heard
	May have heard	Might have heard
	Can have heard	Could have heard
	Must have heard	Must have heard

LECTURE IX.

With one A = *Am* called

With two As = {
  Have been called
  Will be called
  Shall be called
  May be called
  Can be called
  Must be called
}

With three As = {
  Will have been called
  Shall have been called
  May have been called
  Can have been called
  Must have been called
}

⎫ By past participle type of V.

Was called

Had been called
Would be called
Should be called
Might be called
Could be called
Must be called

Would have been called
Should have been called
Might have been called
Could have been called
Must have been called

(*b*).—*Passive.*

With one A = *Am* loving or thinking   } By P. P. type of V.

Was loving or thinking

(*c*).—*Progressive* or *Incomplete.*

(*i*).—*Active* or *neuter.*

(i).—*Progressive Active or neuter.*

With two As =
{
Have been thinking
Will be thinking
Shall be thinking
May be thinking
Can be thinking
Must be thinking
}
By Present Participle type of V.

{
Had been thinking
Would be thinking
Should be thinking
Might be thinking
Could be thinking
Must be thinking
}

With three As =
{
Will have been loving
Shall have been loving
May have been loving
Can have been loving
Must have been loving
}
By Present Participle type of V.

{
Would have been loving
Should have been loving
Might have been loving
Could have been loving
Must have been loving
}

(ii).—*Progressive Passive.*

With one A = Am being loved — By *passive* present participle type of V.

Was being loved

LECTURE IX.

			(a).—*Active or neuter.*
With one A	=	*Have* to go or tell	Had to go or tell
With two As	=	{ *Will have* to go	Would have to go
		Shall have to go	Should have to go
		May have to go	Might have to go
		Can have to go	Could have to go
		Must have to go }	Must have to go
			(b).—*Passive.* (No. 1.)
With one A	=	*Am* to see	Was to see
With two As	=	{ *Will be* to see	Would be to see
		Shall be to see	Should be to see
		May be to see	Might be to see
		Can be to see	Could be to see
		Must be to see }	Must be to see

By present IV type of V.

(b) —*Passive.*

With three As = { *Will have been* to see / Shall have been to see / May have been to see / Can have been to see / Must have been to see } — By present type of IV.

(*No. 1.*) Would have been to see / Should have been to see / Might have been to see / Could have been to see / Must have been to see

With one A = *Have* to be told

With two As = { *Will have* to be told / Shall have to be told / May have to be told / Can have to be told / Must have to be told } — By Passive type of Infinitive.

(*No. 2.*) Had to be told / Would have to be told / Should have to be told / Might have to be told / Could have to be told / Must have to be told

With one A = { *Am* to be told

(*No. 3.*) Was to be told

In the above Table six types of principal Verbs have been shown; namely:—1. Present type of V, 2. Past participle type of V, 3. Present participle type of V, 4. Present passive participle type of V, 5. Present infinitive type of V, 6. Present passive infinitive type of V.

B.—Voice and Tenses of IVs.

(a).—*With intimate preposition and present type and past participle type of V.*

(With one A.)
1. To love, to go
2. To have loved or gone } Active or neuter.

(b).—*Auxiliaried, preceded by intimate preposition and past participle type of V.*

(With one A.)
(„ two As.)
1. To be loved
2. To have been loved } Passive.

C.—Voice and Tenses of PVs.

(a).—*With intimate preposition and "ing" terminal type of V or of A.*

(With one A.)
1. In loving, from running &c.
2. In having loved } Active or neuter.

(b).—*Auxiliaried with intimate preposition and past participle type of V.*

(With one A.)
(„ two As.)
1. From being deceived
2. From having been deceived } Passive.

(With two As.)
1. To doing
2. To have been teaching } Progressive.

LECTURE X.

STUDENTS AND GENTLEMEN,

In previous lectures we have dwelt upon the Mono-simple Principals and Mono-simple Subordinates, the latter of which were shown to be dependent upon the former and could not stand by themeselves. We come presently to the next class of structures, the **Di-simple Principals**, each Simple of which is headed by a Co-ordinate conjunction which forms the *5th Class of Conjunctions.* A Mono-simple P might stand alone but not so the Mono-simple S, while here both the Simples are Principals and must co-ordinate, *i. e.*, stand as colleagues,—the presence of the one foreboding the presence of the other. The initial conjunctions of each of the Di-simples may be pure conjunctional, pure adverbial, pure adjectival. Let the triple brackets embrace the Di-simple Principals (*Co-ordinate Principals*) in the Graphic, and C'-C'' head the respective Principals in the Rational Formulæ.

Illustrations of Di-simple sentence.
With Graphic and rational Formulæ.

1. [*Though* | he | is poor] [*yet* | he | is respectable.]
   $\ _{C'}$ $\quad \ _1 \quad \ _2 \qquad \qquad \ _{C''} \quad \ _2 \quad \ _2$

   $[\ C' \mid \underset{1}{N} \mid \underset{2}{V} \ 2\ ] [\ C'' \mid \underset{1}{N} \mid \underset{2}{V} \ 2\ ] = C'P_2,\ C''P_2$

2. [*As* | the tides | obey | the moon] [*so* | should | our
   $\ _{C'}$ $\quad \ _1 \quad\quad \ _2 \quad\ _3 \qquad \ _{C''}$

   passions | bend to our Judgment.]
   $\ _1 \qquad\quad \ _2$

   $[\ C' \mid \underset{1}{1^1\, N} \mid \underset{2}{V} \mid \underset{3}{1^1\, N}] [\ C'' \mid A \mid \underset{1}{1^3\, N} \mid \underset{2}{V}\ 3\ ] = C'P_3,\ C''P_2$

LECTURE X.

3. [*The-more-carefully* | nature | has been studied] [*the-more-*
   c' 1   2 c''

   widely | has | order | been found | to prevail.]
           1   2   4

   $[\ C'\ |\ \underset{1}{N}\ |\ A A \underset{2}{V}\ ]\ [\ \underset{2}{C''}\ |\ A\ |\ \underset{1}{N}\ |\ A \underset{2}{V}\ |\ \underset{4}{IV}\ ] = C'P_2\ C'P_4$

4. [*Although* | she | was still at that period sufficiently | an
         c' 1   2

   orthodox Unitarian | to perform | this augmentative exploit
                  3   4

   to the satisfaction and admiration of the leader of the sect]
   [*yet* | she | had long before emancipated | her mind | to some
    c'' 1   2   3

   extent from even the comparatively light chains of that
   faith.]

   $[C'\ |\ \underset{1}{N}\ |\ \underset{2}{V}\ 1\,3\,1\ |\ 1^1 2 \underset{3}{N}\ |\ \underset{4}{IV}\ |\ 1^2 2 \underset{5}{N}\ 3\,3\,3\ ]\ [C'\ |\ \underset{1}{N}\ |\ A\ 1\,1\ \underset{2}{V}\ |\ 1^3 \underset{3}{N}\ |\ 3\,3\,3]$
   $= C'P_5\ C'P_3$

5. [*Where-there* | is | a will] [*there* | is | a way.]
                      2   1   2   1

   $[\ C'\ |\ \underset{2}{V}\ |\ 1^1\ \underset{1}{N}]\ [C''\ |\ \underset{2}{V}\ |\ 1^1\ \underset{1}{N}\ ] = C'P_2\ C'P_2$

6. [*Because* | A | is | the centre of the circle BCD] [*therefore*
               1   2   3

   | AC | is equal to AB.]
      1   2

   $[\ C'\ |\ \underset{1}{N}\ |\ \underset{2}{V}\ |\ 1^1\ \underset{3}{N}\ s\ n\,n]\ [C''\ |\ \underset{1}{N}\ |\ \underset{2}{V}\ 2\,3\ ] = C'P_3\ C'P_2$

7. [*The-more* | I | see | you] [*the-more* | I | love | you.]
                1   2   3   1   2   3

   $[\ C'\ |\ \underset{1}{N}\ |\ \underset{2}{V}\ |\ \underset{3}{N}\ ]\ [\ C''\ |\ \underset{1}{N}\ |\ \underset{2}{V}\ |\ \underset{3}{N}\ ] = C'P_3\ C'P_3$

The initial Conjunction of 2nd Co-ordinate may in certain cases remain *understood* and simulate the Mono-simple Complex by C' subordination which is initial.

Illustrations of Di-simples with 2nd co-ordinate conjunction understood.

1. [*Though* | the elephant | is commonly quiet and harmless]
   c' 1   2

   [(c'') | no one | dares | to attack | a herd of elephants
          1   2   4   5
   marching through the forest.]

   $$[C' \mid 1^1 \underset{1}{N} \mid \underset{2}{V} \; 1 \; {}_{2+2}] \; [(C'') \mid 2 \underset{1}{N} \mid \underset{2}{V} \mid \underset{4}{IV} \mid 1^1 \underset{5}{N} \; 3 \; 4 \; 3 \mid]$$
   $$= C'P_2 \; (C'')P_5$$

2. [*Although* | the moral character | depends in a great degree
   c' 1   2
   on temperament and on physical health as-well-as on domestic and early training and the example of companions] [it | is also in the power of each individual | to
                   1   2
   regulate, to restrain and to discipline * | it | * by watchful
      4   4   4   5
   and persevering self-control.]

   $$[C' \mid 1^1 \; 2 \underset{1}{N} \mid \underset{2}{V} \; 3 \; 3+3+3 \; (2+2n+1^1 n) \; 3]$$
   $$[(C'') \mid \underset{1}{N} \mid \underset{2}{V} \; 1 \; 3 \; 3 \mid \underset{4}{IV}, \; \underset{4}{IV} + \underset{4}{IV} \mid \underset{5}{N} \mid 3]$$
   $$= C'P_2 \; (C'')P_5$$

The second co-ordinate conjunction 'yet' is understood in the above two examples.

Analogous to the subordinations of Mono-simples by Mono-simples to form Complexes, *Di-simples* may be subordinated to certain extent only by medial and terminal position of these Subordinates to those of the Ps and even by full extent of sub-subordination. Another point to be remembered is that each of the Di-simples may be *equally* or *unequally* subordinated as circumstances occur.

I.—Complex of the Di-simple by Fractional subordination.

1. [*Just-as* { the energy of the horizontal stream | diminished}
    c' 1   2

   (as | the level of the water | became lower,)^{s}] [*so* | does |
        1   2 c''

   the energy of the vertical stream | diminish.]
   1   2

   [C' { 1^1 N 3 | V } (C | 1^1 N 3 | V 2)^{s}] [C'' | A | 1^1 N 3 | V]
           1   2   1   2   1   2

   = C'P$_2$ 2C$^{s}_2$ C''P$_2$

2. [*Although* { | this | was contained in the atomic theory of
     c' 1   2

   Democritus} (as | expounded by Lucretius)] [*yet* { | it | will
                1   c'' 1

   be found by any one } (*who* | examines further | the
        2   1   2

   consequences)^{s} (*which* | are drawn from it)^{2s} (*that* | it |
        3   1   2   1

   very soon diverges from the truth of the things)^{s} (as
              2

   we | might naturally expect)^{2s} (it | would.)^{3s}]
   1   2   1   2

   [C'{ N | AV 3 3 n } (C | N | A V 3)^{s}][(C''{ N | AAV 3 n } (R | V 1 | 1^1 N)^{s}
        1   2   1   2   1   2   1 2   3

   (R | AV 3)^{2s} (C | N | 1 1 V 3 3)^{s} (C | N | A 1 V)^{2s}
    1   2   1   2   1   2

   ((C) | N | A (V))^{3s}]
          1   2

   = C'P$_2$C$^{s}_2$ C''P$_2$ $\frac{2}{3}$ R$^{s}_3$ 3 R$^{2s}_2$ 2 C$^{s}_2$ C$^{2s}_2$ C$^{3s}_2$

3. [*If* the measures | are graduated accurately], [*then* (whatever
    c' 1   2 c''

   volume of the same water | is put into one)^{s}, {an exactly
         1   2

   similar volume of the same water | must be put into other
            1   2   4

   | to make | the beam | level.}]
        4   5

   [C' | 1^1 N | AV 1]
              1   2

   [C'' (2 N 3 | AV 3)^{s} { 1^1 1 2 N 3 | A V 3 | IV | 1^1 N | 2 }]
          R 1   2   1   2   4   1   5

   = C'P$_2$ C''(R$^{s}_2$ P$_5$)

188   STYLOGRAPHY OF ENGLISH LANGUAGE.

4. [*Although* { it | was | a popular belief } (*that* | no slave |
     c'   1   2   3   1

could breathe in England)] [{ there were | legal men of
                 2   2   1
eminence } (who | expressed | a directly contrary opinion.)]
             1   2   3

[C' { $\underset{1}{N}$ | $\underset{2}{V}$ | $1^1\ 2\ \underset{3}{N}$ | } (C | $2\ \underset{1}{N}$ | $\underset{2}{AV}\ 3$ |)$^{\scriptscriptstyle \bullet}$]

[(C") { | $1\ \underset{2}{V}$ | $2\ \underset{1}{N}\ 3$ | } ($\underset{1}{R}$ | $\underset{2}{V}$ | $1^1\ 1\ 2\ \underset{3}{N}$)$^{\scriptscriptstyle \bullet}$]

$= C'P_3\ 3C^{\bullet}_2\ (C'')P_2\ 1\ R^{\bullet}_3$

We have seen complexity of a Mono-simple P by a Mono-simple Subordinate—P C$^{\bullet}$; we have seen also complexity of P by a complex Subordinate too—P,C(P C$^{\bullet}$)$^{\bullet}$; we come now to the 3rd class of complexity of P by the Di-simple or co-ordinate variety of Subordinate—P C(C'P C"P)$^{\bullet}$. This you might consider as another combination by substitution in place of the Mono-simple S, in which the assertive Conjunction 'that' stands prominent. A direct non-substitutive variety without the interference of 'that' is visible also—P (C'P C"P)$^{\bullet}$.

II—Complex of P by substitutive co-ordinate subordination.

1. { $\underset{1}{You}$ | will $\underset{2}{observe}$ } (that [*though* | $\underset{1}{water}$ | $\underset{2}{occupies}$ | $\underset{3}{space}$]
                                           c'

[$\underset{1}{it}$ | $\underset{2}{has}$ | no definite $\underset{3}{shape}.$])$^{\bullet}$

{ | $\underset{1}{N}$ | $\underset{2}{AV}$ | } (C [C' | $\underset{1}{N}$ | $\underset{2}{V}$ | $\underset{3}{N}$] [(C") | $\underset{.1}{N}$ | $\underset{2}{V}$ | $2\ 2\ \underset{3}{N}$])$^{\bullet}$

$= P_2\ C\ (C'P_3\ C''P_3)^{\bullet}$

2. { $\underset{1}{It}$ | $\underset{2}{seems}$ } (*that* [*the greater* | the bulk of $\underset{1}{water}$ | $\underset{2}{is}$] [*the*
                                                 c'

$\underset{c''}{more}$ | $\underset{1}{it}$ | $\underset{2}{weighs}.$])$^{\bullet}$

{ | $\underset{1}{N}$ | $\underset{2}{V}$ | } (C [C' | $1^1\ \underset{1}{N}\ 3$ | $\underset{2}{V}$] [C" | $\underset{1}{N}$ | $\underset{2}{V}$])$^{\bullet} = P_2\ C\ (C'P_2\ C''P_2)^{\bullet}$

LECTURE X. 189

III.—Complex of P by direct co-ordinate subordination.

1. $\{$It$_1$ | does not matter$_2\}$ ([whether | we$_1$ | watch$_2$ | a shower$_3$
   c'
   | in calm weather here,] [or | we$_1$ | watch$_2$ | it$_3$ | in New Zeal-
   c''
   and.])*

$\{|\ N_1\ |\ A_1\ V_2\ |\ \}$ ([C' | N_1 | V_2 | $1^1\ N_3$ | s_1] [C'' | N_1 | V_2 | N_3 |s])*

$= P_2\ (C'P_3\ C''P_3)$*

This variety of direct *Co-ordinate Subordinate Di-simples* may transform itself to the *first* term in the P, and may altogether become a N Analogue.

Di-simple Principals as N Analogue.

1. [*Whether* | we$_1$ | gain$_2$ | the victory$_3$] [*or* | our enemy$_1$ |
     c' c''
   obtain$_2$ | the day$_3$] N$_1$ | remains for the battle$_2$ | to decide$_4$.

   $\overbrace{[C'\ |\ N_1\ |\ V_2\ |\ 1^1\ N_3]\ [C''\ |\ 1^3\ N_1\ |\ V_2\ |\ 1^1\ N_3]}\ |\ V_2\ 3\ |\ IV_4\ |$

   $= (C'P_3\ C''P_3)^N$ in P_4

2. [*Whether* | it$_1$ | shall be$_2$ | walking$_3$] [*or* (it shall be) some
     c' c''
   vigorous exercise at home$_3$] N$_1$ | is$_2$ | a matter of choice$_3$.

   $\overbrace{[\ C'\ |\ N_1\ |\ AV_2\ |\ N_3\ ]\ [C''\ (N_1\ |\ AV_2)\ |\ 2_2\ N_3\ ]}\ V_2\ |\ 1^1\ N_3\ |$

   $= (C'P_3\ C''P_3)^N$ in P_3

We arrive now to the last variety of Complex structure, the "*conjoined complex.*" This is the complexity of P both by the Mono-simple and the Co-ordinate Subordinates.

14

190   STYLOGRAPHY OF ENGLISH LANGUAGE.

IV.—Complex of P by conjoined Mono- and substitutive Di-simple subordinations.

1. (*When* | we | come | to consider about the position of man
    c   1   2   4

in the gradation scale of nature) {we | find} (that [*though* |
                                    1   2   c′

he | stands prominently independent there] [*yet* | his position
 1   2   c″   1

| is in all respects dependent on every object around him.])
 2

$$(C \mid \underset{1}{N} \mid \underset{2}{V} \mid \underset{4}{IV} \, 3\,3\,3\,3 \,)\cdot \{ \mid \underset{1}{N} \mid \underset{2}{V} \}$$

$$(C \,[\, C' \mid \underset{1}{N} \mid \underset{2}{V} \, 1\,2\,1 \,] \, [\, C'' \mid 1^3 \underset{1}{N} \mid \underset{2}{V} \, 3\,2\,3\,3 \,] \,)\cdot$$

$$= 2 \, C\cdot_4 \; P_2 \; 2C(C'P_2 \; C''P_2 \,)\cdot$$

The complexity of P by Mono-simple Substitute made up of Co-ordinate Ps, the 2nd of which is Co-ordinately subordinated, is also seen. For example :—

1. { We | thus see } (that [| in-a-country-where-there | is
     1   2   c′   2

much industry] [there | are | far-more people (than | in
      1   c″   2   c′   1   c″

one)· (where | there is | no industry.)²·])
         R   2   1

$$\{\underset{.1}{N} \mid 1 \underset{2}{V} \} (C \,[\, C' \mid \underset{2}{V} \mid 2 \underset{1}{N}] \, [\, C'' \mid \underset{2}{V} \mid c' \underset{1}{N}$$
$$(C'' \,(1 \underset{2}{V} \mid \underset{1}{N}) \, 3 \,) \,(\, \underset{R}{1} \mid 1 \underset{2}{V} \mid 2 \underset{1}{N})])$$

$$= P_2 \; 2C \; (C'P_2 \quad C''P_2 \quad c'C'''\cdot_2 \; \tfrac{2}{3}R^{2\cdot}_2)\cdot$$

Here R²· is second Subordinate to the Co-ordinate Subordinate.

The *Substitutes* of Mono-simple Subordinate have thus gradually been shown to be—*first* the Mono-complex, *secondly* the Di-complex, *thirdly* the Co-ordinate P-complex, and *fourthly*, as just shown, the Co-ordinate P-complex co-ordinately subordinated and sub-subordinated.

V.—Complex of the whole Di-simple by integral Subordinate.

1. [*Although* | water | is continually being-evaporated from the
   c' 1   2

surface of the earth and continually restored to it again
                                      2

by condensation] [*yet* | on the whole and in the course of
                    c''

years there seems | to be | no considerable gain or loss of
           2   4   1   1

water in our seas, lakes, and rivers] ; (*so that* | the two
processes of evaporation and condensation | balance | each-
   1   2   3
other.)*

$[\mid C' \mid \underset{1}{N} \mid A \ 1 \underset{2}{V} \ 3 \ 3 \mid + \mid 1 \underset{2}{V} \ 3 \ 1 \ 3 \mid]$

$[C'' \mid 3 + 3 \ 3 \ 1 \underset{2}{V} \mid \underset{4}{IV} \mid 2 \ 2 \underset{1}{N} + \underset{1}{N} \ 3 \ 3]$

$(C \mid 1^1 \ 2 \underset{1}{N} \ 3 \mid \underset{2}{V} \mid \underset{3}{N})^* = \overbrace{C'P_2 \ C''P_4} \ C'_3$

When the 1st term N in the 2nd Co-ordinate is antecedent to its PP proxy in the 1st Co-ordinate, this antecedent N takes the 1st seat in the structure, and *precedes* the 1st Co-ordinate, which is followed by the 2nd co-ordinate conjunction and the rest of the 2nd co-ordinate structure. For example :—

Transposition of the 1st term in the 2nd Principal co-ordinate to 1st seat.

Noun Pronoun.

1. [The *sea*, [though *it* | bears | no harvests on its bosom,] yet
          1   c' 1   2   3 c''

sustains | all the harvest of the world, and make | all the
   2   3   2

wildernesses of the earth | to bud and blossom (as the
   3   4   4

rose.)*]

$[1^1 \underset{1}{N} [C' \mid \underset{1}{N} \mid \underset{2}{V} \mid 2 \underset{3}{N} \ 3] \ C'' \mid \underset{2}{V} \mid 1^3 \ 1^1 \underset{3}{N} \ 3 \mid$

$+ \mid \underset{2}{V} \mid 1^2 \ 1^1 \underset{3}{N} \ 3 \mid \underset{4}{IV} + \underset{4}{IV} \ (C \mid 1^1 \underset{1}{N} \mid (\underset{2}{V}))^*]$

$= \overbrace{C''P_4 \ 4C'_2} \ C'P_3$

192   STYLOGRAPHY OF ENGLISH LANGUAGE.

Similarly, in Co-ordinates with R and its antecedent PP proxy, the 1st term R of the 2nd co-ordinate takes the 1st seat as an antecedent to the PP 1st term in the 1st co-ordinate, and *precedes* this 1st co-ordinate structure, which is followed by the 2nd co-ordinate conjunction and the rest of the 2nd co-ordinate structure. For example :—

Transposition of the 1st term in the 2nd sub-subordinated Co-ordinate to 1st seat in that Co-ordinate.

Relative before Personal Pronoun.

1. {No one in our own country | has deserved | warmer or more
      1 2

loving esteem} (than Helen Walker, the Scottish maiden,)*
      3

([*who*, [though *she* | would not utter | a word of untruth | to
  1 c' 1 2 3

save | her sister | from being sentenced to death,] yet came
  4 5 6 c' 2

on foot from Edinburgh to London, made | her way | to
                                           2 3

the Duke of Argyle, $\langle$ being introduced by him, $\rangle$ by her
                                4

entreaties obtained | that sister's pardon | from Queen
      2 3

Caroline, (*who* | was acting | as Regent in the absence of
            1 2

George II.)])^{2*}

$\{2 \underset{1}{N} 3 \mid A\underset{2}{V}|c' + c' \underset{3}{2 N}\} (C' \mid \underset{1}{N} \mid 1^1 \underset{1}{2 N} \mid (\underset{2}{V}))^*$

$([\underset{1}{R} \mid [\underset{1}{C'} \mid N \mid A \underset{2}{1 V} \mid 1^1 \underset{3}{N 3} \mid \underset{4}{IV} \mid 1^3 \underset{5}{N} \mid \underset{6}{PV 3}]$

$C'' \mid \underset{2}{V 3 3 3} \mid \underset{2}{V} \mid 1^3 \underset{3}{N 3 3} \langle \underset{4}{PV 3} \rangle \mid 3 \underset{2}{V} * \mid 1^2 1^5 \underset{3}{N} \mid *3 |$

$(\underset{1}{R} \mid A\underset{2}{V} * \mid + \underset{3}{N} \mid 3 3)^*])^{2*}$

$= P_3 \, c'C''_2 \, 1(C'R_3 \, \langle 4 \rangle \, \tfrac{3}{4}R'_3 \, C'P_6)^{2*}$

REMARKS :—N is antecedent to PP, while N or PP is antecedent to R as a general rule, but the N of the 2nd co-ordinate precedes the PP of the 1st co-ordinate, thus showing regularity in the position of the antecedent in the one example by inversion, and in the other example of transposition, R has become antecedent in position to PP, as a rare instance, breaking this general rule.

LECTURE XI.

STUDENTS AND GENTLEMEN,

I have shown to you before, that pronominal adjectives under certain circumstances in the Mono-simple do neither take any punctuation nor conjunction in their increased number of repetitions of 2 or 3. I have shown to you also that certain punctuation and simple conjunction become necessary in the increased numbers of two or more than two of any term in the Mono-simple or in its *joiners*. You have seen also in the latter that some of these simple conjunctions though not all, are copulative, alternative, adversative, adversative-negative, negative or co-ordinate-adversative, and pure co-ordinate; and that all these unite parts of speech and phrases only. I have come presently to show to you the same and other punctuations, the same conjunctions; or both punctuations and conjunctions in combination of two or more increased sentences of the Mono-simple P, of the Mono-simple S or Co-ordinates; or Subordinates of the Co-ordinate subordinates; and of each co-ordinate in the Di-simple Ps respectively,—which go to form as it were compounds of each of them with the same conjunctions, now named as **compound conjunctions** or *conjunctions of the 6th class*. Unlike the subordinate and co-ordinate-subordinate conjunctions, they bear no *heading* relation whatever to the simple sentences that follow them or between whom they are placed, and are represented in the formulae by large isolated *plus*. Let these Compounds of Ps, Subordinates, and Co-ordinates each to each be called "un-mixed" or *similar Compounds*, and let me go now to demonstrate them.

A.—SYMMETRICAL COMPOUNDS.

I.—COMPOUND OF MONO-SIMPLE Ps.

1.—Punctuative by , ; : —

1. $\{$Only $\mid$ one of these $\mid$ need $\mid$ occupy $\mid$ our attention,$\}\{$it
   $\quad\quad\;\;\;\;_1\quad\;\;\;\;_2\quad\quad\;_4\quad\;\;\;\;_5\quad\quad\quad\quad\quad\quad\quad\;\;_1$
   is $\mid$ the salamandar.$\}$
   $_2\quad\quad\;\;_3$

$$\{*_1\mid\underset{1}{N}_3\mid\underset{2}{V}*\mid\underset{4}{IV}\mid {}_1{}^3\underset{5}{N}\}\{\mid\underset{1}{N}\mid\underset{2}{V}\mid {}_1{}^1\underset{3}{N}\mid\}$$
$$=P_5\, , \, P_3$$

2. $\{$At one hour of the day $\mid$ it $\mid$ reaches to the upper part of
   $\quad\quad\quad\quad\quad\quad\quad\quad\quad\quad\quad\quad\;_1\quad\;_2$
   the sloping beach ;$\}$ $\{*$ some six hours afterwards $\mid$ it $\mid$ has
   $\quad\quad\quad\quad\quad\quad\quad\quad\quad\quad\quad\quad\quad\quad\quad\quad\quad\quad\quad\quad\;_1$
   retired $*$ to the lower part.$\}$
   $\;\;\;\;_2$

$$\{\mid *_{33}\mid\underset{1}{N}\mid\underset{2}{V}*_{33}\}\{*_{31}\mid\underset{1}{N}\mid A\underset{2}{V}*_3\mid\}$$
$$=P_2\, ; \, P_2$$

3. $\{$ Do not flatter $*\mid$ yourself $\mid *$ with the hope of perfect
   $\quad\quad\quad\quad\quad\;\;_2\quad\quad\quad\;\;_3$
   happiness :$\}\{$there is $*\mid$ no such thing $\mid *$ in the world. $\}$
   $\quad\quad\quad\quad\quad\quad\;\;_2$

$$\{\mid A_1\mid\underset{1}{(N)}\mid\underset{2}{V}\mid\underset{3}{N}\mid {}_{33}\mid\}\{\mid {}_1\underset{1}{V}\mid {}_2{}_1{}^2\underset{2}{N}\mid {}_3\mid\}$$
$$=P_3 : P_2$$

4. $\{\underset{1}{I}\mid$ do not $\underset{2}{\text{fear}}\mid\underset{3}{\text{them}}\},-\{\underset{1}{\text{they}}\mid$ cannot $\underset{2}{\text{hurt}}\mid\underset{3}{\text{me.}}\}$

$$\{\underset{1}{N}\mid A_1\underset{2}{V}\mid\underset{3}{N}\},-\{\underset{1}{N}\mid A_1\underset{2}{V}\mid\underset{3}{N}\}$$
$$=P_3\,,-P_3$$

5. { Alas ! | she | bleeds } — { her mouth | is torn sadly. }
         1   2   1   2

$$\langle ! \rangle \{ \underset{1}{N} \mid \underset{2}{V} \} - \{ \mathbf{1^3} \underset{1}{N} \mid A \underset{2}{V} \mathbf{1} \}$$

$$= \langle ! \rangle P_2 - P_2$$

6. { No impure thought | entered | their imaginations } — { her
           1   2   3
   bosom | heaved against his chest } — { her beautiful cheek,
     1   2   1
   now tinged with a slight colour, | rested upon his. }
                                              2

$$\{ 2\ 2\ \underset{1}{N} \mid \underset{2}{V} \mid \mathbf{1^3} \underset{3}{N} \mid \}$$

$$- \{ \mathbf{1^3} \underset{1}{N} \mid \underset{2}{V}\ 3 \mid \}$$

$$- \{ \mathbf{1^3}\ 2\ \underset{1}{N}\ 1\ 4\ 3 \mid \underset{2}{V}\ 3 \mid \}$$

$$= P_3 - P_2 - P_2$$

2.—CONJUNCTIONAL.

1. { Stand-up before the light here } *and* { let | me | see | you
           2   +   2   3   4   5
   breathe.}
      6

$$\{ \underset{2}{V} \mid \underset{1}{(N)} \mid 3\ 1 \} + \{ \underset{2}{V} \mid \underset{1}{(N)} \mid \underset{3}{N} \mid \underset{4}{IV} \mid \underset{5}{N} \mid \underset{6}{IV} \}$$

$$= P_2 + P_6$$

2. { Serve | God } *and* { be cheerful.}
        2   3   +   2

$$\{ \underset{2}{V} \mid \underset{1}{(N)} \mid \underset{3}{N} \mid \} + \{ \underset{2}{V} \mid \underset{1}{(N)} \mid 2 \}$$

$$= P_3 + P_2$$

3. { At such times, | the flies | enter | the passage } *and*
                         1   2   3   +
   { maggots in the nose | is | the result.}
            1   2   3

$$\{ 3 \mid \mathbf{1^1} \underset{1}{N} \mid \underset{2}{V} \mid \mathbf{1^1} \underset{3}{N} \} + \{ \underset{1}{N}\ 3 \mid \underset{2}{V} \mid \mathbf{1^1} \underset{3}{N} \}$$

$$= P_3 + P_3$$

3.—Both Punctuative and Conjunctional.

1. $\{$ I | took * | your Arithmetic | * away ten minutes ago, $\}$ *and*
   $\quad$ 1 $\quad$ 2 $\qquad$ 3 $\hspace{11em}$ +

   $\{$ you | knew * | nothing | * about it.$\}$
   $\quad$ 1 $\qquad$ 2 $\qquad$ 3

   $\{\,|\,\underset{1}{N}\,|\,\underset{2}{V}\,|\,1^3\underset{3}{N}\,|\,1\,3\,|\,\}+\{\,|\,\underset{1}{N}\,|\,\underset{2}{V}\,|\,\underset{1\delta}{N}\,3\,|\,\}$

   $= P_3, + P_3$

2. $\{$ The elephant | bore * | this | * for some time well enough ,$\}$
   $\hspace{5em}$ 1 $\qquad$ 2 $\qquad$ 3

   but $\{$ at last * | it | got * angry.$\}$ (*But* is Adversative.)
   $+\hspace{6em}$ 1 $\quad$ 2

   $\{\,|\,1^1\underset{1}{N}\,|\,\underset{2}{V}\,|\,\underset{3}{N}\,|\,3\,1\,2\,|\,\}+\{\,|\,1*\,|\,\underset{1}{N}\,|\,\underset{2}{V}*2\,\}$

   $= P_3, + P_2$

3. $\{$ There was | *no* wind, $\}$ *but* $\{$ snow | had begun | to fall
   $\hspace{5em}$ 2 $\qquad$ 1 $\hspace{3em}$ + $\quad$ 1 $\hspace{4em}$ 2 $\hspace{3em}$ 4

   softly all round. $\}$ (*But* is Negative-adversative.)

   $\{\,|\,1\,\underset{2}{V}\,|\,2\,\underset{1}{N},\,\}+\{\,\underset{1}{N}\,|\,\underset{2}{AV}\,|\,\underset{4}{IV}\,1\,3\,\}$

   $= P_2, + P_4$

4. $\{$ They | shout, $\}$ *but* $\{$ there is | *no* answer.$\}$
   $\quad$ 2 $\hspace{3em}$ 2 $\quad$ + $\hspace{4em}$ 2 $\qquad$ 1

   (*But* is Adversative-negative.)

   $\{\,|\,\underset{1}{N}\,|\,\underset{2}{V}\,|\,\}+\{\,|\,1\,\underset{2}{V}\,|\,2\,\underset{1}{N}\,|\,\}=P_2, + P_2$

5. $\{$ * There | he | will stand * | flapping | his ears | to drive
   $\hspace{5em}$ 1 $\qquad$ 2 $\hspace{5em}$ 4 $\hspace{4em}$ 5 $\hspace{4em}$ 6

   away | the flies ;$\}$ *or* $\{$ he | will pull-down | a bough from
   $\hspace{3em}$ 7 $\hspace{4em}$ + $\hspace{6em}$ 2 $\hspace{6em}$ 3

   a tree | to fan | himself.$\}$ (*Or* is Alternative.)
   $\hspace{2em}$ 4 $\hspace{3em}$ 5

   $\{\,|\,1\,|\,\underset{1}{N}\,|\,\underset{2}{AV}\,|\,\underset{4}{PV}\,|\,1^3\underset{5}{N}\,|\,\underset{6}{IV}\,1\,|\,1^1\underset{7}{N}\,|\,\}$

   $+\{\,|\,\underset{1}{N}\,|\,\underset{2}{AV}\,|\,1^1\,\underset{3}{N}\,3\,|\,\underset{4}{IV}\,|\,\underset{5}{N}\,|\,\} = P_7; + P_5$

LECTURE XI.

6. {Here are | 4 facts about the sea :—} { 1st, | it | has | a restless surface disturbed by ripples and waves : } { 2nd, it | is constantly heaving with the ebb and flow of the tide : } {3rd, its surface-waters | drift with the wind : } and {4th, it | possesses | deep and wide currents.}

$$\{\,|\,_1\underset{2}{V}\,|\,_2\underset{1}{N}\,_3\,|\,\}\{\,_1\,|\,\underset{1}{N}\,|\,\underset{2}{V}\,|\,_{1^1}\,_2\underset{3}{N}\,pv\,_3\,|\,\}$$

$$\{\,_1\,|\,\underset{1}{N}\,|\,A\,_1\underset{2}{V}\,_3\,_3\,|\,\}\{\,_1\,|\,_{1^3}\underset{1}{N}\,|\,\underset{2}{V}\,_3\,|\,\}$$

$$+\{\,_1\,|\,\underset{1}{N}\,|\,\underset{2}{V}\,|\,_2+_2\underset{3}{N}\,|\,\}$$

$$=P_2:\!—$$

$$\overbrace{P_3:P_2:P_2:P_3}$$

This Compound of the detail Ps is in *apposition* with the above P_2.

7. {Bodies | do *not* fall on account of the laws of gravitation ;} *nor* {does | gravitation | explain | their fall.}

(*Nor*=Negative-copulative.)

$$\{\,|\,\underset{1}{N}\,|\,A\,_1\underset{2}{V}\,_3\,_3\,|\,\}+\{\,|\,A\,|\,\underset{1}{N}\,|\,\underset{2}{V}\,|\,_{1^3}\underset{3}{N}\,|\,\}$$

$$=P_2\,;\,+P_3$$

8. { I | have selected ; } *while* {you | are engaged with Pearson and Arnold.} (*While*=Adversative.)

$$\{\,\underset{1}{N}\,|\,\underset{2}{AV}\,\}\,;\,+\{\,\underset{1}{N}\,|\,\underset{2}{AV}\,_3\,(n+n)\,\}$$

$$=P_2\,;\,+P_2$$

9. { The animal or vegetable substances- devoured | are taken }
   $\quad\quad\quad\quad\quad\quad\quad\quad\quad\quad\quad\quad\quad\quad\quad\quad_1\quad\quad\quad\quad\quad\quad\quad\quad_2$
into the animal's stomach ;} { they | are there digested or
$\quad\quad\quad\quad\quad\quad\quad\quad\quad\quad\quad\quad_1\quad\quad\quad\quad\quad\quad\quad\quad\quad_2$
dissolved ;} *and* {thus they | are fitted | to be distributed to
$\quad\quad_2\quad\quad\quad\quad +\quad\quad\quad\quad\quad_1\quad\quad\quad\quad_2\quad\quad\quad\quad\quad\quad\quad_4$
all parts of the fowl's own body, and applied to its main-
$\quad\quad\quad\quad\quad\quad\quad\quad\quad\quad\quad\quad\quad\quad\quad\quad\quad\quad\quad_4$
tenance and growth.}

$$\{ 1^1\ 2 + 2\ \underset{1}{N}\ 4\ |\ \underset{2}{AV}\ 3 \};\ \{\ \underset{1}{N}\ |\ A\ 1\ \underset{2}{V} + \underset{2}{V}\ \};$$

$$+ \{\ 1\ |\ \underset{1}{N}\ |\ \underset{2}{AV}\ |\ \underset{4}{IV}\ 3\ 3\ |\ +\underset{4}{IV}\ 3\ \}$$

$$= P_2\ ;\ P_2\ ; + P_4$$

10. {The cold glass- brought into the warm room | has first | a
    $\quad\quad\quad\quad\quad_1\quad\quad\quad\quad\quad\quad\quad\quad\quad\quad\quad\quad\quad\quad\quad_2$
fine film of mist- formed upon it, } *and-then-by-degrees*
$\quad\quad\quad\quad_3\quad\quad\quad\quad\quad\quad\quad\quad\quad\quad\quad\quad\quad\quad\quad\quad\quad\quad +$
{ the clear drops of water | come.}
$\quad\quad\quad\quad\quad\quad\quad_1\quad\quad\quad\quad\quad\quad\quad_2$

$$\{\ |\ 1^1\ 2\ \underset{1}{N}\ pv\ 3\ |\ \underset{2}{V}\ 1\ |\ 1^1\ 2\ \underset{5}{N}\ 3\ pv\ 3\ \}$$

$$+ |\ \{\ |\ 1^1\ 2\ \underset{1}{N}\ 3\ |\ \underset{2}{V}\ |\ \}$$

$$= P_3 + P_2$$

4.—By Increased Copulatives.

1. { * In the early morning | the sky | was bright*, } *then* {the
   $\quad\quad\quad\quad\quad\quad\quad\quad\quad\quad\quad\quad\quad\quad_1\quad\quad\quad_2\quad\quad\quad\quad\quad\quad +$
clouds | appeared,} *and after that* { | came | the rain.}
$\quad_1\quad\quad\quad_2\quad\quad\quad\quad\quad +\quad\quad\quad\quad\quad\quad_2\quad\quad\quad_1$

$$\{\ |\ 3\ |\ 1^1\ \underset{1}{N}\ |\ \underset{2}{V}\ 2\ |\ \} + \{\ |\ 1^1\ \underset{1}{N}\ |\ \underset{2}{V}\ |\ \} + \{\ |\ \underset{2}{V}\ |\ 1^1\ \underset{1}{N}\ |\ \}$$

$$= P_2, + P_2 + P_2$$

2. { It | is very easy | to split* | the craystals |* lengthwise ;}
   $_1$ $_2$ $_4$ $_5$

   while {| much more force | is needed | to cut* | them |*
   $+$ $_1$ $_2$ $_4$ $_5$

   crosswise} *and then* { they | do not split, } but break.}
   $+$ $_1$ $_2$

   { $\underset{1}{N}$ | $\underset{2}{V}$ 1 2 | $\underset{4}{IV}$ | $1^1 \underset{5}{N}$ | 1 } + { 1 2 $\underset{1}{N}$ | $\underset{2}{AV}$ | $\underset{4}{IV}$ | $\underset{5}{N}$ | 1 }

   $+$ { $\underset{1}{N}$ | A 1 $\underset{2}{V}$ + $\underset{2}{V}$ }

   $= P_5 + P_5 + P_2$

5.—By Copulative and Adversative or *vice versa*.

1. { $\underset{1}{I}$ | thank * | $\underset{3}{you}$ | * all the same ; } *but* { $\underset{1}{I}$ | love | tran-
   $_2$ $+$ $_2$

   quillity}—*and* { $\underset{1}{I}$ | find * | $\underset{2}{it}$ | * in the hotel. }
   $_3$ $+$ $_3$

   { $\underset{1}{N}$ | $\underset{2}{V}$ * | $\underset{3}{N}$ | * 1 } ; + { $\underset{1}{N}$ | $\underset{2}{V}$ | $\underset{3}{N}$ } + { $\underset{1}{N}$ | $\underset{2}{V}$ * | $\underset{3}{N}$ | * 3 }

   $= P_3 ; + P_3 -+ P_3$

2. { *Not* a mine | is opened,} *nor* { a heap of shale | thrown-
   $_1$ $_2$ $+$

   out,} | *but* {there occur | fragments of its stem- marked ex-
   $+$ $_2$ $_1$

   ternally with small rounded impressions and in-the-centre
   slight tubercles with a quincuncial arrangement.}

   (*Nor- but*=Negative-copulative and adversative.)

   { 1 | $1^1 \underset{1}{N}$ | $\underset{2}{AV}$ | }, + { | $1^1 \underset{1}{N}$ 3 | (A) $\underset{2}{V}$ | }

   + { | 1 $\underset{2}{V}$ | $\underset{1}{N}$ 3 pv 1 3 + 3 3 3 | }

   $= P_2 + P_2 + P_2$

6.—By Expression Ps.

1. {Let (N) | the Cossacks | go back,} or { $\underset{1}{I}$ | shall fire.}
   $_2$ $_1$ $_3$ $_4$ $+$ $_2$

   $= P_4 + P_2$

2. {Buy-off $|$ the fight,} and {we $|$ will ratify $|$ the peace with gold.}
$\quad_2\qquad\quad\ _3\qquad\ _+\quad _1\qquad\quad\ _2\qquad\qquad\ _3$

$$=P_3+P_2$$

3. { Try $|$ the same experiment with a tea-kettle instead- of a saucepan, } but { only put $|$ a little water in the tea-kettle,} and { shut $|$ the lid $|$ * well down.}
$\ _2\qquad\ _3\qquad\qquad\qquad _+\qquad\qquad _2\qquad\qquad\ _3\quad _+\quad\ _2\qquad _3$

$$\{\underset{2}{V}\mid\underset{1}{(N)}\mid 1^1\ _2\underset{3}{N}\mid 3\ 3\} + \{\ _1\mid\underset{2}{V}\mid\underset{1}{(N)}\mid 1^1\ _2\underset{3}{N}\ _3\mid\ \}$$
$$+\{\underset{2}{V}\mid\underset{1}{(N)}\mid 1^1\underset{3}{N}\mid 1\ 1\}=P_3+P_3+P_3$$

II.—COMPOUND OF MONO-SIMPLE SUBORDINATES.

1.—OF C* SUBORDINATES.

1. {We $|$ say of all these things, or objects,} $(that$ $|$ they $|$ are $|$
$\ _1\quad\ _2\qquad\qquad\qquad\qquad\qquad\qquad\qquad\qquad\ _1\qquad\ _2$
the causes of the sensations in question,)* and $(that$ $|$ the
$\qquad\qquad\ _3\qquad\qquad\qquad\qquad\qquad\ _+$
sensations $|$ are $|$ the effects of these causes.)*
$\ _1\qquad\qquad\ _2\qquad\ _3$

$$\{\underset{1}{N}\mid\underset{2}{V}\ 3\}\ (C\mid\underset{1}{N}\mid\underset{2}{V}\mid 1^1\underset{3}{N}\ 3\ 3)^* + (C\mid 1^1\underset{1}{N}\mid\underset{2}{V}\mid 1^1\underset{3}{N}\ 3)$$
$$=P_2\ \overbrace{2C^*_3+2C^*_3}$$

2.—OF R* SUBORDINATES.

1. $(All\text{-}the\text{-}time\text{-}that\mid$ we $|$ are awake) { we $|$ are learning
$\qquad\qquad\qquad\qquad\qquad _1\qquad\ _2\qquad\qquad\quad _1\qquad\ _2$
by means of our senses $|$ something about the world } $(in$
$\qquad\qquad\qquad\qquad\qquad\qquad _3$
$which$ we $|$ live)* and $(of\ which$ $|$ we $|$ form $|$ a part.)*
$\qquad _1\quad _2\quad\ _+\qquad\qquad\qquad\ _1\qquad _2\qquad\ _3$

$$(C\mid\underset{1}{N}\mid\underset{2}{V}\ 2\mid)^*\{\mid\underset{1}{N}\mid\underset{2}{AV}\ 3\ 3\mid\underset{3}{N}\ 3\mid\}$$
$$(3\ r\mid\underset{1}{N}\mid\underset{2}{V})^*+(3\ r\mid\underset{1}{N}\mid\underset{2}{V}\mid 1^1\underset{3}{N})$$
$$=2\ C^*_2,\ P_3,\ \tfrac{2}{3}\ \overbrace{R^*_2+\tfrac{2}{3}\ R^*_3}$$

3.—OF INCREASED C· OR R· SUBORDINATES.

1. { It | is quite fair and proper } (that | one person | should
     $_1$ $_2$ $_1$
give | credit)· and (another | contract | debt)· (when | it | is
$_2$ $_3$ $_+$ $_1$ $_2$ $_3$ $_1$ $_2$
for their mutual convenience | to do so)$^{2·}$ and (when there
                              $_4$ $_+$
is | little reason | to fear)$^{2·}$ (that | the debtor | will be able |
$_2$ $_1$ $_4$ $_1$ $_-$
to make | payment at the proper time.)$^{3·}$
$_4$ $_5$

$$\{ \underset{1}{N} \mid \underset{2}{V} \; 1\, 2 + 2 \} \overbrace{(C \mid 2\underset{1}{N} \mid A\underset{2}{V} \mid \underset{3}{N})^{·} + (\underset{1}{N} \mid \underset{2}{V} \mid \underset{3}{N})^{·}}$$

$$\overbrace{(C \mid \underset{1}{N} \mid \underset{2}{V} \; 3 \mid IV \; 1)^{2·} + (C \mid 1\underset{2}{V} \mid 2\underset{1}{N} \mid IV)^{2·}}_{4}$$

$$(C \mid 1^1 \underset{1}{N} \mid A\underset{2}{V} \; 1 \mid \underset{4}{IV} \mid \underset{5}{N} \mid 3)^{3·}$$

$$= P_2 \; \overbrace{2C·_3 + 2C·_3} \; \overbrace{2C^{2·}_4 + 2C^{2·}_4} \; 4C^{3·}_5$$

2. { It | is | the *sea*} (*that* | lays | the iron track,)· (*that* | builds |
     $_1$ $_2$ $_3$ $_1$ $_2$ $_3$ $_1$ $_2$
the iron horse,)· (*that* | fills * | his nostrils | * with fiery
$_3$ $_1$ $_2$ $_3$ $_-$
breath,) *and* (*that* | sends | his tireless hoofs | thundering
         $_+$ $_1$ $_2$ $_3$ $_4$
across the continents.)·

$$\{ \underset{1}{N} \mid \underset{2}{V} \mid 1^1 \underset{3}{N} \mid \} (\underset{1}{R} \mid \underset{2}{V} \mid 1^1 \; 2 \underset{3}{N})^{·}$$

$$(\underset{1}{R} \mid \underset{2}{V} \mid 1^1 \; 2 \underset{3}{N})^{·} \; (\underset{1}{R} \mid \underset{2}{V} \mid 1^3 \; \underset{3}{N} \; 3)^{·}$$

$$+ (\underset{1}{R} \mid \underset{2}{V} \mid 1^3 \; 2 \underset{3}{N} \; pv \; 3 \;)^{·}$$

$$= P_3 \; \overbrace{3R·_3, \; 3R·_3, \; 3R·_3,} + 3R·_3$$

202   STYLOGRAPHY OF ENGLISH LANGUAGE.

4.—Of Co-ordinate Subordinates either by increased Subordinates or increased joiner Co-ordinates.

1. { He | was *so pious,*} (that | he | under-took | nothing
    $_1$ $_2$ $_{c'}$ $_{c''}$ $_1$ $_2$ $_3$

without asking | counsel of the gods;)* *so just* } (that
                $_4$ $_5$ $_{c'}$

he | never did | the smallest injury to any one but ren-
$_1$ $_2$ $_3$ $+$ $_2$
dered | essential services to many;)* *so temperate* } (that
                      $_3$ $_{c'}$

he | never preferred | pleasure to virtue;)* *and so wise*}
$_1$ $_2$ $_3$ $+$ $_{c'}$

(that | he | was able even in the most difficult cases with-
         $_1$ $_2$

out advice | to judge (what)* | was expedient and right.)²*
                    $_4$ $_5$ $_1$ $_2$

{N | V c' 2} (C" | N | V | N | PV | N 3)*;
 $_{.1}$ $_2$ $_1$ $_2$ $_3$ $_4$ $_5$

{...c' 2} (C"| N | $_1$ V | 1^1 $_2$ N 3 | + | V | 2 N 3)*;
                      $_1$ $_2$ $_3$ $_2$ $_3$

{...c' 2} (C" | N | $_1$ V | N 3 |)*;
                        $_1$ $_2$ $_3$

{... + c' 2} (C" | N | V 2 1 3 3 | IV | N)* (R | V 2+2)²*
                          $_1$ $_2$ $_4$ $_5$ $_1$ $_2$

= P_2 $c'C''^*_5$; $c'C''^*_3$; $c'C''^*_3$; + $c'C''^*_5$ R^{2*}_2

2. { It | both boils and freezes at a much lower temperature
   $_1$ $_2$ $_4$ $_2$ $_{c'}$

(than | water | does,)* and at a higher temperature} (than
 $_{c''}$ $_1$ $_2$ $+$ $_{c'}$ $_{c''}$

alcohol | does.)
$_1$

{ N | $_1$ V + V 3 c'} (C* | N | A(V + V))*
  $_1$ $_2$ $_2$ $_1$ $_2$ $_2$

+ 3 c' } (C* | N | A(V+V))*
                      $_1$ $_2$

= P_2 c' C'''^*_2

+c' C'^*_2

3. { The current of the other portion of our story | however
         １
has so swollen upon us,} { the condition of the characters
   ２ c′   １
| has gathered such | a depth and urgency,} and { the de-
   ２   c′   ３   +   ３   +
nouncement | becomes so ominous of grave issues} (any
   １   ２   c′
one of which | may one day or another come nearly home
   １   R   ２
to the experience of almost every person in this age of
commingled, endlessly ramified and absorbing interests)
(that | it | is impossible | to grasp | the case of each of
  c″   １   ２   ４   ５
the actors at the same moment or to keep | the whole with
                                +   ４   ５   -
an adequate care constantly before the reader.)•

$$\{1^1 \underset{1}{N} \ 3 \ 3 \ | \ 1 \ A \ c' \ \underset{2}{V} \ 3 \ | \ \},$$

$$\{ 1^1 \underset{1}{N} \ 3 \ | \ A \ \underset{2}{V} \ | \ c' \ 1^1 \underset{3}{N} + \underset{3}{N} \}$$

$$+\{ 1^1 \underset{1}{N} \ | \ \underset{2}{V} \ c' \ 2 \ 3 \ \} (1^2 \underset{1}{N} \ 3 \ r \ | \ A \ 3+3 \ \underset{2}{V} \ 1 \ 1 \ 3\text{-}3\text{-}3\text{-}3)\bullet$$

$$(C' \ | \ \underset{1}{N} \ | \ \underset{2}{V} \ 2 \ | \ \underset{4}{IV} \ | \ 1^1 \underset{5}{N} \ 3\text{-}33 \ |$$

$$+ \underset{4}{IV} \ | \ 1^1 \underset{5}{N} \ 3 \ 1 \ 3)\bullet$$

$$\left. \begin{matrix} =P_2 \ c' \\ , P_3 \ c' \\ +P_2 \ c' \end{matrix} \right\} \tfrac{2}{3} \ R\cdot_2 \ C''\cdot_5$$

5.—Of Expression Subordinates.

1. { Chemistry | tells | us exactly } (how | bodies | combine,)•
       １   ２   ３   １   ２
(what | comes of their combination,)• and (how compounds|
   １   ２   +   １
| may be separated into their constituents.)•
   ２

$$\{\underset{1}{N} \ | \ \underset{2}{V} \ | \ \underset{3}{N} \ | \ 1 \} (C \ | \ \underset{1}{N} \ | \ \underset{2}{V})\bullet \ (\underset{1}{R} \ | \ \underset{2}{V} \ 3)\bullet + (C \ | \ \underset{1}{N} \ | \ AAV_3)\bullet$$

$$=P_3 \ 2C\cdot_2, \ 2R\cdot_2, + 2C\cdot_2$$

2. {Miss Jayne | related} (*how* Emily | arrived at the hotel with-
$\quad\;\;$ 1 $\quad\quad$ 2 $\qquad\quad\;\;$ 1 $\qquad\qquad\quad$ 2
out any kind of luggage,) (*how* | she| was so very wretched,)
$\qquad\qquad\qquad\qquad\qquad\qquad\quad\;\;$ 1 $\quad$ 2
and (*how* Mrs Pembroke | came and took | her into the
$+\qquad\quad$ 1 $\qquad\qquad$ 2 $\qquad\quad$ 2 $\qquad\;\,$ ⌊3
country.)

$$\{\underset{1}{N}\mid\underset{2}{V}\}(C\mid\underset{1}{N}\mid\underset{2}{V}\;3\;3\text{-}3),^*$$

$$(\,C\mid\underset{1}{N}\mid\underset{2}{V}\;1\;1\;2\,)^{\prime}\!+\!(\,C\mid\underset{1}{N}\mid\underset{2}{V\!+\!V\!*}\mid\underset{3}{N}\mid*3\,)$$

$$=P_2\;2\;\overbrace{C^{\prime}_2\,,\,2\;C^{\prime}_2+2\;C^{\prime}_3}$$

III.—COMPOUND IN BOTH Ps AND SUBORDINATES.

1. (*Whether* Simplizio | had obeyed | some private signal from
$\qquad\qquad\qquad$ 1 $\qquad\qquad$ 2 $\qquad\qquad\qquad\quad$ 3
Assunta,) *or* (*whether* his own delicacy | had prompted | him
$\quad\;\;+\qquad\qquad\qquad\qquad\qquad\;\;$ 1 $\qquad\qquad$ 2 $\qquad\;\,$ 3
| to disappear,) {he | was now again in the stable,} and {the
$\;\;$ 4 $\qquad\qquad\;\;\;$ 1 $\quad\;\;$ 2 $\qquad\qquad\qquad\qquad\qquad\qquad\;\;+$
manger | was replenished with hay.}
$\;\;\;$ 1 $\qquad\quad$ 2

$$(\,C\mid\underset{1}{N}\mid\underset{2}{AV}\mid 2\;2\;\underset{3}{N}\;3\,)$$

$$+(C\mid 1^3\;2\;\underset{1}{N}\mid\underset{2}{AV}\mid\underset{3}{N}\mid\underset{4}{IV})^{\prime}\{\underset{1}{N}\mid\underset{2}{V}\;1\;1\;3\,\}+\{1^1\;\underset{1}{N}\mid\underset{2}{AV}\;3\}$$

$$=\overbrace{C^{\prime}_3+C^{\prime}_4}\,,\;\overbrace{P_2+P_2}$$

IV.—COMPOUND OF MONO-COMPLEXES.

1.—BY P AND R' SUBORDINATE.

1. { She | had at any rate ministered to the relief of a family }
$\quad\;\;$ 1 $\qquad\qquad\qquad\qquad\qquad$ 2
(*which*, but for her, | appeared | to have been on the brink
$\quad\;\;$ 1 $\qquad\qquad\qquad$ 2 $\qquad\quad$ 4
of a shocking death;)* *and* { she | was now seated along
$\qquad\qquad\qquad\qquad\quad\;\;+\quad\;\;$ 1 $\qquad\qquad\quad$ 2
with them within the walls of a ruined tower} (*whose* cheer-
$\qquad\qquad\qquad\qquad\qquad\qquad\qquad\qquad\qquad\qquad\;\,$ r

less walls and aspect | might have entitled | her | to be
 1   +   1   2   3   4

taken for a captured princess in the hands of the gipsy or bandit race.)*

$$\{ \underset{1}{N} \mid A \; 3 \; \underset{2}{V} \; 3 \; 3 \} \; (\underset{1}{R} (1 \; 3) \mid \underset{2}{V} \mid \underset{4}{IV} \; 3 \; 3)^* \; ; \; + \{ \underset{1}{N} \mid A \; 1 \; \underset{2}{V} \; 1 \; 3 \; 2 \; 3 \}$$

$$(1^5 \; (r) \; 2 \underset{1}{N} + \underset{1}{N} \mid A \; A \; \underset{:2}{V} \mid \underset{3}{N} \mid A \; \underset{4}{IV} \; 3 \; 3 \; 3)^*$$

$$= \overbrace{P_2 \; \tfrac{2}{3} R^{\centerdot}_4} \; ; \; + \overbrace{P_2 \; \tfrac{2}{3} R^{\centerdot}_4}$$

2.—BY P AND C* SUBORDINATE.

1. (*When* | the sky | is clear overhead*) { rain | hardly ever
            1   2   1

falls,} *but* (*when* | it | becomes- overcast)* { rain | often
 2   +   c   1   2   1

appears.}
  2

$$(C \mid 1^1 \underset{1}{N} \mid \underset{2}{V} \; 2 \; 1 \mid)^* \{ \mid \underset{1}{N} \mid 1 \; 1 \; \underset{2}{V} \mid \}$$

$$+ (C \mid \underset{1}{N} \mid \underset{2}{V} \; 4 \;)^* \{ \mid \underset{1}{N} \mid 1 \; \underset{3}{V} \mid \}$$

$$= \overbrace{2 \; C^{\centerdot}_2 \; P_2} + \overbrace{2 \; C^{\centerdot}_2 \; P_2}$$

2. (*When* we | are catching | the sun's light,)* { we | have |
          1   2   3   1   2

Day ; } (*when* | we | are on the dark side,)* { we | have |
 2   1   2   1   2

Night.}
  3

$$(C \mid \underset{1}{N} \mid \underset{2}{AV} \mid 1^1 1^5 \underset{3}{N})^* \{ \mid \underset{1}{N} \mid \underset{2}{V} \mid \underset{3}{N} \mid \} \; (C \mid \underset{1}{N} \mid \underset{2}{V} \; 3) ;$$

$$\{ \mid \underset{1}{N} \mid \underset{2}{V} \mid \underset{3}{N} \mid . \}$$

$$\overbrace{2 \; C^{\centerdot}_3 \; P_3} \; ; \; \overbrace{2 \; C^{\centerdot}_2 \; P_2}$$

3.—By P and co-ordinate subordination.

1. { The air in the room | is much *warmer* } (*than* | that out
    1   2   c'   1
side,) and { there is mixed with it | *nearly as much* water,
    +   2   c'   1
derived from the breath and the evaporation of moist
surfaces,} (*as* | can maintain* | itself |* in the gaseous state
             1   2   3
at the temperature.)*

$$\{ \mid 1^1 \text{ N } 3 \mid V \text{ } 1 \text{ } c' \} (C'' \mid N \mid 1 (V))^*$$

$$+ \{ 1 \text{ AV } 3 \mid c' \text{ N } 4 \text{ } 3+3-3 \} (R'' \mid AV^* \mid N \mid^* 3 \text{ } 3)^*$$

$$= P_2 \text{ } c'C'''_2 + P_2 \text{ } c'R'''_3$$

4.—By P and both R' and C' subordinates.

1. {A law of man | tells (*what*) we | may expect) (society |will
    1   2   3 3   1   2   1
do under certain circumstances ;) *and* { a law of nature |
   2   +   1
tells | us (*what* } we | may expect) (natural objects | will
   2   3   3   1   2   1
do under certain circumstances.)
   2

$$\{ 1^1 \text{ N } 3 \mid V \mid N \}(R \mid N \mid AV)^* ((C) \mid N \mid AV 3)^{2*} ;$$

$$+ \{ 1^1 \text{ N } 3 \mid V \mid N \text{ N} \}(R \mid N \mid AV)^* ((C) \mid 2 \text{ N} \mid A \text{ V } 3)^{2*}$$

$$= P_3 \text{ 2 } R'_3 \text{ 2 } C^{2\prime}_2 ; + P_3 \text{ 3 } R'_2 \text{ 2 } C^{2\prime}_2$$

5.—By P and both R' and Co-ordinate Subordinates.

1. {That (which | is lighter)* (than | water)^{2*} floats,} and {that
       1   1   2   c'   c'   1   2   +   1
(which | is heavier bulk-for-bulk)* sinks.}
    1   2   2

LECTURE XI.

$$\{N_1 (R_1 | V_2 c')\cdot (C'' | N_1 | (V)_2)^{2\cdot} V_2\}$$
$$+ \{N_1 ((R)_1 V_2 c')\cdot (C'' | N_1 | (V)_2)^{2\cdot} V_2\}$$
$$= \overbrace{P_2 1 R\cdot_2 c' C^{\prime 2\cdot}{}_2} + \overbrace{P_2 1 R\cdot_2 c' (C^{\prime 2\cdot}{}_2)}$$

Compound of Complex by $R\cdot$ and Co-ordinate sub-subordinate, the $C^{\prime 2\cdot}{}_2$ being understood in the 2nd Complex.

V.—COMPOUND OF DI-SIMPLE Ps.

1.—PUNCTUATIVE AND CONJUNCTIONAL.

1. [*Where* | females | are honored] [*there* | the dieties | are
     c' 1   2 c'' 1
pleased ;] *but* [*where* | they | are dishonored] [*there* | all
         2   c' 1   2 c''
religious acts | become fruitless].
       1   2

$$[C' | N_1 | AV_2] [C'' | 1^1 N_1 | AV_2]$$
$$+ [C' | N_1 | AV_2] [C'' | 1^2 {}_2 N_1 | V_2]$$
$$= \overbrace{C'P_2 \; C''P_2} + \overbrace{C'P_2 \; C''P_2}$$

2.—COMPOUND IN EITHER CO-ORDINATES OF DI-SIMPLE.

1. [If the student | is | out of order,] [if his digestion | is
    c' 1   2 c' 1   2
wrong,][if his feelings | are agitated,] *or* [(c) he | is benum-
 c'' 1   2   1   2
bed by want of exercise] [*then of course* | he | must betake*|
                            c''' 1   2
himself | * to the best means | of setting * | himself | *
   3   4   5
to right.)

$$[C' | 1^1 N_1 | V_2 | 1 {}_3] [C' | 1^1 N_1 | V_2] [C' | 1^3 N_1 | AV_2]$$
$$+ [(C') | N_1 | AV_2 {}_3 {}_3] [C'' | N_1 | AV_2 | N_3 | {}_3 | PV_4 | N_5 | {}_3]$$
$$= \overbrace{C'P_2, \; C'P_2, \; C'P_2 + C'P_2 \; \; C''P_5}$$

2. [*The*-more | it | was examined,] [*the*-more | it | surpassed |
    c' 1   2 c' 1   2
the idea-formed of its size and beauty,] [the-more-worthy |
                3   + c''
{the portico | seemed of all | the admiration} (which | has
     1   2   3
for centuries been bestowed upon it.)]
                           2

$$[C' \mid \underset{1}{N} \mid A\underset{2}{V}] [C' \mid \underset{1}{N} \mid \underset{2}{V} \mid \underset{3}{N} pv \; s \; s]$$

$$[C'' \{ 1^1 \underset{1}{N} \mid \underset{2}{V} s \mid 1^1 \underset{3}{N} \} (\underset{1}{R} \mid A \; s \; A \underset{2}{V} s)]$$

$$= C'P_2 \; \overbrace{C''P_3 \, , \, C''P_3 \; 3 \; R^{\cdot}}_{2}$$

The last of the increased Disimple here is rendered Complex by R*.

Simulation of Di-simples to compound by semicolon.

1. [If | a short pipe-bent at right-angles like the letter L | is
   c' 1
fitted by one arm on to the end of the tap,] *while* [(if) |
      2   +
the other | is turned vertically upwards,] and [(if) the vat |
     1   2   + c' 1
is full as before;] (*when* | the tap | is turned,) [(*then*) | the
      2   c 1   2 c''
water | will shoot up into the air, *and* | after rising for a
  1   2   +   4
certain distance | will stop, and then fall.]
                     2   +   2

                                        (Asymmetrical.)

$$[C' \mid 1^1 2 \underset{1}{N} \; 4 \; s \; s \mid A \underset{2}{V} \; 3 \; 1 \; s \; s] + [(C') \mid 1^1 \underset{1}{N} \mid A \underset{2}{V} \; 1 \; 1]$$

$$+ [(C') \mid 1^1 \underset{1}{N} \mid \underset{2}{V} \; 2 \; 1 \; 1]; \; (C \mid 1^1 \underset{1}{N} \mid A \underset{2}{V})^{\cdot}$$

$$[(C^{\cdot}) \mid 1^1 \underset{1}{N} \mid A \underset{2}{V} \; 1 \; s + \mid P\underset{4}{V} \; s \mid A\underset{2}{V} + 1 \underset{2}{V} \mid]$$

$$= \overbrace{C'P_2 + C'P_2 + C'P_2}; \; \overbrace{2C^{\cdot}, \, C'P_4}$$

This is Compound of 1st Co-ordinate and Complex of the 2nd.

2. [{*Just-as* | any quantity of steam | has | exactly the same
   c' 1   2 c'
   weight (as the water) (which | was converted into it by
   3   c'' 1   1   2
   heat)] ; [*so* | the ice | has | exactly the same weight | (*as* |
        c'' 1   2 c' 3 c''
   the water) (which | has been converted into it | by taking
        1   1   2   4
   away | heat.)] (Symmetrical.)
        5

[{C' | 1^2 N 3 | V | 1 1^1 c' N} (C'' | 1^1 N | (V) | (N))·(R | A V 3 2)·];
      1   2   3   1   2   3   1   2

[C' { 1^1 N | V | 1 1^1 c' N} (C'' | 1^1 N | (V) | (N))·
      1   2   3   1   2   3

(R | A A V 3 | PV 1 | N)].
 1   2   4   5

$= \overbrace{C'P_3 \; c'C''_3 \; 1 \; R^{2·}_2}$; $\overbrace{C''P_3 \; c' \; C''_3 \; 1 \; R^{2·}_5}$

This simulates Compound of each Co-ordinate co-ordinately
subordinated and sub-subordinated, by semicolon.

VI.—COMPOUND OF COMPOUND Ps.

1. { The struggle with America | was over, } *and* { trade |
              1   2   +   1
   went- on briskly ; } { India | opened a new market for
        2   1   2   3
   English goods,} {machinery | enabled | the manufacturer |
                         1   2   3
   to produce | everything | much-more rapidly,} *and* { the
        4   5   +
   factories | gave | work | to large numbers of people.}
        1   2   3

{ 1^1 N 3 | V 1 } + { N | V 1 }
        1   2   1   2

{ N | V | 1^1 2 N 3 } { N | V | 1^1 N | IV | N | 1 1 }
  1   2   3   1   2   3   4   5

+ { 1^1 N | V | N | 3 3 }
         1   2   3

$= \overbrace{P_2, + P_2}$; $\overbrace{P_3, P_5, + P_3}$

210   STYLOGRAPHY OF ENGLISH LANGUAGE.

Having now shown to you the six varieties of structures thus compounded like to like, or as they may be called the similar or un-mixed Compounds, we come thus to such Compounds which combine dis-similarly as to structures, and let us call them "mixed" or *dissimilar Compounds*.

B.—ASYMMETRICAL COMPOUNDS.

I.—COMPOUND OF MONO-SIMPLE Ps AND MONO-SIMPLE SUBORDINATES.

1.—Between P and R⁎ Subordinate.

1. { Such | was | the question | put | to Dimock, } and (to
                                1   2   +
which | he | returned | these sterning words.)
         1   2   3

$$\{ 1 \mid A \mid 1^1 \underset{1}{N} \mid \underset{2}{V} 3 \}, +(3r \mid \underset{1}{N} \mid \underset{2}{V} \mid 1^2 2 \underset{3}{N}) = P_3, + R^*_3$$

2.—Between P and C⁎ Subordinate.

1. { They | are ignorant, } *and* (therefore | bazar reports about
        1   2   +   c   1

Russia | gain ⁎ | credence | ⁎ amongst them.)⁎
         2   3

$$\{ \underset{1}{N} \mid \underset{2}{V} 2 \} + (C \mid 2 \underset{1}{N} 3 \mid \underset{2}{V} \mid \underset{3}{N} \mid 3)^* = P_2, + C^*_3$$

2. { Every body | uses | water in one way or another every
            1   2   3

day; } *and* (*consequently* | every body | possesses | a store
      +   c   1   2   3

of loose information- of common knowledge about it.)⁎

$$\mid 1^2 \underset{1}{N} \mid \underset{2}{V} \mid \underset{3}{N} \mid 3\ 3 \mid ; + (C \mid 1^2 \underset{1}{N} \mid \underset{2}{V} \mid 1^1 \underset{3}{N}\ 3\ 3\ 3)^*$$

$$= P_3 ; + C^*_3$$

3. {You | are glad | to get out-side again,} and (so | we all |
   $\quad$ 1 $\quad$ 2 $\quad\quad$ 4 $\quad\quad\quad\quad\quad\quad\quad$ + $\quad$ c $\quad$ 1 $\quad$ 1

sally-forth for a walk.)^s
$\quad$ 2

$$\{ \underset{1}{N} \mid \underset{2}{V} \, 2 \mid \underset{4}{IV} \, 1 \, 1 \mid \} + (C \mid \underset{1}{N} \underset{1}{N} \mid \underset{2}{V} \, 3 \mid)^s = P_4 , + C^s{}_2$$

4. { A true natural law | is | an universal rule,} and, (as such,
   $\quad\quad\quad\quad\quad\quad\quad$ 1 $\quad$ 2 $\quad\quad\quad\quad\quad$ 3 $\quad$ + $\quad\quad$ c

it | admits-of | no exception.)
1 $\quad\quad$ 2 $\quad\quad\quad$ 3

$$\{ 1^1 \, 2 \, 2 \, \underset{1}{N} \mid \underset{2}{V} \mid 1^1 \, 2 \, \underset{3}{N} \} + \{ \underset{1}{N} \mid \underset{2}{V} \mid 2 \, \underset{3}{N} \}$$

$$= P_3 + C^s{}_3$$

All the above Subordinates are integral.

II.—COMPOUND OF MONO-SIMPLE Ps AND MONO-SIMPLE COMPLEXES AND *vice versa*.

1. { By day | the sky | is filled with light, } *but* (when | the
   $\quad\quad\quad\quad$ 1 $\quad\quad$ 2 $\quad\quad\quad\quad\quad\quad\quad\quad$ + $\quad\quad\quad$ c

sun | sinks in the west)^s { darkness | begins.}
1 $\quad$ 2 $\quad\quad\quad\quad\quad\quad\quad\quad$ 1 $\quad\quad$ 2

$$\{ 3 \mid 1^1 \underset{1}{N} \mid A\underset{2}{V} \, 3 \} + (C \mid 1^1 \underset{1}{N} \mid \underset{2}{V} \, 3)^s \{ \underset{1}{N} \mid \underset{2}{V} \}$$

$$= P_2, + \widetilde{C^s{}_2 \, P_2}$$

2. (*If* | it | were taken out of the air)^s { everything | would
   $\,$ c $\,$ 1 $\quad\quad\quad\quad$ 2 $\quad\quad\quad\quad\quad\quad\quad\quad\quad$ 1

be dried-up on the land, } *and* { life | would be impossible. }
$\quad\quad\quad$ 2 $\quad\quad\quad\quad\quad$ + $\quad\quad$ 1 $\quad\quad\quad\quad\quad\quad$ 2

$$(C \mid \underset{1}{N} \mid A\underset{2}{V} \, 1 \, 3)^s \{ \underset{1}{N} \mid AA\underset{2}{V} \, 3 \} + \{ \underset{1}{N} \mid A\underset{2}{V} \, 2 \}$$

$$= \widetilde{C^s{}_2 \, P_2}, + P_2$$

3. {Some times | the air | is busy | drinking-up | vapour every
            1   2   4   5
where,} *or*, (as | we | say,) { there is | great drought, | } *and*
         +   1   2   2   1   +
then {the clothes | dry quickly.}
              1   2

$\{1 \mid 1^1 \underset{1}{N} \mid \underset{2}{V} 2 \mid \underset{4}{PV} \mid \underset{5}{N} 1\}$

$+ (C \mid \underset{1}{N} \mid \underset{2}{V}) \{1 \underset{2}{V} \mid 2 \underset{1}{N}\} + \{1^1 \underset{1}{N} \mid \underset{2}{V} 1\}$

$= P_5, + \widetilde{(C\raisebox{2pt}{.}_2)\, P_2} + P_2$

Here the 2nd P is complex by paranthetic C⋅.

4. { Thus | the surface of a sheet of fine white paper |
                 1
looks perfectly even and smooth to the eye; } *but* { a
    2   +
magnifying glass of no great power | will show | the minute
                   1   2
woody fibres} (of *which* | it | is made-up ;) *while*, {under
            3   1   2   +
a powerful microscope, | the paper | looks like a coarse
                          1   2
matting.}.

$\{1 \mid 1^1 \underset{1}{N} 3 3 \mid \underset{2}{V} 1 2 + 2 3\};$

$\div \{1^1 2 \underset{1}{N} 3 \mid \underset{2}{AV} \mid 1^1 2 2 \underset{3}{N}\} (3 r \mid \underset{1}{N} \mid \underset{2}{AV});$

$+ \{3 \mid 1^1 \underset{1}{N} \mid \underset{2}{V} 3\}$

$= P_2; + \widetilde{P_3\, R\raisebox{2pt}{.}_2}; + P_2$

III.—COMPOUND OF MONO-COMPLEXES AND P.

1. (*So long as* | both scale-pans | are empty) { the beam | is
             1   ,2   1   2

horizontal,} *but* (if | you | put | any thing (*which* | has |
           +   1   2   3   1   2

weight)²· into one,)· {that one | goes down} and {the other |
       3   1   2   +   1

rises.}
     2

$$(C \mid 1^2 \underset{1}{N} \mid \underset{2}{V} 2)^{\cdot} \{ 1^1 \underset{1}{N} \mid \underset{2}{V} 2 \}$$

$$+(C \mid \underset{1}{N} \mid \underset{2}{V} * \mid 1^2 \underset{3}{N} \ (\underset{1}{R} \mid \underset{2}{V} \mid \underset{3}{N}) * 3)$$

$$\{ 1^2 \underset{1}{N} \mid \underset{2}{V} 1 \} + \{ 1^1 \underset{1}{N} \mid \underset{2}{V} \}$$

$$= \overbrace{2 \ C^{\cdot}_2 P_2} ; \ + \ \overbrace{C^{\cdot}_2 \ 3 \ R^{2 \cdot}_3 \ P_2 + P_2}$$

Compound of complex and complex in which, the 2nd is compounded in Ps.

2. (If, on the other hand, | the liquid in the bulb | is cooled,)
                                  1   2

{its volume | is | diminished ;} *and*, (*as* | it | shrinks,)· {the
         1   2   +   1   2

column of liquid in the tube | flows back into the bulb,}
      1   2

and {the level of the top of the column | is lowered.}
             1   2

$$(C \ s \mid 1^1 \underset{1}{N} \ 3 \mid \underset{2}{AV})^{\cdot} \{ 1^2 \underset{1}{N} \mid \underset{2}{AV} \} ; \ + (C \mid \underset{1}{N} \mid \underset{2}{V})^{\cdot}$$

$$\{ 1^1 \underset{1}{N} \ s \ s \mid \underset{2}{V} \ 1 \ s \} + \{ 1^1 \underset{1}{N} \ s \ s \mid \underset{2}{AV} \}$$

$$= \overbrace{2C^{\cdot}_2 \ P_2} ; \ + \overbrace{2C^{\cdot}_2 \ P_2 + P_2}$$

The latter Complex has got compounded in its Ps.

IV.—COMPOUND OF DIFFERENT MONO-COMPLEXES.

1.—OF R^a AND C^a COMPLEXES.

1. { There is | a substance composed of water, proteids, fat,
$\quad\quad\quad\;_2\quad\;\;_1$

amyloids and mineral matters } (which | is found in all
$\quad\quad\quad\quad\quad\quad\quad\quad\quad\quad\quad\;\;_1\quad\quad\quad\quad\;_2$

animals and plants ;)^a and, (when these | are alive,)^c { this
$\quad\quad\quad\quad\quad\quad\quad\;\;+\quad\;\;c\quad\;_1\quad\quad\;\;_2$

substance | is termed | protoplasm.}
$\quad_1\quad\quad\quad\;\;_2\quad\quad\quad\;_3$

$$\{{}_2^1 V \mid {}_1^{11} N \; 4\; 3\} ({}_1 R \mid {}_2 A\, V\, 3)^c ; + (C \mid {}_1 N \mid {}_2 V\, 2)$$

$$\{ 1^2 \underbrace{N}_{1} \mid A \underset{2}{V} \mid \underset{3}{N}\} = \overbrace{P_2 \tfrac{1}{4} R^a{}_2} ; + 2 \overbrace{C^a{}_2 \, P_3}$$

2.—OF MONO-COMPLEX AND COMPOUNDED MONO-COMPLEX.

1. {We | call * | people (who | possess | much muscular or other
$\quad\;\;_1\quad\quad_2\quad\quad\quad\;\;_3\quad\;\;_1\quad\quad\quad\;_2$

power)^c * energetic } ; and { we | estimate | their energy |
$\quad\quad\quad\quad\quad\quad\quad\quad\;\;+\quad_1\quad\quad\quad_2\quad\quad\quad\;\;_3$

* by the obstacles ((R) they | overcome)^c or, in-other-words
$\quad\quad\quad\quad\quad\quad\;_3\quad\;_1\quad\quad\;_2\quad\quad\quad\;+$

by the work } ((R) they | do.)^c

$$\{\underset{1}{N} \mid \underset{2}{V} * \mid \underset{3}{N} (\underset{1}{R} \mid \underset{2}{V} \mid 1\,2, + 1^2 \underset{3}{N})^c\, 2\};$$

$$+ \{\underset{1}{N} \mid \underset{2}{V} * \mid 1^2 \underset{3}{N} \mid *\cdot 3\,\} \begin{matrix}((R) \mid \underset{1}{N} \mid \underset{2}{V})^c \\ +\,3\, ((R) \mid \underset{1}{N} \mid \underset{2}{V})^c \end{matrix}$$

$$= P_3\, 3\, R^a{}_2 \;;\; + \overbrace{P_3 \tfrac{2}{3} R^a{}_3 + \tfrac{2}{3} R^a{}_3}$$

In the 2nd Complex here, the R^a is compounded.

LECTURE XI.   215

3.—Of Mono-simple Complex and Mono-Co-ordinate Complex or *vice versa*.

1. { Mr. Benson | was so pleased with the boy's conduct }
      $_1$ c' $_2$

(*that* | he | made | him | a present of the money,)[^a] *and* (*as*
c'' $_1$ $_2$ $_3$ $_3$ +

he | had | no children of his own)[^a] { he | soon after adopt-
$_1$ $_2$ $_3$ $_2$ $_2$

ed | Leonard as his son *and* left | him | the whole of his
$_3$ $_3$ + $_3$ + $_2$ $_3$ $_3$

fortune.}

$\{\underset{1}{N} \mid A\, c'\, \underset{2}{V}\, _3 \} (\, C'' \mid \underset{1}{N} \mid \underset{2}{V} \mid \underset{3}{N} \mid _{1^1}\, \underset{3}{N}\, _3\,)$[^a]

$+ (C \mid \underset{1}{N} \mid \underset{2}{V} \mid _2 \underset{3}{N}\, _3)\, \{\underset{1}{N} \mid _{1\,1} \underset{2}{V} \mid \underset{3}{N} + _{1^3} \underset{3}{N} \mid + \underset{2}{V} \mid \underset{3}{N} \mid _{1^1} \underset{3}{N}\, _3 \}$

$= \overbrace{P_2\, c'C'''_{\,3}} + \overbrace{C'_{\,3}\, P_3}$

2. { We | obtain indeed | most of (*what* } we | need of these
     $_1$ $_2$ $_3$ $_3$ $_1$ $_2$

materials from our solid food ;) yet {spring-water | (in-so-
                                    + $_1$

far-as | it | contains | them) | is healthier for drinking and
        $_1$ $_2$ $_3$ $_2$

cooking} (*than* | rain-water | would be.)[^a]
                    $_1$ $_2$

$\{\mid \underset{1}{N} \mid \underset{2}{V}\, _1 \mid \underset{3}{N}\, _3 \mid \,\} (R \mid \underset{1}{N} \mid \underset{2}{V}\, _{3\,3}),$

$+ \{\mid \underset{1}{N} \mid (C \mid \underset{1}{N} \mid \underset{2}{V} \mid \underset{3}{N}) \underset{2}{V}\, c' \mid P\underset{4}{V} + P\underset{4}{V} \}(C'' \mid \underset{1}{N} \mid A \underset{2}{V} \mid)$

$= \overbrace{P_3\, \tfrac{2}{3}\, R'_{\,3}} \,\,;\, + \overbrace{P_4\, (C'_3)\, c'C''_{\,2}}$

4.—Of DI-SUBORDINATE AND BI-SUBORDINATE COMPLEXES.

1. (If | two equal tendencies | exactly oppose | one-another,)*
   $\quad\quad\quad\quad\quad\quad\quad\quad 1\quad\quad\quad\quad\quad 2\quad\quad\quad\quad 3$

{ the body (upon which they | act)* | does not move at
  $\quad\;\; 1\quad\quad\quad\quad R\quad\quad\; 1\quad\quad\; 2\quad\quad\quad\quad\quad\quad\quad 2$

all;} *while,* (*if* | one | is stonger)* (than | the other)²* { the
  $\quad\quad\quad +\quad c\quad\; 1\quad\; 2\quad\quad c'\quad\quad\quad\; c''\quad\; 1$

body | moves in the direction of the stronger.}
$1\quad\quad 2$

$$(C \mid {}_{2\,2}\, N \mid {}_1 V \mid N)^*\, \{{}_{1^1}\, N \mid (*\, {}_3\, r \mid N \mid V\, *)^* \mid A\, {}_1\, V_1 \}$$
$\quad\quad\quad\quad 1\quad\quad 2\quad 3\quad\quad\quad 1\quad\quad\quad\quad\quad 1\quad 2\quad\quad\quad\quad\quad 2$

$$+ (C \mid \underset{1}{N} \mid \underset{2}{V}\, c'^*)^* \, (C'' \mid {}_{1^1}\, \underset{1}{N} \mid (\underset{2}{V}))^{2*}\, \{{}_{1^1}\, \underset{1}{N} \mid \underset{2}{V}\, {}_3\, {}_3\}$$

$$= \overbrace{2C^*{}_3\, P_2\, 1R^*{}_2} + \overbrace{C^*{}_2\, c'C''^{2*}{}_2\, P_2}$$

V.—COMPOUND OF MONO-COMPLEX AND MONO-SIMPLE POLY-SUBORDINATES.

1. { *What* | is | true of water | is | true of all kinds of matter, }
   $\quad 1\quad\; 1\quad\; 2\quad\quad\quad\quad\quad 2$

and (we | therefore say) (*that* | it | is | a law of nature)²*
$+\quad\quad 1\quad\quad\quad\quad\quad\quad 2\quad\quad 1\quad 2\quad\quad 3$

(*that* all kinds of matter | possess | gravity.)³*
$\quad\quad\quad\quad\quad 1\quad\quad\quad\quad 2\quad\quad\quad 3$

$$\{\underset{1}{N}\, ((R) \mid \underset{2}{V}\, {}_{2\,3})^* \mid \underset{3}{V}\, {}_{2\,3\,3}\} + (C \mid \underset{1}{N} \mid \underset{2}{V})^*$$

$$(C \mid \underset{1}{N} \mid \underset{2}{V} \mid {}_{1^1}\, \underset{3}{N}\, {}_3)^{2*}\, (C \mid {}_{1^2}\, \underset{1}{N}\, {}_3 \mid \underset{2}{V} \mid \underset{3}{N})^{3*}$$

$$= \overbrace{P_2\, 1\, R^*{}_2} + \overbrace{C^*{}_2\, 2\, C^{2*}{}_3\, 2\, 3\, C^{3*}{}_3}$$

LECTURE XI.   217.

VI.—COMPOUND OF MONO-SIMPLE Ps AND DI-SIMPLE Ps OR *vice versâ*.

1. { We | arrived at the village very late in the evening, } *and*
   $\;\;\;\;1\;\;\;\;\;\;2$ $\;+$

[though | our arrival | was by no means formally made
$\;\;$c′$\;\;\;\;\;\;\;\;\;\;\;1\;2$

known to the villagers] [*yet* | they | came in small parti-
$\;$c″$\;\;\;\;\;\;1\;\;\;\;\;\;\;2$

es at a time | to visit | us in our camp.]
$\;4\;\;\;\;\;\;\;\;\;\;\;\;\;5$

$$\{ \underset{1}{N} \mid \underset{2}{V} \text{3 1 2 3} \} + [C' \mid 1^3 \underset{1}{N} \mid A \text{ 3 1 } \underset{2}{V} \text{ 4 3}]$$

$$[C'' \mid \underset{1}{N} \mid \underset{2}{V} \text{3 3} \mid \underset{4}{IV} \mid \underset{5}{N} \text{3}] = P_2 + \overbrace{C'P_2 \; C''P_5}$$

2. [If {the bulk of one drop, | were (greater} than that of the
   $\;\;\;$c′$\;\;\;\;\;\;\;\;\;\;\;\;\;\;\;\;\;1\;2\;1$

other drop),] [then the larger | would move more slowly,]
$\;\;\;\;\;\;\;\;\;\;\;\;\;\;$c″$\;1\;2$

and {the point of meeting | would be by so- much nearer
$\;1\;2$

the larger drop.}

$$[C' \{ 1^1 \underset{1}{N} \text{ 3} \mid \underset{2}{V} (c') C'' \mid \underset{1}{N} \text{ 3} \mid (\underset{2}{V}))^*]$$

$$[C'' \mid 1^1 \underset{1}{N} \mid A \underset{2}{V} \text{ 1 1}] + \{ 1^1 \underset{1}{N} \text{ 3} \mid \underset{2}{A} V \text{ 3} \}$$

$$= \overbrace{C'P_2 \; c'C''\cdot_2 \; C''P_2} + P_2$$

Here the 1st Co-ordinate is co-ordinately subordinated and the 2nd Co-ordinate compounded in its l's.

3. [*Not only* | was | a larger capital | brought | to bear upon the
   c' 1   2   4

land,] [*but* | the mere change in the system | introduced | a
   c'' 1   2

taste for new and better modes of agriculture ;] { the breed
   3   1

of horses and of cattle | was improved,} and { a far greater
                    2

use | made of manure and dressings. }
 1   2

$$[C' \mid \underset{2}{A} \mid 1^1 \; 2 \; \underset{1}{N} \mid \underset{2}{V} \mid \underset{4}{IV} \; 3 \;]$$

$$+ [C'' \mid 1^1 \; 2 \; \underset{1}{N} \; 3 \mid \underset{2}{V} \mid 1^1 \; \underset{3}{N} \; 3 \; 3 \;] \; ;$$

$$\{ \mid 1^1 \; \underset{1}{N} \; 3+3 \mid \underset{2}{AV} \} + \{ 1^1 \; 1 \; 2 \; \underset{1}{N} \mid (A) \; \underset{2}{V} \; 3 \}$$

$$= \overbrace{C'P_4 \; C''P_3} \; ; \; \overbrace{P_2 + P_2}$$

VII.—COMPOUND OF DI-SIMPLE AND MONO-COMPLEX.

1. [If now | you | either pull or push * | the empty scale | *
   c' 1 c' 2 c'' 2   3

downwards,] [(*then*) | the beam | may be brought into the
   c'' 1   2

horizontal position again,] and { the effort required- to
                          +   1

bring it into the horizontal position | will be the-greater, }
                               2   c'

(the-greater | the weight of the body in the opposite
   c'' 1

scale.)*

$$= [C' \mid \underset{1}{N} \mid c' \; \underset{2}{V} \; c'' \; \underset{2}{V} \; * \mid 1^1 \; 2 \; \underset{3}{N} \mid * \; 1 \;] \; [(C'') \mid 1^1 \; \underset{1}{N} \mid AA$$

$$\underset{2}{V} \; 3 \; 1 \;] + \{ \mid 1^1 \; \underset{1}{N} \; 4 \; 6 \; 7 \; 3 \mid A \; V \; \underset{2}{c'} \} \; (\; C'' \mid 1^1 \; \underset{1}{N} \; 3 \; 3 \mid (A\underset{2}{V}))\text{·}$$

$$= \overbrace{C'P_3 \; (C'')P_2} \; + \; \overbrace{P_2 \; c' \; C''\text{·}_2}$$

Compound of co-ordinate Ps and co-ordinated subordinate Complex.

VIII.—COMPOUND OF DI-SIMPLES WITH COMPOUND OF THE 1ST CO-ORDINATE P.

1. [*The-greater* | the mass of the stream (is)] *and* [*the-more* |
    c' 1   2   + c'

rapidly | it | moves] [*the-more* | motion will * | it | * com-
         1   2 c'' 3   1

municate to the ball,] *or* [the heavier | the ball | (is)]
                   2   + c' 1   2

[(c'') it | will move.]
      1   2

$$[\; C' \; | \; 1^1 \; \underset{1}{N} \; 3 \; | \; (\underset{2}{V}) \;] + [C' \; | \; 1 \; | \; \underset{1}{N} \; | \; \underset{2}{V}] \; [C'' \; | \; \underset{3}{N} \; | \; A \; | \; \underset{1}{N} \; | \; \underset{2}{V} \; 3 \;]$$

$$+ [C' \; | \; 1^1 \; \underset{1}{N} \; | \; \underset{2}{V}] \; [\; C' \; | \; \underset{1}{N} \; | \; \underset{2}{AV} \;]$$

$$= \overbrace{C'P_2 + C'P_2} \; \overbrace{C''P_3 + C'P_2} \; C'P_2$$

In conclusion, I may be permitted to say that the division of *Compounds* into symmetrical and asymmetrical as shown above, though it may appear artificial, is no doubt observational. The Rational Formulæ of those already depicted may be greatly diversified, but they would by no means deviate from the general principles thus laid down, as similarly observed before in the case of Mono-Simple Complexes.

LECTURE XII.

STUDENTS AND GENTLEMEN,

Upto yet all structures have been shown to be *terminated by Period*. Parts of Speech relations of antecedents to personal pronoun and pronominal adjectives are shown to exist within the limit of the Period, and the various Simple, Complex, Co-ordinate, and Compound Sentences have been shown to do the same. Presently we come to see that these *Parts-of-Speech relations* along with certain Adverbial relations do extend to structures *beyond the Period*, and the same holds good with the Subordinates, Co-ordinates, and Compounds too.

A.—Personal pronoun relation beyond the Period.

1. { A sailor | once went ashore on the coast of South America.}
       1   2
   { *He* | had with him | a number of red wollen caps for sale.}
      1   2   3

$$= P_2 . P_3$$

The relation here is between 'sailor' and 'he'.

B.—Pronominal adjective relation beyond Period.

1. { *In the Island of Ceylon | there are* | large herds of wild
                                    2   1
   elephants. } { *Many* | have been caught | and tamed and
                      1   2   +   2   +
   made useful | in helping | to build | bridges, houses, and,
       2   4   6   7   7   +
   churches.}
       7

$$= P_2 . P_7$$

The relation here is between 'elephants' and 'many.'

LECTURE XII.

2. { He | had not | far to go} (for * within a quarter of a mile
   ₁   ₂   ₄   c
   | he | met * with two riders)⁽ (whom | * from their dress
   ₁   ₂   ₃
   | he | knew * | to be | Jews.)²⁽ {One of them | he | at once
   ₁   ₂   ₄   ₅   ₃   ₁
   recognized | as Rebecca's father.}
   ₂   +   ₃

$$= P_4 \; C^{\cdot}{}_2 \; \tfrac{3}{8} R^{2 \cdot}{}_5 \cdot P_3$$

The relation here is between 'two riders' and 'one of them.'

C.—Demonstrative Adjective relation beyond Period.

1. ⟨ Tired and wretched ⟩ { he | sat-down on a large stone by
     ₄   +   ₄   ₁   ₂
   the road-side.} { This stone | from his having rested | him-
                         ₁   ₄
   self upon it | is called | Whittington's Stone to this day. }
   ₅   ₂   ₃

$$= \langle PV + PV \rangle \; P_2 \cdot P_5$$

The relation here is between ' large stone ' and ' this stone.'

2. (While | Wamba and Gurth | were talking about the
   c   ₁   +   ₁   ₂
   capture of Cedric and his party)⁽ { a third person |
                                        ₁
   suddenly appeared.} {This | was | Locksley, the archer.}
   ₂   ₁   ₂   ₃   ₃

$$= 2C^{\cdot}{}_2 \; P_2 \cdot P_3$$

The relation here is between 'a third person' and 'this.'

D.—Adverb relation beyond the Period.

1. ⟨ In-gratitude-for having protected | him ⟩ { he | arranged
                                ₄   ₅   ₁   ₂
   | to provide * | him | * with a splendid steed and a suit of
     ₄   ₅
   new armour.} ⟨ Thus accoutred ⟩ { the Pilgrim | (who
                        ₄   ₁   ₁

16

| had at the castle revealed | himself to the swine-herd)·
soon after made | his way to the lists at Ashby | attended
by Gurth- diguised as his square.}
                                +

$$=\langle\ 4\ 5\ \rangle\ P_5\ .\ \langle\ PV\ \rangle\ P_4\ 1\ R'_3$$

The relation here is between 'with a splendid steed and a suit of new armour' and 'thus.' The latter adverb may be considered as a *connective* showing its analogy with conjunction.

2. {A little further on, we | came to an elevated spot,} (which|
overlooked | the whole scene). {*Here* we | found | a painter-
seated on a rock, and busy in sketching its horrors}.

$$=P_2\ \tfrac{2}{3}\ R'_3\ .\ P_3$$

The relation here is between 'spot' and 'here'.

3. { * In England in the olden time | people | used * | to
drink | ale and a sweet kind of wine called mead.}
{Great tankards of *ale* | stood on the breakfast table.}
{*Now* | we | use | tea and coffee.}

$$=P_5\ .\ P_2\ .\ P_3$$

The relation here is between 'in the olden time' and 'now.'

4. { * In Norway | the winter | is * very long.} {*There* | the
deep snow and the hard frost | last for 8 or 9 months of
the year.}

$$=P_2\ .\ P_2$$

The relation here is between 'in Norway' and 'there.'

E.—Preposition phrase relation beyond the Period.

1. {Every part of the top | is spinning round this central line,} (which | is called | the axis of rotation.} { * *In a similar way* | the earth | is spinning * rapidly on its axis.}

$$= P_2 \tfrac{2}{3} R^{\bullet}{}_3 \cdot P_2$$

The relation here is between the whole previous sentence and 'in a similar way.'

2. {* From the distance | it | appears * | as a conical mountain with its top- cut off.} { * *From this truncated summit* | a white cloud | rises *} ; but {not quite such a cloud} (as | may be seen on an ordinary hill-top.)·

$$= P_3 \cdot P_2 \,;\; + P_2\, 1\, R_2{}^{\bullet}$$

The relation here is between " a conical mountain with its top cut off " and " from this truncated summit."

F.—Mixed relation of the foregoing beyond the Period.

1. (If half a pint of water, coloured-by-putting-a-little-ink-into-it | is added to the same quantity of clean water,)· {the two | will readily mingle;} {the total quantity of water | will be | a pint } ; and {*its* colour | will be just half as dark } (*as* that of the coloured half-pint.)· { *This* | is | a case of simple mixture. } { The volume of *the* mixture | equals | the sum of the volumes of the things,- mixed,} and {there is | no change in the properties of these things.}

(*So* (when | water | evaporates,) { the gaseous water or
              1   2   1 +

vapour | mixes with the air, } ⊂ in the same way, | the
 1   '2

molecules of the one body | dispersing | themselves between
 1   4   5

the molecules of the other ⟩ (until | there is | the same pro-
                             c   2

portion of each everywhere.)*)* { *In like manner* | sand and
 1   1 *1*

sugar | may be mixed, without any change in the proper-
 1   2

ties of either, or in the space } (which | they | primitively
                                    3   1

occupied.)*
 2

$= 2 C\cdot_2 P_2 ; P_3 ; + P_2 c'C'''\cdot_2 . P_3 . P_3 + P_2.$

$C (2 C\cdot_2 P_2 ⟨1\ 4\ 5⟩ 2 C\cdot_2)\cdot . P_3\ \tfrac{2}{3}\ R\cdot_3$

The relation here is between the first sentence and "this" in the 2nd. Again there is relation between the above two sentences and "so" beginning the 4th, and "in the same way" also in it. This 4th sentence, on the other hand, bears relation to "in like manner" beginning the 5th sentence.

It would not be out of place here to show the relations that exist *within* each of the sentences where they exist. For instance in the 1st sentence between "the two" and "half a pint" and "the same quantity", between "of water" and "into it," and between "the quantity of water" and "its colour." In the 3rd between "of the things mixed" and "of these things," &c. &c.

Having now shown the above parts of speech and phrase relations of one sentence *beyond* its 'period' termination to another that follows, we go now to see that Complexes, Co-ordinations, and Compounds of sentences extending *beyond* their Period do likewise exist

LECTURE XII. 225

I.—Complex by Subordination beyond the Period.

1. { The burning of coal and wood | produces | heat, } and
         $_1$ $_2$ $_3$ +
   { the heat thus given out | warms | the air. } (*Hence*
         $_1$ $_2$ $_3$ c
   | it | is | by the giving off on radiation of the heat from
     $_1$ $_2$ $_4$
   some burning substance)ᵃ (that | the air of our houses | is |
                                      $_1$
   made warmer)²ᵃ (than the air outside.)³ᵃ
       $_2$

$$=P_3+P_3 \cdot C^a{}_4 \tfrac{a}{3} C^{2a}{}_2 \; c' \; C''^{3a}{}_2$$

2. { ∗ By the motion of rotation | time | is divided ∗ into
                                $_1$ $_2$ c
   days and nights, }—{ ∗ by that of revolution, | it | is marked
                                                   $_1$ $_2$
   off ∗ into years. } (*So that* in this way | the earth | is
                          c $_1$ $_2$
   our great time-keeper.)
          $_3$

$$=\overbrace{P_2, P_2} \cdot C^c{}_3$$

3. { ∗ By this continual up and down movement of the water,
   | the sand and stones on the beach | are kept ∗ | grinding
     $_1$ $_1$ $_2$ $_4$
   against each other as in a mill. } (*Consequently* | they
                                          c $_1$
   | are gradually ground smooth and worn away.)ᵃ
       $_2$ $_2$

$$=P_4 \cdot C^a{}_2$$

4. { Damocles | gladly accepted | the offer. } (*Upon which*,
     $_1$ $_2$ $_3$
   the king | ordered,) (that | a royal banquet | should be
     $_1$ $_2$ c $_1$
   prepared,)²ᵃ and (a gilded couch ∗ | placed for him, ∗ cover-
     $_2$ $_1$ $_2$
   ed with rich embroidery,)²ᵃ and (side-boards- loaded with
   gold and silver plate of immense value.)²ᵃ

$$=P_3 \cdot R^c{}_2 \; 2\, C^{2a}{}_2 + 2\, C^{2a}{}_2 + 2\, C^{2a}{}_2$$

5. {Animals in breathing | give-out | carbonic acid gas into
   the air ;} and (when they | die)· {the decay of their bodies
   | returns | the same substance again to the soil and the
   atmosphere. } (Hence | the carbonic acid gas of the air
   | passes into the structure of plants and then of animals,
   | and is once more restored to the air)· (when | these
   living things | die,)²· and (their remains | begin | to decay.)²·

$= P_3 \; ; \; +2C^{\cdot}_2 \, P_3 \, . \, C^{\cdot}_2 \; 2 \, C^{2\cdot}_2 + 2 \, C^{2\cdot}_4$

6. {Material substances, (the parts of which | are so movable)·
   (that | they | fit | themselves exactly to the sides of any
   vessel)²· (which | contains | them,)³· and (which | flow)·
   (when | they | are not supported,)²· | are called | fluids ; }
   and { fluids | (the parts of which | do not fly off
   from one another, but hold together)· (as | those of water
   | do,)²· |. are called | liquids. } (Water | *therefore* is | a
   liquid.)

$= P_3 \, 1 \, R^{\cdot}_2 \, c'C''^{2\cdot}_3 \, \tfrac{2}{3} \, R^{3\cdot}_3 + 1 \, R^{\cdot}_2 \, 2 \, C^{2\cdot}_2 \; ; \; +P_3 \, 1 \, R^{\cdot}_2 \, 2 \, C^{2\cdot}_2 \, . \, C^{\cdot}_3$

7. [If | we | fall into the sun] [then | we | shall be fried,]
   [if | we | go away from the sun or the sun | goes out]
   [then | we | shall be frozen]. (*So-that* (so-far-as | the
   earth | is concerned) { we | have | no means | of deter-

mining | (what) will be | the character of the end,) but
   4   5 1   2   3   +
{we | know } (that | one of these two things | must take |
  1   2   1   2
place in time.)*)*
        3

$$= C'P_2 \; C''P_2 \; ; \; \overbrace{C'P_2 + (C')P_2} \; C''P_2.$$

$$C(C'_2 \; P_5 \; 5R'_3 + P_2 \; 2C'_3)*$$

8. {1 | shall endeavour | to show} (that in this case [although |
    1   2   4   c   c'
we | might still have | a feeling of moral approbation or
 1   2   3
reprobation towards action] [yet | we | could not reason-
                                      c''   1
ably praise or blame | men for their deeds | nor regard *
      2   +   2   3   +   2
| them | * as morally responsible.]) (So that (if | my con-
     3   c
tention | is | just to deprive | us of the scientific method)
  1   2   4   5
{ it | is | practically to deprive | us of morals altogether.})
  1   2   4   5

$$= \overbrace{P_4 \; C \; \overbrace{(C'P_3 \; C''P_3)}^*} \cdot C(C'_5 \; P_5)^*$$

This Subordinate has also other structures before (not here given), to which it is a conjoined subordinate.

9. { The driver | could not hold * | it | * in.} (So | he |
            1   2   3   1.
wrapped * | the rein | * around his wrists | in his efforts
   2   3
to hold | the animal.)*
 4   5

$$= P_3 \cdot C'_3$$

The relation here is between the whole previous sentence and 'so' which may be reckoned as a connective.

II.—Co-ordination of 2nd co-ordinate in Di-simples beyond the Period.

1. [*Neither* | will | sand nor iron filings | mix with water;
   c' 1   +   1   2

   as heavier bodies they | also sink to the bottom.] [*Nor* |
            1   1   2 c''

   does | powdered ice (though | it | is | water in another
                 2   c 1   2   3

   shape) mix with ice-cold water; as a lighter body it |
         2   1   1

   floats at the top.]
     2

$$= \overbrace{C'P_2}; \; \overbrace{P_2 \cdot C'P_2 \, (C^{\cdot}{}_3)}; \; P_2$$

The word "also" has reference to preceding structures.

2. [*In the one case* | the water | trickles down the cold glass.]
           c' 1   2

   [*In the other case* | it | gathers into drops of rain] (that |
             c'' 1   2   1

   fall through the air.)
     2

$$= C'P_2 \cdot \overbrace{C''P_2 \, \tfrac{3}{3} \, R^{\cdot}{}_2}$$

III.—Compound beyond the Period.

1.—Between P and P.

1. {The explosions of a volcano | shake | the ground sometimes
                    1   2   3

   with great violence.} *But* { | the solid earth | is affected
                                 +   1   2

   by movements even remote, from any volcano.}

$$= P_3 \cdot + P_2$$

2. {Even the loose stones in the mould itself | are continually
                                      1

   crumbling down | and making | new earth.} *And* { ∗ thus-
            2   2   3   +

LECTURE XII.   229

day-by-day | the soil | is slowly renewed, *} and {the
              1   2   +

balance required for the continued growth | is preserved.}
1   2

$$= P_3 . + P_2 + P_2$$

The word "thus" refers to the 1st P integrally.

2.—BETWEEN MONO-COMPLEX AND P OR vice versa.

1. {We | cannot indeed examine | the sea-bottom with any-
    1   2   3

thing like the same minuteness} (as the surface of the
                        c'   c''   1

land.)   Yet and {great deal | may be learnt regarding it.}
          +   1   2

$$= P_3 \, c' C''_3 . + P_2$$

2. {One | cannot be pedantic all day.} But (if | we | choose
    1   2   +   c   1   2

for once | to be pedantic)· {the matter | is after all very
    4   1   2

simple.}

$$= P_2 . + 2 C·_4 \, P_2$$

3.—BETWEEN COMPLEX AND COMPLEX.

1. {We | say} (that anything | has | weight)· (when | on
    1   2   c   1   2   3   c

trying | to lift | it from the ground, or on holding | it
   4   6   7   4   5

in the hand | we | have | a feeling of effort.)²· Or-again
       1   2   3   +

(if | anything (which | is supported at a certain height above
 c   1   1   2

the ground)²· falls)· (when | the support | is taken away,)²·
        2   c   1   2

{we | say} (that | it | has | weight.)
  2   1   2   3

$$= P_2 \, 2 C·_3 \, 2 C^{2·}_7 . + 2 C·_2 \, 1 R^{2·}_2 \, 2 C^{2·}_2 \, P_2 \, 2 C·_3$$

4.—BETWEEN MONO-SIMPLE AND A DI-SIMPLE.

1. {A great deal of the underground water | must no doubt
                        1
descend far below the level of the valleys and even
   2
below the level of the sea.} *And* [yet [though | it | should
                              +   c″   c′ ·   1
descend to a considerable depth] it | comes at last to
   2   1   2
the surface again.]

$$= P_2 \cdot + C''P_2\, C'P_2$$

The 2nd co-ordinate conjunction "yet" is transposed here to the first seat in the Co-ordinate.

Compound by other Conjunctions beyond the Period.

1. (When therefore | the Lord ¹ knew)* (how | the Pharisees |
                      1   2   1
had heard)²* (that Jesus | made and baptized | more dis-
     2   1   2   3   c′
ciples)³* (than | John)⁴*, { he | left | judæa, and departed
    3   1   1   2   3   2
again into Galilee.} *And* { he | must needs go through
                       +   1   2
Samaria.} *Then* { cometh | he | to a city of Samaria}
           +   2   1
(which | is called | Sychar,)* near to the parcel of ground,
   1   2   3
(that | Jacob | gave to his son Joseph.)* *Now* { Jacob's
   3   1   2   +
well | was there.} { Jesus | therefore, being wearied with
  1   2   1
his journey, sat thus on the well :} and { it | was | about the
             2   +   1   2
sixth hour.}

$$= 2\overbrace{C'_2\, 2C^2_2\, 2C^3_3\, c'C''^4_2}, P_3 \cdot + P_2 \cdot + \overbrace{P_2\, \tfrac{3}{3}R'_3\, \tfrac{3}{3}R'_3}$$
$$+ P_2 \cdot P_2 \left\langle PV \right\rangle : + P_2$$

Connectives "then" and "now" have been shown to belong to this class.

LECTURE XII.   231

2. { For some time the struggle | was most amusing }—(the
         1   2
fish | pulling, and the bird | screaming with all its might)—
  1   4   +   1   4
(the one | attemping | to fly and the other | to swim,
    1   4   6   +   1   4
from the invisible enemy) — (the gander | the one
                                            1
moment losing and the next regaining | the centre of
           4   4   4   5
gravity, and casting between whiles | many a rueful look
                    4   5
at his snow white fleet of geese and goslings, (who | cack-
led forth | their sympathy for their afflicted commodore.))
        2   3
At length { | victory | declared in favour of the feathered
       +   1   2
angler, } (who (bearing away for the nearest shore,) |
               1
landed on the smooth green grass | one of the finest pikes-
              2   3
ever caught in the castle-loch.)

$= P_2 \,(1\ 4+1\ 4) - (1\ 4\ 6+1\ 4) - (1\ 4 + 4\ 5 + 4\ 5\ \tfrac{5}{3}\ R'_3).$

$+ P_2 \tfrac{2}{3} R'_3 \,(PV)$

Here the first sentence has a *Compound of a Compound
absolute*, a compound co-ordinate absolute and a complex
absolute.

3. { Our heroine Miss Hellen Convolvulus | had | no aversion
        1   2   3
to a lover, especially to *so* handsome a lover *as* Mr. Fer-
dinand Fitzroy. } *Accordingly* { she | neither accepted nor
                             +   1   2   +
discarded | him ; but kept | him on hope, and suffered | him |
    2   3   +   2   3   +   2   3
to get into debt with his tailor, and his coach-maker, | on-
                  4
the-strength-of becoming | Mrs. Fitzroy Convolvulus.}
           6   7

$P_3 \cdot + P_7$

4. {The skull of the negro | is narrower,} {his brain less capa-
   $\quad$ 1 $\qquad$ 2
   cious,} {his muzzle | more projecting,} { his arms longer}
   (than those of the average European man.) *Still* { he | is
   $\qquad\qquad\qquad\qquad\qquad\qquad\qquad\qquad\qquad$ + $\quad$ 1 $\quad$ 2
   essentially | a man; and separated by a wide gulf from the
   $\qquad\qquad\quad$ 3 $\qquad\qquad$ 2
   chimpanzee or gorilla. }

$$= P_2, P_2, P_2, P_2 \, c'C''_2 \, . \; + P_3$$

Here three Ns form three *elliptical* Ps with a C'' to four Ps.

5. { Years | may pass over our heads, | without affording | any
   $\quad$ 1 $\qquad\quad$ 2 $\qquad\qquad\qquad\qquad\qquad$ 4
   opportunity for acts of high beneficience, or extensive
   $\qquad\qquad$ 5
   utility.} *Whereas* {not a day | passes,} but {in the common
   $\qquad\qquad\quad$ + $\qquad\quad$ 1 $\quad\;\;$ 2 $\;$ +
   transactions of life, and especially in the intercourse of
   domestic society, gentleness | finds | place | for promo-
   $\qquad\qquad\qquad\qquad$ 1 $\qquad$ 2 $\qquad$ 3 $\qquad$ 4
   ting | the happiness of others, and for strengthening in our-
   $\qquad\qquad$ 5 $\qquad\qquad\qquad$ + $\qquad\qquad\qquad$ 4
   selves | the habit of virtue. }
   $\qquad$ 5

$$= P_5 \, . \, + \widetilde{P_2, + P_5}$$

6. { Many things, (though | they | resist,)* can be easily
   $\qquad$ 1 $\qquad\qquad\quad$ 1 $\qquad$ 2
   squeezed or compressed into a smaller volume.} { This,
   $\quad$ 2 $\qquad\qquad$ 2 $\qquad\qquad\qquad\qquad\qquad\qquad\qquad$ 1
   however, is not * | the case | * with water,} (which like
   $\qquad\qquad$ 2 $\qquad\qquad$ 3 $\qquad\qquad\qquad\qquad$ 1
   other liquids | is almost incompressible.)
   $\qquad\qquad\quad$ 2

$$= P_2 \, 2 \, C'_2 \, . \; + P_3 \, \tfrac{1}{2} R'_2$$

7. {We | are much obliged by your kindness | in coming so
   $\quad$ 1 $\qquad\qquad\qquad$ 2 $\qquad\qquad\qquad\qquad$ 4
   far | to tell | us all these things } (which | you | have heard
   $\;$ 6 $\qquad$ 7 $\qquad\quad$ 7 $\qquad\qquad\qquad$ 3 $\qquad$ 1 $\qquad\qquad$ 2
   from your mothers.)* *In return*, { I | will tell | you some
   $\qquad\qquad\qquad\qquad\qquad\qquad\qquad$ + $\;$ 1 $\qquad$ 2 $\qquad$ 3 $\quad$ 3
   of those } (which | we | have heard from ours.) *
   $\qquad\qquad\;\;$ 3 $\qquad\;\;$ 1 $\qquad$ 2

$$= \widetilde{P_7 \, 7R'_3} \, . \, + \widetilde{P_3 \, 3R'_3}$$

LEOTURE XII. 233

8. ("That | pleasure," replied | the merchant, { "I | believe,}
      1   2   1   1   2
proceeds from sympathy)* : { it | is scarce possible,
    2   1   2
(unless | you | have | some peculiar cause of misery,)| not
           1   2   3
to be pleased } (when | you | see | every thing around you
       4   1   2   3
happy.) *On the contrary*, (if you | go into the mansion
                          +   1   2
of sorrow,) { it | will be impossible | to withstand | the
                1   2   4
infection of it." }
       5

$= $ " $2C^*_2$," P_2, " P_2 : $\overparen{P_4 \ (C^*_3) \ 4C^*_3}$. $+C^*_2 \ P_5$ "

* In the last two examples "in return" and "on the contrary"
are *preposition phrase connectives*.

LECTURE XIII.

STUDENTS AND GENTLEMEN,

Structures bearing *no relation* to each other by noun-pronoun, pronominal adjective, certain adjective, and preposition phrase formed by all of them, and at the same time *terminated* by Period as in Mono-simples have first been considered. All these may be termed Independent structures terminated by Period, and those bearing *such relation* under the same condition have also been shown. In the last lecture we have seen the extension of these relations and structural combinations to go *beyond* the Period. Now we proceed to see the same relations and structural **Combinations between Para. (¶) and Para. (¶).** You have seen extra compound conjunctions to develope, in the last lecture, and it is the same extra conjunctions, besides the ordinary compound conjunctions, that we have to utilize here too. I will point out to you here, in the analysis, the consecutive *Independent structures*, those that bear parts of speech and phrase relations *beyond* Period; and those that go to form *stuctural combinations* together, before pointing out to you the *paragraph relations and combinations* which fall under this lecture.

A.I. Consecutive Independents in a Para.

(*i. e.* without structural relation to each other.)

Ex. 1. ¶ 1. { The sun was setting upon one of the rich grassy glades of the forest } (we have mentioned.) { Hundreds of broad-headed, short-stemmed, wide-branched *oaks* (which in former times had witnessed perhaps the stately march of the Roman soldiery,) flung their gnarled arms over a thick carpet of the most delicious greensward. } { In some places *they* were intermingled with beeches, hollies and copse-wood of various descriptions so closely as totally to intercept the level beams of the sinking sun. }

¶ 1. $= \overbrace{P_2 \tfrac{2}{3} R'_3} . \overbrace{P_2 \, 1R'_3} . P_5$

REMARKS.—Here the three sentences are consecutive Independents : the 1st being a complex by Relative subordination in which the relative is understood, the 2nd, the same with an expressed Relative. The 3rd sentence is a mono-simple up to 5th term, the 3rd being absent, and bearing N P relation between "oaks" and "they". "Grassy glades" and "delicious greensward" bear only *meaning relation* here.

¶ 2. { The human figures (which completed the landscape) were in number two-partaking in their dress and appearance of that wild and rustic character } (which belonged to the woodlands of the West-riding of Yorkshire at that early period.) {The elder of *these* men had a stern savage and wild aspect.} { *His* garment was of the simplest form imaginable,} ⟨being a close jacket with sleeves composed of the tanned skin of some animal⟩ (on which the hair had been originally left,) but (which had been worn off in so many places) (that it would have been difficult to distinguish from the patches) (that remained) (to what creature the fur had belonged.)

¶ 2. $= P_3 \, 1R'_3 \, \tfrac{2}{3} R'_2 . P_3 .$

$\overbrace{P_2 \langle 1 \, 5 \rangle \tfrac{5}{3} R'_2} + \overbrace{\tfrac{4}{3} R'_2 \, c' C''^{2s}_4 \, \tfrac{4}{3} R^{3s}_2 \, R^{3s}_2}$

REMARKS :—The 2nd para is consecutive to the preceding, and is independent. The 1st sentence is both medially and terminally subordinated in its mono-simple P by two R' subordinates. The 2nd sentence is related to the 1st by pronominal adjective "these" in its post-joining preposition phrase to first N. The 3rd sentence is related to the 2nd by personal pronoun "his" ;

and bears relation subordinated by two R^s to the absolute, the latter of which is co-ordinately sub-subordinated by a C^{2s}, which is again sub-subordinated by R^{3s}.

CRITICISM :—The author here has used one mono-simple independent sentence, two relatively connected mono-simples, each related by a personal pronoun and a pronominal adjective to its preceding sentence, respectively. Of the Complex structures, two are complex by relative subordination, while the last is a complex by poly-subordination up to 3rd sub-subordination in all of which cases the Subordinates have been four times relative, and once only co-ordinate conjunction subordinate. The author has, therefore, shown more fondness for R^s than that for C^s. He has shown also two varieties of combination, the "simple" and the "locked".

II. Personal Pronoun relation between Paras.

Ex. 1. ¶ 1. {Alone in her mountain dwelling the poor mother lay watching and waiting.} (As the snow and the wind beat around the cottage) { *she* sometimes feared } (that her husband too might perish in the glen.)

¶ 2. { *She* felt } (that the lives of both her husband and her son depended on the sagacity of the dog.) But { she knew } (that God could guide the dumb creature's footsteps,) and { she fervently prayed to Him in her time of need.}

$$\P\ 1. = P_4 \cdot \overparen{C^s_2\ \ P_2\ 2\ C^s_2}\ .$$

$$\P\ 2. = \overparen{P_2\ 2\ C^s_2} \cdot + \overparen{P_2\ 2\ C^s_3} + P_2.$$

REMARKS :—The first sentence here extends its relation to 2nd by "she," and the 1st para to the 2nd by "she" too. The 2nd sentence of the 2nd para is compounded to its 1st sentence by compound conjunction "but."

CRITICISM: — The 1st sentence is an independent mono-simple. The 2nd is a Complex by Di-subordination, both the subordinates being C⁸. The 1st sentence in para 2 and a part of the 2nd are each a complex by C⁸. The author seems to be fond of C⁸ subordination; by the last sentence he has shown compounds beyond and within the Period.

III. Pronominal Adjective relation between Paras.

Ex. 1. ¶ 3. { A grand dinner was provided for the occasion ;} and { the king and his guests showed great good humour and kind feeling. }

* * * *

¶ 7. { *Another* dinner which had been prepared and served up, was just about to be attacked in the same way } (as the former one) (when puss sprung in a moment among the crowd of rats and mice,) (killing several and making the rest run off in less than a minute.) *But* (when the dishes were placed on the table) { the white visitors were astonished at the appearance of rats and mice in great numbers } (which came from their hiding-places and ate up nearly everything on the table in a very short time !)

¶ $3. = P_2 + P_3$.

¶ $7. = P_4 \ 1R'_2 \ c'C''{}'_2 \ 2C'_2 \ (4\ 5\ 6)$. $+2C'_2 \ P_2 \ \frac{2}{3}R'_3$!

REMARKS :—" Another dinner" relates to the "grand dinner." And "the former one" refers to "grand dinner" too.

Ex. 2. ¶ 1. {In that pleasant district of merry England (which is watered by the river Don) there extended in ancient times a large forest- covering the greater part of the beautiful hills and valleys } (which lie between Sheffield and the pleasant town of Doncaster.) { *Here* were fought many of the most desperate battles during the Civil wars of the Roses: } and { here also flourished in ancient times those bands of gallant outlaws } (whose deeds have been rendered so popular in English song.)

17

¶ 2. (*Such* being our chief scene) {the date of our story refers to a period towards the ebb of the reign of Richard the First} (when his return from his long captivity had become an event-rather wished than hoped for by his despairing subjects) (who were in the meantime subjected to every species of oppression.)

¶ 1.$=\frac{2}{3}$ R$'_2$ P$_2$ $\frac{1}{3}$ R$'_2$. P$_2$: $+$ P$_2$ $\frac{1}{2}$ R$'_2$.

¶ 2.$=($ 4 5 $)$ P$_2$ $\frac{2}{3}$ C$'_3$ $\frac{1}{3}$ R$^{2s}_2$

REMARKS :—The 1st sentence is an independent complex : the 2nd is related to the 1st by means of the adverb "here". Both are subordinated by R$'$, the former di- and the latter mono-subordinated. The absolute adjective "such" refers to the whole of the 1st para.

CRITICISM :—All the sentences are subordinated by R$'$ except the sentence in the 2nd para which is subordinated by C$'$, and sub-subordinated yet by R$'$.

IV. Adverbial relation between Paras.

Ex. 1. ¶ 1. { Cyrus, (who with the chief officers of his court was present) was curious to know} (why Crœsus pronounced that name with so much vehemence.) (Being told the reason, and reflecting upon the uncertainty of all sublunary things) { he was touched with commiseration, ordered the monarch to be taken from the pile, and treated him afterwards with honour and respect.}

¶ 2. {*Thus* had Solon the glory of saving the life of one king and giving a wholesome lesson of instruction to another.}

¶ 1.$=$P$_4$ 1 R$'_2$ 4 C$'_3$. $($4 5 $+$ 4$)$ P$_4$
¶ 2 $= +$P$_5$.

REMARKS :—"Thus" relates integrally to the whole of the 1st para. The integrally connected parts of speech and phrases may also be considered as *Conjunctions*, and hence adverbs, conjunctions, and certain preposition phrases become *connectives* by analogy.

V. Preposition phrase relation between Paras.
(a)—Of "Time."

Ex. 1. ¶ 1. {*The next morning* (when Cheery went to feed the pony in the manger) there lay the 20 gold pieces in the bin, the very same} (that Cheery had paid the day before.)

¶ 2. {*From that day* all went well at the mill.} {The flour was always the earliest in the market and brought the highest price. } { There were *more* sacks on the pony's back *than* three horses could carry.} {Cheery bought a cart and let him fill it *as* heavily } (*as* he would,) { the pony never slacked his pace but trotted on and seemed *as* fresh and *as* fat after a day's work } (as-when he was first taken out of the stable.)

¶ 3. { *In a year's time* Cheery married a merry little wife *as* lively and sprightly}(*as* himself ;) and {things went on *so* very well} (*that* Grumble got worse- tempered than ever at having nothing to find fault with.) {Above-all he had the strongest dislike for the pony;} (for (not-long-after he had been taken to the mill) {Grumble tried to ride him, and the pony ducked him in the pond, dragged him through the briers and soused him at last into a ditch. })* (So Grumble for a long time brooded over this but could not not find an opportunity for his revenge.)

¶ 4. { *After three years* (as the little old man had declared,) Cheery's affairs were *so* thriving } (*that* he and Grumble were nearly the headmen of the parish,) and {they were both made overseers of the poor.} { Cheery was always for kindness to the poor old people, } but { Grumble was a harsh tyrant and would never give them a bit *more* help) (*than* he could not avoid.)

¶ $1. = +C'_5 P_2 1 R'_3$

¶ $2. = + P_2 . P_3 . P_2 \, c'C''_2 . P_5 \, c'C''_2 , P_3 \, c'C''_2$

¶ $3. = + P_3 \, c'C''_2 + P_2 \, c'C''_7 . P_3 ; C \, (2C'_2 P_5 + P_3)' . + C'_2$

¶ $4. = +(C'_2)P_2 \, c'C'''_3 + P_3 . P_2 + P_3 \, c'C'''_2$

REMARKS :—Here all the paras begin with preposition phrases of time progressing by degrees, and thus relate to each-other, so that the paras may be said to be connected with them as with conjunctions.

CRITICISM :—The author has used here seven times co-ordinate Subordinates or "locked" combinations so that inference as to his fondness for them may safely be drawn.

(b)—OF "PLACE."

Ex. 1 ¶ 1. { *In the Pyrenees*, the ancient glaciers have occupied all the principal valleys of this chain both on the French and Spanish sides, especially the valleys of the centre } (which comprehend those of Luchon, Aude, Bareges, Cauterets, and Ossun.) { *In the Cantabrian an extension of the Pyrenees*, the existence of ancient glaciers has also been recognized. }

¶ 2. { *In the Vosges and the Black Forest*, they covered all the southern parts of these mountains.} { *In the Vosges* the principal traces are found in the valleys of Saint-Amarin, Giromagny, Munster, the Moselle, &c. }

¶ 3. { *In the Carpathians and the Caucasus* the existence of ancient glaciers of great extent has also been observed. }

¶ 4. { *In the Sierra Nevada* in the south of Spain, mountains upwards of 11,000 feet high (the valleys of which descend from the Picacho de Veleta and Mulhacen) have been covered with ancient glaciers during the quaternary epoch. }

$$\P\ 1. = + \overbrace{P_3\ 3\ R'_3} . P_2 \qquad \P\ 2. = + P_3 . P_2$$

$$\P\ 3. = + P_2. \qquad \P\ 4. = + \overbrace{P_2\ 1\ R'_2}.$$

REMARKS :—As the *preposition phrases* of "time" obtained the 1st seat in each para and *simulated as connectives* in series in the first illustration, so here also the transposed preposition phrases of "place" took the 1st seat and simulated as connectives in series. You must not omit observing "the next morning", "from that day," "in a year's time," and "after three years" in the preceding example, and here the preposition phrases "in the pyrenees," "in the Vosges and the Black Forest," "in the Carpathians and the Caucasus," and "in the Sierra Nevada" as *para connectives.*

(c)—Of "Number" or conjoined "Number" and "Place."

Ex. 1. ¶ 1. { I will only point-out a few analogies between Egyptian and Hebrew customs. }

§ I. { Moses took the name, conception, and idea of a special national god for the guide and ruler of his specially chosen children from the Egyptians, } (who in the valleys of the Nile far distanced all other nations in sciences and arts and consequently had at least apparently some right to that proud assumption.) {With the Egyptians only, the priests of the highest caste of Amn or Amn-ra (to which Moses belonged) were considered the chosen children of the highest concealed God.}

§ II. { The division of the Jews into 12 tribes was in imitation of the primitive 12 *nomes-* of Egypt} (*which* took their origin in the 12 signs of the Zodiac.)

§ III. { The establishment of a special priest caste (the Levites) among the Hebrews was in imitation of the Egyptians.} {In addition to this, the Levitic organization, customs, and ceremonies, their very division and classification were entirely framed according to the Egyptian laws.} * * * *

¶ 1.=P_3.

§ 1.= +P_3 ⅔ R'_3 . P_3 ⅓ R'_2 .

§ 2.= +P_2 ⅔ R'_3.   § 3.= +P_2 . P_2 .

Remarks :—Except the 1st, all the paras here are arranged numerically and consecutively in detail.

Ex. 2. ¶ 2. (When a school-globe is turned slowly round on its axis,) { we not only see at a glance (how much *larger* the surface of water is) (*than* the surface of land,) but may notice several other interesting features in the distribution of land and water. }

¶ 3. { *In the first place*, the water is all connected together into one great mass- called the sea.} {One might sail from any part of the sea to any other part without having to cross land. } { The land on the other hand, is much *broken up by the way*, } (the sea runs into it,) and {some parts are cut off from the main mass of land, so as to form islands in the sea.} { One cannot pass from every part of the land to every other part without crossing the sea. }

¶ 4. { *In the second place*, much land lies on the north than on the south side of the equator. } ⟨Turning the globe so-as-to look straight down on the site of London,⟩ { you will find } (that most of the land comes into sight ;) *whereas*, (if from the opposite side you look straight down on the area of New Zealand,) { you will see most of the sea.} {London *thus* stands about the centre of the land-hemisphere, midway among the countries of the earth. } *And no doubt* { this central position has not been without-its-influence-in fostering the progress of British commerce. }

¶ 5. { *In the third place*, (by-the-way- in which the masses of land are placed,) parts of the sea are to some extent separated from each-other.} {These masses of land are called continents, and the wide sheets of sea between are termed oceans.} { The surface of the solid part of our globe is uneven, } ⟨ *some-portions* rising into broad swellings or ridges, ⟩ ⟨ *others* sinking into wide hollows or basins. ⟩ Now, { into these hollows the sea has been gathered, and only those upstanding parts (which rise above the level of the sea) form the land.}

¶ $2. = 2\,C'_2\,P_2\,2\,C'_2\,c'C''_2$.

¶ $3. = +P_2 \cdot P_7 \cdot P_2\,2C'_2, +P_5 \cdot P_5$.

¶ $4. = +P_2 \cdot \langle 4\ 5\ 6\rangle\,P_2\,2C'_2 ; +C'_2\,P_3 \cdot +P_2 \cdot +P_5$.

¶ $5. = +\tfrac{3}{4}R'_2\,P_2 \cdot P_3, +P_3 \cdot P_2 \langle 14, 14 \rangle \cdot +P_2, +P_3\,1\,R'_2$.

LECTURE XIII.   243

REMARKS :—You see here that to the last portion of the 1st sentence from "but—to water," the three paras beginning with "in the 1st place," "in the 2nd place," and "in the third place" are related each to the other.

In para 5, the 3rd sentence contains a N | PV *co-ordinate absolute* structure.

From mere relation we come now to the combination of structures between paras. *Para-complexes* and *Para-compounds* (analogous to such Complexes and Compounds beyond Period and *within* a para) are visible.

B.—Para-complexes.

Ex. 1. ¶ 1. (As frost sets in) {this pervading moisture freezes.} Now, { precisely the *same* kind of action takes place with each particle of water} (*as* in the case of a burst water-pipe or a cracked jar.) { It does not matter } [*whether* the water is collected into some hole or crevices,] [*or* is diffused among the grains of the rock and the soil.] (When it freezes) {it expands, and-in-so-doing tries to push-asunder the walls} (between which it is confined.)

¶ 2. { *Hence* arise some curious and interesting effects of frost upon the ground.} {After a frosty night the small stones upon a road or footpath may often be seen to have been partly pushed out of their beds } (as the ground ;) { thus the surface of the road is covered with a layer of fine mud. } { The frost separates the grain of sand and clay by freezing the moisture between them} (so-that (when the frozen moisture melts) {the particles of soil no longer adhere to each-other but seem} (as-if they had been pounded down in a mortar.))*

¶ 1.$=2 C'_2 P_2 . +P_3 c'C''_3 . P_2 C'P_2 C''P_2 . 2C'_2 P_4 5 R'_2$.

¶ 2.$=C'_2 . P_4 2 C'_4 ; +P_2 . P_5 C (2 C'_2 P_2 2 C'_2)$*.

Ex. 2. ¶ 1. { A carpenter could not (as we say) make a chair} (unless he knew something of the properties and power of wood,)

{ a blacksmith could not make a horse-shoe } (unless he knew) (that it is a property of iron to become soft and easily hammered into shape) (when it is made red-hot.) { A brickmaker must know many of the properties of clay, and a plumber could not do his work } (unless he knew) (that lead has the properties of softness and flexibility) and (that a moderate heat causes it to melt.)

¶ 2. (*So-that* the practice of every art implies a certain knowledge of natural causes and effects,) and (the improvement of the arts depends upon our learning more and more of the properties and powers of natural objects, and discovering how to turn the properties and the powers of things and the connections of cause and effect among them to our own advantage.)

¶ $1. = P_3 (C'_2) 2C'_3, P_3 2C'_2 2C^2{'}_4 4C^3{'}_2.$

$P_3, + P_3 2 C'_2 2 C^2{'}_3 + 2 C^2{'}_4.$

¶ $2. = C'_3 + C'_7.$

REMARKS :—In the two preceding examples the integral subordinate conjunctions "hence" and "so-that" construct para-complexes by forming combinations with their paras respectively.

Ex. 3. ¶ 1. {*In other words*, the dimensions of the Earth (large as it is) are simply imperceptible when compared with the vast distance } (which separates the Stars from the Earth.)

¶ 2. (*If then* the Stars were so immensely distant and of such enormous size,) (as they were thus shown to be,) { (to suppose that they could nevertheless revolve round the Earth in 24 hours)^N is rationally inconceivable. } { To the theological type of mind this difficulty of conception was of course as nothing, } but { to the scientific type of mind the difficulty is insuperable } (for, science, (being based on the conviction of the uniformity of nature,) views the heavenly bodies and their movements not-as-without but-as-within the pale of analogy and experience, and regards Astronomy not-as a mystery but-as a science of cause and effect.)

LECTURE XIII. 245

¶ 3. (*When therefore* about the year 1537 Copernicus propounded his geometrical conception) ⟨based upon the supposition of the Earth's double motion, ⟩ ⟨its rotation on its axis, ⟩ and ⟨its translation through space in an orbit round the Sun, ⟩ { a rationally conceivable account was given of every motion } (that the Heavens presented to the Astronomer,) ⟨an account showing⟩ (that they could all intelligibly cohere without contradicting each-other and without any violation of the nature of things) (as concluded from human experience.) { It was indeed, though not altogether original, a marvelous conception—for Copernicus neither did nor could in the then state of science) explain the mechanical origin of the movements (he supposed,) or assign them any dependence on physical causes.) {That, however, was subsequently done,} (as we shall presently see,) ⟨when glancing at the discoveries of Kepler, of Galileo, and of Newton.⟩

¶ 1.=P_2 (C'_2) ⅔ R'_3.

¶ 2.=C'_2 (C'_4) $P_2 \cdot P_3 + P_2 C'_3$ ⟨4⟩.

¶ 3.=C'_3 ⟨ PV ⟩, ⟨ 3 3 ⟩+⟨ 3 3 3 3 ⟩

P_2 ⅔ R'_3 ⟨N | PV (4C'_5 ⅔ $R^{2'}_2$)⟩.

$P_3 C'_3$ ⅔ $R^{2'}_3 \cdot + P_2$ (C'_2) ⟨PV⟩.

REMARKS :—In para 2 the integral subordinate conjunction "then" forms the subordination to para 1, and in para 3 the conjunction "therefore" combines this para with para 2, but in both the instances their initial positions have been given to each of the subordinate conjunctions "if" and "when" which form the subordinates in the complexes following.

C.—Para-compounds.

Ex. 1. ¶ 1. {Scarcity alone, *however,* would not make a thing valuable} (if there were no reason) (why any one should desire to possess it.) {There are some kinds of stone} (which are scarce but of no value)⁎ (because they have neither use nor beauty.)²⁎ {You would not give anything in exchange for such a stone} [not-because you cannot easily get it] [but-because you have no wish for it.]

¶ 2. *But* { a stone (which is scarce and very beautiful) may be of great value } (though it is of *no* use *but* to make an ornament for the person.)

¶ 3. *And* {they desire these things the-more} (because ⟨besides being beautiful to the eye,⟩ they are reckoned a sign of wealth in the person) (who wears them.) { A bunch of wild flowers will often be a prettier ornament} (than a fine ribbon or a jewel,) (but a woman likes better to wear these last to show) (that she can afford the cost of them) whereas (the wild flowers may be had for picking.)

¶ 1. $= +P_3 \; 2\,C^{\cdot}{}_2 \; 2\,C^{2\cdot}{}_5 \, . \, P_2 \; \tfrac{1}{4} R^{\cdot}{}_2 \, C^{2\cdot}{}_3 \, . \, P_3 \; C'P_3 \; C''P_3$

¶ 2. $= +P_2 \; 1\,R^{\cdot}{}_2 \; 2C^{2\cdot}{}_5.$

¶ 3. $= +P_3 \; c'C''{}_3 \, \langle c\,4 \rangle \, \tfrac{3}{8} R^{2\cdot}{}_3 \, . \, P_3 \; c'C''{}_2$
$\quad + P_6 \; 6\,C^{\cdot}{}_3 + P_2 .$

REMARKS :—Para 1 is compounded with the preceding one not given here, and does so by "however" transposed but not initially placed. Para 2 is compounded with para 1 by "but" and para 3 compounded with the 2nd by "and". The latter two conjunctions have not shifted from their initial places.

Ex. 2. ¶ 1. (When the psalm ceased,) { an echo, like a spirits' voice, was heard dying away high up among the magnificent architecture of the cliffs, } and { once more might be noticed in the silence, the reviving voice of the water fall. }

¶ 2. *Just then* { a large stone fell from the top of the cliff into the pool, } { a loud voice was heard,} and { a plaid hung over on the point of a shepherds' staff.}

¶ 1. $= 2C^{\cdot}{}_2 \; P_4, \, + P_2.$
¶ 2. $= +P_2 , \; P_2 , \, + P_3.$

Ex. 3. ¶ 1. * * * { From these gentlemen I have received familiar calls, and the most pressing invitations ; } and [though I wished to accept their offered friendship,] [I have repeatedly excused myself under-the-pretence-of not being quite settled ;] (for, the truth is,) (that (when I have rode or walked, with full intention to return their several visits,) { my heart has failed me } (as I approached their gates ;) and { I have frequently returned homeward, } ⟨resolving to try again to-morrow.⟩)⸱

¶ 2. { *However,* I at length determined to conquer my timidity and three days ago, accepted of an invitation to dine this day with one, } (whose open easy manner left me no room to doubt a cordial welcome.)

¶ 1. $= P_3$; $+C'P_5\ C''P_3$; $C'_2\ C\,(2C'_5,\ P_3\,2C'_3$; $+P_2\,(4\ 6))$⸱

¶ 2. $= +P_4\ \tfrac{1}{3} R'_5$.

Ex. 4. ¶ 1. { The water then flows over in a stream and falls to the ground, } (where it spreads out and runs to the lowest accessible place, or gradually soaks up into crevices.)

¶ 2. *Nevertheless,* [although the parts of the water thus loosely slip and slide upon one another,] [yet they hold together to a certain extent.]

¶ 1. $= P_2\ \tfrac{2}{3}\ R'_2$.

¶ 2. $= +C'P_2\ C''P_2$.

Ex. 5. ¶ 1. { We have now seen } (what a wonderful change is brought about by heating water.) At first, { it expands gradually and slightly, } but (when it reaches the boiling point,) { it suddenly expands enormously, and is no longer a liquid, but a gas. }

¶ 2. *On the other hand,* (if warm water is allowed to cool,) { it gradually contracts } (till it reaches the ordinary temperature of the air in mild weather ;) but (if the weather is very cold,) or (if the water is cooled artificially,) { it goes on contracting only down to a certain temperature (39°), and then begins to expand again. }

¶ 1.=P_2 R'$_2$. + P_2 + 2C'$_3$, P_3 .

¶ 2.= +2C'$_4$ P_2 2C'$_3$; + 2C'$_2$ + 2C'$_2$ P_4.

Ex. 6. ¶ 1. {The emotions (I felt on the receipt of this letter)* can only be conceived by those} (who, in the midst of despairing love, have beheld a gleam of hope.)* { The tumult of my heart hurried me to the place appointed, long before the time ;}{ I walked backward and forward in the utmost confusion totally regardless of every object about me :} (*sometimes* raising my hands and eyes in the sudden effusions of transport, and *sometimes* smiling with the complacency of delight.)

¶ 2. *At length* { the day departed,} and { Zara came, } { my heart bounded at her sight :} {I, was unable to speak, and threw myself at her feet.}

¶ 1.=P_2 1R'$_3$ ⅔R'$_3$. P_3 ; P_2 : (c'4 5 + c''4).

¶ 2.= +P_2+P_2 , P_2 : P_4.

Ex. 7. ¶ 1. {Shah Abbas the First, king of Persia, (being one day hunting, and having wandered from his attendants,) found a young shepherd- playing on a pipe.} {The king spoke to him, and, after some conversation, was *so* struck with his solid understanding, } (*that* he committed him to the care of teachers, to be properly educated.)* { The shepherd made *such* wonderful progress,} (*that* he excited the admiration of the court and of his patron,)* (who gave him the name of Mohammed Ali Bey, together with the office of Nazar, or intendant of the household.) {The king sent him twice as ambassador to the Great Mogul, and was much pleased with his negotiations,} (for he had the firmness to resist bribes, a thing very uncommon among the Persians.)* {The favor (he enjoyed) raised him up a host of enemies, but none would venture to speak to the sovereign, } (who had so high an opinion of his fidelity.)*

LECTURE XIII.

¶ 2. {After the death of the king, *however*, the enemies of Mohammed endeavoured to effect his ruin with Shah Sefi, the successor, } (who, (being a young man,) was more easily persuaded.) {They represented to the king,} (that (as Mohammed had built at his own expense several Caravanseras and a magnificent palace,)* { he could not have done so without employing some of the public money. })*

¶ 1.=$P_5 . P_2 c'C''_4 . P_3 c'C''_3 \frac{3}{3} R^{2*}_3 . P_3 C^*_5 . P_3 1R^*_3 + P_4 \frac{4}{3} R^*_3$.

¶ 2.=$+P_5 \frac{4}{3} R^*_2 . P_2 2C(C^*_3 P_5)^*$.

REMARKS :—Of the five sentences in Para 1, the first is a simple sentence, the 2nd is a Complex by co-ordinate subordination, the 3rd is the same with Bi-subordination, the 4th is a Complex by C*, and the last is a Compound of Complexes with R* subordination. In Para 2, the first sentence is a Complex by R* subordination, while the 2nd is a Complex by substitutive Complex. "However" connects the last sentence of Para 1 to Para 2.

CRITICISM :—The author has given here six varieties of structures which are distinct in each case; but he has shown twice, fondness for co-ordinate subordinates which follow one another very rarely.

LECTURE XIV.

STUDENTS AND GENTLEMEN,

I have shown to you in the preceding lectures that the *maximum mono-simple sentence* in its full stretch consists of 9 chief terms, 5 of which are Ns and 4 of which are Vs, and that they alternate with each other except in the case of N, which may sometimes be absent. The same extent and alternate arrangement of Ns and Vs hold good in *other structures* too, the different Subordinates, Sub-subordinates, and the Co-ordinates. We have seen *Proxy Part of Speech* the PP, as chief term somewhat *distantly* placed within the period, or actually distant beyond the period from the N to which it is a proxy. We have seen the *proximate* proxy part of speech the Relative Pronoun, proxy to N or PP, which goes to place itself at the head of the subordinate Relative structure as a chief term or as a joiner to its N or V terms within the period of the principal structure, though the period may also terminate it. We have seen this approximation of the antecedent and the Relative, in the instance of a compound Relative, to be riveted words. We have seen compound PPs, the proxy colleagues to Ns or PPs, as chief emphatic terms or joiners within the principal. All these *pronouns of the three varieties* possess antecedents of reference.

We have seen the *different joiners* as adjuncts to Ns and Vs which may be regarded as clothings or dependents to these chief terms; while the PA and adjective ante-joiners to N, when Ns are understood, have been considered as *N substitutes*. We have seen also that IV or PV (not its past) chief terms go to form post-joiners to Ns along with their suite of Government respectively, alone or alternately together. We have seen analogous joiner roll played by the past participle, which may be considered as post-adjective to Ns and Vs. Past participle with 'have' and 'be' has gone by us principal verb or as chief term.

Like the Relative, as with the other pronouns, the article adjective "the" has been shown to possess its *antecedent of reference*. The PA by virtue of its pronominal designation has been shown to possess antecedents, while certain adjectives as "same, like, similar, analogous," &c., and certain adverbs such as "thus, so," &c. have been shown to possess also their antecedents of reference.

There were shown to exist the *three varieties of Government* in parsing 1st, between terms and terms, 2nd, of adjective relation between terms and their respective joiners, or in certain instances only between joiners and joiners, and 3rdly of antecedent and Relative relations between terms and terms or between parts of speech and structures.

On the other hand, outside the pale of the Mono-simple principal at its extreme positions were seen the *absolute parts of speech* or *terms*, the interjections, the case of address nouns and pronouns (the vocatives sometimes subordinated by R*) and the absolute incomplete N structures. This absolute incomplete structure has been seen also to stand as independent one terminated by its own Period. Similarly the absolute IVs and suite have been seen within the Period of the principal or as independent by its own period termination. The absolute participle structures have been seen to head the Mono-simple, and it must be remembered that the term "absolute" is given to all the above for their want of Government in parsing whether within the principal or whether within their own isolated period termination.

We have seen also *parenthetic parts of speech, phrases*, or *structures* within the pale of the principal, having no parsing relation with it like the "absolutes," or having such relation within its own complete or incomplete structure. Direct-Narrative structures having the Narrative within the pale of the Direct, simulate in appearance the paranthetics, each having its distinct government in parsing, or better that the whole of the Direct, may be considered as 3rd term of Government after V, the 2nd term of the Narrative.

Analogues of 1st term N by certain post-terms and structures as IVs, PVs, C^s, R^s, C'P C"P were shown, for we should remember that whatever is governed may on its turn govern also.

Transposition of terms or their joiners with or without collateral transposition were shown in the Narrative ; while *inversion* of the 1st two terms in the imperative, interrogative, and sometimes in the exclamatory expressions were shown as a rule. In the analogues of post-terms for 1st N, no Transformations of them occured. *Transformations* however *of the 3rd term* into the 1st, and *of the 1st* to a preposition phrase joiner to the 2nd with consequent transposition of them, were shown in the changes of the active to passive expressions and *vice versa*.

In *Direct-Narrative* structures you have observed the narrative to be almost always a Minimum mono-simple sentence with the 1st and 2nd terms naked or clothed to which the Direct structure viewed as a whole has been regarded as its 3rd term. *Transformation of the Direct* (Simple, complex, or Co-ordinate) to narrative in continuation of the original Narrative has been shown by conversion of it into a subordinate by introducing the narrative or assertive conjunction " that" at its head, and thus rendering the whole a C^s to the narrative P. No changes occured in the Direct structure when the V term of the P was in the present tense and the N term of Direct, a 3rd person N or PP. However, when the V term of the P was present or past and the N term a pronoun of the first person, the change of this pronoun to 3rd person and the V of the Direct to past were seen. Besides these *person and tense changes*, pronominal possessive joiners of the first person changes to those of the 3rd. When the 2nd term of the original narrative is post-joined by a pronominal preposition phrase of the 1st person, the 2nd person pronominal term of the Direct changes to that of the 1st person pronoun with the changes of the Direct V of the *present* into that of the *past* and the original Narrative V into a different but adequate V of the past.

In the case of the post-joined preposition phrase of the 2nd person, the 2nd person pronoun of Direct does not change, though the V of Direct will change from the present into the past with adequate narrative V change. In the case of the post-joined preposition phrase of the 3rd person noun or pronoun, the 2nd person pronominal term of the Direct changes into that of the 1st with its usual V changed into past, and the narrative V changes adequately. We see that the above were good for the narrative or assertive as well as for the interrogative expressions of the Direct. When again, an imperative Direct follows the preposition phrase joiner to the narative V, the Imperative 2nd V is changed into IV 4th term in case of the 3rd person phrase, but in case of the 1st person phrase, the pronominal 3rd term of the 1st person changes into the 3rd, and the pronoun possessive joiner of the 3rd into that of the 1st. In the exclamatory variety of Direct speech, the same *word and tense changes* of the PP or PA joiner with tense change of V in the Direct were visible, but in the optative, you have seen at times another way of doing so by changing the Direct 1st term into the narrative 3rd term and the Direct 2nd into narrative 4th. *Transpositions* of joiners and *transformations* of structures had also been shown in equations.

We have seen Conjunctions (one of the *Connective Parts of speech*) as Mono-groupal or Bi-groupal (co-ordinates) in the Mono-simples called for the sake of distinction "Minor Conjs." We have spoken of subordinate conjunctions as Fractional, Integral, and Co-ordinate subordinate heading such so-called structures. We have seen also the co-ordinate conjunctions to head the principals in the Co-ordinate structures. We have seen also the position and functions of *compound conjunction* (for *compound structure as distinct is a myth*) placing between and connecting words, phrases, analogous words and phrases in the mono-simple, and placing between and connecting mono-simples, mono-subordinates, complexes and each or both of the Co-ordinates or between each other of all these. Compound conjunctions have thus been shown as typical or general, for they concerned themselves with words or terms, phrases, or adjuncts, and all structures. The whole class of conjunctions in fact from its pure variety to those borrowed from other parts of speech as the prepositions, adverbs single or co-ordinate, preposition phrases single or co-ordinate, and from the definite article adjective "the" with comparative adjectives as co-ordinates have been narrated. *The Article* "the" also was shown to form with certain PAs co-ordinate terms of N as in instances of "the former—the latter," "the one—the other," and hence they may be reckoned in all these cases as co-ordinate connectives. Co-ordinates without connectives, like Co-ordinate Relative Subordinate were found also in the Pronominal Adjective class alone, as in "this"—"that," "some—others".

Having thus cursorily shown to you, in a **retrospective view** all the parts of speech, phrases, and structures together with their transpositions where feasible, and the connectives as pure and derivative under the head of conjunctions, it remains now for me to point out to you what else amongst the parts of speech may be reckoned as connectives in their further dealings, though such dealings have not been generally accepted as connective ones. I mean to allude to the *connective ability of prepositions* bearing analogy to conjunctions in their various stretches by variety of connective powers. I go now therefore to illustrate to you this analogy, and hope to be understood.

Analogy between Conjunctions and Prepositions as Connectives.

I.—As REGARDS Ns. (SYMMETRICAL.)

(a) — *Mono-Groupal.*

N	Conj.	N	N	Prep.	N
Man	or	beast.	Parts	of	speech

(b)—Bi-groupal (co-ordinates.)

Conj.	N	Conj.	N	Prep.	N	Prep.	N
Neither	poverty	nor	riches.	From	youth	to	age.

II.—As regards Vs, IVs, and PVs. (Symmetrical.)

(a)—Mono-Groupal.

V	C.	V		V	P.	V
Sees	and	loves.		Loves	to	see

(b)—Bi-Groupal.

C.	V	C.	V		P.	V	P.	V
Either	likes	or	dislikes.		In	going	to	see.

III.—Conj. between dissimilars.

(Vide Lecture IV.)

IV.—Prep. between dissimilars.

	V.	P.	PV.			Adj.	P.	N.
1.	Used	in	constructing		7.	Weak	in	intellect
	V.	P.	N.			Adj.	P.	IV.
2.	Remained	in	darkness		8.	Anxious	to	go
	IV.	P.	N.			Adj.	P.	PV.
3.	(To) go	to	club		9.	Afraid	of	getting
	PV.	P.	N.			Adv.	P.	N.
4.	Shining through	window		10.	Constantly	in	pursuit
	N.	P.	PV.			Adj.	P.	N.
5.	Delight	in	doing		11.	Bent	upon	mischief
	N.	P.	IV.					
6.	Desire	to	govern					

Having thus shown to you the connective powers of prepositions with relation though otherwise than that of conjunctions, I go now to point out to you the *dual connection of preposition phrases and prepositions, of preposition phrases and conjunctions, of conjunctions and preposition phrases, and of conjunctions and adverbs.*

Analogy of dual connection of preposition, conjunction and adverb as connective.

Prep.	*Prep.*	*Prep.*	*P.rep.*
1. From	among	2. Up	to

P. Phrase.	*P.*	*P. Phrase.*	*P.*
1. In order	to	2. With a view	to
3. With the purpose	of	4. For the sake	of
5. With the object	of	6. In the event	of

Conj.	*Conj.*	*Conj.*	*Conj.*
1. As	if	2. And	yet

P. Phrase.	*Conj.*	*P. Phrase.*	*Conj.*
1. At the time	that	2. At the moment	that

Prep.	*Conj.*	*Adv.*	*Prep.*
1. In	that	1. Partly	through
2. In	as-much-as	2. Long	before
Adv.	*Conj.*	*Adv.*	*Adv.*
1. Just	as-much-as	1. So	often
2. Only	when	2. Very	politely

Conj.
1. And
2. At last
3. If
4. Nevertheless
5. That

Prep. Phrase.
at the same time
by the advice of (his physicians)
for instance
in *such* cases, *as* in all others
for the shake of (our fellow-creatures)
as well as for (ourselves).

Conj.	*Adv.*	*Conj.*	*Mixed.*
1. And	chiefly	1. And	the more so, because
2. And	so far	2. And	even when
Conj.	*Prep.*	3. If	at all possible
1. As	to	4. And	in a couch too
2. Because	of		

The *affinity of Adverbs and Preposition phrases to Conjunctions* is so much that they leave their proper seats very often and go close to them by *transposition*, hence they are as connectives like conjunctions though not exactly so in sense.

LECTURE XV.

STUDENTS AND GENTLEMEN,

We have seen in some of the preceding lectures, that transpositions of different joiners and chief terms, as well as their certain Transformations with attendant transpositions, do occur in the mono-simples. I have shown to you also that sentence structure as the Direct of the Narrative-direct gets transformed and even sometimes transposed in continuation of the Narrative as C⁰ subordinate, and thus forms complex structure out of the Narrative-direct. We go now presently to show to you the mono-simples and the absolutes where they can transform themselves into complex, co-ordinate, or compound structures and *vice versa*.

A.—Transformation of N Analogues in P.

1.—IV ANALOGUE OF N CHANGED INTO C⁰.

1. { (*To be* always attentively observing what is passing around them)^N is one of the means } (by which men improve their circumstances.) = P_3 ⅔ R⁰$_3$

1. {(*That men should* be always attentively observing what is passing around them)^N is one of the means } (by which they improve their circumstances.) = P_3 ⅔ R⁰$_3$

2.—PV ANALOGUE OF N CHANGED INTO C⁰.

1. (*His being* in town)^N is certain. = P_2
1. (*That he is* in town)^N is certain. = P_2

3.—C⁰ ANALOGUE OF N CHANGED INTO N.

1. (*Whether he has arrived*)^N is not known. = P_2
1. *His arrival* is not known. = P_3

4.—IV ANALOGUE OF N CHANGED INTO N.

2. (*To extend* human happiness)^N is the aim of the philanthropist. = P_3
2. *The extension of* human happiness is &c. = P_3

5.—PV ANALOGUE OF N CHANGED INTO N.

3. (His *being ruined*)^N was the cause of his death.=P_3
3. His *ruin* was the cause &c.=P_3

B.—Transformation of several simple Ps into a P.

1.—Ps CHANGED INTO A P WITH COMPOUND Vs.

1. {Honest Jack adhered to his resolution notwithstanding the jeers of his companions.} { *He ceased* to go to taverns.} { *He spent* all his earnings on the things necessary for the comfort of his home.}=$P_2 . P_4 . P_3$

1. { Notwithstanding the jeers of his companions, Honest Jack adhered to his resolution, *ceased* to go to taverns, *and spent* all his earnings on the things necessary for the comfort of his home.}=P_4

2. {He caught the infection probably from her, *and became* one of its victims.} { *He was burried* in the neighbourhood of Cherson} (where some years after, the Emperor Alexander caused a monument to be erected to his memory.)=$P_3 . P_2$ ⅔ R'$_4$

2. {He caught the infection probably from her, *became* one of its victims, *and was buried* &c.}=P_3 ⅔ R'$_4$

2.—P WITH COMPOUND Vs RESOLVED INTO DISTINCT Ps.

1. { Young men should train themselves to marshal their ideas in good order, *and keep* a firm grip of them without the help of paper.}=P_5

1. {Young men should &c., to marshal their ideas in good order.} { *They should keep* a firm grip of them &c.}=$P_5 . P_3$

2. {The same bee, for example, markets and bakes beebread, and manufactures sugar, *and makes* wax, and builds storehouse, and plans apartments, *and nurses* the royal infants, and waits upon the queen, *and apprehends* thieves, and smites to the death the enemies of the amazons.}=P_8

2. { The same bee, for example, markets, bakes bee-bread, and manufactures sugar. } { *She makes* wax, builds store-houses, and plans appartments. } { *She nurses* the royal infants, and waits upon the queen. } { *And lastly, she apprehends* thieves, and smites to the death the enemies of the amazons.}

$$=P_3 \cdot P_3 \cdot P_3 \cdot + P_3$$

C.—Transformation of complex into complex and P.

1.—PR' CHANGED INTO DISTINCT PR' AND P.

1. {Jack Simpkin, *a sailor* who worked in the dock-yards at Portsmouth, *was* at one time much given to drinking.}=P_2 1 R'$_2$

1. { Jack Simpkin *was a sailor* } (who worked in &c) { *He was* at one time much given to drinking.}=P_3 3 R'$_2$. P_2.

D.—TRANSFORMATION OF A SIMPLE INTO COMPLEX STRUCTURE.

(*By change of Adj., Adv., Prep. ph., IV, and PV joiners to N or V, and of terms.*)

I.—P changed into P R' and Vice Versa.

1.—PV JOINER TO N CHANGED INTO R'.

1. The city was managed for sometime by a set of men-*elected* by the people.=P_2.

1. {The city was managed for some time by a set of men} (*who were elected* by the people.)=P_2 ⅔ R'$_2$

2. The generous merchant put young Adorno into a vessel-*bound* for Italy.=P_3

2 {The generous merchant put young Adorno into a vessel} (*which was bound* for Italy.)P_3 ⅔ R'$_2$

3. The ship-*containing* their sons had foundered at sea.=P_2

3. {The ship (*that contained* their sons) had foundered at sea .}=P_2 1R'$_2$

4. The only persons- *composing* the funeral company were four poor-looking old men.=P_3

4. {The only persons (*that composed* the funeral company) were four poor-looking old men.}=P_3 1R'$_3$

In the above examples PV post-joiner of N changed into R'.

1.—R' CHANGED INTO PV JOINER TO N.

1. {The next faculty of the mind (*that demands* special culture) is memory.}=P_3 1 R'$_3$

1. The next faculty of the mind- *demanding* special culture is memory.=P_3

2. {Accomplished speaking, like marching or dancing is an art,} (*for the exercise of which* in many cases a special training is necessary.)=P_3 3 R'$_2$

2. Accomplished speaking, like marching or dancing is an art- *necessitating* in many cases a special training *for its exercise.*=P_3

In these examples R' changed into PV post-joiner of N.

2.—IV JOINER TO N CHANGED INTO R'.

1. The design- *to honour* Mr. Howard in this way was afterwards abandoned.=P_2

1. { The design (*which was to honour* Mr. Howard in this way) was afterwards abandoned. }=P_2 1 R'$_5$

2.—R' CHANGED INTO IV JOINER TO N.

1. {The first lesson (*that a young man has to learn*) is not to find fault but to perceive beauties.}=P_5 1R'$_5$

1. The first lesson- *to be learnt by a young man* is not &c. =P_5

In this example R' active changed into PV passive joiner to N.

3.—IV TERM CHANGED INTO R'.

2. A small quantity was brought *to allay* the thirst of Sir Philip.=P_5

2. {A small quantity was brought} (*which was to allay* the thirst of Sir Philip.)=P 1 R'$_5$

LECTURE XV. 261

4.—Apposition N changed into R• and vice versa.

1. { Mr. Holt (who was a man of good sense and considerable benevolence) resolved to try } (if he could manage the men by some better means than the fear of the lash.)=P_4 1 $R^{\bullet}{}_2$ 4 $C^{\bullet}{}_3$

1. { Mr. Holt, a man of good sense &c.}=P_4 4 $C^{\bullet}{}_3$.

2. This rule, the source of all our troubles, is much disliked.=P_2

2. {This rule (which is the source of &c.,) is &c.}=P_2 1$R^{\bullet}{}_2$

5.—Adverb joiner to V changed into R•.

5. The brook murmured *pleasantly*.=P_2.

5. {The brook murmured *in-a-manner*} { *that was pleasant*.} =P_2 $\frac{2}{3}$ $R^{\bullet}{}_2$.

6.—Prep. ph. joiner to V changed into R•.

1. Country gentlemen would not vote for so large and so expensive an army.=P_2

1. {Country gentlemen would not vote for, an army} (which is so large and so expensive.)=P_2 $\frac{2}{3}$ $R^{\bullet}{}_2$

7.—Prep. ph. joiner to N changed into R•.

1. A boy with a large head is generally intelligent.=P_2

1. {A boy (who has a large head) is &c.}=P_2 1$R^{\bullet}{}_3$

II.—P changed into PC• and Vice Versa.

1.—Adjective joiner to V changed into C•.

3. He arrived *safe*.=P_2

3. { *He was safe*} (*when* he arrived.)=P_2 2$C^{\bullet}{}_2$

2.—Prep. ph. joiner to V changed into C•.

5. {A constant formation of the mould *is always going* on by the *crumbling* of the surface of the land.}=P_2

5. (*As the crumbling* of the surface of the land is always going on) {*there is* a constant formation of the mould.}=2$C^{\bullet}{}_2$ P_2

5. {A constant formation of the mould is always going on} (as the surface of the land *crumbles down*.)=P_2 $C^{\bullet}{}_2$

2.—C⁽ CHANGED INTO PREP. PH. JOINER TO V.

1. {The man died} (*before* the doctor arrived.)$=P_2$ 2 $C^{\cdot}{}_2$
1. {The man died before *the arrival of* the doctor.}$=P_2$
2. {I walked} (*after* the moon rose.)$=P_2$ 2 $C^{\cdot}{}_2$
2. {I walked after *the rising of* the moon (moon-rise).}$=P_2$
3. {This fellow will be a cripple} (*till* he dies).$=P_3$ 2 $C^{\cdot}{}_2$
3. {This fellow will be a cripple till *his death*.}$=P_3$
4. {I have been very happy} (*since* you arrived.)$=P_2$ 2 $C^{\cdot}{}_2$
4. {I have been very happy since *your arrival*.}$=P_2$

2.—PV JOINER TO IV CHANGED INTO C⁽.

1. { We should always be anxious to avoid *provoking* the rebel spirit of the will in those } (who are entrusted to our guidance.)$=P_7 \tfrac{7}{3} R^{\cdot}{}_2$

1. {We should always be anxious to avoid} (*that we do not provoke* the &c.)$=P_4$ 4 $C^{\cdot}{}_3$ $\tfrac{3}{2} R^{2\cdot}{}_2$

3.—3RD TERM CHANGED INTO C⁽.

1. They found the Act no longer tying, but actually strangling them.$=P_3$
1. { They found } (that the Act was no longer tying &c.) $=P_2$ 2 $C^{\cdot}{}_3$

4.—PV TERM CHANGED INTO C⁽.

1. {*In promoting* the welfare of others we must toil.}$=P_5$.
1. {We must toil} (*that we might promote* the welfare of others.)$=P_2$ 2 $C^{\cdot}{}_3$.
2. I am certain of giving you satisfaction.$=P_3$
2. { I am certain } (that I shall give you &c.)$=P_2$ 2$C^{\cdot}{}_3$

4.—C⁽ CHANGED INTO PV TERM.

1. { This applies more particularly } (*when the advice is wanted* for some matter) (which is not of a temporary nature.)
$=P_2$ 2 $C^{\cdot}{}_2$ $\tfrac{2}{3} R^{2\cdot}{}_2$.

1. {This applies more particularly *when wanting the advice* for some matter} (which is not of a temporary nature.)
$=P_5 \tfrac{5}{3} R^{\cdot}{}_2$.

LECTURE XV.

2. (*If we are industrious*){we shall never starve.}=$2C'_2\ P_2$.
2. {We shall never starve *by being industrious.*}=P_4

5.—IV TERM CHANGED INTO C'.

1. { He deemed it best *to conform* in some measure to the superstitions of his fellow-citizens and to conceal his real opinion.} =P_6.

1. { He deemed it best } (*that he might conform* in some measure to the superstitions &c.) =$P_3\ 2\ C'_3$.

2. { It would be nearer the truth *to say* } (that few people are in-the-habit-of employing their imagination in the service of charity.) =$P_4\ 4\ C'_5$.

2. { It would be nearer the truth } (*when we say*) (that few &c.)=$P_2\ 2\ C'_2\ 2\ C^{2'}_5$.

3. { I do not mean *to suggest* } (that truth and right are always to be found in middle courses.)=$P_4\ 4\ C'_4$.

3. { I do not mean } (*that I suggest*) (that truth and right &c.)=$P_2\ 2C'_2\ 2\ C^{2'}_4$.

5.—C' CHANGED INTO IV TERM.

1. { We may remember } (*that sorrow is* at once the lot, the trial, and the privilege of man.)=$P_2\ 2\ C'_2$.

1. { We may remember *sorrow to be* at once the lot, the trial, and privilege of man.}=P_5.

2. { The French accordingly took that without suspecting } (*that he had* any larger sum in his possession.)=$P_4\ 4\ C'_3$.

2. { The French accordingly took that without suspecting *him to have* any larger sum in his possession.)=P_7.

REMARKS :—IV after active V as a rule is transformable into C'. IV after passive V is almost generally not transformable into C' unless the passive expression is rendered into an active.

IV immediately after 'be' and 'have' is not generally transformable into C' when the IV is cheif in its sense or gerundial, and the 'be' and 'have' are like auxiliaries in the combination. Grammarians admit the auxiliary character of 'have' and 'be' when they are followed by present and past participles of the chief verbs, but this auxiliary character is disowned when the IV follows them.

Illustrations.

Am	loving	Have (Present part : wanting)
Am	loved	Have loved
Am	to love	Have to love
Was	to be loved	Had to be loved

That the IVs are *chief* verbs in these instances cannot be denied as they can by no means be transformed into a subordinate C*. IV after certain immediate neuter V cannot be transformed into a C* owing to its Gerundial and inseparable character.

C* is not transformable into IV when its tenses are all potential as also indicative future and future perfect.

As IVs and PVs have no future and potential tenses, while the R* and C* have (except for "may" and "might"), such transformations between them and each other are not allowed in the language. *Joiners* as well as *governed terms* and *governed subordinate structures* are therefore *analogues*, and where their transformations are admissible they show forth slight or no modification in their sense. For examples :—

1. He loves *to seek* the truth.$=P_5$
1. He loves *in seeking* the truth.$=P_5$
1. He loves *that he might seek* the truth.$=P_2\ 2\ C^*_3$

2. Plants also help *to form and renew* the mould.$=P_5$
2. Plants also help *in forming and renewing* the mould.$=P_5$
2. Plants also help *that they may form and renew* the mould.$=P_2\ 2\ C^*_3$

3. I wish *all men's happiness.*$=P_3$
3. I wish *the happiness of all men.*$=P_3$
3. I wish *that all men should be happy.*$=P_2\ 2C^*_2$
3. I wish all men *to be* happy.$=P_4$
3. I wish all men *in being* happy.$=P_4$

III.—P Changed into P c' C"* and Vice Versa.

1.—Prep. phrase joiner to V changed into c' C"*.

1. The earth is round *like* a ball.$=P_2$
1. { The earth is (*as* round } *as* a ball.)$=P_2\ c'\ C'''_2$

LECTURE XV. 265

2.—JOINER AND TERM CHANGED INTO $c'C''^s$.

2. He is *too* honest *to accept* a bribe.$=P_5$
2. {He is *so* honest} (*that he will not* accept &c.)$=P_2$ c' C''^s_s

3.—ADJECTIVE JOINER TO N CHANGED INTO c' R''^s.

3. *Hard-working* pupils may win a prize.$=P_3$
3. { *Such* pupils (*as* work hard)^s may win &c.}$=P_3$ c' R'''^s_2

IV.—Mutual transformation of P into Mono-complexes.

1. The *industrious people* live in a much better style.$=P_{2}$.
1. (*When* the people are industrious) { *they* live in a much better style.}$=2$ C^s_2 P_2
1. { The people (*who are industrious*)^s live in a much better style. }$=P_2$ 1 R^s_2.
1. { *Such* people (*as* are industrious)^s live &c.}$=c'$ P_2 R'''^s_2
2. The *people-not working* but living on fruits or wild animals are said to be in a savage condition.$=P_4$.
2. (*When* the people do not work but live on fruits or wild animals) { *they* are said to be in a savage condition. }$=2$ C^s_2 P_4
2. { The people are said to be in a savage condition } (*who* do not work but live on fruits or wild animals.)$=P_4$ 1 R^s_2
2. { *Such* people (*as* do not work but live on fruits &c.) are said &c. }$=c'.P_4$ R''^s_2
3. An *industrious man* is happy.$=P_2$.
3. A man (*that is industrious*) is happy.$=P_2$1R^s_2.
3. (*When* a man is industrious) {*he* is happy.}$=2$ $C^s_2P_2$.
3. {*Such* a man (*as* is industrious) is happy.}$=c'$ P_2 R''^s_2

E.—Transformation of Absolute united to P into P, Complex, or Compound.

1.—$(N \mid PV)$ CHANGED INTO A PREP. PH. IN P, OR C^s.

1. $($*Winter approaching*,$)$ { he returned to town. }
$=(N \mid PV)P_2$
1. *On the approach of winter* he returned to town.$=P_2$
1. (*When the winter approached*) {he returned &c.}$=2C^s_2P_2$

2.—$\langle$N | PV$\rangle$ United to P changed into P+P or PC'.

1. {James and Robert were brothers,} $\langle$*the one* being about 7 years of age and *the other* less than 5.$\rangle$=P$_2$ $\langle$ N | PV+N $\rangle$

1. { James and Robert were brothers, } { *the one was* about 7 years of age, } and { *the other was* less than 5.}=P$_3$, P$_2$+P$_3$

1. { James and Robert were brothers. } { *James was* about 7 years of age, } and {*Robert was* less than 5. }=P$_2^1$. P$_2^{\cdot}$+P$_2$

2. { He allowed them for some time to eat out of his own plate ; } but $\langle$their habits *being* rather slovenly$\rangle$ { he was afterwards glad to give them a separate dish.}=P$_4$+$\langle$ N | PV $\rangle$ P$_5$

2. { He allowed them &c. out of &c. } but (*as* their habits *were* rather slovenly) { he was afterwards glad &c.}=P$_4$+C'$_2$ P$_5$

2. {He allowed &c.} but {their habits *were* rather slovenly,} *and* {he was &c.}=P$_4$+P$_2$+P$_5$

2.—$\langle$N | IV$\rangle$ Absolutes changed into compound Ps.

1. { It is therefore incumbent upon us all both as individuals and as nations to take an interest in each other, } $\langle$the strong *to help* the weak,$\rangle$ $\langle$the good *to correct* and improve the bad,$\rangle$ $\langle$the rich *to help* the needy,$\rangle$ and $\langle$the enlightened *to impart* their knowledge to the ignorant.$\rangle$

=P$_6$ $\langle$ 1 4 5 $\rangle$,$\langle$ 1 4 5 $\rangle$ $\langle$ N | IV | N $\rangle$ + $\langle$1 4 5$\rangle$

1. { It is therefore incumbent &c., in each other, } { the strong *should help* &c.,} { the good *should correct* &c.,} { the rich *should help* &c.,} and { the enlightened *should impart* &c.}

=P$_6$, P$_3$, P$_3$, P$_3$+P$_3$

3.—PV Absolute changed into C'.

1. $\langle$ *Reflecting* upon this decay and renewing of soil,$\rangle$ { we perceive } (that-in-reality the whole surface of the land may be looked upon as travelling down to the sea.)

=$\langle$PV$\rangle$P$_3$ 2 C'$_4$

LECTURE XV.   267

1. (*If we reflect* upon this decay and renewing of soil) { we perceive } (that &c.)=$C'_2 P_3 2 C'_4$

2. $($*Sitting* on the river side,$)$ { I saw a boat-passing by.} =$($PV$)P_3$.

2 (*As I sat* on the river side,) {I saw a boat-passing by.} =$C'_2 P_3$.

3. $($*Hearing* this,$)$ {he advanced.}=$($PV$|$N$)P_2$.

3. (*As he heard* this,) {he advanced.}=$C'_3 P_2$.

3.—C' CHANGED INTO PV ABSOLUTE.

1. (*When you have arrived* at your decision) {you have to consider} (how you shall convey it.)=$4C'_2 P_4 4C'_3$

1. $($*Having arrived* at your decision$)$ {you have to consider} (how you shall convey it.)=$($ PV $) P_4 4C'_3$

Remarks :—C' in instances with Indicative Future and Pot. as said before are not transformable.

4.—PV ABSOLUTE CHANGED INTO $c' C'$.

1. $($At length *seeing* the other rat eat so heartily,$)$ { she rushed forward, seized a piece, and immediately retreated. }

=$($ 4 5 6 $) P_3$

1. { At length *she saw* the other rat eat *so* heartily } (*that* she rushed forward &c.)=$P_4 c' C''_3$

5.—$($PV+N $|$ PV$)$ UNITED TO P CHANGED INTO P+PC'.

1. $($*Clogged* in his wings, enfeebled in his legs, and his whole *frame* totally *enervated.*$)$ { he was but just able to bid his friends adieu and to lament with his latest breath } (that [though a taste of pleasure may quicken the relish of life,] [an unrestrained indulgence brings inevitable destruction.]

=$($ 4, 4, + 1 4 $) P_5 2C(C'P_3 C''P_3)'$

1. {*He was clogged* in his wings, enfeebled in his legs,} and {his whole *frame was* totally *enervated*,} (*so that he was* but &c.)

=$P_2+P_2 C'_5 2 C (C' P_3 C'P_3)'$

F.—Transformation of Complex into Co-ordinate or Compound and *Vice Versa*.

1.—P Complex changed into C′P C″P or P+P.

1. (*If* the repast was homely) {the welcome was hearty.}
= $C'_2 P_2$

1. [*Though* the repast was homely] [*yet* the welcome was hearty.] = $C'P_2 C''P_2$

1. {The repast was homely,} *but* {the welcome was hearty.}
= $P_2 + P_2$

2.—Di-simple C′P C″P changed into Complex.

1. Thus [the sea [*though* it bears no harvest on its bosom] *yet* sustains all the harvests of the world and makes all the wilderness of the earth to bud and blossom as the rose.]
= $+C''P_4 4C'_2 \ C'P_3$

1. Thus {the sea (*which bears* no harvest on its bosom) sustains all &c.} = $+P_4 \ 1 \ R'_3 \ 4C'_2$

3.—Di-simple C′P C″P changed into compound P+P.

1. [{*Though* Isaac Newton was wiser} (than most other men)] [{ *yet* he said } (a-little-before he died) (that all his knowledge was as nothing-when compared with (what) he had yet to learn.)]
= $C'P_2 \ c' \ C''_2 \ C''P_2 \ 2 \ C'_2 \ 2 \ C'_3 \ \tfrac{3}{3} \ R^2 \cdot_5$

1. {Isaac Newton was wiser than most other men,} *and yet* {he said} (a-little-before he died) (that all his knowledge &c.)
= $P_2 \ c' \ C'''_2 + P_2 \ 2 \ C'_2 \ 2 \ C'_3 \ \tfrac{3}{3} \ R^2 \cdot_5$

2. [*Though* the magnificent romance of the sack of Rome be not fact] [*yet* it is certainly history and well worthy of note and remembrance as one of the finest extant traditions of a whole chain of Golden Deeds.] = $C'P_2 \ C''P_3$

2. {The magnificent romance of the sack of Rome *may* not be a fact} *but* {it is certainly history &c.} = $P_2 + P_2$

4.—Compound changed into Complex.

1. {Speak the truth,} and {you need no fear.}$=P_3+P_3$.
1. (*If you* speak the truth,) {you need have no fear.}$=C^{\bullet}P_5$.

G.—Mutual Transformation of all structures.

1. { It is necessary in reading verse to trust a great deal to ear, } *but* { we must be careful not to do so to the detriment of the sense.} $=P_5 + P_5$. (*Compound.*)

1. [*Though* it is necessary &c.,] [*yet* we must be careful &c.]$=C'P_5$ $C''P_5$ (*Co-ordinate.*)

1. {It is *not only* necessary in reading verse to trust &c.,} (*but* we must be careful &c.)$=P_5$ $c'C''_5$ (c' C''• *Complex.*)

1. (*As* it is necessary in reading verse to trust a great deal to ear,) { we must be careful &c.}$=C^{\bullet}_5\ P_5$ ($C^{\bullet}$ *Complex.*)

1. {To trust a good deal to ear is necessary in reading verse} (in which we must be careful &c.)$=P_2\ R^{\bullet}_5$ ($R^{\bullet}$ *Complex.*)

1. In reading verse we must necessarily trust a great deal to ear, *and* be careful not to do so &c.$=P_5$ (*Simple.*)

1. {In reading verse we must trust &c. to ear,} ζ taking care not to do so &c.$\rangle=P_5$ $\langle 4\ 5\ 6\ 7\rangle$ (*Simple with Absolute.*)

2. { John is strong} *but* {he is sickly.} $P_2 + P_2$
2. [*Though* John is strong,] [*yet* he is sickly.]$=C'P_2\ C'P_2$
2. {John (who is strong) is yet sikly.}$=P_2\ 1R^{\bullet}_2$
2. {John is sickly} (*though* he is strong.) $=P_2\ 2C^{\bullet}_2$
2. {*Such* a strong man (*as* John)• is sickly.}$=c'\ P_2\ C''_3$
2. John is strong but sickly.$=P_2$
2. Being a strong man, John is yet sickly.$=\langle 4\ 5\rangle\ P_2$

Having thus shown to you the feasible Transformations so far as above, let us now enter into *more complicated structures*, and try to transform them *into less complicated* but increased or distinct ones.

H.—Transformation of more complicated into less complicated structures.

1. {The moral nature like every thing else (*if it is to grow* into any sort of excellence) demands a special culture ;} *and* (*as* our passions by their very nature like the winds are not easy of

control) and (our actions are the outcome of our passions) $\{i^f$ follows,$\}$ (*that moral excellence* will in no case be an easy affair and in its highest grades will be the most arduous, and as such the most noble achievement of a thoroughly accomplished humanity.)= P_3 $C^{\bullet}_4 + 2C^{\bullet}_2 + 2C^{\bullet}_3$ P_2 $2C^{\bullet}_3$

1. {The moral nature like every thing else *in-order-to grow into any sort of excellence demands a special culture.*} {Our passions by their very nature like the winds are not easy of control} and {our actions are the outcome of our passions.} {*Moral excellence therefore* will in no case be an easy affair, and in its highest grades will be the most arduous and *hence* the most noble achievement of a thoroughly accomplished humanity.}

$$= P_3 \cdot P'_2 + P_3 \cdot C^{\bullet}_3$$

2. {It was an easy thing for Lord Byron to be a great poet;} {*it was* merely indulging his nature,} {he was an eagle and must fly;} but {(to have curbed his wilful humour, soothed his fretful discontent and learned to behave like a reasonable being and a gentleman)^N *that was* a difficult matter} (*which he does not seem even seriously to have attempted.*)

$$= P_5 ; P_3 ; P_3 ; + P_3 \, 3R^{\bullet}_5$$

2. {It was an easy thing for Lord Byron to be a great poet} (*for it was* merely indulging his nature.) {He was an eagle and must fly.} But {(to have curbed his wilful humour, soothed his fretful discontent and learned to behave like a resonable being and a gentlemen)^N *was* a difficult matter *never seemingly been attempted even seriously by him.*}= P_5 $C^{\bullet}_3 \cdot P_3 \cdot + P_3$

3. {Another flaring beacon of the rock (*on which great wits are often wrecked* for want of a little kindly culture of unselfishness) is Walter Savage Landor, *the most finished master* of style perhaps} (that ever used the English tongue;) but {*a person* at the same time so imperiously wilful and so majestically crossgrained} (*that with all his polished style and pointed thought* he was constantly living on the verge of insanity.)

$$= P_3 \, 1R^{\bullet}_2 \, 3R^{\bullet}_3 ; + P_3 \, c' \, C''^{\bullet}_2$$

3. {Another flaring beacon of the rock-*wrecking great wits* for want of a little kindly culture of unselfishness is Walter Savage Landor} (*who was the most finished master* of style perhaps) (that ever used the English tongue.) But {*he was a person* at the same time so imperiously wilful and so magestically crossgrained *in spite of* all his polished style and pointed thought} (*that* he was constantly living on the verge of insanity.)

$$= P_3 \ 3R\text{'}_3 \ 3R^{2\text{'}}{}_3 \ . + P_3 \ c' \ C''\text{'}_2$$

4. {Money is *not needful*;} {power is *not needful*;} {cleverness is *not needful*;} {fame is not needful;} {liberty is not needful;} {even {health is *not the one thing needful*;} but {character alone, *a thoroughly cultivated will*, is that which can truly save us;} and (if we are not saved in this sense) {we must certainly be damned.}

$$= P_2 \ ; \ P_2 \ ; \ P_2 \ ; \ P_2 \ ; \ P_2 \ ; + P_3 \ ; + P_3 \ 3R\text{'}_3 + 2C\text{'}_2 \ P_2$$

4. {We need *neither* money *nor* power, cleverness *nor* fame;} {we need *no* liberty *nor* even (what} we call health.) {(What we need the most) is character} (*which is but another name for* a thoroughly cultivated will.) {*By this alone* we can be truly saved,} and {*it must certainly be damnation to us*} (*if* character cannot save us.)

$$= P_3 \ ; \ P_3 \ 3 \ R\text{'}_3 \ . \ P_3 \ 1R\text{'}_3 \ 3R\text{'}_3 \ . \ P_2 + P_3 \ 3C\text{'}_3$$

5. At length (one of the most hardy lifting up his head above the surface of the lake,) "Ah, dear children!" said he, "why will you learn so soon to be cruel?"

$$= + \langle \ N \ | \ PV \ \rangle \ P_2, \ "\langle \ ! \ N \ \rangle \ P_4" \ ?$$

5. At length {one of the most hardy- lifting up his head above the surface of the lake *said*} ⟨" Ah, dear children,⟩ {why will you learn so soon to be cruel?"} $= + P_2 \ "\langle \ ! \ N \ \rangle \ P_4" \ ?$

Thus you see structures may be cast and recast from one another, and these under specified rules. The various *Transformations* are by no means arbitrary, some being castings and others Recastings.

LECTURE XVI.

STUDENTS AND GENTLEMEN,

I have already by concise and stray criticism shown to you that there is always an unconscious tendency with each writer to produce particular structural repetitions in his style; and his peculiarity, if carefully traced out, might possibly isolate him from the rest of his class very much in the same way as we do distinguish different individuals by their respective features or lineaments.

This *philologico-structural feature of an author* then can only be arrived at, by going very deeply into his writing by constant reference to the Graphic and Rational formula as shown in this work.

Upto yet the *system of analysis* taught in schools is a more expansive process, while the stylographic system as divulged herein, brings you to a compact and rational one in the same. I hope, therefore, that more than the rapid stride of phonography, the short-hand *conventional system* of speech representation by linear symbols, Stylography or the contracted system of style representation by formulae may one day come to be taken as a part and parcel of philology, for it is evidently a thoroughly scientific system applicable to all languages as I have found its applicability to the French and German as well as to some of the Indian languages. But before I conclude the work I must assert that as there is structural distinction in the writings of different authors, the *various subjects* themselves, on the other hand, necessitate *varieties of style*, so that volumes might be written on them.

I give you below only a tentative table of five subjects— Mathematics, Science, Law, Medicine, and Poetry of which the illustrations will show forth distinct peculiarities of each subject and similarity if any between the many members of the same subject.

Table of subjects with their distinguishing structures.

SUBJECTS.	BRANCHES.	PORTIONS.	PREDOMINATING STRUCTURES FOUND.
1. Mathematics	Geometry Conics Trignonetry Mensuration Astronomy Mechanics Algebra Arithmetic	Problem Book Articles	IV Absolute, Imperative Ps, and C⁎ or C'P C''P with conjunctions of reason.
2. Science	Botany Zoology Physics Chemistry	Systematic Classification Experimental Do.	N Absolutes, rarely Assertive Ps. Inp. Ps, C⁎ with conjs. of reason, and rarely Assertive Ps.
3. Law	Criminal	Indian Penal Code	Alternative (rarely copulative) increase of terms or joiners.
4. Medicine	Materia Medica	Pharmacopœa	Inp Ps, rarely Assertive Ps.
5. Literature	Poetry	Rhyme, Blank Verse	Transposition & ellipsis of terms, joiners, and connectives.

I.—Mathematics.

A.—Geometry.

Problem.

To describe an equilateral triangle on a given finite straight line.=⦃ I V | N ⦄

Let AB be the given straight line. It is required to describe an equilateral triangle on AB.=P_5. P_5

Construction.—From centre A, with radius AB, describe the circle BCD.=P_3

From centre B, with radius BA, describe the circle ACE. =P_3

From the point C at which the circles cut one-another, draw the straight lines CA and CB to the points A and B.=P_3 $\frac{2}{3}$ R$^{\bullet}_3$

Then shall ABC be an equilateral triangle.= +P_3

Proof :— *Because* A is the centre of the circle BCD, *therefore* AC is equal to AB.=C′P_3 C″P_2

And *because* B is the centre of the circle ACE, *therefore* BC is equal to BA.= +C′P_2 C″P_2

But it has been shewn that AC is equal to AB ;
therefore AC and AB are each equal to AB.= +P_2 2 C$^{\bullet}_2$; C$^{\bullet}_2$

But things which are equal to the same thing are equal to one another.= +P_2 1R$^{\bullet}_2$

Therefore AC is equal to BC.=C$^{\bullet}_2$

Therefore CA, AB, BC are equal to one-another.=C$^{\bullet}_2$

Therefore the triangle ABC is equilateral; and it is described on the given straight line AB. Q. E. F.=C$^{\bullet}_2$;˙ +P_2 . R$^{\bullet}_4$

REMARKS :—In Geometry the *General enunciation* of a problem as you see here, is an absolute structure beginning with an IV 4th term. The *particular enunciation* is an imperative followed by an assertive Mono-simples. *Construction* brings on the imperative and assertive again, while *proof* introduces Co-ordinate P structure or Integral sub-ordinate structure with conjunction of reason 'because—therefore" or only integral " therefore". The Compound stuctures are initiative with 'and,' 'but' and lastly, you see the assertive, "which was to be done."

II.—Science.

A.—SYSTEMATIC BOTANY.

Anonaceæ.

Diagnosis.—⟨Trees or shrubs with naked buds and no stipules;⟩ ⟨thalamus usually prominently convex;⟩ ⟨calyx of three sepals;⟩ ⟨corolla of six petals in two circles, usually valvate in the bud, hypogynous, sometimes coherent:⟩ ⟨stamens with an enlarged connective, mostly indefinite, on a large torus:⟩ ⟨carpels usually numerous, separate or cohering:⟩ ⟨seed with ruminated perisperm.⟩

= ⟨N⟩ ⟨N⟩ ⟨N⟩ ⟨N⟩ ⟨N⟩ ⟨N⟩ ⟨N⟩.

Dicotyledones.

CHARACTER.—⟨ Flowering Plants, with stems-having pith and bark-separated by a compact layer of wood,⟩ (which, in perennial plants, receives annual additions on the outside, beneath the bark;)* ⟨leaves with the ribs- mostly distributed in a netted pattern and generally diminishing in size⟩ (as they branch ;)* ⟨parts of the floral circles mostly 5 or 4, or some multiple of those numbers, rarely 3;⟩ ⟨embryos with a pair of cotyledons and a radicle,⟩ (which is devolped into a tap-root in germination.)* { The typically complete floral formula, ⟨supposing the parts to be uncomplicated by adhesions, irregular growth, multiplication, &c.,⟩ is S5 P5 A5 G5, in regular alternation. }—

A. Henfrey.

= ⟨N⟩ $\frac{1}{3}$ R'$_s$ ⟨ N ⟩ $\frac{1}{4}$ C'$_2$ ⟨N⟩ ⟨N⟩ $\frac{1}{3}$ R'$_2$.

P$_3$ ⟨ 4 5 6 ⟩

How to describe a Plant.

Description of a flower.

ORCHIS.—⟨Flower irregular.⟩ ⟨Perianth irregular, of 6 very unequal pieces.⟩ ⟨Stamens, confined with the style.⟩ ⟨Pistil of 3 carpels confined into 1-celled ovary.⟩

= ⟨N⟩ . ⟨N⟩ . ⟨N | PV⟩ . ⟨N | PV⟩

Description of a fruit.

MULBERRY.—(A head of fruits,) (each consisting- of a dry 1-seeded little indehiscent nut- inclosed in four juicy perianth pieces.)—*J. D. Hooker.* (Vide also Roxburgh's Flora indica.)

$$=(N) (N \mid PV\ N).$$

B.—Zoolgy.

NATURAL SYSTEM OF CLASSIFICATION.

Infusoria.

Diagnosis.—(Protozoa with a definite form and provided with an external membrane, bearing either flagella or cilia.) (Mouth and anus usually, contractile vacuole and one or more nuclei always present.)

$$=(N \mid PV \mid N).(N + N \mid N + N)$$

Scyphomedusæ.

Diagnosis.—(Medusæ of considerable size, with gastric filaments.) (The edge of the umberella lobed.) (The sense organs covered.) {The embryonic stages are not hydroid stocks but scyphistoma and strobila forms.}

$$=(N) \cdot (N \mid PV) \cdot (N \mid PV) \cdot P_3$$

Xiphosura.

Diagnosis.—(Gigantostraca) (whose body is divided into three parts,)·(which are movably articulated together ;)^{2*} (a large shield-shaped cephalo-thorax,) (an abdomen with five pairs of lamellar feet and a long movable caudal spine.)

$$= (N) 1\ R\cdot_2\ \tfrac{2}{3}\ R\cdot_2\ ; (N), (N).$$

Asteroidea.

Diagnosis.—(Echinoderms with dorso-ventrally compressed pentagonal or star-shaped body.) (The ambulacral feet are confined to the ventral surface.) (Internal skaletal pieces in the ambulacra articulated together like vertebræ.)—*Claus-sedgwick.*

$$=(N) \cdot P_2 \cdot (N \mid PV)$$

C.—Experimental Physics.

EXPERIMENT.—{To prove osmose.} { take two glass jars, one larger than the other ;} {put into the larger one a certain quantity of water, and into the other water (to which sugar and some soluble colouring matter have been added.) {Tie a a piece of parchment over the smaller one, *and then* invert it into the larger one, as shown in the figure.} {After a few hours, on removing the smaller jar the water in the larger one will be seen to be coloured, and also to be less than before,} *whereas* {the fluid in the smaller one will be found to be lighter in colour and increased in volume.} *Thus* {we see that osmose has taken place.}

$$= \{ IV \mid N \} P_3 \; ; \; P_3 \; \S \; R^{\cdot}{}_2 \cdot P_3 + P_3 \cdot P_4 + P_4 \cdot + P_2 \; C^{\cdot}{}_2$$

D.—Experimental Chemistry.

EXPERIMENT.—{Hold a wide mouthed bottle or cylinder- filled with hydrogen with the mouth downward.} {Insert into the vessel a lighted taper- held on a bent wire, as shown in the figure.} {The gas takes fire at the mouth of the vessel, but the taper is extinguished.}—*Ira Remsen.*

$$= P_3 \cdot P_3 \cdot P_3 + P_2$$

EXPERIMENT.—{ Place a few drops of wood spirit on the deflagrating spoon, and set fire to the liquid ; } *now* { lower the spoon into a dry jar of air, allow the combustion to proceed for a short time, *then* remove the still burning spirit and cover the mouth of the jar with the hand. } { Note that some moisture has condensed on the sides of the jar, and the residual gas-when shaken up with some lime-water, ·causes the usual turbidity- indicative of the presence of carbon dioxide. } (*Therefore* the wood spirit contains carbon :) {hydrogen is *also* present in it, (*as* the moisture-produced is water.)

$$= P_3 + P_3 \; ; + P_3^{\cdot}, \; P_4, + P_3 + P_3 \cdot P_2 \; 2 \; C^{\cdot}{}_2, + 2 \; C^{\cdot}{}_3 \cdot C^{\cdot}{}_3 \; ;$$
$$+ P_2 \; C^{\cdot}{}_2$$

EXPERIMENT.—{Add some nitric acid to an aqueous solution-containing some glycolic acid, and warm in a test tube ;} {ruddy fumes are evolved, indicating oxidation.} (When the chief action is over,) {boil for a short time, and evaporate a few drops of the liquid on a watch-glass;} {colourless crystals separate,} (which consist of *oxalic acid.*)—*J. E. Reynolds.*

$$= P_3 + P_2;\ P_2 \cdot C'_2\ P_2 + P_3;\ P_2\ 1\ R'_2$$

III.—Law.
Indian Penal Code.

{ (Whoever hires, *or* engages *or* employs *or* promotes *or* connives at the hiring, engagement *or* employment of any person to join *or* become a member of any unlawful assembly,) shall be punishable as a member of such unlawful assembly *and* for any offence } (which may be committed by any such person as a member of such unlawful assembly, in pursuance of such hiring, engagement *or* employment in the *same* manner (*as if he had been a member of such unlawful assembly*) *or* (himself had committed such offence.)

$$= P_3\ 1R'_5\ \tfrac{2}{3}\ R'_3\ c'\ C''_3 + C'''_3.$$

REMARKS :—In $1R'_5$ you find five alternative increase of the 2nd term, three alternative increase of the post-joiner 3 of the 2nd term, and two alternative increase of the 4th term—by alternative conjunction " or."

In P_3, the 3rd term and the post-joining Prepositional phrase of the 2nd term have been compounded by "and."

In $\tfrac{2}{3}\ R'_3$, the final post-joiner 3 of 2nd term has three alternatives and lastly, the 2nd term post-joiner of P_3 bears a co-ordinate subordinated by two alternative increase of C''_3.

Thus you see in the principal and subordinate structures, *alternative increase of terms and joiners predominate* while once only a copulative compound increase is visible.

IV.—Medicine.
BRITISH PHARMACOPŒA.

Santonium.

A crystalline principle prepared from Santonica.$= (N\ |\ PV)$
It may be obtained by the following process :— $= P_2$

Take of $=P_3$
Santonica, bruised   1 pound
Slaked Lime   7 ounces
Hydrochlor : Acid   a sufficiency
Sol : of Ammon :   a quarter ounce
Rect : spirit   14 f : ounces
Purified : Anim : Charcoal 60 grains
Dist : water   a sufficiency.

Boil the santonica with a gallon of the water and 5 ounces of the lime in a copper or tinned iron vessel for an hour, strain through a stout cloth, and express strongly. Mix the residue with half a gallon of the water and the rest of the lime, boil for half an hour, strain and express as before. Mix the strained liquors, let them settle, decant the fluid from the deposit, and evaporate to the bulk of 2 pints and a half. To the liquor while hot, add, with diligent stirring, the hydrochloric acid until the fluid has become slightly and permanently acid, and set it aside for 5 days that the precipitate may subside.

$=P_3$, P_2+P_2. P_3, P_2, P_2. P_3, P_4, P_3+P_2. P_3 $2C'_2$, $+P_3$ $2C'_2$.

Remove, by skimming, any oily matter which floats on the surface, and carefully decant the greater part of the fluid from the precipitate.

Collect this on a paper filter, wash it *first* with cold distilled water (till the washings pass colourless and nearly free from acid reaction), *then* with the solution of ammonia previously diluted with 5 fluid ounces of the water, and *lastly* with cold distilled water (till the washings pass colourless.)

Press the filter containing the precipitate between the folds of filtering paper, and dry it in a warm place.

Scrape the dry precipitate from the filter, and mix it with the animal charcoal.

Add to the mixture 9 ounces of the rectified spirit, digest for half an hour, and boil for 10 minutes.

Filter while hot, wash the charcoal with an ounce of boiling spirit, and set the filtrate aside for 2 days in a cool dark place to crystallise.

Separate the mother liquor from the crystals, and concentrate to obtain a further product.

Collect the crystals, let them drain, redissolve them in 4 ounces of boiling spirit, and let the solution crystallise as before.

280   STYLOGRAPHY OF ENGLISH LANGUAGE.

Lastly, dry the crystals on filtering paper in the dark and preserve them in a bottle protected from light.

$= P_4 \, 3R'_2 + P_3 \cdot P_3, P_3 \, C'_2 \cdot P_3 + P_3 \cdot P_3 + P_3 \cdot P_3 + P_2 + P_2 \cdot$

$P_2, P_3 + P_4 \cdot P_3 + P_5 \cdot P_3, P_4, P_3 + P_4 \cdot + P_3 + P_3$

Remarks :— The language of Pharmacopœal peparations being directions, 14 out of 16 Sentences terminated by Period have consequently been Imperatives, while of the remaining two, one is absolute and the other an Assertive.

In the 1st imperative, the post-joining preposition phrases of V and the 3rd terms have been repeated without the intervention of punctuation or conjunction. Second term Vs have been repeated in the way of compounds from 2 to 4 in all the sentences with comma and conjunction (and). The imperative Mono-simples have in some instances been extended to the 4th and 5th terms. Their complexities by R• and C• Subordinates are also visible. Post-joining adverbial repetitions of progressive time *first*, *then*, and *lastly* to V were also visible in one instance with punctuation and conjuction. The last sentence is headed by connective "lastly" as conjunction, compounding it with all the previous sentences.

There are seen *no Absolutes, no Integral subordinates*, no compounds of Subordinates, *no co-ordinate Subordinates*, no Sub-subordinate with these Imperatives, nor are Co-ordinate Principals *i.e.*, Di-simples seen to make their possible appearance here.

V.—Poetry.

Rhyme.

1. {∗Not | a drum | was∗heard } {∗not | a funeral note (A∗V)}
(As | his corpse | ∗ to the ramparts | we | hurried ∗;)
{∗Not | a soldier | discharged ∗ | his farewell shot
∗O'er the grave} (where |∗our hero | we | burried∗.)— *Wolfe.*
$= P_2, P_2 \, C'_3. \quad P_3 \, \tfrac{2}{3} \, R'_3.$

2. { Such was the sound, } (when-oft, | ∗ at-evening close,
∗ Up yonder hill | the village murmur rose ∗ ;)
{ There, (as I passed with careless ∗ steps | ∗ and slow,)
The mingling notes came- softened from below : }
{ The swain responsive (as the milk-maid sung,)
The sober herd (that low'd to meet their young ;)

The noisy geese (that gabbled o'er the pool,)
The playful children-just let loose from school,
The watch-dog's voice, (that bayed the whispering wind,)
And the loud laugh (that spoke the vacant mind ;)
These all | * in sweet confusion | sought * | the shade,
And filled each pause } ((R)'the nightingale had made.)—
Goldsmith.

$= P_2 \, 2 \, C'_2 \, ; \ P_2 \, 2 \, C'_2 \, : \ (N \tfrac{1}{2} C'_2, \, N \, 1 \, R'_5 \, ; \ N \, 1 \, R'_2, N,$
$N \, 1 \, R'_3 + N \, 1 \, R'_3 \, ; \,)^N P_3 \, 3 \, R'_3.$

Blank Verse.

1. (Distinguished much by reason, and still more
By our capacity of grace divine,
From creatures) (that exist but for our sake,)
(Which (having served us,) perish,) {we are held
Accountable ;} and { God, some future day,
Will reckon with us roundly for the abuse
Of (what} he deems (IV) no mean or trivial trust.)
(*Superior | as they are *) {they yet depend
Not *more* on human help} (*than* we (V) on theirs.)
{Their strength, or speed, or vigilence, were given
In aid of our defects;}'{ * in some | are found * |
Such teachable and apprehensive parts,}
(*That* man's attainments in his own concerns-
Matched with the expertness of the brutes in theirs,
Are oft times vanquished and thrown far behind.)—*Cowper.*

$= (PV) \tfrac{4}{3} R'_2 \tfrac{4}{3} R'_2 \, (\, PV \, | \, N \,) \, P_2 + P_2 \tfrac{2}{3} R'_5.$
$C'_2 \, P_2 \, c' \, C''_2 . \, P_2 \, ; \ P_2 c' \, C''_2 .$

2. { * Of man's first disobedience, and the fruit
Of that forbidden tree, (whose mortal taste
Brought death into the world, and all our woe,
With loss of Eden,)* (till one greater Man
Restore us, and regain the blissful seat,)²*
| Sing, * } (heavenly muse,) (that | * on the secret top

Of Oreb, or of Sinai, | didst inspire * |
That shepherd,)* (who first taught the chosen seed)²*
(*.In the beginning | how | the heavens and Earth
Rose * out of chaos.)³*—*Milton.*
$= P_2 \tfrac{2}{3} R^{\prime}{}_3 \; 2 \; C^{\prime}{}_3 \; (N) \; 1 \; R^{\prime}{}_3 \; 3 \; R^{2\prime}{}_3 \; 2 \; C^{3\prime}{}_2.$

Examination Questions on Stylography.

1. *Construct* or write down from your text-book illustrations of naked and clothed N , V, IV , and PV term respectively with Graphic Formula of each.

2. *Exemplify* from any book a Minimum Mono-simple Sentence with Graphic and Rational Formulæ, (G. F. and R. F.)

3. *Illustrate* a Medium Mono-simple by 3 terms or by 4, in which the 3rd term may or may not be absent, both graphically or rationally.

4. *Write down* from memory or otherwise an example of Maximum Mono-simple with G. F. and R. F. each.

5. How do you differentiate a Narrative from an Imperative expression P in the G. F. ; an Interrogative from the Exclamatory also if any?

6. *Unite* an Interjection Absolute or a Vocative Absolute to any of the Narrative, Imperative, Interrogative, or Exclamatory Expression P with G. F. and R. F.

7. *Give* a P with transposed 3rd term to the 1st seat or between 2nd term and its post-joiner in the Mono-simple with G. F.

8. Can you exemplify differentiating a Mono-simple by transposed PV term and its union with a PV Absolute with G.F. and R.F. of each.

9. Illustrate an IV absolute union to a mono-simple with Graphical and Rational formulae.

10. Give illustrations of a mono-simple each with N | PV and N | IV absolute union and their G. F.

11. Exemplify a C* and R* giving G. F.

12. *Seek out* PR* or PC* mono-subordinate Complex with any number of terms in the P or Subordinate giving their G. F.

13. What difference is there between a Bi-subordinate and a Di-subordinate Complex ? Exemplify.

14. Exemplify with G. and R. formulae a Poly-subordinate Complex.

15. Give an example of a Mono-simple with increase in the 1st, 3rd or any odd term by Ns of Capacity intervened by a comma-connective with G. and R. formulae.

16. Illustrate mono-simple sentences each with increased

terms, joiners, or sub-joiners respectively with intervention of Mono-groupal conjunction connectives and punctuative commas if necessary. Give their G. F. and R. F.

17. Give similar illustrations with Bi-groupal or Co-ordinate connectives with G. F. and R. F.

18. Give example of post-joiner 3 of second term transposed to 1st seat with G. F.

19. Illustrate IV | PV or alternate IV | PV Analogues of N in the 1st term of mono-simple with G. F. and R. F.

20. Exemplify N | V inversions into V | N in the 4 varieties of expressions, the Narrative, the Imperative, the interrogative, and the exclamatory with G. F. and R. F.

21. Write down from your book a complex PC* substitutive subordination, a Di-complex with C* P C* substitutive subordination.

22. Exemplify from your book a complex of N absolute subordinated by R*, IV or PV absolute by C* either independent or initial to a P.

23. Construct or pick out Illustrations of the following Rational Formula without restriction of terms in each P C* C^{2*}, P C* R^{2*}.

24. Find out and write Graphically and Rationally a P with Parenthetic C* or R* or P.

25. Construct or write down from your text-book a Di-simple structure with G. F. and R. F.

26. Give a Di-simple P structure with equal or unequal subordination of each with G. F. and R. F.

27. *Depict* Graphically and Rationally a Compound of P structures.

28. Give a Complex in which an R* or C* is compounded, with G. F. and R. F.

29. Construct a sentence in way of synthesis the R. F. of which is P_2 $2C^*_3$.

30. *Form* a sentence of which the R. F. is P_9 without heed to the joiners of each of the terms.

31. Give example of a riveted PR* with both kinds of F.

32. Find out from your text a compound of C'P C"P by punctuation or connective with R. fromula of the whole.

33. Construct a sentence with P c' C"* or P c' R*" as R. F.

34. *Produce* a compound of Ps, and 2 other structures of compounds of R*, and C* combined with Ps with option of terms in each.

35. *Convert* an Assertive Direct-Narrative into continued Narrative with Formulae.

36. *Wanted* an Interrogative, an Imperative Direct-Narrative each into continued Narrative conversion with F. of them.

37. Give the Graphic Formulae of the following *Quotation Analogues* of N,—

Ex. 1. "Ask what is unjust", is a good rule where a man hath strength of favour.

Ex. 2. "Be angry, but sin not : let not the sun go down upon your anger", must be limited and confined, both in race and time.

38 Give an example of *Compound Absolute*-structure.

39. How would you *turn* a Principal with joiner co-ordinates into an elliptical Co-ordinate Principal.

40. *Enclose* the following within appropriate brackets with their respective powers where necessary, dividing the terms by perpendicular lines and depicting the transpositions if any by asterisks—"The house fell and great was the fall there of."

41. *Write a letter* to your friend on malaria in which there would be 5 sentences only with the following structures in them. P . PC* . PR* . C'P C"P . and P+P.

42. Illustrate 3 distinct Ps with as many increase of V terms and transform them into a single P with so many terms compounded.

43. Exemplify a P with PV or IV Post-joiner to N transformed into a PR*.

44. Can you *convert* a Negative adversative P+P into C'P C'P.

45. What are the distinctive *peculiarities of style* in Mathematics and Poetry.

46. "When a man is from necessity his own tailor, tent-maker, carpenter, cook, huntsman, and fisherman, it is not probable that he will be expert at any of his callings."—*Comment* upon the peculiarity of structure if any and give the G. F.

47. "Ninety-nine tell lies, impose on people, and rob them of their well earned money, is no reason to believe that hundreth is the same".—Give the G. F. of this *sentence analogue of* N in P.

48. *Turn* into continued Narrative the following :—

1. He said, "We cannot be quite happy in this life."
2. He said, "The earth moves round the sun."—*Comment* upon the peculiarity of tense-change if any.

APPENDIX.

RECOGNITION OF WORDS BY CLASSIFICATION.

First series or Special Ante-joiners to Nouns.

1. Article Adjectives :—A, an, the.
2. Pronominal Adjectives :—

(a.) Distributive :—Each, every, either, neither (no+either) several.

(b.) Demonstrative :—This, that, yon, yonder, these, those.

(c.) Indefinite :—None (no+one) any, one, another (an+other), some, such, other.

(d.) Definite :—Whole, former, latter, all, both.

(e.) Identical :—Same, similar, like.

(f.) Interrogative and Relative :—What, which, whichever, whatever.

(g.) Numeral Adjectives :—One, two, &c. (cardinal) 1st, 2nd, &c. (ordinal) single, double, &c. (multiplier).

REMARKS.—Altogether the number of words in this group is 33. These words do not admit of comparison.

3. Personal pronoun, possessives :—My, mine, thy, thine, his, her, hers, its, our, ours, your, yours, their, theirs.

This group has but 14 words.

4. Relative pronoun, possessive :—Whose.

5. Pronominal adjective, possessive :—One's, other's, another's.

6. Noun, possessive :—Recognised by suffixial 's, s' or only (').

REMARKS.—The total number of words, therefore, in the first series of Ante-joiners to Nouns are 51 and two varieties of the words, *recognizable*.

Ante-sub-joiner series to Nouns.

1. *Non-recognizable Adverbs* (sub-joiners to Adjectives) :— Never, far, once, twice, often, almost, more, much, most, so, too, very, ill, well.

2. Recognizable by suffix "ly".

GENERAL REMARKS.—Altogether in the Ante-sub-joiner series there are 14 words and 1 variety of words.

Second Ante-joiner series to Nouns.

1. *Irregular non-recognizable Adjectives* so called for the appearance of distinct words in their comparison :—

Positive.	Comparative.	Superlative.
Bad, evil or ill	worse	worst.
Down	downer	downmost.
Far	farther	farthest.
Fore	former	foremost or first.
Good, well	better	best.
In	inner	inmost or innermost.
Late	later or latter	latest or last.
Little	less	least.
Many or much	more	most.
Near	nearer	nearest or next.
Nigh	nigher	nighest or next
Old	older or elder	oldmost or eldest.
Up	upper	upmost or uppermost.
Hind	hinder	hindmost, hindermost.
Out	outer	outermost, utmost.

The number of words in these are 59.

REMARKS.—Traces of regular suffixial regularity (by r, er ; or st, est) in the comparison of non-recognizable Adjectives that go to form the next class begin to appear in some of these.

2. *Regular non-recognizable Adjectives*—the regularity being in the suffixes of comparison (by r, er; st, est,). (Cull out from the list of Non-recognizable Adjectives given herafter).

3. *Uncomparable Non-recognizable Positives.* (Cull out from the same list).

Continual, dead, empty, false, infallible, intolerable, inexpiable, void, royal, circular, perpetual, &c.

4. *Uncomparable recognizable comparatives* by 'ior' or 'or'.

Interior, exterior, superior, inferior, anterior, posterior, prior ulterior, senior, junior, major, minor.

5. *Uncomparable recognizable or Non-recognizable Adjective superlatives* :—Almighty, chief, extreme, supreme, perfect, eternal universal, infinite.

6. *Regular recognizable Adjectives.*—the regularity being in their comparison by help of the irregular higher or lower comparatives, or the highest or lowest superlatives *i.e.* "more" or "less" and "most" or "least" placed before them.

List of NON-RECOGNIZABLE ADJECTIVES.

A.—PURE ADJECTIVES.

Able, adroit, adult, afraid, apt.

Base, big, black, bland, blank, blind, brisk, brown, busy, blunt, broad, bleak, boon, brave, buxom.

Chaste, cheap, clean, clear, cool, crude, crump.

Damp, dank, dark, dead, deaf, dear, deep, dire, divers, diverse, drab, dread, dry.

Earnest, entire, even, evil.

Fain, faint, fair, false, far, fat, few, fierce, fine, firm, fit, flat, fond, four, free.

Gaunt, gay, gilt, glib, glad, grand, grave, gray, grey, great, green, gross, grum.

Hard, harsh, high, hind, hoar, hot, hundred, hush.

Idle.

Just, jocund.

Keen, kind.

Lag, lame, lank, large, lax, left, level, like, loath, long, lorn, loud, lush.

Mad, main, male, manifest, mean meek, mich, milch, mute.

Near, neat, net, neither, new, neuter, nice, no.

Odd, old, one, overt.

Pale, parallel, perk, pert, plain, plump, poor, prime, prone, proper, proud, purblin, pure.

Quaint, queer quick quiet, quit.

Rank, rare, random, rash, rather, raw, ready, real rich, rife, ripe, roan, robust, rotund, round, rude, russet.

Sad, safe, sage, salt, same, savage, scant, scarce, second, secret, secure, serene, set, seven, severe, sham, sharp, sheer, short, shrewd, shrill, shy, sick, sincere, six, slack, slope, solemn, some, soar, spruce, stalwart, starch, stark, steep, stern, stout, straight, strict.

Tame, tart, ten, tense, thick, thin, thrice, thirty, thousand, three, thwart, tranquil, trig, twelve, twenty, two.

Utmost, uttermost.

Very, vague.

Warm, waste, weak, werid, well, welsh, west, white, wide, whole, wise, worth.

Zig-zag.

TOTAL=226.

List of RECOGNIZABLE ADJECTIVES derivative & observational known by suffixes, prefixes or both with examples of each.

A.—SUFFIXIAL PHONETIC GROUP.

(1.) *Of Vowels.*

—y...Sorry, bloody.
—ue...Blue, true.
—ow...Tallow, shallow.
—ough...Thorough.

(2.) *Of Consonants.*

D

—id... Rigid, lucid.
—und...Jocund, moribund.
—oid...Ovoid, typhoid.
—ed...Sacred, kindred.
—dy...Rowdy.
—ld...Cold, mild.

F

—ief...Brief, chief.
—uff...Gruff.
—ough...Rough, tough.

G

—ng...Wrong, strong.
—ing...Governing

K

—ac...Elegiac.
—ic...Rustic, public.
—fio...Terrific.
—esque...Grottesque, picturesque
—ique...Unique, antique

L

—al...Legal, mortal.
—ical...Numerical, inimical.
—eel...Genteel.
—le...Gentle, simple.
—il...Civil, tranquil
—ble...Audible, treble.
—able...Memorable, fordable.
—ible...Sensible, corrigible.
—el...Cruel.

—ile...Fertile, futile.
—ple...Couple, supple.
—ail...Frail.
—ly...Homely, comely.
—ful...Careful, skilful.
—ll...Ill, well, all.
—ley...

M

—im...Dim, grim.
—eme...Extreme, supreme.
—ime...Sublime, maritime.
—dom...Seldom, random.

N

—an...Human, roman.
—gn...Malign, foreign.
—en...Golden, leaden.
—urn...Auburn, taciturn.
—ern...Modern.
—ene...Serene, terrene.
—ane...Mundane, profane.
—een...Thirteen.
—ain...Certain, vain.
—ine,. Devine, canine.

R

—gre...Meagre.
—er...Eager, clever.
—ar...Circular, regular.
—cre...Mediocre.
—ary...Contrary, honorary.
—ory...Migratory, illusory.
—or...Minor, major.

SH

—sh...Foolish, English.
—sy...Tipsy.

S

—ense...Tense, dense.
—arious...Multifarious, gregarious.
—aneous...Simultaneous.

S
—erious...Deleterious.
—orious...Laborious.
—ous...Virtuous, curious.
—ose...Verbose, comatose.
—ise...Precise, concise.
—ise...Hoarse, coarse.

T
—ate...Affectionate, effeminate.
—pt...Prompt, apt, abrupt.
—ant...Errant, observant.
—ert...Inert, expert.
—ute...Resolute, minute.
—st...First, last.
—ect...Elect, correct.
—ete, eet...Complete, discreet.

—ite...Partite.
—ty...Dirty
—ent...Patient, indolent.
—inct...Distinct, succinct.
—ute...Minute, dilute.
—the...Lithe, blithe
—th...Fifth, seventh.

V
—ive...Active, restive.

X
—ex...Complex, convex.

BY WORD.
—like...Godlike, warlike.
—less...Shameless, hopeless,
—some...Handsome, winsome.
—ward...Forward.
—fold...Manifold.

Total=90 Varieties.

Compound Adjectives.
1. Noun+Adj.=Snow-white, sky-blue.
2. Noun+participle=Web-footed, heart-rending.
3. Adj.+Adj.=Red-hot, luke-warm.
4. Prep.+noun=Over-land, Over-time.

(b).—BOTH PREFFIXIAL AND SUFFIXIAL.

Ab-omin-able, ab-origin-al, ad-ventur-ous, ad-vantage-ous, aggress-ive, Bi-pol-ar, bi-nom-ial, Com-mod-ious, com-merc-ial, con-geni-tal, con-form-al, cor-rupt-ible, cor-ross-ive, De-rogat-ory, de-riv-able, di-gest-ible, di-la-tory, dis-allow-able, dis-asterous, E-duc-ible, e-jaculat-ory, en-thusias-tic, e-nunciat-ive, ex-or-bit-ant ex-haust-ible, In-fer-enc-ial, in-fert-ile, il-lustri-ous, il-logic-al, Mani-pulat-ive, mani-fest-ible, Non-sensi-cal, Ob-erv-able, ob-nox-ious, oc-curr-ent. oc-casion-al, op-press-ive, op-po-sable, or-thograph-ic, or-tho-pter-ous, Para-sit-ic, para-graph-ic, per-form-able, per-enn-ial, pre-dict-ive, pro-nom-inal, pro-gress-ive, Re-ligi-ous, re-flect-ive Sub-servi-ent, sub-junct-ive, Trans-fer-able, tra-dition-al, tra-mont-ane.=54.

(c)—PREFIXAL WITH ROOTS.

A...A-ghast, a-ware, a-verse. Ab...ab-ject, ab-rupt, ab-surd, Ad...ad-verse, ad-apt. Bi...Bi-fid. Cor...Cor-rupt. Com...Common, con-cise, con-crescent, Di-lute, dis-mal, dis-tinct, En-tire, ex-empt, ex-tinct, e-lect, Im-mense, il-licit, in-ert, Mani-fest, Non-discript, Ob-solete, ob-tuse, o-cult, op-posite, ortho-dox, Para-llel, per-fect, pre-cise, pro-lix, Re-cluse, re-mote, Sin-cere, se-cure, sub-ject, Trans-parent, tra-verse.=31.

(d).—Prefixial with words.

A-lien, bi-fold, com-pound, con-cave, de-void, ex-act, in-bred, ob-scene, pyri-form.=9

B.—Irregular participle adjectives. (Past)

Broken, chosen, cut, fallen, forbidden, hewn, hidden, known, lost, mis-shapen, said, sold, slain, sown, spent, split, spun, stolen, stung, sworn, swollen, torn, trodden, woven, won, wrought, written, =27.

C.—Their compounds with adjective and adverb united or un-united.

Ill-fed, long-felt, well-knit, highly-let, long-sought, best-set. Twice-told, wide-spread, newly-built.=9.

List of RECOGNIZABLE NOUNS derivative and observational, known by suffixes and prefixes or both with examples of each.

A.—Suffixial phonetic group.

1.—*Of Vowels.*
—a...Macula, malaria
—ee...Payee, nominee
—e,y...Beside, baby.
—y...Party, warranty
—o...Sago, seraglio
—oo...Taboo
—ow...Window, willow

2.—*Of Consonants.*

C
—ic...Garlic, stoic, bishop-ric
—que...Marque, ceque
—iac...Maniac, zodiac

D
—ad...Ballad, salad
—ade...Crusade, cannonade
—ode...Node, geode
—id...Orchid, hybrid
—ide...Parricide
—nd...Wind, friend
—and...Viand, errand
—ard...Sluggard, orchard
—end...Legend

—red...Kindred
—ald...Herald, emarald
—oid...Conoid, rhomboid
—tude...Solitude, gratitude

NG
—ing...Learning
—ling...Sapling
—ong...Throng, song, gong

J
—age...Village, parentage
—dge...Bridge, wedge
—ledge...Knowledge, pledge

G
—logue...Monologue, epilogue
—gue...League, fatigue

J
—ge...Barge
—gy...Clergy

L
—al...Proposal, dismissal
—el...Model, shovel

L

—il...Tendril, nostril
—yl...Beryl, idyl
—le...Chyle
—ail...Detail, tail
—ol...Patrol
—ole...Parole, rigmarole
—cel...Parcel
—cle...Particle, vehicle
—sel...Damsel, morsel
—ule...Globule, plumule
—cule...Animalcule
—ly...Contumely

M

—em...Theorem, problem
—eme...Scheme, raceme
—im...Pilgrim, maxim
—yme...Chyme
—om...Venom, ransom
—dom...Kingdom, wisdom
—um...Opium
—asm...Spasm, sarcasm
—ism...Hinduism

N

—an...Organ, orphan
—ain...Chaplain, villain
—san...Partisan, courtisan
—en...Chicken, warden
—zen...Denizen, citizen
—in...Tannin, tiffin
—gin...Origin, margin
—lin...Goblin
—ine...Turpentine, pepsine
—kin...Lambkin
—one...Ozone
—on...Union, weapon
—sin...Tocsin
—oon...Cartoon, monsoon
—gon...Pentagon, hexagon
—une...Fortune, tribune
—ny...Tyranny
—ney...Journey
—mony...Testimony, sanctimony
—ern...Lantern, postern
—urn...Saturn

R

—ar...Liar, beggar
—er...Maker, temper
—ber...October, November
—cer...Grocer, necromancer
—der...Spider
—ter...Laughter, sister
—re...Ombre, sabre
—ogre...Ogre
—yre...Eyre, gyre, lyre
—tre...Spectre, theatre
—or...Curator, doctor, tenor
—er...Maker, saddler, order
—ery...Vinery, finery
—our...Endavour, flavour
—ier...Terrier, fusilier
—ure...Verdure, tenure
—cre...Nacre, massacre
—chre...Sepulchre, ochre
—ture...Signature, mature
—ry...Ovary, vestry
—ar...Scholar, vicar, templar
—ory...Victory, wory
—ary...Dignitary, vagary
—ter...Daughter, laughter
—ster...Songster, youngster
—ray...
—cer...Necromancer, grocer
—ther...Mother, weather
—der...Spider, rudder
—ir...Nadir
—oir...Memoir
—eer...Volunteer
—ury...Treasury, usury
—ire...Satire, empire
—yr...Satyr, zephyr

S

—acious...Audacius, sagacious
—aceous...Herb-aceous, farinaceous
—ess...Prowess, progress
—ness...Sickness, kindness
—cess...Process, access
—sy...Gipsy, heresy
—cy...Mercy, secrecy
—us...Genius, genus
—aneous...Extraneous

S
—is...Basis, glottis
—ise...Devise, franchise
—pse...Eclipse, ellipse
—ous...Amorous

T
—t...Sight, height
—at...Aristocrat, democrat
—eight...Weight, freight
—ment...Amendment,
             condiment
—ant...Warrant, tyrant,
             infant.
—ent...Talent, tangent
—ette...Etiquette
—ity...Christanity, gravidity
—ite...Favorite, satellite
—ate...Pirate, protectorate
—et...Signet, wicket, tablet
—ot...Zealot, patriot
—it...Orbit, cubit
—ute...Statute, tribute
—Phyte...Zoophyte, neophyte

ST
—ist...Linguist, botanist
—ast...Enthusiast, bombast

MIXED.
—ph...Paragraph, epitaph

—the...Tithe, scythe
—th...Stealth, health
—ics...Statistics, tactics
—scape...Landscape, escape
—scope...Telescope
—ause...Pause, cause
—ock...Hillock, bullock
—sis...Oasis, synopsis
—isk...Basilisk, asterisk
—esque...Burlesque
—ige...Vestige, prestige
—ch...Church, watch, match
—sh...Thrush, brush, bush
—ll...Bull, bell
—ex...Vortex, vertex
—ix...Matrix, affix
—iff...Mastiff, bailiff

BY WORDS.
—lock...Wed-lock, pad-lock
—wright...Ship-wright
—monger...Fish-monger
—let...Ring-let, rivu-let
—ship..Friend-ship wor-ship
—hood..Boy-hood, man-hood
—head...God-head
—sphere...Atmo-sphere,
             hemi-sphere
—aster...Poet-aster
—arch..Mon-arch, patri-arch

TOTAL=170 VARIETIES.

List of RECOGNIZABLE NOUNS known by prefixes or words or roots or both by prefixes and suffixes.

A...A-spect, a-theist
Ab...Ab-use, ab-erra-tion
Abs...Abs-ence, abs-truc-tion
Ac...Ac-anthus, ac-cumula-tion
Ad...Ad-jective, ad-mira-tion
Acro...Acro-bat, acro-gen
Af...Af-fix, af-flux
Ag...Ag-grega-tion
Al.. Al-arm, al-cohol
Ambi...Ambi-gu-ity, ambi-tion
Amphi-Amphi-theatre
Ampli...Ampli-fica-tion
An...An-archy
Ana...Ana-tomy
Ante...Ante-room, ante-penult

Anti...Antipathy
Ap...Ap-posi-tion, ap-horism
Apo...Apo-logy, apo-logue
Arch...Arch-duke, arch-angle
Ar...Ar-rogance
As...As-sent, as-sail-ant
At...At-trac-tion, at-tempt
Auto...Auto-cracy, auto-graph

Be...Be-ginn-er, be-liev-er
Bene...Bene-dic-tion,
             bene-fact-or
Bi...Bi-ped
Bis...Bi-sec-tion, bis-cuit
By...Bypath, byword.

APPENDIX.

Cent...Cent-age, centi-ped
Circum...Circum-fer-ence, circum-ci-sion
Co...Co-erc-ion, co-herence
Col...Col-leag-ue, col-loquy
Com...Compass, com-pact
Con...Con-sort, con-trast
Contro...Controversy
Cor...Cor-rect-ion
Coun...Council
Counter...Counter-part
Cis...Cis-alpine
Cata...Cata-comb, cata-log-ue
De...De-bate, de-cad-ence
Deca...Deca-gon, deca-log-ue
Des...Des-sert
Deuter...Deuter-otgami, Deutero-nomy
Dexter...Dexter-ity
Dia...Dia-lect, dia-tribe
Dif...Dif-fus-ion, dif-fer-ence
Demi...Demi-god
Di...Di-lemma, di-lu-tion
Dis...Dis-temper, dis-cord
Dys...Dys-entery, dys-pepsia
E...E-bull-ition, e-carte
Ec...Eccentricity
Ec...Eclipse
Ef...Ef-fect, ef-figy
El...El-ixir
Em...Em-blem, em-brocat-ion
En...en-croach-ment
Enter...Enter-prise
Epi...epi-taph, epi-lepsy
Es...es-cape, es-planade
Eso...eso-teric
Eu...eu-phony, eu-logy
Ex...ex-odus, ex-perience
Exo...exo-gen, exo-tic
Extra...extra-vasation

For...for-bearance
Fore...fore-castle, fore-closure
Hemi...hemi-sphere, hemi-stich
Hiero...hiero-glyph, hiero-phant
Homo...homo-logue, homo-type
Hepta...hepta-rchy, hepta-gon
Hyper...hyper-bole, hyper-trophy
Hypo...hypo-tenuse, hypo-crisy

I...I-gnominy
Il...Il-lumination
Im...Im-port, im-post
In...In-come, in-crustation
Intel...Intel-lect, intel-ligence
Inter...Inter-course, inter-jec-tion.
Intro...Intro-duction
Ir...Ir-regularity
Juxta...Juxta-position
Mal...Mal-position, mal-aria
Met, meta...Met-hod, meta-physics
Mis...Mis-hap, mis-conduct
Mon, mono...Mon-arch, mono-syllable
Multi-Multi-plication, multi-tude
Ne...Ne-penthe
Neg, nec...Neg-ation, neg-lect nec-tar
Non...Non-suit, non-plus
Ob...Ob-ject, ob-sequies
Oc...Oc-currence, oc-cupation
Octa...Octa-hedron, octa-gon
Off...Off-set, off-spring
On...On-set, on-slaught
Out...Out-break, out-cry
Over...Over-coat, over-weight
Pan...Pan-theism, pan-orama
Par, para...Par-enthesis, para-site
Panto...Panto-mime
Pen, pene...Pen-insula, pene-tration
Per...Per-fection, per-fume
Peri...Peri-carp, peri-phery
Phono...Phono-graphy, phono-type
Photo...Photo-sphere, photo-graphy
Pol...Pol-lution
Poly...Poly-glot, poly-gamy
Post...Post-script, post-pone-ment
Port...Port-manteau, port-folio
Pro...Pro-cess, pro-phet
Preter...Preter-mission
Pre...Pre-caution, pre-tention
Pros...Pros-elyte, pros-ody

Proto...Proto-type, proto-zan
Pseudo...Pseudo-nyme
Pur...Pur-port
Retro...Retro-spect, retro-grade
Re...Re-call, re-move, re-union
Se...Se-cure, seduce
Sed...Sedition
Semi...Semi-circle, semicolon
Sine...Sine-cure
Sub...Sub-treasury, subject
Suc...Suc-ceed
Suf...Suffix
Sug...Sug-gestion
Subter...Subter-fuge
Sup...Sup-port, sup-plication
Sur...Sur-mise, sur-face
Super...Super-stition

Sus...Sus-pense, sus-tenance
Sys...Sy-stem
Syl...Syl-lable, syl-labus
Sym...Sym-bol, sym-pathy
Syn...Syn-tax, syn-thesis
Tele...Tele-phone, tele-gram.
Tra...Tra-dition, tra-ducer
Tran, trans...Tran-sit, trans-port.
Tres...Trestri-pod
Tres..Tres-pass
Tri...Tri-angle, tripod
Ultra...Ultra-montanist
Un...Un-animity
Uni...Uni-form
Vice...Vice-roy
Vis...Vis-count.

Total=147 Varieties.

Compound Nouns.

1. Noun+noun=Ring-finger, washer-man,
2. Participle+noun=Looking-glass, Shoe-making.
3. Adverb+noun=By-word, by-path.
4. Verb+noun=Tell-tale, turn-key.
5. Adverb+verb=Out-look, run-away.
6. Adjective+noun=Noble-man, strong-hold.
7. Prep.+noun=After-noon.

Personal pronouns or Noun-proxies in the 1st term in the Mono-simple.—I, we, thou, ye or you, he, they, she, it.

Personal pronoun or noun-proxies in the 3rd term of the mono-simple.—Me, us, thee, you, him, them, her, it.

List of NON-RECOGNIZABLE NOUNS.

Ace, ache, ado, adz, adze, aerie, ail, air, ale, acme, adult. agate, april. ague. alms. aloe. aloes, alum, ankle, annals, ant, ape. apex, apple, apse, arch, arm, arson, art, ash, asp, ass, aunt, awn, axe, azote.=37.

Babe, bait, barb, bark, barn, beer, bawl, bean. bear, beard, beck, bee, belt, bay, bey, bias. bier. bin, bird, bit, bitch, bliss, blood, boar, bout, bomb. bond, boon, boor, bourse, bowels, bom, boy, bread, breeze, brill, brink, brog, brook. brink. brunt, brute, buck, buff. bug, bull, bulk, bur, burr, burin, bust.=47.

Cab, cad. calx. cane, cone, car. cates, caul. cave, celt, cent, chalk, chaos, chart, cheese, chest, cheek, chick. child, chin, chit, choir,

APPENDIX. xi

chord, chub, chit, clan, clause, clef, clerk, click, clock, clod, clove, clump, cob, cock, cod, coif, coke, coir, cob, column, cone, coom, coot, core, clown, clue, colt, corps, costume, cot, cote, course, cowl, crab. craft, crage, crane, crape, crate, crake, crane, creed, creek, creel, cress, crime, crock, croft, crone, croup, cruse, cud, cue, culm, cult, cur, curd, casp, cyst, czar.=80.

Dace, dad, dais, dale, dam, dame, dance, dare. day, dean, dear, debt, deed, delf, den, derm, desk, duce, dew, dice, diet, dill, dint, dirge, dirt, doe, dog, doge, dole, doll, dolt, dome, don, door, dose, dough, dove, draff, drake, dregs, drone, dross, duck.=38.

Earl, east, eaves, edge, eft, eld, elf, elk, ell, elm, era, eve, ewe, eye.=14.

Fact, Fad, Fair, fame, fane, fang, farce, fast, fate, fault, faun, fawn, fay, feat, feint, fell, fen, fern, fete, fiat, fib. fief. filly, fin, firm, fisc, fist, fit, fine, flail, flask, flax, flea, fleam, fleet, flesh, flight, flint, flip, fluke, flume, fool, fop, foe, fog, folk, font, food, fort, fosse, fount, fox. fraud, fray, frenzy, fresco, friend, frieze, frock, frog, frond. front, fund, fungus, fur, fury, furze, fuss.=68.

Gail, Gale, gallows, gand, goal, gaol, gap, garb, gas, gate, gaul, gauge, gauze, gawk, germ, ghost, gist, gift, gig, gill, gimp, girl, girt, glair, gland, glass, glave, glebe, glee, gleet, glen, globe, glove, glue, gnat, goat, god, gold, golf, goose, gorse, gourd, gown, gout, grade, grail, grange, grape, grass, grate, grave, grease, greaves, grief, grig, grime, grip, grist, grit, groat, grog, groin, grot, grotto, grouse, grout, grove, gruel, grunt, guest, guild, guile, guilt, guise, gulf, gun, gust.=78.

Hades, haft, hag, hair, hake, half, hall, halt, ham, hank, hap, hare, harl, hart, hat, havoc, hay, haze, hearse, heart, heir, helix, hell, helm, hemp, hen, hop, herb, hill, hind, hoax, hob, hock, hod, holm, holt, home, hoof, horde, horn, horse, house, host, hound, hour, houri, hue, hulk, hump, humus, hurt.=50.

Ibex, idea, ides, idol, ilex, inn, iota, ire, iris, iron, ivy.=11.

Jack, jag, jail, jam, jamb, jaw, jay, jean, jest, jess, jet, jen, jig, joint, jowl, juice, june, junk, jute.=19.

Kail, kale, keg, kelp, kern, kerne, key, kibe, kid, kiln, kilt, kin, kind, kine, king, kiosk, kirk, kit, knack, kite, knag, knave, knee, knife, knob, knoll, knop, knout, kyrie.=29.

Lac, lad, lady, lair, lake, lamb, lamp, lar, lard. lark, lass, lava, law, lawn, lay, ledge, lee, leek, lees, leet, leg, lemur, lens, lent, lethe, liar, lias, lice, lid, lien, life, lieu, light, like, lily, links, lint, lion, lip, litmus, lobe, loch, lode, loft, log, loin, loo, loaf, loom, loon, lord, lore. loss, louse, lout, luce, luck, lump, lune, lung, lye, lymph, lynch, lynx, lyre.=64.

Mab, mace, maid, main, maize, malt, mane, mange, mana. manse, mare, mart, martyr, mauve, maw, mead, menses, mere, merle, mews, mica, midge, mien, miff, mile, milt, mime, mina, minx, mist, mite, mode, mole, monk, mood, moon, moor, moose, morn, mote, mow, moxa, muff, mug, mule, mum, mumps, musea, mush, myrrh.=50.

Nag, nap, nape, naught, nave, naze, neap, neb, neck, negro, nerve, nest, news, nib, niece, nit, nob, node, nook, noon, noun, nudge, nun, nymph.=24.

Oaf, oak, oar, oat, ocean, odds, ode, olive, omen, orange, ore, oven, owl, ox.=14.

Pact, pail, pair, pall, palm, pan, pane, pang, pap, papa, paper, par, pard, park, part, pate, pawl, pea, peace, peak, pear, peat, pelf, pell, pelt, penny, pest, pew, phase, phlegm, phrase, pica, pier, pike, pill, pint, pip, pix, plane, plank, plea, plumb, plus, poem, poet, point, poise, pole, pome, pomp, pond, pool, pope, pore, pork, port, poult, pox, prank, prey, priest, prig, prism, prince, prod, proof, prop, prow, puck, pug, pulp, pulse, psalm, pup, pus, puss, pigmy, pyre, pyx.=79

Quack, quag, qualm, quart, quay, queen, quern, quest, quib, quid, quince, quirk, quoit, quota.=14.

Radix, raff, raft, rag, rage, raid, ram, rand, rank, rape, rash, raven, ray, realm, ream, rear, reed, reef, reel, reeve, reign, reins, rhomb, rice, rick, rind, riot, rite, road, rod, roe, rope, rood, rook, room, rose, ross, rote, rounce, roup, rout, ruck, rud, rug, rum, rump, rune, runt, ruse, rusk, ruth, rye.=51.

Sac, sage, sago, saint, sake, salt, salve, scab, scall, scarp, scene, sconce, scope, scrag, scrap, scribe, scrip, script, scroll, scurf, sea, sect, sedge, see, seine, self, sense, sept, serf, serge, sex, shad, shaft, shag, shale, sham, shark, shaw, sheaf, sheave, shed, sheen, sheep, sheer, sheers, shelf, shin, shire, shive, shoad, shock, shoe, shop, shore, shot, shrew, shrift, shrimp, shrine, shrub, side, siege, sieve, silk, sill, silt, sine, sir, sire, site, skein, skull, sky, slag, slat, slaw, sleave, sled, sledge, sleight, slime, sloe, sloop, slope, slot, slug, sluice, slut, smalt, smock, snag, snail, snake, snipe, snob, snood, snot, snout, sock, sod, sofa, soda, sol, sole, son, song, soot, sore, sot, soul, sound, soup, source, sow, space, spade, spark, specie, species, sperm, sphere, sphinx, spice, spile, spine, spire, spirit, spleen, spoon, spore, spouse, sprat, sprig, sprit, spud, spurge, squad, squib, squill, squint, stack, staff, stag, stage, stair, stamen, stanza, state, statue, stead, steak, steed, steel, step, stern, stigma, stile, stilt, stinge, stipend, stoat, stole, stone, stool, stork, strand, strap, straw, streak, stream, street, stress, stride, strife, strophe, stum, sty, suds, suet, suite, sulphur, summons, surd, surf, swab, swain, swamp, swan, swarm, swell, swine, sword.=192.

Tabby, table, taboo, tact, tail, tale, tang, tank, tape, tare, tarn, tart, tavern, tea, teak, teal, team, teat, term, text, thane, thew, thigh, thing, thole, thong, thorn, thorp, thrall, threat, throat, thug, thumb, thump, thyme, tic, tier, tierce, tiger, till, 'tilt, tithe, title, toad, toe, tomb, tomp, ton, tongs, tool, tooth, tope, torch, tory,

APPENDIX.   xiii

tour, town, tract, trait, trance, trash, trass, trave, tray, tree, tress, tret, trial, tribe, trice, tripe, trope, trough, trout, troy, truce, truck, trull, trump, trunk, trus, trust, tryse, tub, tuft, tun, tup, turk, tusk, twain, tweed, twig, twin, type, tyro.=94.

Udder, ulcer, umbel, uncle, unit, urchin, urine.=7.

Vails, vale, valet, valise, valley, value, valve, van, vane, vase, vat, veal, venue, verb, verge, vermin, verse, verst, verve, vesper, vessel, vesta, vestry, veto, vial, viand, vicar, vice, victim, vigil, villa, vine, viol, viper, virgin, virtue, virus, vista, vitals, vixen, void, volley, volt, vowel.=44.

Wady, wafer, wager, wages, wagon, waif, wain, waist, wale, wand, ware, wart, wasp, waste, way, weal, web, week, weft, weir, weird, weld, well, wen, west, wey, whale, wharf, wheat, whelk, whey, whig, while, whim, whin, whit, white, whore, wick, wife, wig, wight, wile, wine, wisd, witch, withe, woad, woe, wolf, womb, woof, wool, world, wort, wrack, wren, wretch, wright, wrist.=50.

Yacht, yak, yam, yard, yarn, yawl, year, yeash, yew, yolk, yore, yule.=12.

Zany, zeal, zeand, zenith, zero, zest, zinc, zone.=8.

Total=1181.

DI-PARTS OF SPEECH GROUP OF WORDS.—Adjectives and Nouns known by their Suffixes.

SUFFIXES.   WORDS.

—ory...access-ory, judicat-ory, purgat-ory, sternutat-ory, suspens-ory, sudat-ory.

—ary...capill-ary, centen-ary, lapid-ary.

—ar...capitul-ar, circul-ar, irregul-ar, mol-ar, perpendicul-ar, secul-ar, jugul-ar, famili-ar, scapul-ar, particul-ar.

—or...exteri-or, interi-or, maj-or, min-or, pri-or, superi-or.

—er...bould-er, count-er, neut-er, premi-er, fronti-er.

—ure...az-ure, fut-ure, leis-ure.

—ant...conson-ant, dorm-ant, expectant, expectorant, gallant, infant, instant, intolerant, irritant, litigant, malignant, mendicant, merchant, mordant, najant, peasant, protestant, radiant, recreant, recusant, ruminant, secant, stimulant, brilliant, conversant.

—ent...antecedent, astringent, consequent, constituent, contingent, correspondent, crescent, current, diluent, discontent, deponent, dissentient, dissident, efficient, effluent, emollient, expedient, gradient, impenitent, incumbent, innocent, insurgent, intent, intercipient, lenient, malcontent, orient, patient, precedent, proficient, regent, resident, trident.

—ic...ascetic, catholic, caustic, characteristic, climacteric, eclesias-
tic, ecbolic, ecliptic, electric, empiric, encaustic, enclitic,
epic, epidemic, iambic, intrinsic, lunatic, magic, mosaic,
paralytic, mystic, pacific, pontific, prognostic, sceptic,
schismatic, scolastic, septic, splenitic, stoic, stomachic,
styptic, sudorific, tonic, tropic, public, cynic, fanatic,
rubric.

—al ..cannibal, capital, ceremonial, constitutional, corporal, cre-
dential, criminal, crystal, decimal, decretal, dental, dia-
gonal, frontal, funeral, general, imperial, infinitismal, integral, labial, lachrymal, lacteal, liberal, lingual, littoral,
material, memorial, menial, numeral, nasal, neutral, normal,
oval, pastoral, potential, primordial, principal, prodigal,
proportional, provincial, radical, reciprocal, serial, spiral,
udal, bacchanal, cordial.

—ern...northern.

—ive...conservative, correlative, dative, definitive, derivative,
diminutive, dissuasive, exclusive, executive, expletive,
incarnative, incrassative, interrogative, invective, laxative,
lenitive, locomotive, maturative, motive, narrative, objective, offensive, operative, sedative, subjunctive, sub-
stantive, superlative, corrosive, fugitive.

—ly...orderly.

—ian...christian, indian, latitudinarian, machiavelian, plebian,
pedestrian, quotidian, sabbatarian, saurian, unitarian, meri-
dian, tertian, fustian, patrician, ruffian, barbarian, hyper-
borian.

—an...mahomedan, pagan, partisan, republican, roman, german.
—ite...exquisite, favorite, infinite, jacobite, requisite.
—o...octavo, folio, quarto.
—on...carrion, common, poltroon, saxon, felon, saffron.
—ow...fallow, shallow.
—ate...literate, graduate, intestate, ordinate, private, profligate.
—id...acid, invalid, liquid, fluid, rapid, solid.
—ine...intestine, libertine, saline, supine, marine, nervine, palatine,
ultramarine.

—in...latin, matin.
—en...craven, maiden, mizzen, raven.
—ile...reptile, projectile, gentile, missile.
—cript...manuscript, conscript.
—esque...arabesque, grotesque.
—ard...bastard, coward, dastard, standard.
—eate...chalybeate.
—ing...fencing, folding, hanging, landing, living, lying, morning,
mouring, parting, riding, running, saving, standing.

Total=30 Varieties.

List of Adjectives and Nouns with common Suffixes.

COMMON SUFFIXES.	ADJECTIVES.	NOUNS.
—ac	Elegiac	Maniac
—al	Mortal	Emerald
—ant	Repentant	Sergeant
—ent	Patient	Student
—ate	Private	Graduate
—ern	Southern	Cistern
—ary	Honorary	Secretary
—ic	Public	Sceptic
—id	Tepid	Liquid
—ile	Puerile	Gentile
—ine	Divine	Iodine
—ing	Loving	Farthing
—ish	Outlandish	Irish
—le	Idle	Beadle
—oty	Prefatory	Purgatory
—ew	Narrow	Marrow
—er	Bitter	Timber
—red	Kindred	Hatred
—right	Downright	fright
—ute	Minute	Tribute
—teen	Fourteen	Canteen
—th	Fourth	Month
—tory	Migratory	Dormitory
—ty	Dainty	Quality
—ward	Homeward	Reward
—ple	Simple	Example
—oid	Avoid	Rhomboid
—id	Lucid	Orchid
—dy	Rowdy	Body
—ald	Bald	Herald
—ble	Audible	Marble
—el	Cruel	Model
—om	Seldom	Thralldom
—an	Human	Organ
—ign	Malaign	Sign
—en	Golden	Omen
—urn	Auburn	Saturn
—ern	Modern	Pastern
—ain	Certain	Villain
—gre	Meagre	Agre
—cre	Mediocre	Acre
—or	Minor	Doctor
—sys	Tipsy	Gypsy
—ene	Immense	Sense
—ise	Concise	Devise
—tinct	Extinct	Instinct

STYLOGRAPHY OF ENGLISH LANGUAGE.

COMMON SUFFIXES.	ADJECTIVES.	NOUNS.
—ithe	Blithe	Tithe
—ough	Rough	Slough
—ex	Convex	Vertex
—dy	Bloody	Body
—ue	Blue	Hue
—ong	Wrong	Song
—ild	Wild	Child.
—uff	Gruff	Stuff
—ail	Frail	Detail
—ale	Sable	Table
—ly	Comely	Orderly

Total=57 Varieties.

List of NON-RECOGNIZABLE VERBS of the Regular group.

Add, amble, argue,

Bable, baffle, bake, bask, baste, bathe, batter, beckon, beg, bless, bloat, blurt, bluster, bob, bode, borrow, bow, brag, breathe, brew, budge, busk.

Calk, cancel, carry, carve, cater, cease, cede, ceil, cere, champ, chew, choke, chuckle, cite, clamber, climb, clinch, cram, crackle, craze, creak, cringe, cruise, crumble, crumple, crunch, cull, curdle, curl, curry.

Dabble, daggle, dandle, daunt, dawn, daze, dazzle, deem, deign, delve, dibble, dig, dine, ding, dive, dote, douse, drape, dribble, drill, drip, drivel, drizzle, droop, drown, drowse, drudge, dub, dure, dwell, dwindle.

Earn, eat, eke, err, etch.

Fade, fail, feign, fell, fend, filch, fix, flay, flicker, flirt, flit, flog, flout, flutter, foist, found, founder, freeze, frizzle.

Gabble, gamble, garble, geld, gender, gild, gird, gloat, gloze, gloze, gnar, gnarl, gnash, gnaw, gobble, goggle, govern, grab, grant, grapple, grasp, grave, graze, greet, grieve, grill, grain, groin, grope, grovel, growl, grumble, grunt, guide, gulp, gurgle, guzzle.

Haggle, halt, halve, hamper, harass, hark, harry, heal, hew, huggle, hinder, hobble, hockle, hom, hurry, hurtle, hustle.

Ignite, imagine, irk.

Jam, jangle, jog, join, jostle, judge, juggle, jumble, justle, jut.

Kill, kindle, knead.

Lave, learn, lean, levy, lick, limn, live, loathe, loll, lug, lurk.

Manage, mar, marry, meddle, melt, mend, merge, mince, mingle, mix, mizzle, moil, molest, moot, mope, moult, mourn, mull, mumm, mump, munch, mute, mutter, maunder, mete, mumble,
Nestle, nibble, nuzzle.
Ope, own, owe, oust, ogle.
Pamper, pant, pare, parry, parse, patter, pave, peddle, pelt, pester, piddle, pierce, pilfer, pill, pleach, plead, please, plod, ply, poach, poise, ponder, pore, potter, pour, pout, prattle, pray, preach, preen, prove, prowl, pry, pucker, puke, pule, pup, purge, purr.
Quack, quaff, quash, quell, quench, quit, quote.
Raise, rally, rankle, rap, rase, rasp, rat, ratten, rave, ravel, raze, rear, reave, reck, reckon, reel, reeve, rely, retch, rifle rinse, rip, roam, rove.
Sate, save, scan, scare, scorch, scotch, scour, scrawl, scrub, sear, seem, seethe, seize, serve, sever, sheer, shelve, shift, shirk, shove, shrive, shun, shift, shimmer, simper, singe, skim, skulk, slake, slump, smatter, smirch, snarl, sniff, snivel, snooze, snort, snub, snuffle, soak, soar, sob, solicit, solve, soothe, sound, sour, spare, spin, splay, sprawl, sprinkle, squat, squeal, stagger, stalk, stanch, stare, starve, steep, stew, stifle, still, stow, straggle, strain, strangle, stray, stretch, strip, strum, study, stun, stunt, suckle, sue, sulk, sully, sunder, swaddle, swagger, swallow, swathe, swelter, swerve, swop.
Tamper, taper, tarry, tease, ted, teem, tempt, tend, tender, thieve, thrash, thwart, tickle, tilt, tinge, tingle, tipple, titter, toddle, totter, tout, trample, trash, trawl, tremble, trickle, trim, trow, truck, truckle, trudge, try, twit.
Unite, urge, usurp, utter.
Vary, vaunt, veer, vend, verge, vex, vie, view, visit, vouch, vow.
Waddle, wade, waft, wag, wager, waggle, wait, waive, wander, warble, ward, warn, waul, wean, wed, ween, weigh, weld, welter, wend, wheedle, wheeze, whelm, whimper, whine, wield, wimble, win, wince, wipe, wither, wive, woo, wreak, wreathe, wrestle, wriggle, writhe.
Yean, yearn, yelp, yield.

Total=478.

List of NON-RECOGNIZABLE VERBS of the Irregular group.

A.—ALL THREE ALIKE.

(a) Terminated by D.

Ind. Pres.	Ind. Past.	Part. Past.
Read	read	read
Rid	rid	rid
Shed	shed	shed
Shred	shred	shred
Spread	spread	spread

(b) Terminated by T.

Beat	beat	beat
Cast	cast	cast
Cost	cost	cost
Burst	burst	burst
Cut	cut	cut
Hit	hit	hit
Hurt	hurt	hurt˙
Knit	knit	knit
Let	let	let
Put	put	put
Quit	quit (quitted)	quit R.
Set	set	set
Shut	shut	shut
Slit	slit (slitted)	slit R.
Split	split	split
Sweat	sweat	sweat
Thurst	thurst	thurst

B.—LAST TWO ALIKE.

By adding D to 1st.

Hear	hear-d	hear-d

By adding T to the 1st.

Deal	deal-t	deal-t
Mean	mean-t	Mean-t
Pen	pen-t	pen-t

D changed into T.

Bend	bent	bent
Build	built	built
Gild	gilt	gilt
Gird	girt	girt
Lend	lent	lent
Rend	rent	rent
Send	sent	sent
Spend	spent	spent

Double L changed into single, then adding T.

Dwell	dwelt	dwelt
Spill	Spilt	spilt

Dropping all letters except one or two initials and adding "aught" or "ought" to the 1st.

Catch	c-aught	c-aught
Teach	t-aught	t-aught
Beseech	bes-ought	bes-ought
Bring	br-ought	br-ought
Buy	b-ought	b-ought

Fight	f-ought	f-ought
Seek	s-ought	s-ought
Think	th-ought	th-ought
Work	wr-ought	wr-ought R.
Ring	rang or rung	rung
Shrink	shrank or shrunk	shrunk
Sing	sang or sung	sung
Sink	sank or sunk	sunk
Slink	sl-ank or sl-unk	sl-unk
Stink	st-ank or st-unk	st-unk
Swim	sw-am or sw-um	sw-um
Swing	sw-ang or sw-ung	sw-ung
Spin	sp-an or sp-un	sp-un
Sling	sl-ang or sl-ung	sl-ung
Spring	sp-rang or spr-ung	spr-ung
Shoot	shot (oo into o)	shot
Hang	hung (a into u)	hung
Cling	clung (i into u)	clung
Dig	dug	dug R.
Fling	flung	flung
Sting	stung	stung
String	strung	strung
Wring	wrung	wrung
Stick	stuck	stuck
Bind	bound (i into ou)	bound
Find	found	found
Grind	ground	ground
Wind	wound	wound
Creep	crept (ee into e)	crept
Feel	felt	felt
Keep	kept	kept
Kneel	knelt	knelt
Sleep	slept	slept
Sweep	swept	swept
Weep	wept	wept

Last two irregularly alike.
Still terminal by D or T, rarely Phonetic.

Have	had	had
Flee	fled	fled
Make	made	made
Lose	lost	lost
Shoe	shod	shod
Stand	stood	stood
Berieve	bereft	bereft
Cleave	cleft	cleft
Leave	left	left

Light	lit	lit
Bleed	bled (ee into e)	bled
Breed	bred	bred
Feed	fed	fed
Meet	met	met
Speed	sped	sped
Lead	led (ea into e)	led -
Hold	held (o into e)	held
Be-hold	be-held	be-held or be-hold-en

Remarks :—Phonetic N appears here as termination of the Past Participle.

Abide	abode	abode
Shine	shone	shone
Win	won	won
Lay	la*id*	la*id*
Pay	pa*i*-d	pa*i*-d
Say	sa*i*-d	sa*i*-d
Sel*l*	so*l*d	so*l*d
Chide	chid	chid or chid*den*
Hide	hid	hid or hid*den*
Bite	bit	bit or bi*tt*-en
Slide	slid	slid or sli-d*d*-en
Stride	strid (strode)	strid or stri-d*d*-en
Sit	sat	sat or si-*tt*-en
Get	got	got or go*tt*-en
Forget	forgot	forgot or forgo*tt*-en
Spit	spit or spat	spit or spi*tt*-en
	1st and last alike.	
Come	came	come

C.—ALL 3 DIFFERENT.

Take	took	take-n
Shake	shook	shake-n
Forsake	forsook	forsake-n
Shear	shore	shor-n
Forbear	forbore	forbor-ne
Wear	wore	wor-n
Break	broke	broke-n
Steal	stole	stole-n
Bear	bore	born or borne
Speak	spoke or spake	spoke-n
Tear	tore	torn
Swear	swore or sware	swor-n
Bid	bad or bade	bi*d*-d-en

Eat	ate	eat-en
Arise	arose (i into o)	arise-n
Drive	drove	drive-n
Rise	rose	rise-n
Strive	strove	strive-n
Thrive	throve	thrive-n
Stride	strode	strid-d-en
Ride	rode	rid-d-en
Smite	smote	smit-t-en
Write	wrote	writ-t-en
Weave	wove (ea into o)	woven
Tread	trod	trod-d-en
Cleave	clove	clove-n
Choose	chose (oo into o)	chose-n
Freeze	froze (ee into e)	froze-n
Awake	awoke (a into o)	awake-d, awaken
Blow	blew (o into e)	blow-n
Grow	grew	grow-n
Know	knew	know-n
Throw	threw	throw-n
Crow	crew	crow-ed R.
Draw	drew (a into e)	draw-n
Fall	fell	fall-en
Give	gave (i into a)	give-n
Drink	drank	dr-*unk*
Begin	began	beg*u*-n
Help	help-ed	holp-en
Hew	hew-ed	hew-n
Grave	grave-d	grave-n
Lade	lade-d	lade-n
Mow	mow-ed	mow-n
Seethe	seethe-d or sod	sod-d-en
Saw	saw-ed	saw-n
Shape	shape-d	shape-n
Shave	shave-d	shave-n
Show	show-ed	show-n
Sow	sow-ed	sow-n
Strow	strow-ed	strow-n or strow-ed
Wax	wax-ed	wax-en
Swell	swell-ed	swoll-en
Rive	rive-d	rive-n
Clothe	clothe-d	*clad*
Do	did	do-ne
Go	*went*	go-ne
Dare	d*urst*	dare-d
Slay	sl*ew*	slai-n

STYLOGRAPHY OF ENGLISH LANGUAGE.

Lie	lay	la*i*-n
See	saw	see-n
Strike	str-*uck*	str-*uck* or strick-en
Fly	flew	flow-n
Be	was	be-en
		Total=176.

REMARKS :—*Regular Verbs* take *d, ed*, or *t*, to form both their Indicative past and participle past Tenses which are alike. *Irregular Verbs* on the other hand which are terminated by *d, ed*, or *t*, never take any addition but remain the same under such conditions, all their three conditions being alike. Some of them like the Regular take *d* or *t* to form those two conditions; Others change their terminal *d's* into *t's* in the same. The terminals "ought" or "aught" sometimes mark their recognition in both these conditions. The phonetic *d*, that is, *d, ed, de* and the phonetic *n*, that is, *n, ne, en*, also characterise the two conditions so much so that N Phonetic may be reckoned as the *Regular type of the Irregular Past participles* : In other words what is D of the Regular, N is of the Irregular. Vowel changes of "i" into "a" or " u"; of "i" into " n" or "on"; of "i" into " o"; and of "i" into "a" are visible in the Indicative past, and participle past. Changes of "oo" and "ee" into single "o" are always seen. "A" into "o" or "u" or "oo" becomes visible too. "Ea" into "e" or "o"; "o" into "e" or "a"; "e" into "o", the *medial* into final, "ee" into "o" are observed in the Indicative past. When all the three are different words, the participle past with one or two exceptions are recognized by the phonetic termination of N which proves that D of the Regular is analogous to N of the Irregular. Certain of the Indicative past of the three unlike words are regular in their formation; while the words "went," 'durst', 'slew', 'lay', 'saw', 'struck','flew', and 'was,' are exceptionally irregular. "Sod" belongs to these Irregulars, and the past participle "clad" is exceptionally irregular in its formation. 'Unk,' 'ung,' 'uck,' 'ug' and 'eft,' are sometimes terminals of like words of the Indicative past and the participle past. When the past participle terminal is a D or T before it takes its repetition of N phonetic termination, the D or T is doubled before such addition. The Indicative past may be recognized again by terminations as "-ook, -re, -ke,-le,-de,-te,-se,-ve,-me," and as well as by-aw,-ay,-nd,-s.

It might be remembered also that when of the three different words, the Indicative Past has "o" for its medial vowel the Participle past is derived from it by the addition of phonetic N as a geneal rule, though exceptions with Verbs terminated by "ise", "ive", "ide", and "ite" take place when the past participles are formed from the verbs themselves by the same phonetic addition of N. You will find again the formation of past tenses to be typically Regular, while participle past to be typically N-phonetic.

Vowel changes alone in the three different words with "n" or "nk" terminations are also visible.

APPENDIX. xxiii

List of non-recognizable verbs of the **Auxiliary** irregular group.

A.—Auxiliary from the Irregular group.

Do	did	done
Have	had	had
Be or am	was	been

B.—Pure Auxiliary.

Shall	should
Will	would
May	might
Can	could
Must	must

The pure auxiliaries are *defective* in not having the participles, and infinitives, and their irregularity is visible in the indicative past though all of them at the same time are terminated by T or D.

List of **Defective verbs**, non-recognizable.

A.—Personal
Ought	ought	nil
Quoth	quoth	—
Need	—	—
Beware	—	—
Wis	wist	—
Wit	wot	—

B.—Impersonal
Behoves	behoved
Rains	rained
Methinks	methought

On further irregularities of Verbs.

Both the Regular and Irregular Verbs are regular in the development of words in their Indicative present and past tenses, and they are to number 5. Certain irregular verbs, however, admit increase to more than 5 and some less than this number. For examples.

Verb.	Ind. pres.	Ind. past.	Total words.
Walk	R. walk, walkest, walks or walketh.	walked, walkedst.	5.
Go	Ir. go, goest, goes, or goeth,	went, wentest.	5.
Have	Ir. have, ha(ve)st, ha(ve)s or ha(ve)th,	ha(ve)d, ha(ve)dst.	5.

Have is thus irregular by omission of "ve," were it a regular verb.

Be	Ir. be, am, art, is, are	was, wast, were, went.	9.
Shall	Ir. shall, shalt	should, shouldst.	4.
Will	Ir. will, wilt	would, wouldst.	4.
Must	Ir. must	must, must.	2.

The verb "be" is, therefore, the highest irregular verb in the language, all the auxiliaries the less irregular, and the auxiliary "must" the least. The defectives "ought" and "quoth" like "must" are but single words, and hence least irregular; while "wis" and "wit" are less irregular having two words for each.

List of RECOGNIZABLE VERBS derivative & observational known by suffixes, prefixes, or both.

A.—WITH SUFFIXES.

—ate...create, agitate.
—ite, it...expedite, credit.
—esce...effervesce, coalesce.
—fy...fructify, edify.
—ise...civilise.
—ize...sympathize, monopolize.
—ish...publish, finish.
—en...blacken, sharpen.
—ide...divide, collide.
—er...linger, loiter, glitter.
—om, on...blossom, reckon.
—le...dazzle, wrestle, startle.
—se...cleanse, rinse.
—owl...prowl, growl.

Total=14 Varieties.

B.—WITH PREFIXES.

Prefixes	To other verbs :—	To roots :—
—a...	a-rise, a-mend, a-wake	a-bide, a-venge, a-vert
—ab...	ab-solve, ab-use	ab-rogate, ab-negate
—abs...	...	abs-tain, abs-cond
—ac...	ac-count, ac-company	ac-cept, ac-celerate
—ad...	ad-join, ad-minister	ad-mire, ad-mit
—af...	af-firm, af-fix	af-flict, af-fect
—ag...	ag-grieve	ag-grandise, ag-gravate
—al...	al-lot, al-lay	al-lege, al-ter
—an...	an-nul	an-nex
—ap...	ap-prove, ap-ply	ap-pear, ap-pease
—as	as-sign, as-sail	as-semble, as-sess
—at...	at-tempt, at-test	at-tach, at-tract
—am...	am-putate	...
—ar...	ar-rogate	...
—ante	ante-date	...
—anti...	...	anti-cipate
—be...	be-take, be-head	be-lieve
—bi...	bi-sect	...
—circum...	circum-navigate	circum-cise

APPENDIX.

Prefixes.	To other verbs :—	To roots ;—
—co...	co-agulate, co-operate	co-here
—col...	col-locate	col-lect
—com...	com-press	com-mit
—con...	con-firm	con-fide
—cor...	cor-respond	cor-rode
—contra...	contra-distinguish	contra-dict
—contro...	...	contro-vert
—counter...	counter-act	counter-poise
—de...	de-throne	de-pute
—di...	di-stil	di-vide
—des...	des-cant	...
—dis...	dis-prove	dis-cuss
—dif...	dif-fuse	dif-fer
—e...	e-lapse	e-voke
—ef...	ef-face	ef-fect
—em...	em-power	em-barrass
—en...	en-feeble	en-dure
—ex...	ex-change	ex-haust
—equi...	equi-ponder-ate	equi-librate
—extra...	...	extra-vasate
—enter...	...	enter-tain
—for...	for-give, for-bear	for-sake
—fore...	fore-go, fore-close	...
—gain...	gain-say	...
—il...	il-luminate	il-lude
—im...	im-migrate, im-part	im-merse, im-bue
—in...	in-case, in-close	in-cise, in-cline
—ir...	ir-radiate	ir-rigate
—inter...	inter-knit	intervene
—intro...	...	intro-duce
—mis...	mis-behave, mis-carry	...
—multi...	...	multi-ply
—neg...	...	neg-lect
—ob...	ob-serve	ob-trude
—oc...	...	oc-cur, oc-cupy
—of...	...	of-fend, of-fer
—op...	op-press	op-pose
—os...	...	os-sify
—per...	per-use	per-ceive
—pre...	pre-exist	pre-vent
—pro...	pro-create	pro-mote
—pur...	...	pur-loin, pur-chase
—por...	...	por-tend, por-tray
—pol...	...	pol-lute
—re...	re-fund, re-pay	re-duce
—red...	...	red-eem
—se...	...	se-duce, se-clude
—sub...	sub-scribe	sub-mit

STYLOGRAPHY OF ENGLISH LANGUAGE.

Prefixes.	To other verbs:—	To roots:—
—suc...	...	suc-cumb
—suf...	suf-fix	suf-fice, suf-fer
—sug...	...	sug-gest
—sup...	sup-press	sup-pose, sup-port
—super...	super-abound	super-sede
—sus...	...	sus-tain, sus-pect
—sur...	sur-round, sur-mount	sur-vive
—su...	...	su-spect
—syl...	...	syl-labify, syl-logise
—sym...	...	sym-pathise, sym-bolise
—tra...	...	tra-verse, tra-duce
—trans...	tans-act	trans-fer
—tran...		tran-scend
—tres...	tress-pass	...
—tri...	...	tri-sect
—un...	un-do, un-bind	

Total = 83 Varieties

C.—BOTH PREFIX AND SUFFIX TO ROOTS.

—em...en   em-bold-en
—e...ate   e-long-ate
—sub...ate   sub-ordin-ate

D.—WITH WORD-PREFIXES.

—over...   over-awe, over-take
—under...   under-go, under-take
—with...   with-hold, with-stand
—out...   out-grow, out-strip
—up...   up-set, up-hold

Compound Verbs.

1. Noun+Verb=Hen-peck, back-bite.
2. Adj.+Verb=Safe-guard, white-wash.
3. Adverb+Verb=Over-awe, Over-hear.

Di-Parts-of-speech group of words.—Nouns and Verbs or Vice Versa.

DERIVATIVE BY SENSE OR RARELY DISTINCT WORDS.

    Act, age, aid, aim, arch, awe, address, advance, alloy, appeal, approach, array, arrest, article, assay, attempt, attire, attribute, audit, augur, award.

    Back, bag, bail, bale, balk, band, bandy, bang, bank, bar, barb, barn, bat, beam, bear, beat, bed, beetle, belch, belly, bill, bet, bias, bid, bite, blame, blare, blast, blaze, bleat, blight, blink, bloom, blot, blow, blur, blush, board, boast, boat, boil, bolt, bone, book, boom,

APPENDIX. xxvii

boot, bore, boss botch, bounce, bound, box, brace, bray, braid, brain, branch, brand, brawl, breach, break, breast, breed, bribe, brick, bridge, bridle, brim, bronze, brood, bruise, bruit, brush, bubble, buck, buckle, bud, build, bulb, bulge, bully, bump, bunch, bundle, bungle, buoy, burn, buss, butt, buzz, balance, ballast bargain, ballot, bandage, banquet, barrel, barter, benefit, billow, blazon, blister, blossom, blubber, blunder, bluster, border, bottle, bottom, bracket, brigade, bristle, buffet, burden, burrow, bustle, butcher, buttom, buttress.

Cake, call, camp, cant, cap, card, care, carp, cart, case, cash, cast, catch, cause, caw, cess, chafe, chaff, chain, chair, challenge, chance, change, chant, chap, char, charge, charm, chase, chat, cheat, check, cheer, chime, chink, chip, chirp, chop, chouse, chuck, church, churn, clack, claim, clamp, clang, clap, clash, class, clatter, claw, clay, clew, click, clink, clip, cloak, clog, clot, cloud, clout, club, cluck, clutch, coach, coal, coast, coat, cock, cog, coil, coin, comb, cook, cool, coop, cope, copy, cord, cork, corn, cost, couch, cough, course, court, cove, cow, crack, cramp, crash, cream, crease, crest, cribe, croak, crop, crow, crowd, crown, crush, crust, cry, cub, cup, curb, cure, curse, curve, cut, cabal, cabin, canker, canopy, canton, canvass, capture, caress, caricature, carpet, caution, cavil, cement, censure, centre, certificate, challenge, chaperon, charter, checker, chisel, cipher, circle, clatter, closet, cluster, coffin, collapse, collar, colleague, collect, colour, comfort, command, company, concern, concert, conduct, conflict, consent, consort, contest, contract, contrast, control, convert, convict, convoy, copper, counsel, count, courtesy, covenant, cover, cradle, credit, cribble, cuckold, culture, curtain, carvet, cushion.

Dab, dam, dance, damn, dawn, deal, darn, dart, dash, date, daub, deck, die, dike, din, dip, ditch, dock, dodge, dog, dole, doom, dose, dot, doubt, doze, drab, draft, drag, drain, draught, draw, drawl, dream, dredge, drench, dress, drift, drink, duck, dun, dung, dupe, dust, draft, dye, debate, debauch, debit, decay, decline, decrease, decree, default, defeat, defile, delay, delegate, delight, deluge, demand, demise, deposit, design, desire, despair, despatch, detail, devise, digest, dimple, discipline, discomvour, disgrace, disgust, dish, dispute, disquite, distance, divorce, docket, dovetail.

Ear, earth, ease, ebb, each, echo, eddy, egg, end, envy, eye, eclipse, effect, elbow, embarg, empty, enamel, endeavour, enfilade, entail, escalade, escape, escarp, escheat, escort, essay, esteem, estimate, excise, excuse, exercise, exile, experience, experiment, exploit, export, extract.

Fable, face, fag, fail, fan, fare, farm, fear, feast, fee, feed, felt, fence, fetch, fib, fife, fight, file, fill, film, fire, fish, flag, flake, flame, flank, flap, flare, flash, flaunt, fleck, fleece, fleer, float, flock, flood, floor, flounce, flour, flush, flute, flux, fly, foam, foil, fold, fool, foot, force, ford, forge, fork, form, fowl, frame, freak, freight, fret, fright, frill, fringe, frisk, frizz, frost, frown, fry, fume, fuse, fuzz, farrow, fashion, father, fatigue, favour, feather, ferment, ferret, ferry, fester, fetter, fever, fiddle, fidget, figure, filter, finger, finish, flavour, flounder, fluster, flutter, focus, fodder, forfeit, fracture, franchise, freckle, fresco, fricassee, fritter, furrow.

Gad, gag, gage, gain, gall, game, gape, gash, gasp, gaze, gear, gem, gibe, gin, glare, glance, glaze, gleam, glean, glide, gloom, gloss, glow, glut, goad, gore, gorge, gouge, grace, graft, grain, groom, groove, ground, group, grub, grudge, guard, guess, guide, gull, gum, gush, gut, gyve, gallop, gambol, gangrene, garden, gargle, garter, gazette, gibbet, giggle, gimlet, girdle, glimmer, glimpse, glitter, gossip, graduate, guarantee, gutter, grin, growl.

Hack, hail, hand, handle, harm, harp, hash, hasp, haste, hatch, hate, haul, haunt, haw, hawk, head, heap, heat, heave, hedge, heed, heel, help, hem, herd, hide, hinge, hint, hip, hire, hiss, hit, hitch, hive, hoard, hoe, hog, hoist, hold, hole, hone, hood, hook, hoop, hoot, hop, hope, horse, hough, house, howl, huddle, huff, hug, hull, hum, hunt, hurt, hurl, husk, hut, hymn, habit, hackle, hackney, halloo, hammer, hamper, handcuff, harangue, harbour, harness, harpoon, harrow, harvest, havoc, hazard, hiccough, honey, honour, hovel, huddle, humble, humbug, humour, hunger, hurdle, hurry, husband.

Ice, imp, ink, image, impact, import, impress, imprint, incense, incline, increase, indent, indenture, influence, instance, institute, insult, interest, intrigue, invoice, issue, item.

Jade, judge, jug, jar, jaunt, jeer, jerk, joke, joist, jolt, jot, job, joy, joust, jump, jabber, japan, jewel, jib, jilt, jingle, jockey, jointure, journey, juggle, jumble, junket.

Kedge, keel, keep, ken, kick, kiss, knell, knight, knock, knot, kennel, kipper, kitten, knuckle.

Lace, lack, lance, land, lap, lapse, lash, latch, laugh, launch, lead, leaf, leak, leap, lease, leash, leave, leech, leer, lie, lift, lilt, limb, lime, line, link, lisp, list, load, loaf, loam, loan, lock, lodge, look, loop, loot, lop, lord, lot, lounge, love, luff, lull, lunch, lurch, lure, lust, lute, label, labour, lackey, lacquer, lament, lampoon, lantern, lasso, lather, lattice, leaven, lecture, letter, levy, libel, licence, limber, limit, litter, lumber.

Mail, maim, make, mall, man, map, march, mark, marl, mash, mask, mass, mast, mat, match, mate, may, maze, mesh, mess, mew, might, milk, mill, mind, mine, mint, mire, miss, moan, moat, mob, mock, mop, moss. mould, mound, mount, mouse, mouth, move, mow, muck, mud, muse, musk, manacle, mangle, manoeuvre, mantle, manufacture, manure, market, marline, marshall, martyr, masquerade, massacre, matter, meander, measure, mention, merit, minister, mirror, muzzle, model, monger, mortise, motion, mulct, mullion, mummy, murder, murmur, muster, mutiny, muzzle.

Nail, name, need, neigh, nerve, nick, nip, nod, noise, noose

APPENDIX.

nose, note, notch, nurse, nut, neglect, neighbour, nettle, nick, name, notice, number, nurture.

Oil, oose, orb, object, occasion, offer, offset, order, ornament, overture.

Pace, pack, pad, page, pain, paint, pair, part, pass, paste, pat, patch, pause, paw, pawn, pay, peal, peck, peel, peep, peer, peg, pen, perch, pet, pick, piece, pig, pile, pimp, pin, pinch, pine, pink, pipe, pique, pit, pitch, pity, place, plague, plait, plan, plant, plash, plate, play, pledge, plight, plot, plough, pluck, plug, plume, plunge pod, poke, poll, poop, pop, pout, pose, post, pot, pounce, pound, praise, prate, press, price, prick, pride, print, prize, prune, puff, pull, pump, pun, punch, punt, purl, purse, push, packet, paddle, pander, panel, parade, parcel, pardon, parley, parody, pasture, patrol, pavilion, pencil, pension, pepper, perfume, permit, pestle, physic, picket, pickle, picnic, picture, pilot, pillory, pinnacle, pioneer, pirate, piroutte, plaster, pleasure, plunder, pocket, poison, pommel, poniard, portion, postulate, posture, pother, poultice, powder, precaution, prejudice, premise, principle, privateer, privilege, probe, produce, proffer, profit, progress, puddle, puncture, puzzle.

Quail, quake, quiz, quarrel, query, quaver, question, quibble, quill, quilt, quiver,

Race, rack, rate, rail, rain, rake, ram, ramp, range, rant, rap, rat, reach, reap, reer, reek, rein, rent, rest, rib, ridge, rift, rig, rill, rim, ring, rise, risk, roar, roast, rob, robe, rock, roll, romp, roof, root, rope, rot, rouge, rouse, rout, row, rub, rue, ruff, ruin, rule, run, rush, rust, rut, rabbet, racket, raffle, rafter, ramble, ransom, rattle, ravage, reason, rebuff, rebuke, receipt, recompense, record, recruit, redress, refrain, regale, regard, regress, regret, relish, remedy, render, repeal, repeat, reply, report, repose, repute, request, rescue, reserve, resolve, resort, respect, respite, result, retail, retort, retouch, retreat, return, revel, revenge, reverence, revolt, reward, rhyme, ribbon, riddle, ridicule, rustle, ripple, rivet, roost, ruffle, rumble, rummage, rumour, rumple, rupture, rustle.

Sack, sail, sand, sad, sash, sauce, saw, scald, scale, scalp, scamp, scar, scarf, scathe, (scath) scent, scheme, school, scoff, scold, scoop, score, scorn, scourge, scout, scowl, scrape, scratch, scream, screech, screen, screw, scruple, scud, scull, scum, seal, seam, search, seat, seed, shade, shake, shame, shape, share, shawl, sheet, shell, shield, shift, ship, shirt, shoal, show, shred, shriek, shrink, shroud, shrug, shunt, sigh, sight, sign, sin, sip, size, skate, sketch, skid, skill, skin, skip, skirt, slam, slap, slouch, slate, slave, sleep, sleet, sleeve, slice, slide, sling, slip, slit, slop, slouch, slough, slur, smack, smash, smell, smelt, smile, smirk, smoke, smut, snap, snare, snatch, sneak, sneer, sneeze, snip, snore, snow, snuff, soap, sob, soil, sop, sort, sorgh, souse, sow, span, spar, spawn, spear, speed, spell, spike, spill, spin, spit, spite, splash, splice, splint, split, spoil, sponge, spool, sport, spot, spout, sprain, spread, sprig, spring, springe, sprout, spum, spur, spurn, spurt, sputter, spy, squall, squash, squeak, squeere, squirt, stab, stack, stain, stake, stalk, stall, stamp, stand, star, stare, start, stave, stay, steam, steer, stem, slip, stew, stick, sting, stink, stint, stir, stitch, stock, stoop, stop, store, storm, stove, strike, string, stripe, stroke, stroll, strop, strut, stub, stud, stuff, stump, style, suck, suit, sum, sun, sup, surge, sway, sweat, sweep, swell, swig, swill, swim, swing, swoon, swirl, switch, swoop, swop, sabre, sacrifice, saddle, sally, salute, sample, sanction, saunter, savour, scaffold, scallop, schedule, scamble, scuffle, scuttle, season, sentence, serenade, settle, shadow, shelter, shingle, shiver, shower, shudder, snuffle, silence, skirmish, slander, slaughter, slumber, smother, smuggle, sojourn, solace, soldier, spangle, spume, sputter, squabble, stammer, startle, station, stencil, stockade, stomach, stopper, stopple, straddle, struggle, stucco, stumble, stutter, subpoena, substitute, succour, sugar, summer, supplement, surfeit, surmise, survey, swindle, syringe.

Tack, tag, taint, talk, tan, tap, tar, task, taste, taunt, taw, tax, tear, tent, term, test, thank, thatch, thaw, thist, thread, thrill, throb, throne, throng, throw, thrum, thrust, tick, tide, tie, tile, time, tin, tint tip, tire, toast, toil, toll, tone, top, toss, touch, tow, trace, track, trade, trall, train, tramp, trap, tread, trench, trend, trick, trill, trip, troll, troop, trot, tube, tuck, tuft, tug, tune, turf, turn, twang, tweak, twill, twine, twinge, twirl, twist, twitch, table, taboo, tabor, (tabour), tackle, tailor, tallow, tally, tambour, tangle, tapestry, tattle, tattoo, teasel, temper, tenant, tenon, tentor, terrace, tether, thunder, thwack, timber, tincture, tinkle, tissue, title, today, tomhawk, torment, torture, tower, traffic, trammel, transfer, trapan, travel, treasure, trephine, trifle, triumph, trouble, truncheon, trundle, trumble, tunnel, tutor, twinkle, twitter.

Use, usher, upset.

Vamp, vault, veil, vein, vent, vest, view, vaunt, vote, vow, valance, value, vapour, veneer, venture, vermilon, veto, visit, voice, volley, vomit, voyage.

Ward, waft, wail, wad, wage, wake, walk, wall, waltz, wane, want, war, warp, wash, watch, wave, wax, wear, wedge, weed, welt, wench, wheel, whelp, whet, whiff, whip, whir, whirl, whisk, whiz, whoop, will, wind, wing, wink, wife, wire, wish, wit, witch, wood, work, word, worm, wound, wrap, wreck, wrench, wrest, wainscot, warble, war, winter, witness, wonder, worry, worship, wrangle.

Yawn, yell, yoke.

Total=1691.

List of Adverbs as joiner to Verbs, Infinitives, and Participles.

A.—Recognizable Group.

This group has but one variety, all the words being recognized by their suffix "ly." The minor varieties being by suffix "ward", "ling", "long", "wise" &c.

B.—Non-Recognizable Group.

Time :—Ago, already, always, never, now, sometimes, soon, then, to-day, to-morrw, yesterday. The words "now" and "then" become *Conjunctions* also.=11.

Place :—Above, apart, asunder, below, elsewhere, far, forth, hence, here, hither, near, off, thence, there, thither, up, within, without, yonder. The words "above, below, near, off, up, within, without," are *Prepositions* forming with their subsequent Ns Preposition Phrases also. The words "hence" and "thence" become *Conjunctions* also. The word "far" is an *Adjective* and "yonder" an Adjective pronoun too.=19.

Number :—Once, twice, thrice, first, secondly, again, often. The word "first" is Adjective and "again" is *Conjunction* also.=7.

Quantity:—Almost, enough, more, much, most, so, too, very. The words "more," "much," "most" are adjectives too, and "so" the first of a co-ordinate and an Integral Conjunction.=8.

Quality :—How, ill, well. The word "how" is a fractional Subordinate Conjunction and "ill" is an Adjective too.=3.

Affirmation, negation and doubt :—Ay, nay, yea, yes, not, nowise, doubtless, peradventure, perhaps.=9.

Analogy between Adverbs and Preposition Phrases.

Adverbs.	Preposition Phrases.
Now	At the present time
Elsewhere	In another place
Very	In a great degree
How	In what manner
Generally	In a general way

Di-Parts of speech group of words.

Adjectives and Verbs with common suffix of "ate".

Appropriate, confederate, conglobate, degenerate, desolate, duplicate, elate, glomerate, granulate, incorporate, irradiate, mediate, moderate, prostrate, regenerate, separate.=16.

STYLOGRAPHY OF ENGLISH LANGUAGE.

NON-RECOGNIZABLE ONES.

Wake, corrupt, diffuse, dilute, erect, exempt, expedite, lavish, manifest, select.=10.

Crisp, complete, direct, dizzy droll, dry dull, empty, exact, faint, frank, free, further, glad, idle, lame, live, loose, malign, mature, mean, moot, muddy, near, numb, obscure open, own, patent, perfect, perk, prim, prompt, rough, secure, shy, single, slack, slight, smooth, sober, soar, stanch, steady, supple, tame, thin, triple, utter, weary, warm.=52.

Tri-parts of speech group of words.—Noun, Adjective and Verb.

Average.

Bevel, base, black, blind, bond, bosom, bound, brown, bass.

Calm, chance, chill, compact, converse, crank, cripple, cross.

Damp, desert, dread, double, damask, deligate.

Elect, equal.

Fancy, fast, fat, fawn, fell, fine, fit, fleet, flush, forest, frolic, fallow.

Grave, gallant, goggle.

Halt, hoiden, hallow.

Initial, intimate, iron, invalid.

Joint.

Lag, last, laurente, lay, lavel, light.

Malt, manifest, marble, maroon, master, meet, miniature. minute, mock, mother, mute.

Narrow, negative, net, neighbour..

Pale, paper, parallel, prime, plumb, precipitate, present, prose, prostitute, pearl, purple.

Quack, quadrat, quadruple, quiet.

R^{a}nk, rebel, reverse, right, rival, romance, ruby.

Salt, second, see, saw, set, sham, side, signal, silver, slant, slope, smart, sod, sole, sound, square, starch, state, steel, steep, stereotype, still, subject, sublime, subordinate.

Taper, tabby, tender, thwart, tinsel, traverse, travesty, treble, trim, trust, twin.

Volunteer, void, verge.

Wrong, wont, white, wet, welcome, waste.

Tidy.

Adjective, Adverb and Verb :—
Better, clear, even, long, near, thin.

Adjective, Adverb and Noun :—
Due, evil, enough, impromptu, naught, quarterly.

Noun, Verb and Adverb :—
BACK.   Total=151

Quadri-parts-of-speech group of words.—Noun, Verb, Adjective and Adverb.

Like, plumb, round, sheer.=4

Poly parts of speech.

Above, all, but, by, down, either, fast, off, save, so, still, the, that, till, up, what, while, will.=18

List of Preposition with their Classification.

A.—Position prepostions.

POSITIONS.   WORDS.
Below :—below, beneath, down, under, underneath.
Above :—above, beyond, over, up, upon.
After :—after, behind.
Amid :—amid, amidst, among, amongst, between, betwixt.
With :—along, with, besides.
Without :—except, save, without, but.
Across :—across, athwart, past, into, through, throughout, within.
Before :—before, against.
About :—about, around, round, by, toward.
Beside :—beside, near, nigh, about, towards.
Distant :—off.

B.—Case Prepositions.

Of, in, to, at, from, by, into, unto.

C.—Time Prepositions.

Until, till, since, during, before, about, after.

D.—Reason Prepositions.

For.

E.—Participle or absolute prepositions.

Notwithstanding, regarding, concerning, according, pending, excepting, touching.

III

F.—CO-ORDINATE PREPOSITIONS.

From————to, From————till.
From————into, From————until.

Classification of Conjunctions.

Class 1.

Conjunctions that place themselves between similar parts of speech or parts of speech and phrases or between parts of speech and their analogous phrases in a Mono-simple sentence are called "Minor" or "Mono-simple" Conjunctions.

Mono-simples with their Characters.

A.—MONO-GROUPAL.   B.—BI-GROUPAL.

1.—SINGLE.   DOUBLE-SEPARATE OR CO-ORDINATE.

And...copulative
But...adversative
Though...adversative
Or...alternative
As...examplary and of capacity
Namely...distributive

2.—DOUBLE PROXIMATE.

So as...consequential
As if...of semblance
As though...of semblance
And partly...complex
Such as...examplary

3.—TRIPLE PROXIMATE.

As-well-as...copulative

4.—PHRASIAL.

For example...examplary
For instance...   Do.
As for example... Do.
In like manner...of semblance

Either—or...alternative
Neither—nor...copulative
  negative
Whether...or...alternative, conditional
No—nor...negative-copulative
Not—nor... Do.   Do.
Not—but... negative-adversative
Never—but... emphatic-negative
  and adversative
Not—but only...neg.-adversative
Never—nor...neg.-copulative
Not only—but...emphatic-
  adversative
Not only—but also...Do.
Not merely—but...emphatic-
  adversative
Both—and...double copulative
Both—though...copulative-
  adversative
Such—as .. example-co-ordinate
Both as—and as...double dual
  copulative
Adjective comparative—than...
  comparative
Adverb ,, —than...comparative

As adj.—as adj ...comparison of
  equality
So adj.—as IV   ,,
So V—as IV   ,,

Some of these Conjunctions are pure, and where found doubleproximate, or co-ordinate, or triple, Parts of speech such as adverb, adjective, and pronominal adjective constitute to form parts of them. Hence these three parts of speech go to bear identity here with conjunction. And the identity or closeness of Adverb is so much with conjunction that illustrations as "and besides," "but some times" have proved it elsewhere.

Class 2.
INTEGRAL (STRUCTURE) SUBORDINATES.
Therefore, hence, so, sothat, consequently, as.

Class 3.
FRACTIONAL (JOINER OR TERM) SUBORDINATES.

These conjunctions head the subordinate sentence whether placed initial, intermediate, or terminal, to the principal and bear affinity to it in part.

Single. — Character.

Pure.—If, unless, until, though, although, lest, — Subjunctive.
  Than (always after the principal) — Comparative.
  As, — Conditional
  That, — Assertive, objective
Adverbial.—Ere, when, whenever, whilst, — Of Time
  What (adjective.)
  However, — Adversative.
  How, why, — Of manner or reason.
Prepositional.—Before, after, till, since, until, — Of time.
  Except — Conditional
  For (always after principal,) — Causative.
  Notwithstanding, — Adversative

Double.

Pure.—As-if, as-though, — Of semblance.
Adberbial and pure.—Just-as, now-that, — Point of time
Participle or prep. and pure.—According-as, — Of aggrement.
Phrasial.—In-case, in-so-far-as, — Conditional.

Triple. — Character.

Both pure with adv. intermediates.—
As-soon-as, as-long-as, as-often-as, — Of time.
As-far-as, — Of distance.
As-oftenmuch-as, — Of quantity or circumstance.
Phrasial and pure.—In-order-that, — Of purpose, reason.
From-the-moment-that, at-the-time-that — Of time.

Quadruple.

Prepositional phrase before 1st triple.—
  In-as-much-as, for-as-much-as, — Causative.

It will be seen that prepositional and distinct adverbial conjunctions are special to this class besides the pure ones.

Class 4.
Co-ordinate Subordinate.

As (before adj.)	As.	Comparative of equality.
So (before adv. & adj.)	That,	Quality, consequence.
Such (before noun)	That	do. do.
Not so	As.	Negative Comparative.
Not	Unless.	Do. conditional.
Not	But	Do. adversative.
Not merely	But	Do. do.
So much	That	Quantitative. Consequence.

Class 5.
Co-ordinate Principal (Disimple.)
A.—CONJUNCTION.

1st Co-ordinate.	2nd Co-ordinate.	Character.
Neither	nor	Negative-copulative
No	nor	do do
Either	or	Alternative
Whether	or	do
As	so	Conditional, consequential
Though	yet, still	do adversative
Although	yet	do do
Because	therefore	Cause, consequence

B.—ADJECTIVES.

The-more	the more	Higher comparative.
The more	the less	,, Lower comparative
The-less	the more	Lower higher comparative
The-greater	the lesser	Higher lower do

C—ADVERBS.

Where there	there	Place
When	then	Time

Class 6.
COMPOUND CONJUNCTIONS.
I. A. Within Period.

And...Copulative.   But...Adversative.
As-well-as...copulative   While...Do.

B. Beyond period.

Again, now, yet, or again, then, at length, accordingly, when as, still, in return, however, on the contrary, here, there, nor,

APPENDIX. xxxvii

II. (For para Combination).

The same as Integral subordinates, Class 2.

Hence, so that, if then, when therefore, still, as soon as, for, if therefore, as, when, if.

III. (For para compound).

The same as Compound conjunctions, class 6.

Also, now, however, nevertheless, atlength, on the other hand, at the same time, in like manner, consequently, indeed, thus, lastly, in other words, moreover, next, now, accordingly, again, at last, here, there.

Analogy of Conjunctions in different structures.

FUNCTIONS.   IN SIMPLE STRUCTURE.

Symmetrical unitors
  1. Mono- groupal or singles   Between terms, joiners and subjoiners.
  2. Bi-groupal, or co-ordinates   initial to do   do   do.

Asymmetrical unitors
  1. Singles   Between terms and its joiners or joiners and terms.
  2. Co-ordinates   wanting.

IN INCREASED STRUCTURES.

Symmetrical unitors
  1. Mono-groupal Conjunctions.   In Compounds of mono-simples, mono-subordinates, mono-complexes.
  2. Bi-groupal Conjunctions   In Di-simple.

Asymmetrical Unitors
  1. mono-groupal   In Complex by mono-subordinates.
  2. Bi-groupal   In Complex by co-ordinate subordinates.

Classification of Interjections.

1. Pure :—Alas, ah, ay, oh, ha, O, fy, alak, hurrah, ho, eh, lo !
2. Adjectival :—Strange, bravoe !
3. Noun :—Courage, Non-sense !
5. Varbal :—Smack, see, hold, hush, hail, behold, hark !
4. Adverbial :—Yes, now, well !
6. Phrasial :—By-heaven, farewell, good-bye, adieu !

Unrecognizable Words.

TABLE OF ENUMERATION OF THE SERIES.

Special Ante-joiners of Noun and those common to Noun and Verb.

Series.	Enumeration.
1. Article adjective. A. A.	3
2. Pronomial adjective P. A.	25
3. Personal pronoun possessives P.P.P.	14
4. Pronominal adjective possessives P. A. P.	3
5. Relative pronoun possessive R. P. P.	1
6. Adverbs-joiners to adjectives	15
7. Adjectives, pure	285
8. Irregular past participle adjectives	27
9. Adverb prefixes of above	9

The common Ante-joiners of Noun and Verb from 6 to 9 are their Post-joiners. Post-joiners of Noun are Ante, Inter, and Post-joiners to Verb.

10. Prepositions, or preposition phrases	54
11. Un-recognizable Nouns, pure Regular	1181
12. Ditto Verbs regular, Irregular Verbs, Auxiliaries, Defectives	562
13. Un-recognizable Bi-parts-of-speech group of noun and verb and verb-noun	1691
14. Un-recognizable Tri-parts-of-speech group of N, V, adjectives	139
15. Do Quadri groups	4
16. Personal Pronoun, nominatives	8
17. Do, objectives	8
18. Relative pronoun, nominatives	3
19. Do Relative Pronoun, objectives	3
20. Interjections, unrecognizable pure	18
21. Unrecognizable pure Conjunctions, Monogroupal, Bigroupal, tri- and quadri groupal	79
22. Unrecognizable bi-parts-of speech Adj. & V	62
23. Do Tri parts of speech Adverb, Adjective, V	6
24. Do Do Adverb, Adjective and N	6
25. Unrecognizable poly parts-of-speech	18

Total=4275.

Classification of Parts of Speech.

1.—JOINER PARTS OF SPEECH.

Article, Adverb, Adjective, (*Pronominal Adjective*) (Personal Pronoun, Pron. Adjective, Noun, & Relative Pron. *Possessives*).

2.—TERM (CHIEF) PARTS OF SPEECH.

Noun, (Pronoun), Verbs, (Infinitive and Participle).

3.—CONNECTIVE PARTS OF SPEECH.

Conjunction, Adverb, Preposition.

4.—ABSOLUTE PARTS OF SPEECH.

Interjection, (Vocatives).

NOMENCLATURE OF STRUCTURES AND FORMULÆ, GRAPHIC AND RATIONAL.

A.—Symbols, digits, and signs used in Graphic Formula.

(*a*) *By Symbols.*

N=Noun.   V=Verb.   IV=Infinitive.
PV=Participle.   C=Conjunction.   R=Relative.
c'=Joiner first Co-ordinate. C'=Principal first Co-ordinate.
C''=Principal or joiner 2nd Co-ordinate.

(*b*) *By Digits.*

1^1=Article. 1^2=Pronominal Adj. 1^3=Pers. Pron. Possess.
1^4=Pron. Adj. Possess. 1^5=Noun or Rel. Pron. Possessive.
1=Adverb.   2=Adjective.
3=Preposition Phrase.   4=IV or PV Joiner to N.

(*c*) *By Signs.*

{ }=Principal sentence (Simple or in Complex).

( )^s=Subordinate.

[ ]=Co-ordinate (Di-simple) Principal.

⟨ ⟩=Absolute.

⟨ ! ⟩=Interjection.

⟨ ⟩^{N}=Analogue of N.

REMARKS:—In a complete Ante- or post-joiner to N or V, the Adverb takes the 1st position, Adjective takes the 2nd position, and Preposition phrase, the 3rd. The 1, 2, 3, signifying respectively Adverb, Adjective, Preposition phrase have thus been named by their respective position. The digits 5, 6, 7, 8, 9 when used indicate term suite to IV or PV joiner (4). The digits $1^1, 1^2, 1^3, 1^4, 1^5$ have been so represented according to the respective frequency of occurence of those joiners. Digits *below* symbols of-terms indicate their respective terms and *perpendiculars* have been used to isolate them.

B—Symbols used in Rational Formula.

P=Mono-simple or Principal sentence.

P=Imperative Mono-simple or Principal.

C^s=Conjunction Subordinate.

R^s=Relative Subordinate.

$c'C''^s$=Co-ordinate Conjunction Subordinate.

$c'R'^s$=Co-ordinate Relative Subordinate.

C'P' C"P=Co-ordinate (Di-simple) Principal.

REMARKS:—*Plus*+has been used for compounding of joiners, terms and structures. *Integers* beneath and in advance of symbols in Rational formula denote the total number of Terms in them, and these or fractions *before* the symbols show their respective relation with the terms or joiners of their predecessor. *Integers* with power 's' of symbols show the respective degrees of subordination.

A.—Graphic Formula of Noun.

(SUBJECT OR OBJECT.)

(*a*) Noun without adjuncts (naked). $= |\ N\ |$

(*b*) Noun with adjuncts (clothed). $= \left|\ {}^{1^1}_{1^3}\ 1^2\ 1\ 2\ N\ 1\ 2\ 3\ \right|$
1^4
1^5

(*c*) Noun preceeded by noun-possessive.

$= |\ 1^1\ 1\ 2\ 1^5\ 1\ 2\ N\ 1\ 2\ 3\ |$

B.—Graphic Formula of Verb, Infinitive, and Participle.

(PREDICATE.)

(*a*) Verb without adjuncts (naked). $=|\ V\ |$

(*b*) Verb with adjuncts (clothed). $=|\ 1\ 3\ V\ 1\ 2\ 3\ |$

APPENDIX.

(c) Verb with Auxiliary. (V with A.)
$$= | _{1\,2}A\,_{1\,2}A\,_{1\,2}A\,_{1\,2}V\,_{1\,2\,3}|$$
(COMPLEMENT OF PREDICATE.)

(d) Infinitive, with Auxiliary (clothed).
1. $|_{1\,2\,3}IV\,_{1\,2\,3}|$ 2. $|_{1\,2\,3}A\,_{1\,2}A\,_{1\,2}IV\,_{1\,2\,3}|$

(e) Participle Verb, with Auxiliary (clothed).
1. $|_{1\,2\,3}PV\,_{1\,2\,3}|$ 2. $|_{1\,2\,3}A\,_1A\,_1PV\,_{1\,2\,3}|$

A.—Mono-simple sentences or Ps.
(*In Terms.*)

(a) Narrative or Assertive.   (b) Imperative.
(c) Interrogative.   (d) Exclamatory.

(a) $P_2.\ P_3.\ P_4.\ P_5.\ P_6.\ P_7.\ P_8.\ P_9.$
(b) $P_2 \cdot P_3 \cdot P_4 \cdot P_5 \cdot P_6 \cdot P_7 \cdot P_8 \cdot P_9.$
(c) $P_2?\ P_3?\ P_4?\ P_5?\ P_6?\ P_7?\ P_8?\ P_9?$
(d) $P_2!\ P_3!\ P_4!\ P_5!\ P_6!\ P_7!\ P_8!\ P_9!$

B.—Mono-simple Complexes.

1.—BY ABSOLUTE UNIONS.

N. B. (Integers indicating Terms omitted.)

a.—Narrative or Assertive.

1. $\langle$ N | PV $\rangle$ P.   2. P $\langle$ N | PV.$\rangle$
3. $\langle$ N | PV $\rangle$ P.   4. $\langle$ N | I V $\rangle$ P.
5. $\langle$ P V $\rangle$ P.   6. $\langle$ I V $\rangle$ P.
7. $\langle$ Adj : $\rangle$ P.   8. $\langle$ N, N R' $\rangle$ P.

2.—BY SUBORDINATE MONO-SIMPLE COMBINATIONS.

I.—Mono-subordinate.

a.—Relative subordination :—
1. P R'. (simple combinative.) 2. R' P. (permutative.)

b.—Conjunction subordination :—
1. P C'.   2 . C' P.
(*a*) Co-ordinate Relative Subordination:—P c'R'''*
(combination Locked)
(*b*) Co-ordinate Conjunctional Subordination:— P c'C'''*.

II.—*Di-subordinate.*

(*a*) Conjunction subordination:—C' P C'.
(*b*) Both conjunctional and Relative subordinations :—
C' P R'.

III.—*Bi-subordinate.*

(*a*) Relative Sub-Subordinations :—P R' R²'.
(*b*) Conjunctional Sub-Subordinations :—P C' C²'.
(*c*) Both Relative and Conjunctional or *vice versa* Sub-subordinations :—
  1. P R' C²'.   2. P C' R²'.   3. P c'C''' R²'.
(*d*) Co-ordinate Bi-Subordinate :—P c'C''' R²'.

Alternate or twice-continued Relative and Conjunction Sub-subordinations up to 5th Sub-Subordination.

IV.—*Poly-subordinate.*

1. P C' R²' C³'.   2. P R' C²' C³'.
3. P C' R²' R³'.   4. P R' C²' R³'.

1. P C' R²' C³' R⁴'.   2. P R' C²' C³' R⁴'.
3. P C' R²' R³' C⁴'.   4. P R' C²' R³' C⁴'.
5. P C' C²' R³' R⁴'.   6. P R' R²' C³' R⁴'.

1. P C' R"' C³' R⁴' C⁵'.   2. P C' C²' R³' R ' R⁵'.
3. P R' R²' C³' R⁴' C⁵'.   &c., &c.

(*a*) Co-ordinate Poly-subordinate :—P c'C''' R²' C³'

The above Subordinations and Serial Sub-subordinations are *unions* by Combination and Permutation.

Conjoined Antecedent- Relative Subordination :—
1. P R'   2. PR'. (combination Riveted)

APPENDIX.   xliii

3.—BY SUBSTITUTIVE SUBORDINATION.
1. Mono-complex Subordinate :—P C(P C$^{\bullet}$)$^{\bullet}$. P C(C$^{\bullet}$ P)$^{\bullet}$.
2. Di-complex subordinate :—P C(C$^{\bullet}$,P C$^{\bullet}$)$^{\bullet}$.
3. Bi-complex subordinate :—P C (P R$^{\bullet}$ C$^{2\bullet}$).

By inference a *Poly-complex* is possible as a Subordinate.

4. Mono-complex Co-ordinate Subordinate. P C(P cC$''^{\bullet}$)$^{\bullet}$.

  V.—*Bi-di-subordinate* :—
  C$^{\bullet}$ C$^{2\bullet}$ P R$^{\bullet}$

  VI.—*Di-bi-subordinate* :—
  C$^{\bullet}$ P C$^{\bullet}$ R$^{2\bullet}$

  VII.—*Bi-bi-subordinate* :—
  C$^{\bullet}$ R$^{2\bullet}$ P C$^{\bullet}$ R$^{2\bullet}$

  VIII.—*Di-Bi-Co-ordinate subordinate* :—
  C$^{\bullet}$ P C$^{\bullet}$ c$'$C$''^{2\bullet}$.

IX.—*Complex of the P by conjoined co-ordinate and single conjunctional subordination .—*
  P C-C$'^{\bullet}$ C$''$-C$^{2\bullet}$.

X.—*Complex by both absolute union and subordinate combination* :—
  ⟨ N | PV ⟩ P C$^{\bullet}$.

XI.—*Other Expressions subordinated besides the Narrative.*
 1. C$^{\bullet}$ P ?   2. C$^{\bullet}$ P !   3. P C$^{\bullet}$.

XII.—*Complex of Mono-simple Ps by Parenthetic subordination* :—P (C$^{\bullet}$).

C.—Di-simple or Co-ordinate Principal Sentences.

 1. C$'$P C$''$P.   2. C$''$P C$'$P.

(*a*) Complex of each or both of the co-ordinate Ps subordinated equally or unequally.

 1. C$'$P C$''$P R$^{\bullet}$ R$^{2\bullet}$ C$^{\bullet}$ C$^{2\bullet}$ C$^{3\bullet}$.   2. C$'$P C$^{\bullet}$ C$''$P R$^{\bullet}$.

(b) Complex of conjoined co-ordinate Ps subordinated integrally :—C′P C″P ; C⋅.

(c) Complex of Mono-simple Ps by substitutive co-ordinate Ps to mono-subordinate combinations :—P C(C′P C″P)⋅

(d) Complex of mono-simple Ps both by Mono and Di-simple substitutive Ps subordinations :—C⋅ P C(C′P C″P)⋅.

(e) Complex of Mono-simple Ps by substitutive Ps to Mono-subordinate combinations, the 2nd Co-ordinate co-ordinately Subordinated :—P C(C′P C″P c′C″⋅ R²⋅).

(f) Complex of Mono-simple Ps by direct Co-ordinate Subordinate Ps :—P (C′P C″P)s.

(g) *Transposed* 1st Term of the 2nd Co-ordinate at the first seat before the 1st Co-ordinate in Di-simple Principals :—
C″P C⋅ C′P.

(h) Similar Transposition in Di-simple Subordinates :—
P c′ C″⋅ (C″P R⋅ C′P)²⋅.

D.—Compound of Structures.

(a) Compounds of Mono-simple Ps :—
1. P , P .   2. P ; P .   3. P : P .
4. P . + P .   5. P , P , + P. 6. P ; + P.
7. P , + P , + P. 8. P—P.   9. P+P.

(b) Compound of Mono-simple subordinates :—
1. P R⋅+R⋅.   2. P C⋅+C⋅.
3. P c′C″⋅ ; c′C″⋅ ; c′C″⋅ ; c′C″⋅ ; + c′C″⋅ R²⋅.
4. P R⋅ , R⋅ , R⋅ , + R⋅.

(c) Compounds in Bi- and Poly-subordinates :—
P C⋅+C⋅ C²⋅+C²⋅ C³⋅.

(d) Compound of compound Ps :—P+P ; P+P.

(e) Compound of Mono-complexes :—
1. P C⋅ ; P C⋅.   2. C⋅ P + C⋅ P.

(f) Compound of either or both Di-simple Ps :—
1. C′P , C′P , C′P , + C′P C″P.
2. C′P C″P+C″P.   3. C′P C′P + C′P C″P.

(g) *Compound* of Mono-simple Ps & Mono-subordinates :—
1. P , + C^s.   2. P ; + C^s.   3. P + C^s.
All these Subordinates are Integral ones.

(h) *Compound* of Mono-simple Ps and Mono-complex and *vice versa* :—1. P ,+C^s P.   2. C^s P + P.

(i) Compound of Mono-simple Ps and Di-simple Ps or *vice versa* :—1. P + C′P C″P.   2. C′P C″P +P

(j) *Compound of Mono-co-ordinate Complex and Mono-simple Complex* :—P c′C′^{s} + C^s P.

(k) Other *Expression-compounds*, those of the Narrative and with each other including the Direct-Narrative :—
1. P , P .   2. P C^s , P .   3. P ? + P ?
4. P+P.   5. "P" P.   6. "P C^s" P .

E.—Relation beyond Period.

(a) *Consecutive Parts-of-speech relation* but no structural union or combination of Mono-simple and Di-simple Ps as well as their different Complexes each to each or with each other extending *beyond period* :—C′P C″P R^s . P . P R^s . P R^s P C^s.

(b) *Complex* of Ps *beyond* their period by subordinate combinations :—
1. P . C^s 2. P . P . C^s.   3. P + P . C^s C^{2s} C^{2s}.

(c) *Compound* of P-complex or Complex-complex subordinated *beyond* their period :—1. P+P C^s. C^s C^{2s}+C^{2s}.
2. P R^s C^{2s} R^{3s}+R^{3s} C^{4s} ;+P R^s C^{2s} . P . C^s.

(d) *Di-simples* subordinated *beyond* their period :—
C′P C″P ; C′P + C″P . C^s (C^s) R^{2s} +C^s C^{2s}.

(e) Substitutive co-ordinate complex subordinated *beyond* their period :—P C(C′P C″P)^s . C^s (C^s)

(f) *Co-ordination* of the 2nd co-ordinate beyond the period of the 1st :—1. C′P ; C^s P . C′P (C^s); C^{s}P   2. C′P . C″P R^s.

(g) Compound of Ps beyond their period :—P . + P.

(h) Compound of complexes *beyond* the period :—
   P C⁽ᵃ⁾ C²⁽ᵃ⁾ . + C⁽ᵃ⁾ C²⁽ᵃ⁾ R³⁽ᵃ⁾ C⁴⁽ᵃ⁾.

(i) Compound of Ps with the complex *beyond* the period.
   P . + C⁽ᵃ⁾ P.

(j) Compound of Ps with Di-simples *beyond* the period :—
   P . + C′P C″P.

F.—Structure of Paragraph.

I.—**Para-consecutives** with structural independence :—

¶ 1. P R⁽ᵃ⁾ . P R⁽ᵃ⁾ . P.

¶ 2. P R⁽ᵃ⁾ R²⁽ᵃ⁾ . P . P R⁽ᵃ⁾ R⁽ᵃ⁾ c′C″²⁽ᵃ⁾ R³⁽ᵃ⁾ R³⁽ᵃ⁾.

II.—**Para-complex** the 1st having the P and the 2nd one integrally sudordinated to the preceeding one.—

¶ 1. C⁽ᵃ⁾ P.+ P . C′P C″ P . C⁽ᵃ⁾ P R⁽ᵃ⁾.

¶ 2. +P . P . C⁽ᵃ⁾ P . P C(C⁽ᵃ⁾ P C⁽ᵃ⁾)⁽ᵃ⁾.

Para-complex consecutives by integral subordination and sub-subordination :

¶ 1. P (C⁽ᵃ⁾) R⁽ᵃ⁾.

¶ 2. C(C⁽ᵃ⁾ c′C‴⁽ᵃ⁾)⁽ᵃ⁾ P C⁽ᵃ⁾ . P+P C⁽ᵃ⁾.

¶ 3. C(C⁽ᵃ⁾ P C⁽ᵃ⁾ C²⁽ᵃ⁾)⁽ᵃ⁾ . P C⁽ᵃ⁾ R²⁽ᵃ⁾ . P (C⁽ᵃ⁾).

III.—**Para-compounds** one to another or consecutives.—

¶ 1. P C⁽ᵃ⁾ C²⁽ᵃ⁾ . P R⁽ᵃ⁾ C²⁽ᵃ⁾ . P C⁽ᵃ⁾+C⁽ᵃ⁾.

¶ 2. +P R⁽ᵃ⁾ . C⁽ᵃ⁾ . P.

¶ 3. +P C⁽ᵃ⁾ R²⁽ᵃ⁾ . P C⁽ᵃ⁾+P C⁽ᵃ⁾ +P.

www.ingramcontent.com/pod-product-compliance
Lightning Source LLC
Chambersburg PA
CBHW032045220426
43664CB00008B/864